Solaris™ PC NetLink: Performance, Sizing, and Deployment

Don DeVitt

Sun Microsystems Press
A Prentice Hall Title

The publisher offers discounts on this book when ordered in bulk quantities. For more information, contact: Corporate Sales Department, Phone: 800-382-3419; Fax: 201-236-7141; E-mail: corpsales@prenhall.com; or write: Prentice Hall PTR, Corp. Sales Dept., One Lake Street, Upper Saddle River, NJ 07458.

Editorial/production superviser: *Laura E. Burgess*
Cover design director: *Jerry Votta*
Cover designer: *Kavish & Kavish Digital Publishing & Design*
Manufacturing manager: *Alexis R. Heydt*
Marketing manager: *Bryan Gambrel*
Acquisitions editor: *Gregory G. Doench*

Sun Microsystems Press
Marketing manager: *Michael Llwyd Alread*
Publisher: *Rachel Borden*

10 9 8 7 6 5 4 3 2 1

ISBN 0-13-026686-8

Sun Microsystems Press
A Prentice Hall Title

Acknowledgments

Without the help and support of many people, this book could not have been completed.

First, I would like to thank Chuck Alexander, the manager of Sun's Enterprise Engineering group, for his support, allowing me the time to focus on this project. I would also like to thank both Cathleen Plaziak and Barbara Jugo, who together provided great assistance in coordinating the project.

Thanks to Alice Kemp, Vibha Akkaraju, Wendy Werges, and Shuroma Herekar for technical writing support, and Sue Jackson for editing the book. Thanks to Laura Burgess from Prentice Hall for doing a thorough edit of the book.

Linda Cavanaugh deserves special thanks for incorporating many last minute edits, for converting the book to the latest Blueprint format, and for performing the last of the five updates of Appendix C.

Special thanks to Dany Galgani for his extraordinary illustrations.

Many of the sections of some of the chapters were derived from papers, guides, technical documents, and research that many development engineers and field SEs developed to support the Solaris PC NetLink project. These people include Ron Karr, David Shapiro, Brendan Lynch, Gordon Ross, Jonathan Edwards, Madhavaram Raghunathan, Craig Chan, Ron Graham, Mike Belch, Jairo Cardozo, Eduardo Barron, and Jonathon Driscoll. Peter Belknap, Solaris PC NetLink's engineering manager, Kenneth Leigh, Elizabeth Bermudez, and all the management and staff of Sun's Workgroup Layered Software group deserve special thanks for supporting this project.

Most of the lab work done to support this book was performed in Sun's Enterprise Technology Center (ETC) in Burlington, Massachusetts. The ETC manager, Bob Saitow, and Dave Waite from the ETC staff, deserve recognition for supporting the hundreds of benchmarks and tests that required a multitude of server configurations. Gregory Cross also contributed significantly to the benchmarking effort.

John Lazarus managed the technical review process, which included reviews from many of the people listed above, with special thanks to Ron Karr, David Shapiro, Russell White, and Peter Belknap. With their help this document is as accurate as it can be.

Last on this list, but first in my heart, special thanks to my wife, Barbara, and my daughter, Megan, for their loving support in tolerating my sometimes unpredictable work schedule.

Contents

Figures

Tables

Preface

This book describes many aspects of the Solaris™ PC NetLink product from Sun Microsystems™. This book is intended to help you gain a basic knowledge of the most common areas of the Solaris PC NetLink software functionality and provide best practices for its use.

Sun BluePrints Program

The mission of the Sun BluePrints™ Program is to empower Sun customers with the technical knowledge required to implement reliable, available, extensible, and secure information systems within the data center using Sun products. The Sun BluePrints Program is managed by the Enterprise Engineering Group. This group provides a framework to identify, develop, and distribute best practices information that applies across the Sun product line. Technical subject matter experts in various areas contribute to the program and focus on the scope and usefulness of the information.

The Enterprise Engineering Group is the primary provider of the technical content of the Sun BluePrints Program that includes books, guides, and online articles. Through these vehicles, Sun can provide guidance, installation and implementation experiences, real-life scenarios, and late-breaking technical information.

The monthly electronic magazine, Sun BluePrints OnLine, is located on the Web at http://www.sun.com/blueprints.

Who Should Use This Book

The book is aimed at two types of audiences:

- System Administrators—This book will help system administrators implement best practice procedures with regard to the PC NetLink software in the areas of performance tuning, resource management, backup, and deployment, in large enterprise environments.
- System Planners—This book provides in-depth knowledge of the PC NetLink product for planners to explore before deploying the product. The sizing information helps determine the correct configuration for meeting the requirements of the user community.

This book is primarily written for experienced system administrators and planners who are familiar with UNIX®, the Solaris operating environment, and Microsoft Windows NT.

System Administrators new to Solaris and to the PC NetLink software will find this book useful after they have gained a basic understanding of Solaris administration procedures.

Scope of the Book

This book does not replace the documentation supplied with the Solaris PC NetLink product. Instead, it supplies additional information such as software architecture, server scaling information, performance tuning tips, and best practices that are not generally available in the standard documentation.

Solaris PC NetLink Update Information

This book was written during development and release of Solaris PC NetLink 1.0 and 1.1 software. For up-to-date information and announcements on new versions and capabilities of the PC NetLink software as it evolves, search the Sun web site at http://www.sun.com for the term "PC NetLink".

What's in a Name

After reading the description of the Solaris PC NetLink product in Chapter 1, you may recognize the description but associate it with a different product name. The Solaris PC NetLink product has been known by a variety of names during its development. First, the Solaris PC NetLink product is based on the AT&T Advanced Server for UNIX (AS/U) product. The AT&T product, in turn, was based on Microsoft Windows NT 4.0 source code. The AT&T product ships in various forms for different UNIX environments by several OEMs. When Sun acquired the code to start development, the internal project name was Project Cascade. The product's official name used for the first release of the product was SunLink Server.

The product name was immediately changed to Solaris PC NetLink. Unfortunately, time-to-market issues forced the first versions of the product to ship with the older name, SunLink Server. If you have one of the first versions of Solaris PC NetLink, your product probably is labeled, documented, and implemented in code as SunLink Server. That name still appears in the code and the man pages. Thus, Cascade Project, Sunlink Server, and Solaris PC NetLink all refer to the same product.

Uses of the Term "PC NetLink"

Throughout the book the term "PC NetLink" is used in several contexts. The context of the term changes the meaning. Some of the most common uses of the term are:

- **Solaris PC NetLink**—This is the official name of the product. When the term "PC NetLink" is used in this context it implies the full product. This includes all forms of the software as well as the documentation, packaging, CDROM, and so on.

- **PC NetLink Server**—This refers to the concept of a Solaris server that is running the PC NetLink software. A "PC NetLink Server" supports all the Solaris functionality plus the additional functionality that the Solaris PC NetLink product offers. This includes PC client file and print access, Windows NT domain authentication, WINS services, and all other included client services.

- **PC NetLink Software**—This implies the server software of the Solaris PC NetLink product. This usually means the daemons supplied with the Solaris PC NetLink software. It does *not* include the PC NetLink Server Manager.

- **PC NetLink Server Manager**—This refers specifically to the Java-based GUI that manages the configuration of the PC NetLink software. In initial releases of the Solaris PC NetLink product this software was identified as the "SunLink Server Manager".

How This Book Is Organized

Chapter 1 "Introduction to the PC NetLink Software," provides an overview of the Solaris PC NetLink product and describes its server functionality.

Chapter 2 "The PC NetLink Software Architecture" describes the architecture of the PC NetLink software as well as how it implements its services.

Chapter 3, "Tuning a Solaris System for use with the PC NetLink software" focuses on tuning a Solaris server to best support the PC NetLink software. Benchmarks are used to study how each server subsystem influences PC NetLink software.

Chapter 4 "PC NetLink Tuning Parameters," looks at tuning the server from a PC NetLink software perspective. PC NetLink Registry parameters that control performance are reviewed and procedures for changing and managing these parameters are described.

Chapter 5 "Sizing a Solaris PC NetLink Server," explains how to size a PC NetLink server. Using a methodology applied to specific examples, it takes you step by step through the sizing exercise. A spreadsheet tool, available on the Sun web site, helps summarize and implement sizing.

Chapter 6 "Transitioning to a PC NetLink Server," investigates issues in transitioning from Windows NT servers and other Solaris-based products that offer functionality similar to that of Solaris PC NetLink. This chapter also discusses UNIX and Windows NT user account maintenance.

Chapter 7 "Server Consolidation and Resource Management," investigates how consolidating the services of several servers onto one larger, scalable system that supports multiple services solve system administration and server room requirements.

Chapter 8 "Monitoring the Resources Used by PC NetLink Software," reviews the Solaris commands to monitor system usage. This chapter focuses on tracking resources consumed by the PC NetLink software. The chapter includes scripts to help resolve resource consumption problems by specific users or clients.

Chapter 9 "Printing With PC NetLink," provides procedures for setting up and maintaining printer services with the Solaris PC NetLink product. It highlights issues to be aware of when printing using the PC NetLink software with the different Solaris releases.

Chapter 10 "PC NetLink Setup Maintenance and Troubleshooting Procedures," provides procedures for backing up user data and the databases used by the PC NetLink software. Procedures for setting up Directory Replication, Roaming Profiles, combining UNIX and Windows NT permissions, and other PC NetLink services are also provided.

Appendix A "File Service Benchmark Methodology," explains how the benchmarks are used to support sizing discussed in Chapter 5. It also defines the client, server, and network environment used to execute the Ziff-Davis NetBench benchmark.

Appendix B "A Profile of an Average End User," profiles the end user that the sizing example presented in Chapter 5 was based on.

Appendix C "Man Pages and Help Files," provides the text of all the UNIX man pages that were supplied by the Solaris PC NetLink product. Useful help files for the NET command are also listed.

What Typographic Changes Mean

The following table describes the typographic changes used in this book.

Typeface or Symbol	Meaning	Example
AaBbCc123	The names of commands, files, and directories; on-screen computer output	Edit your .login file. Use ls -a to list all files. machine_name% You have mail.
AaBbCc123	What you type, contrasted with on-screen computer output	machine_name% **su** Password:
AaBbCc123	Command-line placeholder: replace with a real name or value	To delete a file, type rm *filename*.
AaBbCc123	Book titles, new words or terms, or words to be emphasized	Read Chapter 6 in *User's Guide*. These are called *class* options. You *must* be root to do this.

Shell Prompts in Command Examples

The following table shows the default system prompt and superuser prompt for the C shell, Bourne shell, and Korn shell.

Shell	Prompt
C shell prompt	machine_name%
C shell superuser prompt	machine_name#
Bourne shell and Korn shell prompt	$
Bourne shell and Korn shell superuser prompt	#

Related Documentation

The Solaris PC NetLink product ships with several online manuals. The manuals are available in HTML, PDF, and AnswerBook2™ formats:

- *PC NetLink Administration Guide*
- *PC NetLink Installation Guide*

When installation is completed, these sources of information are available to administrators:

- *PC NetLink Server Administration Guide*—Explains critical concepts and describes how to administer a PC NetLink server. To access this information, print the PDF version located in the doc folder on the product CD, or point your browser to one of the following URLs:

  - From the Solaris machine where the PC NetLink software is installed: `file:/opt/lanman/shares/admindoc/TOC.htm`.

  - From a PC client machine: `file://`*servername*`/admindoc/toc.htm` where servername is the name of a PC NetLink server.

- PC NetLink Server Manager Online Help—The PC NetLink Server Manager administration tool includes on-line help to guide you through system administration and configuration tasks. To start PC NetLink Server Manager do the following:

  - On a Solaris system, enter the following command while logged in as root:

```
hostname% /opt/lanman/sbin/slsmgr &
```

  - On a Microsoft Windows client machine, click Start and select PC NetLink Server Manager from the Programs submenu.

Once the PC NetLink Server Manager is running, you can access on-line help topics by clicking the Help Topics button at the lower right part of the window.

- UNIX style man pages for all the utilities and data files are included with the Solaris PC NetLink product. These man pages and the text of the PC NetLink `net help` command are printed in Appendix C.

The following BluePrint books also offer in-depth information on related subjects that may apply to your installation of PC NetLink.

- *Solaris Guide for Windows NT Administrators*
- *Resource Management*

Refer to the BluePrints web site `http://www.sun.com/blueprints` for details.

Ordering Sun Documentation

Fatbrain.com, an Internet professional bookstore, stocks selected product documentation from Sun Microsystems, Inc.

For a list of documents and how to order them, visit the Sun Documentation Center on Fatbrain.com at:

`http://www1.fatbrain.com/documentation/sun`

Accessing Sun Documentation Online

The `docs.sun.com`^{sm} web site enables you to access Sun technical documentation on the web. You can browse the `docs.sun.com` archive or search for a specific book title or subject at:

`http://docs.sun.com`

Accessing BluePrints Updates and Tools Online

Every effort has been made to make this book as accurate as possible. If corrections are made after publication they will be posted on the BluePrints web site (`http://www.sun.com/blueprints`). In addition to updates, the sizing tool described in Chapter is available via a link labeled "Scripts and Tools" on the BluePrints web site. The sizing tool may be updated as new information is acquired about the Solaris PC NetLink product. Check the site for the latest version of the tool before planning a new PC NetLink server.

As information is learned about the Solaris PC NetLink product, BluePrints articles will appear in the online magazine, which is available at: `http://www.sun.com/blueprints`. In addition to the monthly publication, previous articles are listed by date.

The author can be reached via email address don.devitt@sun.com.

Sun Server Performance Information

Many performance-related papers and tools referenced in several chapters of this book are available at the Sun performance web site `http://www.sun.com/sun-on-net/performance`. The paper *Solaris Memory Sizing White Paper* by Richard McDougall, referred to in Chapter 4, explains Solaris memory management as well as the tools to monitor memory usage. You can download the tools from `http://www.sun.com/sun-on-net/performance/`.

SymbEL Toolkit

The SE Toolkit, referred to in Chapter 8, is available at `http://www.sun.com/sun-on-net/performance/se3/`. SymbEL (known as SE) is an interpreted language that provides an extensive toolkit for building performance tools and utilities. If you are frustrated with the limitations of `vmstat`, `iostat` and `sar`, then this is the tool for you. The scripts are improved versions of the basic utilities, with powerful rule-based performance monitors and viewers.

With this too, you can apply performance rules every 30 seconds or so against a running system to check for bottlenecks.

Multi Router Traffic Grapher (MRTG)

The Multi Router Traffic Grapher (MRTG) is a tool to monitor the traffic load on network links via SNMP protocol. It is referenced in Chapter 8 as a method to monitor network activity. For more information, see http://mrtg.hdl.com/mrtg.html

Common Internet File System (CIFS) Web Site

CIFS, or the Common Internet File System, is based on the existing Server Message Block (SMB) protocol that the PC NetLink software supports. The CIFS web site is good source of information. The URL is: http://www.cifs.com/

Ziff-Davis Benchmark Web Site

You can download the documentation and software for the NetBench benchmark used in several chapters of this book from the Ziff-Davis web site at http://www.zdnet.com/zdbop/

## CHAPTER 1

Introduction to the PC NetLink Software

The Solaris PC NetLink product is a fundamental part of Sun's PC interoperability product offering. It is fully compatible with network technology from Microsoft, and provides the network services and resource sharing facilities required by Microsoft Windows 3.11, Windows NT, Windows 95, Windows 98, and Windows 2000 clients. The PC NetLink software is a native implementation of the core Microsoft network services found on Microsoft Windows NT 4.0 Server, but it is also engineered for Sun's scalable servers and the Solaris operating environment. With the PC NetLink software, IT managers can consolidate the functionality of multiple PC servers onto a single, highly reliable Sun platform scaling up through the Sun Enterprise Server product line, as well as Solaris Intel Platform Edition environments.

The PC NetLink software running on scalable Sun servers and the Solaris operating environment itself enables you to configure departmental servers for enterprise levels of reliability, availability, and serviceability. It provides the following benefits to small and large enterprises:

- Increases the reliability of Windows NT environments
- Transparently provides key Microsoft network services to users
- Reduces complexity and lowers total cost of ownership
- Provides throughput and headroom to accommodate demand and growth
- Offers higher scalable systems than traditionally offered in the PCs market
- Enables the consolidation of many applications onto fewer servers, reducing management costs.
- Provides simple, familiar installation and administration tools
- Is fully year 2000 compliant

PC NetLink Versions Available

As of January 2000, the following three versions of the Solaris PC NetLink product have shipped:

- Solaris PC NetLink 1.0 (U.S. Domestic)—Shipped April 1999. This original version of PC NetLink was bundled with Sun Workgroup servers and also sold separately. This version supports the SPARC™ platform only.

- Solaris PC NetLink 1.0 (Global)—Shipped June 1999. This version (part number WE239-0) shipped shortly after the domestic release and superseded the initial release to cover the global market. This version supports the SPARC platform only.

- Solaris PC NetLink 1.1—Shipped September 1999 as part of the Solaris Easy Access Server (SEAS) product. This version (part number WE247-0) requires licensing and will not work without an enabling code. This version supports both Solaris SPARC and Solaris Intel platforms.

Features of the PC NetLink Software

Based on the AT&T Advanced Server for UNIX, Solaris PC NetLink is Sun's PC LAN integration server. While porting the original ASU code to Solaris, Sun engineers took advantage of enhanced Solaris functionality to allow the software to perform and scale better than it does on other platforms.

The PC NetLink software provides transparent access to Microsoft Windows NT 4.0 services, such as file, print, and directory services, in addition to addressing critical enterprise computing needs. The PC NetLink software provides:

- Native Windows NT services and tools to manage key server and network functions

- Print, file, directory, and security services hosted on Sun Enterprise servers of up to 64 processors

- Coexistence of Sun Enterprise servers running the PC NetLink software under the Solaris operating environment with servers running Microsoft Windows NT on the same network

- Flexibility to choose from a wide array of Sun hardware and software options (enterprise storage systems, legacy and high performance networking products, Java technologies)

- Compatibility with Microsoft networking protocols

- Industry-standard networking protocols
  - Security and authentication (SAM/SID)
  - NetBIOS and WINS protocols
  - File and print services (CIFS, SMB)
- Service Pack 3 compliance (Version 1.0 and 1.1), with some SP4 compliance with Version 1.1
- Easy installation using install wizards
- Support for all major PC client operating systems, including Microsoft Windows NT 4.0, Windows 3.11, Windows 95, Windows 98, and Windows 2000

With these features, the PC NetLink software provides PC-based network clients with the main Microsoft Windows NT 4.0 services they need in addition to the familiar Solaris services and applications (see "Solaris Software, PC NetLink Software, and Windows NT Functionality" on page 7 for a more complete discussion, and a more complete list.)

The PC NetLink software from Sun Microsystems implements Microsoft network services in the Solaris operating environment, providing file, print, directory, and security and authentication services to Microsoft Windows clients. The PC NetLink software is fully compatible with Microsoft Windows NT Server 4.0 networking technology. As a result, Solaris servers can take over key roles in a Microsoft Windows NT local area network (LAN), replacing Microsoft Windows NT servers or coexisting with them.

A Solaris server running the PC NetLink software in a LAN enables you to share computing resources among a community of desktop users, and delivers powerful new network administration and enhanced security features. The PC NetLink software interoperates with the following supported client systems running the following operating environments:

- Microsoft Windows NT Server 4.0
- Microsoft Windows NT Workstation 4.0 (SP4 and earlier)
- Windows 2000 Professional
- Microsoft Windows 95
- Microsoft Windows 98
- Microsoft Windows for Workgroups 3.11

The term "support" means many things to many people. Here, a supported client system means a system that Sun has thoroughly tested and will commit to fixing bugs against. In fact, some DOS-based lanman-based software clients may work perfectly well with the PC NetLink software and may be used from time to time by users. However, it is risky to allow production level use of these PC clients because Sun offers no support if something fails.

PC NetLink is based on Microsoft Windows NT Server Version 4.0 Service Pack 3 and provides networking capabilities that are functionally equivalent to those offered by Microsoft Windows NT Servers.

Interoperability With Other Systems

A server running the PC NetLink software can function as a file and print server for a small, isolated community of users, or as the foundation of an enterprise networking scheme for a large network distributed over a wide area network.

Sun supports only PC clients that it has tested with the product. Thus, Sun supports a specific list of PC clients with the PC NetLink software. For those intimately familiar with file and print protocols, the PC NetLink software implements the NTLM 0.12 dialect described in the Common Internet File System (CIFS) specification (available at http://www.cifs.com/spec.html). If a PC client other than those on the above list is compatible with this protocol, then it should work with the PC NetLink software, but it will not be supported by Sun. What "works" and what is officially "supported" are two different things in this context.

You can deploy a server running the PC NetLink software as either a Windows NT style primary domain controller (PDC) or a Windows NT style backup domain controller (BDC) in a network composed of other servers running the PC NetLink software or the Microsoft Windows NT server software.

In most file, print, authentication, and naming (WINS) network services, you can replace existing Microsoft Windows NT servers with Solaris servers running the PC NetLink software. You can do this gradually, by first replacing backup domain controllers and later promoting one to Primary Domain Controller (PDC). Users can benefit immediately from the new resources offered by the PC NetLink software. Your network should continue to behave as it did before. Because there is no change in the way network resources are accessed, both you and your user community will see little or no difference in the methods used to access the system. If the names of the servers and domains are kept the same during the transition, users need not even be aware that a transition has taken place.

A major feature of the PC NetLink software is that you can replace several smaller Microsoft Windows NT servers with a single, larger server running the PC NetLink software. The PC NetLink software scales well as it is placed on Sun Enterprise servers with many processors.

A server running the PC NetLink software can act as a gateway to an NFS-mounted file structure on other Solaris servers, but make sure that no writable file is supported by two servers running the PC NetLink software at the same time. This restriction exists because the extended attributes and ACLs for the file must be supported by only one server running the PC NetLink software. If the file is to be used as a read-only file and you can ensure that write access is denied the second system, then it may be possible for more than one PC NetLink server to use the file.

Security

The PC NetLink software offers a logical administrative model that enables efficient management of large networks. You can set up Windows NT style domains and trust relationships between Windows NT domains to centralize user account and other security information, making the network easier to manage and use. Each user needs only one account and one password. This account can provide the user with access to resources anywhere on the network.

The PC NetLink software incorporates enhanced features that support discretionary access control permissions on individual files, directories, and resources, and also includes comprehensive auditing capabilities. These features provide a fine level of control over user and resource permissions and auditing.

Note that during normal operation, user accounts maintained by the PC NetLink software are maintained independently of user accounts that Solaris supports natively via NIS, NIS+, or locally on the Solaris server itself.

Network Services

After installation, the PC NetLink software starts several network services automatically when the system is booted so that the capabilities of the network are available immediately after installation.

Network Activity Tracking

The PC NetLink software enables you to monitor network activity and track computer usage. For example, you can view servers and see which resources they are sharing; view which users currently are connected to any network server; see which files are open; log and view security auditing entries; keep sophisticated error logs; and specify that alerts be sent to administrators when certain events occur. You can also use Microsoft Windows NT server administration tools to monitor network activity.

Printing

The PC NetLink software supports Solaris-supported printers that are attached and spooled from the server the PC NetLink software is installed on. You can attach a printer to a Solaris server running the PC NetLink software, and it will appear and function the same as other printers in your domain. If you attach a printer to a

Solaris system that is not running the PC NetLink software, it will not be visible to other computers in the domain. See the *PC NetLink Administration Guide* for information about installing a PC NetLink-accessible printer on a Solaris system.

Browsing

You can browse domains, workgroups, and computers to look for shared directories and printers. You can specify a network name to display available domains and workgroups, a domain or workgroup name to display available computers, or a computer name to display its shared directories.

Network File Sharing

The PC NetLink software provides superior performance, reliability, and security for sharing files and directories among network users. Discretionary access controls and the security supported by the PC NetLink software on each file and directory let you specify the groups and users that can access files, define the levels of access that each group or user is permitted, and control auditing. Additional features include file ownership and directory replication.

For best performance and functionality, install the PC NetLink software on systems that have the local file and printer resources that you want to share within the network. Share local UFS file structures rather than NFS file structures, because a file mounted under NFS that is shared by more than one system running the PC NetLink software has a separate Access Control List (ACL) entry for each server. Accessing the same file via two different PC NetLink servers can cause the ACL entries on the two servers to become unsynchronized.

User Environment Management

The PC NetLink software supports Microsoft Windows NT user profiles, which let you control access to network resources and manage Microsoft Windows NT Workstation user desktops.

Remote Administration

The PC NetLink software includes the PC NetLink Manager software that enables you to administer the PC NetLink software from the Solaris server and also from Microsoft Windows client machines on your network. The application runs and appears the same under all supported operating environments. The PC NetLink Manager application is not supported on clients running the Microsoft Windows for Workgroups 3.11 or Microsoft Windows NT 3.51 operating environments, because these older operating systems do not support the Java Runtime Environment (JRE) needed to execute the PC NetLink Manager software. Remote administration is supported for all network functions, including server management, security management, and Solaris printer installation.

The PC NetLink software can operate and be administered regardless of whether Microsoft Windows NT is running on the network. In addition, you can use Microsoft client-based network administration tools running on Microsoft Windows client computers to remotely administer Microsoft Windows NT network services provided by the PC NetLink Manager software. The following Microsoft Windows NT server tools are included in the PC NetLink kit:

- Server Manager
- User Manager for Domains
- Event Viewer
- Policy Editor (Microsoft Windows NT and Microsoft Windows for Workgroups only)
- WINS Manager (Microsoft Windows NT and Microsoft Windows for Workgroups only)

Sun Microsystems does not support Microsoft Windows NT Server Tools. For assistance, refer to the on-line help that accompanies those tools.

Solaris Software, PC NetLink Software, and Windows NT Functionality

TABLE 1-1 defines what is supported by the Solaris operating environment and the Windows NT software directly, as well as the server-level functionality supported by the PC NetLink software. TABLE 1-1 shows the following kinds of functionality and server support:

- Native—Services and functionality natively supported by Windows NT or the Solaris operating environments.
- Solaris + PC NetLink software—Services and functionality available on a Solaris server after PC NetLink is installed. These have been placed at the top of the chart.

- Solaris or Windows NT unbundled—Services and functionality available on a Solaris or Windows NT server after an unbundled or third-party package is installed. This functionality is not provided by PC NetLink but as part of the Windows NT server.

TABLE 1-1 Solaris Software, PC NetLink Software, and Windows NT Functionality

Server Functionality	Solaris Software + PC NetLink Software	Windows NT 4.0
File operations via SMB (CIFS) protocols	Solaris with PC NetLink	Windows NT native
NetBIOS Transport Layer	Solaris with PC NetLink	Windows NT native
Print Operations SMB (CIFS)	Solaris with PC NetLink	Windows NT native
Windows NT Domain directory (PDC or BDC) services	Solaris with PC NetLink	Windows NT native
Windows Internet Naming Service (WINS)	Solaris with PC NetLink	Windows NT native
Security—ACLs (Access control lists), SAM (Security Access Manager), SIDs (Security identifiers)	Solaris with PC NetLink	Windows NT native
File Operations (NFS). Available only to clients with NFS Client code.	Solaris native	Windows NT unbundled or third-party software
NIS (Network Information Service) + NIS	Solaris native	Not available
FTP	Solaris native	Windows NT unbundled or third-party add-on
Telnet command line	Solaris native	Windows NT unbundled or third-party add-on
Email IMAP/POP Protocols	Solaris native	Windows NT unbundled or third-party add-on
SMTP (Simple Mail Transfer Protocol)	Solaris native	Windows NT unbundled or third-party add-on
X11 Client Server application support. X11 package required on Client.	Solaris native	Windows NT third-party software

TABLE 1-1   Solaris Software, PC NetLink Software, and Windows NT Functionality
(Continued)

Server Functionality	Solaris Software + PC NetLink Software	Windows NT 4.0
Solaris SPARC or Intel Platform server application support	Solaris native	Not available
SLIP/PPP Dial-up Support	Solaris native	Windows NT native
DHCP (Dynamic Host Configuration Protocol)	Solaris native	Windows NT native
Web Services (HTML)	Solaris unbundled Sun WebServer™, JavaServer™, or third-party server software such as Netscape™ Enterprise Server or Apache	Windows NT add-on or third-party software
Database operations	Solaris-based database programs such as ORACLE®, or Sybase	Windows NT add-on or third-party software
Software RAID	Solaris native Solaris DiskSuite™ or Veritas	Windows NT native
LDAP, X.500, ESMTP, MIME	Solaris add-on—SIMS	Windows NT add-on
Windows NT Domain Administration	Windows NT-based tools supplied with PC NetLink, or use Windows NT tools that exist. Solaris command line commands	Windows NT based tools supplied with Windows NT
Hardware BUS - PCI or PCMCIA support	Solaris native drivers or third-party drivers	Windows NT native drivers or third-party drivers
Intel Platform Edition system support	Solaris Intel Platform Edition native	Windows NT native
Win 32 Intel Platform-based application support	Solaris add-on or third-party software or hardware	NT native
Lotus Notes or Domino Server support	SPARC Solaris based Notes and Domino Server available from Lotus	NT based Lotus Notes Server software from Lotus

TABLE 1-1 Solaris Software, PC NetLink Software, and Windows NT Functionality *(Continued)*

Server Functionality	Solaris Software + PC NetLink Software	Windows NT 4.0
Microsoft Exchange support	Not available	NT add-on or third-party
Appletalk support	Solaris third-party software Syntax™ Totalnet	NT add-on or third-party
Novell Netware support	Solaris third-party software Syntax™ Totalnet	NT native

PC NetLink Restrictions

PC NetLink is an extremely robust and useful product for solving a variety of problems related to Windows NT domains. PC NetLink does not, however, support all the functions that extend beyond those needed to support Windows NT domains. The following are restrictions to remember when planning servers that use PC NetLink 1.0 software.

Controller Restrictions

During the installation of the PC NetLink software, you must decide whether the server will be the primary domain controller (PDC) or a backup domain controller (BDC) of a Windows NT domain. The PC NetLink software allows only these two options for a server for Versions 1.0 and 1.1.

To work around this restriction, create a new domain that has a one-way trusted relationship with the domain of which you want to be a member. This trusted relationship allows authentications that are not supported locally to be passed through to the trusted domain. A PC NetLink server set up in this way has no user accounts in its own PDC database. Instead, the user authentication is passed through to a BDC or the PDC of the trusted domain.

For example, to set up a Solaris server running the PC NetLink software as a member server of the ENGDOMAIN, you would do the following:

1. When installing the first server running the PC NetLink software, choose the name of a trusting domain member (for this example use MEMBERENGDOMAIN) and use it to define the PC NetLink server as a PDC.

2. After the PC NetLink software is installed, use the Windows NT User Manager tool to administer the trusted domain (ENGDOMAIN). Define the trusting domains using the Policies Trust Relationships dialog.

Once the trusted relationship is established, the servers running the PC NetLink software will pass through all their authentications to the trusted domain. As long as you never enter any account information into this dummy domain, you will have accomplished most of what a member Windows NT server is used for. The down side to this workaround is seeing the extra domain.

Transport Protocol Restrictions

The NetBIOS layer shipped with the PC NetLink software supports NetBIOS over the TCP/IP (Transmission Control Protocol/Internet Protocol). This NetBIOS layer does not support NetBEUI or IPX/SPX transport protocols that are still common on some local area networks (LANS). While NetBEUI is used on small networks, it cannot be used in large networks because it does not route from one subnet to another.

The popularity of the Internet requires most network-aware PCs to be delivered by computer companies with the TCP/IP protocol already installed. The TCP/IP protocol is essential to the use of the Internet. TCP/IP protocol scalability is also a primary consideration for most large enterprise environments that use this protocol for supporting the network infrastructure within the company. Microsoft makes the use of the TCP/IP protocol easy to support because this protocol is included with all its operating systems.

For all of these reasons, the restriction of PC NetLink software access to PCs using the TCP/IP transport protocol is not really a restriction. The simple workaround is to install the TCP/IP protocol on any system that doesn't already have it. If you already use an Internet browser to browse and display HTML on the internet using your PC client, you already have a TCP/IP protocol installed on your PC. Check the Network icon of the Windows 95, Windows 98, or Windows NT Control Panel to verify that your PC has the TCP/IP protocol installed.

PC NetLink Requirements

Before you can install the PC NetLink software, you must have specific Solaris operating environment releases on specific hardware platforms.

PC NetLink 1.0

- Solaris 2.5.1 Hardware: 11/97 or a subsequent compatible version
- Solaris 2.6 or a subsequent compatible version

PC NetLink 1.1

- Solaris 2.5.1
- Solaris 2.6
- Solaris 7 operating environment

Hardware Platform Requirements

- SPARC
  - Sun Enterprise™ 2
  - Sun Ultra™ 5S
  - Sun Ultra 10S
  - Sun Enterprise 250
  - Sun Enterprise 450
  - Sun Enterprise 3000/3500
  - Sun Enterprise 4000/4500
  - Sun Enterprise 5000/5500
  - Sun Enterprise 6000/6500
  - Sun Enterprise 10000

This list of Sun Enterprise servers represents the systems that have been tested with PC NetLink and Sun is willing to officially support. Other Sun servers and even workstations may work equally well with PC NetLink, but they would not fall within the official list Sun has tested fully. If you are compelled to test or use PC NetLink on a system other than those listed, you may not be in a position to ask for support from Sun.

- Intel Platform Edition
  - Any Intel platform supported by the versions of Solaris Intel Platform Edition listed previously.

System Resource Requirements

Before you can successfully install the PC NetLink software, your system must have the following minimum requirements:

- 78 Mbytes (40 Mbytes in Version 1.0) of free space in the /opt directory.
- 15 Mbytes of free space in the /var/opt/ directory.
- No other program that uses a NetBIOS stack is running on the Solaris. This includes programs like Syntax Totalnet or Samba. Chapter 6 offers techniques for transitioning from these products to Solaris PC NetLink.

PC Clients Supported by PC NetLink

- Windows NT Workstation 4.0
- Windows 95
- Windows 98

Recommended Patches

To use the PC NetLink software in the most problem-free environment possible it is best to use the latest version, including the current updates of patches for that version. Read the patch descriptions fully to determine if it applies to your system. Patch revision numbers change regularly. Try to install the latest revision if possible. Also read the release notes shipped with each version for other recommended patches.

- PC NetLink 1.0 Domestic
  - 107897-01: Bug Fixes
- PC NetLink 1.0 Global
  - Patch 108164-01: Netbios Bug fixes patch
  - Patch 108235-01: PC NetLink jumbo patch
- PC NetLink 1.1 Domestic/Global
  - Patch 108246-01: Netbios patch
  - Patch 108274-02: PC NetLink jumbo patch
- Solaris 2.6
  - Patch 106235-04: LP patch fixes several printing related problems

## CHAPTER 2

The PC NetLink Software Architecture

This chapter provides an overview of the Solaris PC NetLink software and describes its server functionality.

The four basic components of the PC NetLink software are:

- PC NetLink base code—This software consists of several processes that support the fundamental functionality of the Solaris PC NetLink server.

- PC NetLink Server Manager software—This application, based on Java, lets you configure the Solaris functionality to administer the PC NetLink servers and clients. It consists of both a client and server code as well as all the support software required to execute the application.

- NetBIOS driver—This driver supports requests from both the clients and the PC NetLink server and is installed as a network driver. While included with the PC NetLink software, the NetBIOS driver works independently of other PC NetLink software components.

- PC NetLink utilities—These are the WIN16 and WIN32 utilities used to configure the Windows NT domain items in the PC NetLink server. These are the same tools used on Microsoft Windows NT 4.0 server to administer Windows NT servers.

Knowing what is and is not required by the PC NetLink server base software can help keep the /opt directory as small as possible. TABLE 2-1 shows the software components in each package and whether the package must be installed on all PC NetLink servers, or is optional and can be installed elsewhere. Large Solaris servers sometimes contain over 100 packages.

TABLE 2-1   PC NetLink Server Software Packages

Package Name	Content	Optional
SUNWlzac— PC NetLink Server Adm Common	Java Runtime Environment needed to support both the client and server sides of the PC NetLink Manager. Also contains the uninstaller for the entire product	Not optional
SUNWlzag— PC NetLink Server Adm GUI	PC NetLink Server Manager client Java application	Optional only if you have access to the package from some other server or do not plan to use PC NetLink Server Manager to configure your server.
SUNWlzas— PC NetLink Server Adm Srv	The server side of the PC NetLink Server Manager application	This package requires the SUNWlzac. Optional only if you will not use the PC NetLink Server Manager.
SUNWlzcl— PC NetLink Server-Client Utilities	A TCP/IP stack used by the PC NetLink environment	Required only if you will not perform system administration tasks from Windows for Workgroup 3.11 machines.
SUNWlzd— Administration Documentation	The full PC NetLink Server documentation	Required only if the documentation has not been installed on another accessible server.
SUNWlzm— PC NetLink Server Man Pages	The man pages for every Solaris command-line executable that installed with the PC NetLink Server	Needs to be installed on only one server at a site. The man pages can then be exported to all other servers.
SUNWlznb— Sun NetBIOS Transport	The code needed to create the /dev/nb and /dev/nbdg driver that support the NetBIOS interface layer	Required for basic functionality.

TABLE 2-1   PC NetLink Server Software Packages *(Continued)*

Package Name	Content	Optional
SUNWlzs— PC NetLink Server base	The base Sun Link Server functionality	Required for basic functionality.
SUNWlzst— PC NetLink Server Tools	The Win32 and Win16 utilities for performing Windows NT Server Administration. They consist of the User Manager, System Manager, and Event Manager	Required if the Windows NT 4.0 workstations, or Win 9X PCs will be used to configure PC NetLink.
SUNWlzsr— Data configuration information	This package was introduced in Version 1.1. The files in this package were in the SUNWlzs package in Version 1.0	Required in every PC NetLink 1.1. Does not exist in Version 1.

At a bare minimum, only the SUNWlzs and SUNWlznb and SUNWlzsr (for Version 1.1) packages must be installed if the following restrictions apply:

- You can configure Solaris and PC NetLink Server using the command-line options only.
- You have access to Windows NT 4.0 server tools User Manager, System Manager, and Event Manager.

PC NetLink Server Manager Architecture

The PC NetLink software is a layered product that requires some unique administration requirements. These requirements are met by the PC NetLink Server Manager tool—PC NetLink server manager software (also known as SunLink Server Manager, path =opt/lanman/sbin/slsmgr). Knowing something about its architecture may help avoid problems that can occur with complex server configurations.

The PC NetLink Server Manager software consists of client and server Java applications. Its user interface was designed to be familiar to Windows NT administrators. The client component of the PC NetLink Server Manager is supported on Solaris clients as well as Windows NT 4.0, Windows 95, Windows 98, and Windows 2000. The software uses Remote Method Invocation (RMI) and the rmiregistry to bind the client to the server.

The PC NetLink Server Manager software supports the administrative tasks normally performed during the initial installation and configuration of a Windows NT server, such as:

- Setting the name, domain name, and role (PDC vs. BDC) of the server
- NetBIOS configuration, including B or H node and WINS address
- Configuration of Solaris printers, which must be done to map Windows NT printers to Solaris printer queues

These various services can be started and stopped with this tool.

The PC NetLink software provides configuration parameters that allow access from both Solaris and Windows NT environments. The PC NetLink Server Manager software supports the configuration of these parameters together with a rich set of informational and help text that describes their effects.

While standard Windows NT tools can be used to manage the PC NetLink server after it is installed and working, they cannot control the Solaris administration that may be required to support the PC NetLink server software. Solaris commands facilitate monitoring the Solaris resources needed by the PC NetLink software. The functionality offered by the PC NetLink Server Manager duplicates the functionality provided by the Solaris or the PC NetLink command-line interface. The man pages for these command-line interfaces are documented in Appendix C.

Note – The Java Runtime Environment is required only if you want to use the PC NetLink Server Manager GUI. It is not required for base level Solaris PC NetLink software support that PC clients require.

Runtime Architecture

The GUI, which is based on Java, runs on all the PC clients that the server supports (except for Windows for Workgroup 3.11), as well as the Solaris clients or servers. The PC NetLink Server Manager server code is installed by default when you install the Solaris PC NetLink software via the install script, or, in the case of PC NetLink 1.1, during the Solaris Easy Access Server (SEAS) installation. The client portion of the PC NetLink Server Manager software is shipped with PC NetLink server software and is available in the /opt/lanman/shares directory after a standard installation.

PC NetLink Server Manager software requires the use of the Java Runtime Environment (JRE) software that comes with a specific version of the Java Development Kit (JDK™). If you have a previously installed version of JDK that does not work with the JRE software required by the PC NetLink Server Manager software, in some instances you can install the required version of the JDK in addition to any version required by other software. Special attention should be made to issues that may exist by having two different versions of the JDK existing on the same server at the same time. If these issues become too difficult to resolve, you can install and administrate the Solaris PC NetLink software without the need of the PC NetLink Server Manager software. This requires administrating the PC NetLink software via command-line options alone.

The PC NetLink Server Manager client application, while based on a specific version of the JDK, does not interfere with other client applications based on Java. It is developed and installed in such a way that the JDK virtual machine (VM) and Java support libraries are used privately by the PC NetLink Server Manager client software. The JRE running on a PC client may require additional memory resources, so be sure to run the PC client Java code on a PC with sufficient memory.

Client-Server Architecture

Remote Method Invocation (RMI) is the framework used by the client portion of the software to initiate a PC NetLink Server Manager session (see FIGURE 2-1). After a standard installation of the PC NetLink server software, the Session Manager process will start as part of a normal PC NetLink server startup. Its role is to handle a secure login by a system administrator on a PC or Solaris client. Once you are logged on, the Session Manager process acts as remote object factory to support your requests, using the PC NetLink Server Manager client software. While the actual API interface used by client and server portions of the software to communicate is not documented, Appendix C provides a well-documented set of commands. You can use these commands to develop tools to extend PC NetLink Server administration. Chapter 8 shows how to combine these commands in scripts to perform a variety of functions.

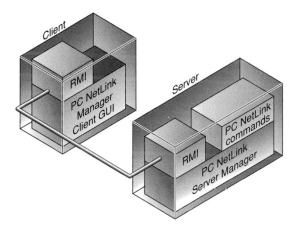

FIGURE 2-1   PC NetLink Server Manager Client-Server Architecture

PC NetLink Server Manager Security

The PC NetLink Server Manager software implements a security envelope above the RMI layer using the Java Cryptography API of the JDK. This API enables:

- Client connection is authenticated at login.
- No password is ever transmitted in clear text.
- All client-server communications are authenticated.
- Required access level is verified for all client requests.
- All client-server communications have the option of data integrity.

Installing PC NetLink Server Manager on Microsoft Clients

The PC NetLink server media contains a `setup.exe` file that installs the PC version of the PC NetLink Server Manager client. It was constructed with InstallShield. An auto-run file automatically invokes this installer when the CD is placed in the drive if the PC is running Windows NT 4.0, Windows 95, or Windows 98. This software's use of the Microsoft Registry conforms to the requirements listed in *Meeting Windows Logo Requirements With InstallShield 5.5*. The software is installed in the appropriate software directory (determined by the ProgramFileDir Registry parameter). The Solaris PC NetLink software installation creates the Registry parameters in TABLE 2-2.

TABLE 2-2   Installation Data Parameter Keys

InstallLocation	The path of the installation executable
JavaRuntimeVersion	The version of Java Runtime installed by this product

Solaris PC NetLink Server Architecture

Under normal operation, no one needs to be concerned with the architecture for simple installations of the Solaris PC NetLink software. However, for server consolidation and some of the tuning techniques to improve performance, an understanding of the architecture may be necessary. FIGURE 2-2 shows a functional diagram of the Solaris PC NetLink server architecture.

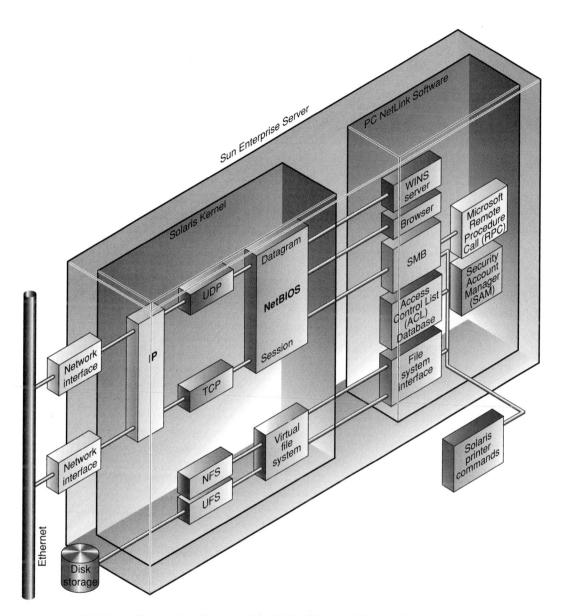

FIGURE 2-2   Interaction Between the PC NetLink and Solaris Software

FIGURE 2-2 shows how the various services are layered. In addition it shows where the PC NetLink Server functionality ends and the Solaris functionality begins. Important points to note from FIGURE 2-2 are:

- Most of the PC NetLink server code runs in user mode. Only the supplied NetBIOS layer runs at the kernel level. This feature protects all other Solaris processes from any possible problem the PC NetLink server might have. Outside of resource allocation, these user-level processes cannot directly interfere with other user processes on the system.

- The PC NetLink server software makes its calls to and from the network layer through the NetBIOS layer.

- The NetBIOS layer, in turn, uses TCP and UDP protocols through the IP layer.

- The Access Control List (ACL) and Security Account Manager (SAM) are supported by the PC NetLink server privately maintained database. On a Windows NT machine, this Windows NT domain style ACL is stored in the NTFS file system.

- File lock information is handled at the user level and is maintained inside shared memory.

- The actual server processes that support this functionality are not shown, but will be explained later in this chapter.

Supported Windows NT Network Services

File and print sharing services require implementation of the Server Message Block (SMB) protocol. Many versions of this protocol have been released over the years. Documentation of the most recent version, renamed the Common Internet File System (CIFS), was released by Microsoft. The CIFS protocol was implemented in Windows NT 4.0 and is supported by the PC NetLink server. The CIFS specifications are available at http://www.cifs.com/. The specific version of the CIFS protocol that comes closest to what the PC NetLink software supports is the NTLM 0.12 version.

This information may be useful if you need to diagnose some obscure problem that requires sniffing the network wire. Knowing the specific protocol the PC NetLink software supports is of little value to customers that know only that they are running a specific operating system. It is not always easy to determine which network protocol version a PC client operating system supports. Sun Microsystems bases its support in terms customers can relate to, namely the PC Client operating systems that will be using the PC NetLink functionality. For example, it is stated by the Solaris PC NetLink specifications that it supports the file and print operations originating from PCs running the Microsoft Windows 98 operating system (among others). Without knowing the exact protocol designation, you know that if you have a Windows 98 PC Client it is officially supported by Sun.

The NTFS security model associates ACLs with each file and directory. While the PC NetLink server maps file and directory paths to the Solaris file system name space, it maintains a separate database of ACLs associated with the paths. This enables the PC NetLink server to provide NTFS semantics over the network. The PC NetLink server also maintains DOS file attributes for each file. The attributes are maintained in special Solaris group ownerships assigned to the file, rather than in a separate database as the ACLs are. The PC NetLink server installation creates these special Solaris groups (DOS----, DOS---h, and so on) in the /etc/group file if they do not already exist in the naming service.

Naming and network address services require NetBIOS, WINS, DNS, and DHCP. NetBIOS supports the registration and lookup of NetBIOS name/IP mappings on a subnet. WINS extends this service across subnets. Microsoft extended its DNS server so that it will communicate with WINS servers for lookups that cannot be resolved from its static database. Therefore, after a client has registered its NetBIOS name/IP mapping with the WINS server, it can be located using the Microsoft DNS. The PC NetLink server supports NetBIOS and WINS, but does not support DNS or DHCP directly. However, both DNS and DHCP support are provided by the Solaris platform. The lack of a WINS interface in Solaris DNS is a drawback that can be mitigated by a combination of the Solaris Dynamic DNS and DHCP.

The Windows NT Browser service publishes lists of shared resources (printer and file shares) that are available in a workgroup or Windows NT Domain. The familiar Network Neighborhood listing is derived from a browser. The PC NetLink server includes a port of the Windows NT Browser service.

The Windows NT Directory Replication Service supports export and import for directories. If a directory is exported, the contents of the files and directories below it are periodically copied to remote systems that imported that directory. The PC NetLink server includes a port of the Windows NT Directory Replication Service.

The Windows NT Authentication service supports user authentication within a Windows NT Domain. The Windows NT Security Account Manager (SAM) is the store of user accounts for the domain. A copy of the SAM must exist on any server designated as a domain controller capable of authenticating a user. Updates to the SAM are directed to the primary domain controller (PDC). Changes to the PDC's SAM are periodically sent to the Backup Domain Controllers (BDC). A PDC can be demoted to a BDC, and a BDC can then be promoted to the PDC (only one per domain). The PC NetLink servers can be configured as either a PDC or BDC, and fully support the Windows NT network authentication protocols.

The Windows NT management protocols are layered on the Microsoft RPC (MS-RPC). The PC NetLink server includes an implementation of MS-RPC along with the RPC procedures that implement the server side of the Windows NT management protocols. Therefore, the PC NetLink server supports the common Windows NT management GUIs (run from a PC client), including Event Viewer, User Manager, Registry Editor, and Server Manager. Support for Windows NT management interface means that the PC NetLink server supports a large subset of the Microsoft

WIN32 API because it relies upon these management interfaces.

FIGURE 2-3 provides an architectural overview of the implementation of services and protocols.

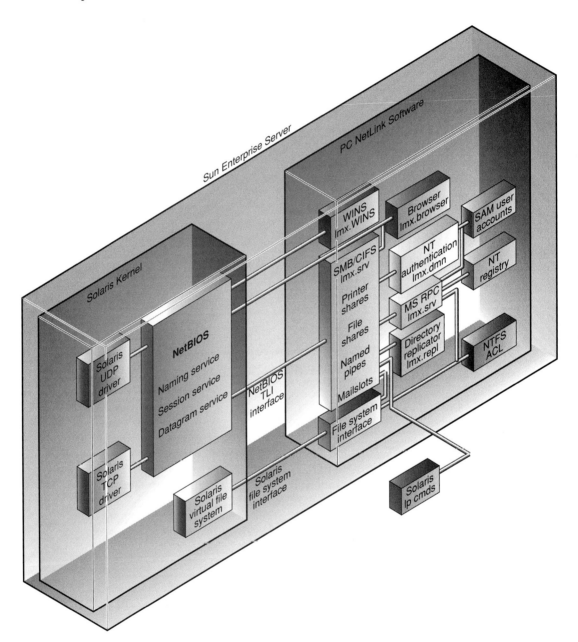

FIGURE 2-3 Relationships Between Major PC Netlink Components

FIGURE 2-3 illustrates the relationships between the major components of the portion of the PC NetLink server that supports the Windows NT protocols and services. The name of the PC NetLink server daemons (`lmx.browser`, `lmx.srv`, etc.) are seen within the block labeled "PC NetLink Server". The lines from the "PC NetLink Server" block are shown going to and from the "Solaris Kernel" block which highlights the primary interfaces the PC NetLink software uses to support it's functionality.

The Registry maintains configuration and tuning parameters for nearly all of the services. Even though lines were not drawn between the Registry and the other services, the services do query the Registry.

The lines from MS-RPC to the ACL, Registry, and SAM support the APIs used to manage those components from client management tools.

The interfaces between the Browser, Authentication, MS-RPC, and Replication services and the SMB/CIFS modules are *named pipes* and *mailslots*, which are network communication endpoints. The services create well-known named pipes or mailslots in the SMB name space, and service the requests that arrive on them through connections from the client. The SMB connection is layered on a NetBIOS connection created by the NetBIOS Session service. Mailslots (class 2) are layered on the NetBIOS Datagram service. The NetBIOS session and datagram services use the TCP and UDP drivers respectively.

The alerter is an Windows NT service that sends alert messages to clients or to specific users. For example, a server can be configured to send a message to a particular client if a power failure occurs. The alert is displayed in the center of the client's monitor.

The daemons that provide the various services are controlled by the control daemon—`lmx.ctrl`. The control daemon spawns (and stops) the others as appropriate and communicates with them through a Named Streams pipe. A client request for a connection is initiated with a request to the control daemon, which creates a NetBIOS connection and passes the corresponding file descriptor to the appropriate daemon. Each `lmx.srv` process can support connections to more than one client. However, additional `lmx.srv` daemons are spawned as the number of connections per daemon reaches a threshold. The number of file descriptors per daemon is set to a hard limit—1024 in the default Solaris configuration.

The states of open files and locks are maintained in a shared memory segment. This shared memory segment also contains the set of shared resources and client connections. Each daemon maps this segment.

Shared libraries contain code that implements the ACL, Registry, and SAM subsystems, as well as the file system and printer interfaces. The `libasusec.so` library implements the ACL and Registry subsystems. The `libsam.so` library implements the SAM. Much of the file and print system is implemented in the `liblmx.so` library. The `lp_ops.so` library is used to support the PSI functionality while the PSI API itself is supported by the `libmxpsi.so` library. Portions of the `lmx.srv` process that make the PSI calls are in the `liblmx.so` library.

The ACL, Registry, and SAM data are stored in what are known as Binary Large OBject (or BLOB) files. The format of a BLOB file consists of a free block map, a key map that maps keys to blocks, three hash lists that map some searchable value to a key, and the data blocks themselves. This format is intended to support efficient lookups, but updating a record requires updates to many structures within the BLOB file. Because of the small chance that the structures of the BLOB file could become inconsistent as a result of a crash, the PC NetLink software provides command-line utilities that restore the consistency of BLOB files—`acladm`, `regadm`, and `samcheck`. You can use the PC NetLink Server Manager GUI to run these utilities.

The administration of the WINS service is unique in that the WINS RPC management interface is layered directly on TCP/IP, rather than on Named Pipes over SMB. Without a well-known Named Pipe name, the WINS service needs the help of the endpoint mapper, which maps a request for the WINS administration interface to the TCP/IP port that the WINS service has registered. The endpoint mapper is implemented as the daemon `lmx.ep` and listens at port 135.

Integrating Solaris and Microsoft Environments

The PC NetLink server software provides services that are usually provided by the operating system, such as user authentication and file locking. The relationships between these PC NetLink services and the Solaris services are configurable in order to support two general types of environments—one in which users access the server resources only from a Microsoft client, and the other in which users can access resources from either Solaris or Microsoft clients.

User Account Mapping for Microsoft-Only Accounts

For Microsoft-only accounts, users have an identity in the Windows NT Domain (the PC NetLink server SAM) and have no identity in any Solaris naming service. Files created by any user in this environment are owned by the Solaris user `lmworld`— one of the password accounts created by the PC NetLink software installation. (The PC NetLink server installation also creates `lmxadmin` and `lmguest` accounts to which the special Windows NT accounts Administrator and Guest are mapped.) File locking is provided solely by the PC NetLink server, without support of Solaris locking.

User Account Mapping for Solaris and Microsoft Accounts

In accounts mapped for both Solaris and Microsoft accounts, users can have an identity in both the Windows NT Domain (SAM) and a Solaris naming service. You can create mappings between the Windows NT (SAM) account and a Solaris account using the mapuname command. Newly created files are owned by the Solaris user to which the Windows NT account is mapped. You can also configure locking so that the PC NetLink Server locks are propagated to Solaris locks.

For dual-mapped accounts, the PC NetLink server provides the tools passwd2sam and sam2passwd to maintain mappings between Windows NT and Solaris user accounts. If updates to accounts are made to the Solaris naming service, the passwd2sam utility migrates these updates to the Windows NT SAM. Since passwords cannot be migrated, this tool can create a file with a list of random passwords for the new accounts, or assign a single password to all of the new Windows NT accounts. Use sam2passwd utility in environments where the updates are made to the Windows NT SAM. The utility will generate a file in /etc/passwd format that can be merged with an /etc/passwd file or with NIS maps.

NetBIOS Transport Support

The PC NetLink server supports network protocols by way of the NetBIOS over the TCP/IP layer. This layer is based on the RFC1001/1002 NetBIOS protocol and is a standard networking protocol used primarily by PCs. It is one layer below the SMB (Server Message Block) protocol used by Windows NT networking, and one layer above the TCP/IP protocol. In the PC NetLink server, the NetBIOS protocol is implemented in kernel space using the standard STREAMS framework (FIGURE 2-4.)

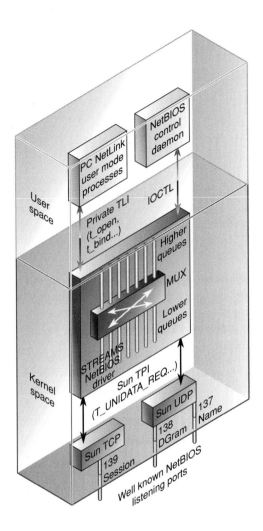

FIGURE 2-4 Network Paths and Components

The PC NetLink server NetBIOS kernel component is a regular kernel STREAMS multiplexing network protocol device driver that implements the RFC1001/1002 NetBIOS protocol. It exposes a private TLI interface to the user mode PC NetLink server components. It uses regular TPI STREAMS messages to communicate with Sun TCP and UDP STREAMS drivers. It is controlled by a user mode daemon that starts up at boot time to control and manage the multiplexing STREAMS driver. The daemon controls the driver through private I_STR ioctls. It has no dependency on other PC NetLink server components and can be viewed as a self-contained software component (FIGURE 2-5.)

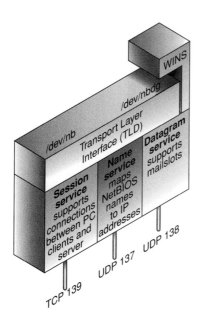

FIGURE 2-5 NetBIOS Architecture

The NetBIOS layer attaches to specific TCP/IP sockets on the system and also responds to specific broadcasts to support NetBIOS naming requests. For this reason, only one NetBIOS layer can be active on a server at one time. Neither SunLink PC (Syntax Totalnet), nor Samba can have active NetBIOS functionality while the PC NetLink software is running. See Chapter 6 for help with making a transition to and from these environments.

When Sun Microsystems started developing the Solaris PC NetLink software, it evaluated many UNIX-based NetBIOS layers. The one chosen to bootstrap the work was from NCR, which had been used to support other AT&T AS/U implementations. This NetBIOS layer has since undergone many changes to make it more robust and better able to take advantage of multiprocessor environments. Little of the original code now exists in the current shipping product.

NetBIOS is typically supported on three different transport layers. The PC NetLink 1.0 software only supports NetBIOS over TCP. Use of the TCP transport is the most scalable solution, so it is the preferred transport for any large organization. Microsoft Windows operating systems (Windows 95, 98, and Windows NT 4.0) all support the TCP protocol. Users who have been using other protocols on their PC clients (such NetBEUI, and NetBIOS over IPX) and have *not* installed TCP, must install the TCP protocol from the appropriate OS CD-ROM or diskette. This situation is highly unlikely, however, as all web browsers and Internet-aware applications use the TCP protocol, exclusively requiring the installation of the TCP layer.

The PC NetLink software NetBIOS supports both B- and H-node types. A full description of these node types is beyond the scope of this book. Refer to Windows NT 4.0 documentation for a full description of B- and H-node types.

The important points to keep in mind about the NetBIOS architecture is its use of specific TPC and UDP sockets to support its functionality. Specifically these sockets are:

- TCP Socket 139 Session Service
- UDP 137 Name Service (WINS involvement)
- UDP 138 Datagram Service mail slots

Note that the NetBIOS layer used by Sun Microsystems is a multi-threaded version of NetBIOS. This means that as the number of concurrent PC client operations are processed by a multiprocessor PC NetLink server, multiple processors can process instructions within the NetBIOS layer without interfering with one another (FIGURE 2-6.) One processor handles the request for one PC client, while another processor handles a request for another PC client without slowing down because of resource contention. It does, however, maintain `mutex` locks around data memory that maintains NetBIOS state information. The code executed while these `mutex` are in effect is small, and will cause only slight delays as threads running on other processors attempt to flow through the code and are blocked by the `mutex`.

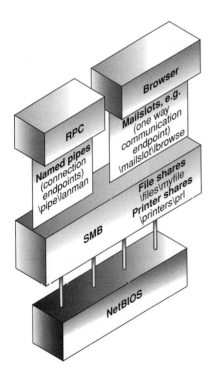

FIGURE 2-6   NetBIOS Named Pipes and Mailslots

NetBIOS Changes to the Solaris Operating Environment

When the PC NetLink server NetBIOS is installed, the following changes are made to the Solaris environment:

1. The netbios script is placed into /etc/init.d. The /etc/rc2.d/S98netbios and /etc/rc1.d/K20netbios symbolic links are created to point back to this script. This script is used to start and stop the NetBIOS layer.

2. /kernel/drv—The nbx driver and the configuration file are placed in the directory.

3. Device links /dev/nb, /dev/nbdg are created.

4. The NetBIOS control daemon is installed into /opt/SUNWlznb/sbin/nbdaemon

5. Configuration and monitoring utilities are installed: /opt/SUNWlznb/sbin/...

6. Network interface related config files are created and initialized: /etc/opt/ SUNWlznb/...

7. Other config files are installed: /var/opt/SUNWlznb/...

8. The NetBIOS man pages are added. /opt/SUNWlznb/man

NetBIOS Relationship With the Java Admin Tool

In addition to allowing the user to configure the NetBIOS component through command-line utilities, the Java-based PC NetLink Server Manager (slsmgr) enables the user to change parameters through a Graphical User Interface (GUI). Any change requiring a restart of the NetBIOS layer will require the user of the GUI to give permission for the restart. The GUI can be used remotely.

PC NetLink Server Printer Architecture

The PC NetLink server's role in handling printing requests for PC clients falls into two categories. First, the security measures are enforced to allow users to access a particular printer. Second, the PC NetLink software works with Solaris software to maintain a printer spooler to accept print jobs. The PC NetLink server only moves the data from the client to the printer. It has little notion of what kind of printer it is spooling output to. If the PC client creates a network printer using the wrong printer driver, the PC NetLink software will send this incorrectly matched printer output to the printer, resulting in garbage output or a confused printer.

FIGURE 2-7 PC Netlink Printing Subsystem

The PC NetLink server printing system has four layers (FIGURE 2-7.) Each lmx.srv process can handle printer-related functions. Within a server process is a full set of Windows-style printer server components, such as the spooler. The Printer Subsystem Interface (PSI) layer is the API that the server process uses to contact the underlying Solaris print services. Support for PSI calls are scattered throughout the parts of the server that need access to the printing subsystem. PSI is completely ignorant of the print subsystem. The PSI layer simply calls the corresponding functions in the PSI library for each function in PSI that was called by the lmx.srv process.

The PSI library is the interface library between the PSI API and Solaris print services. The PSI library, which is implemented as a shared library, converts each PSI function call into its corresponding Solaris lp command. All communication between the PC NetLink software and Solaris software within the printing subsystem occurs inside the PSI library. Unlike the PSI layer above, the PSI library from the original AS/U code was rewritten for PC NetLink to take full advantage of Solaris software.

Printer Names

Four different names appear in the printing subsystem of the PC NetLink server. Each name has its own purpose and restrictions.

- Solaris Printer Name—This is the name of the Solaris print queue that prints the requests passed in from the PC NetLink server PSI library. As with any other lp print queue, this name must adhere to the lp naming restrictions. Legal characters are [A–Z], [a–z], [0–9], and "_". This name must be between 1 and 14 characters long. No other characters or white space are permitted in an lp printer name. Follow instructions in the *PC NetLink Server Administration Guide* to avoid problems with the naming rules.

- Windows Printer Name—This is the actual name that Windows clients will interact with. This name is a Windows NT-style long name, and it can have any of the following characters: [A–Z], [a–z], [0–9], and "_". Unlike Solaris printer names, Windows printer names can have white space, and can be as long as the Windows NT long name limit (255 characters). Downlevel clients, however, may not be able to see the entire name.

- Windows Share Name—Every PC NetLink server printer consists of both a printer and a share. The printer share name must adhere to the DOS 8.3 naming length (that is, 12 characters). The share name for a printer is automatically created from the first 12 characters of that printer's Windows printer name. Users never directly interact with the Windows share name of a printer from Windows clients. It is visible while browsing the root level of the PC NetLink server from a Windows client. It is also visible from other commands, such as net share.

- Solaris Class Name—Each Windows print queue is mapped on a one-to-one basis with a Solaris printer class. This printer class is generated automatically whenever a Windows printer is created by the PC NetLink server. The name of this class is the first 14 characters of the Windows printer name, with the white space converted to underscores. This class is never seen from the Windows side, but it should not be removed from the Solaris server.

Printer Installation With the PC NetLink Software

Printer installation is a three-step process, and is covered in the *PC NetLink Server Administration Guide*. This section describes only the architectural details of printer installation.

1. Solaris Printer Install—To be used by the PC NetLink software, a Solaris printer must be configured so that it is locally spooled. The Install Solaris Printer task in the PC NetLink Server Manager was created to ensure proper configuration of Solaris printers. Any printer properly set up with the PC NetLink Server Manager is a potential PC NetLink shared printer.

The PC NetLink software supports only locally spooled printers because the PC NetLink software must have access to the spool directory of the Solaris server that is actually doing the printing. Without this access, it would not be possible for Windows clients to have job control.

A locally spooled printer is not the same as a local printer. Network printers can be locally spooled, in fact, to many different machines at the same time. The PC NetLink Server Manager correctly configures lp print queues for network printers so that they are locally spooled. Using other tools for this task, such as Solaris Admintool, is not recommended because they do not force users to set up a local spool for their network printer.

A Solaris printer that is being used as a PC NetLink shared printer is still a viable Solaris printer for use by Solaris clients.

2. PC NetLink Printer Installation—The creation of a PC NetLink server shared print queue is basically the construction of a link between a Windows print queue and a Solaris lp print queue. This link takes the following form:

Upon completion of the Add Printer Wizard on Windows, three new entities are created: a Windows print queue, a Windows printer share, and a Solaris printer class. The Windows printer name is entered by the user, and the share and lp class are constructed based on that name, adhering to the naming rules. Note that while the Windows Add Printer Wizard also asks for a printer share name, the information entered there is ignored. The share name that the PC NetLink software uses is constructed from the Windows printer name.

Note also that the Windows printer name cannot be the same as the Solaris printer name because of the Solaris class that is constructed. lp uses a single name space for class names and printer names. Because the Solaris class name for the printer is constructed from the Windows printer name, if the Windows printer name was the same as the Solaris printer name, the PC NetLink software would attempt to create a Solaris class with that name, which is not possible in lp.

After a successful installation, browsing the PC NetLink server from the Network Neighborhood on a Windows NT client will display the printer in two locations. The printer share appears at the root level of the server. This printer icon has the Windows share name for that printer. Inside the printers folder is the Windows print queue. This printer icon has the full length Windows printer name. The Solaris printer class is not visible from the Windows side. If you look at the Solaris lp configuration, you can see that an lp class was created, and its members are the Solaris printers that are to receive the print jobs from that particular Windows printer. This is usually one printer, but can be more if multiple Solaris printers were mapped to a single Windows print queue.

The printers folder of a the PC NetLink server is not visible from Windows 95 or 98 clients. These clients can see the printer only at the share level.

3. Client Printer Install—Each client uses the full length Windows NT long name as the printer name when performing the local install. The printer driver must match that of the actual printer.

Printing Queues and Communication

The PC NetLink software maintains the list of Windows printer queues internally. Information about the Solaris print queues is available from lp. Communication between the PC NetLink software and lp is a critical issue because they do not use the same name space. The PC NetLink software only uses the Windows printer and share names, while lp is only aware of the Solaris class name(FIGURE 2-8.) This can be a problem. If the PC NetLink software sends an API call with the Windows printer name, everything is fine because the Windows printer name can be used by the PSI library to construct either the Windows share name or the Solaris lp class name as needed. However, if the PC NetLink software sends an API call with the Windows share name, there will be a problem. From the 12-character share name, it is not possible to reconstruct either the full length Windows printer name or the Solaris lp class name. The solution is to ensure that all communication between the PC NetLink software and the PSI library uses the long Windows printer name.

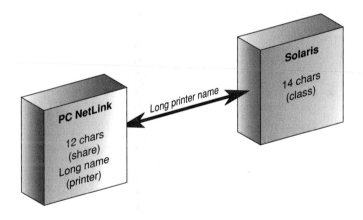

FIGURE 2-8 PC Netlink Printer Communication

A potential problem with this mechanism, which the PC NetLink software deals with, is that when an lmx.srv process starts (either because a new one was spawned to deal with the load, or because the server was restarted), the server process must be able to rematch lp class names with Windows printer names. To solve this problem, a storefile provides stable storage of (longname, classname) pairs. This file is located at /var/opt/lanman/datafiles/.lpstorefile.

Because the `lpstorefile` is written to each time a printer is created, and multiple `lmx.srv` processes can create printers at the same time, the `lpstorefile` is protected by a write-lock mechanism. This is a straightforward exclusive write-lock. Any number of `lmx.srv` processes can read the `lpstorefile` at once, but only one at a time can write to it.

lpstat

In the PC NetLink 1.0 software, all time consuming calls to `lpstat` (such as those with the `-s`, `-t`, or `-v` flags) were replaced with a PC NetLink software specific function, referred to here as pseudo-lpstat. Pseudo-lpstat returns only the names of locally spooled printers. In Solaris networks that use both Solaris print servers and the PC NetLink print servers, this saves a lot of time because the machine acting as a PC NetLink server does not have to contact all the Solaris print servers on the network to generate a list of names.

Pseudo-lpstat works by listing all the printers that have directories inside `/etc/lp/printers` (by a call to `ls`). This is a complete listing of all the locally-spooled printers (and therefore all the printers that can potentially become PC NetLink shared printers). Pseudo-lpstat is much faster than a call to the traditional `lpstat` for these purposes, especially when the number of print queues is large.

The creation of pseudo-lpstat also solves a conflict between the PC NetLink server and the `lp` interest list. The `lp` interest list is the list of Solaris print queues returned by `lpstat`. While you can create and use printers that are not on the interest list, they will not be returned by `lpstat` even when `lpstat` is set to list all printers. The `lp` interest list can be modified by either the `lpset` command or by directly editing `/etc/printers.conf`. Because the PC NetLink software no longer uses `lpstat` to list the Solaris print queues, users need not worry about adding printers created by the PC NetLink Server Manager to the `lp` interest list. The `lp` interest list does not interact with the PC NetLink software in any way. The PC NetLink software can continue to use the `lp` interest list to control the list of printers that Solaris clients see when using that machine as a Solaris print server.

Printing Registry Keys

A variety of registry keys are associated with printers. The most important thing to note about the keys is that the registry always uses the share name for permanent storage. By using the smallest name in the registry, you can find the proper key regardless of whether the procedure doing the search has the share name or the long name.

Print Jobs

Each PC NetLink server print job corresponds to a specific lp print job. However, the life cycle of a PC NetLink server print job is more complicated than that of an ordinary Solaris print request. The following operations occur:

1. Starting a Job—When a PC NetLink server receives a print request from a Windows client, the PSI library starts an lp job request. A paused lp job is created to hold the information for the print job, and resumes in order to print it. This paused lp job is simply created by a call to lp with the -H hold flag.

At the time of job creation, a Solaris job is assigned a *jobid* that is unique to the lp system on that Solaris server. A full Solaris *jobid* consists of a number and the name of the Solaris print queue. For example, job number 10 on printer prntbw has a Solaris *jobid* of prntbw-10. The numerical portion of the *jobid* is unique among *all* printers on that server. In other words, if you have a job prntbw-10, there will not be a job prntcol-10, but there could be a prntcol-9 or prntcol-11.

When Solaris lp creates a job, it creates two files in the spool directory for that job (for reference: the lp spool directory is /var/spool/lp/tmp/*uname*, where *uname* is the Solaris hostname). The two files have names *jobid*-0 and *jobid*-1, where *jobid* is the numerical portion of the Solaris *jobid* of that job. For example, for Solaris job prntbw-10, the two files created are 10-0 and 10-1. The *jobid*-0 file is the lp status file. This file contains a variety of fields reflecting the status of the job in lp. The *jobid*-1 file (hereafter referred to as the lp spool file) is the corresponding data file for that lp job.

When the PC NetLink server creates the paused print request, it must supply lp with a filename. Ideally, this would be the name of the lp spool file, but the PC NetLink software cannot get an lp *jobid* before submitting the job. Therefore, the PC NetLink software creates a unique filename to provide to lp. These files are named lptmp*pid-nonce* where *pid* is the pid of the lmx.srv process that started the job, and *nonce* is the job's PC NetLink server *jobid*. This file will hereafter be referred to as the PC NetLink server spool file.

Each job actually has two different *jobids*. The PC NetLink server *jobid* is taken from an internal counter held by each lmx.srv process. Each lmx.srv process starts counting with job 1, and the counter rolls over after 8192 jobs on a particular process. The Solaris *jobid* is created by lp. Because the PC NetLink server *jobids* are not unique, two different lmx.srv processes can be concurrently using the same PC NetLink server *jobid*. Therefore, all translations from the PC NetLink server *jobid* to Solaris *jobid* also require the pid of the server process. With a pid and a PC NetLink server *jobid*, the PSI library can figure out the Solaris *jobid* by looking in the PC NetLink server status files.

The PC NetLink server status file is the fourth (and final) file involved in a print job. The PC NetLink server status files have names similar to the PC NetLink server spool files: lptmp*pid-nonce*-0. The PC NetLink server status files have three lines.

The first is the corresponding Solaris job number. The second is the name of the Solaris class that is going to print that job. The third line contains a string with the user name in the format *username* on *Windows client*. This information is needed so that the PC NetLink software can perform security checks and identify the Windows user associated with the print job. This allows only the submitter of the job or a system administrator to cancel a print job.

The group ID of the PC NetLink server status file is used to store the Windows job bits (paused, q_paused, and others). These are the same group IDs used by the PC NetLink software to store the Windows file attributes for shared files (hidden, archived, and so on). The use of the group ID to store status was inherited from AS/ U. The group ID of the PC NetLink server status file is used rather than the lp status file, because Solaris lp changes the group of an lp status file back to lp whenever it is touched by lp. This would cause loss of status information if they were not stored in a file that was not actually being used by lp.

2. Spooling—The PC NetLink software spools directly to the lp spool file. The lp job, instead of printing that file, prints the PC NetLink server spool file. To make sure that lp prints the correct data, the PC NetLink software copies the contents of the lp spool file into the PC NetLink server spool file, once it has finished spooling the data. After the PC NetLink server spool file is correct, the lp spool file is deleted.

While a job is spooling, the spooling status bit is set. It is turned on when the first function call is made that indicates a job is going to start, and it is turned off when the spool file has been written to the spool directory on the server.

3. Printing—Once the PC NetLink server spool file has the data to be printed, unless the job is paused on the Windows side, the PSI library tells lp to resume that job. Solaris lp takes control of the job and activates it to be printed. Sometime after lp has sent the job to the printer, the PC NetLink software will detect that lp has done this, and the PC NetLink software will delete the PC NetLink server status file. Once the printer is printing, the spool directory no longer contains any of the four files for that print job.

Printer Job Status

The group IDs of the PC NetLink status files for each job are used to store the job status. These are the same group IDs used by the PC Netlink software to store Windows file system attributes. The meanings on spool files are shown in TABLE 2-3.

TABLE 2-3   Group IDs as Job Status

Group ID	File System Attribute	Meaning on Spool File
DOS-a--	Archived	Queue Paused
DOS--s-	System	Job Paused
DOS---h	Hidden	Spooling

There are actually two different pause bits. One represents the actual pausing of a job, and the other the state of a job on a queue that has been paused. A job can have both pause bits set at the same time. The job will not resume and print until both pause bits are cleared.

Supported Printer Types

The three main categories of printers supported by the PC NetLink software are: PostScript™, PCL, and non-PostScript non-PCL (RAW). Through the PC NetLink Server Manager, you can properly configure a Solaris printer queue for any of these types. The Solaris printer queues appear as shown in TABLE 2-4.

TABLE 2-4   Solaris Printer Queues

Queue	Content Type	Printer Type
PostScript	simple	PS
PCL	simple	hplaserjet
RAW	simple	unknown

The content type is left as simple for all types of printers. This prevents lp from using any of its filters on the data, possibly corrupting the data in the process. The nobanner flag can be set on printer queues created via the PC NetLink Server Manager (Please refer to Chapter 9 for methods for turning banner pages off and on.) The reasoning for this is that RAW printers should print without Solaris banner pages, but the PC NetLink software cannot detect the printer type each time a job is sent off (lp requires the nobanner flag to be sent with each job as well, to prevent it from printing a banner.) Users who want to have Solaris banner pages on their PC NetLink printers can force them manually by using the command `lpadmin -p` *printername* `-o banner`.

PC NetLink Software Use of Solaris File Systems

The PC NetLink software uses normal Solaris files, supported by UFS (UNIX file system), to support PC client files. Unfortunately, there is not a one-for-one match between Solaris and Windows NT-style ACLs and Solaris file permissions. For this reason, the PC NetLink software allocates eight Solaris group IDs (GIDs) to represent the eight possible bit patterns of the DOS attributes (hidden, system, or archive). As the DOS attributes are changed by PC client applications, the PC NetLink software will store the files into the Solaris UFS files with the appropriate GIDs to represent the correct DOS attribute bit pattern. By default, the PC NetLink software allocates GIDs below 100 unless most of the GIDs below 100 have already been used. When this happens the PC NetLink software will use other unused GIDs to support this function. Therefore, the GIDs needed to support this functionality can vary from server to server. Always login to a PC NetLink server directly to see what GIDs have been used to support this function.

PC NetLink Server Processes

Once the PC NetLink software is installed and running, several processes and drivers work in concert to support PC clients. These processes are started at boot time by scripts in the `/etc/init.d` directory. The following processes run when needed to support the various functionality of the Solaris PC NetLink product:

- `lmx.ctrl`—This process is the master process for all PC NetLink functionality running on the server. It controls all other processes, listens to connection requests, and spawns `lmx.srv` processes as needed to support PC client requests to the server.

- `lmx.srv`—This process is spawned repetitively to support PC clients. A PC client is assigned to a specific `lmx.srv` process for the duration of its connection to the server. One `lmx.srv` process typically will support more than one PC client at a time. Chapter 4 describes this algorithm in detail.

- `lmx.repl`—This process supports the directory replication services supported by the PC NetLink software.

- `lmx.browser`—This process supports the browser requests made by PC clients of the PC NetLink server.

- `lmx.dmn`—This is the net login daemon that handles the authentication of users attempting to login to PC clients on the domain (PDC or BDC) of which the PC NetLink server is a member.

- `lmx.alerter`—This process supports Windows NT style Alerter service which logs system-level messages in the PC NetLink software.

- `lmx.ep`—This process acts as the endpoint mapper which maps a request for the WINS administration interface to the TCP/IP port that the WINS service has registered. The endpoint mapper listens at port 135.

- `lmx.wins`—This process supports the Windows Internet Naming Service (WINS).

Control of these processes, especially `lmx.srv`, is crucial for obtaining maximum performance in your Solaris server.

SAM Database

The Security Account Manager (SAM) database is maintained as a *BLOB* file. The data storage is composed of 128-byte fragments, and a hash table is used to map search values into the database. The key mapped values are offsets into the data file. Any data larger than 4 Kbytes is stored in a separate file named by the BLOB and the key value becomes the name of the file (for example, `registry.55`).

The SAM database stores user and group accounts keyed by Security ID (SID). Other secret accounts are also stored in the database. These accounts are used during such procedures as directory replication service, handling PDB/BDC synchronizing, and handling trusted domains.

The database resides in `/var/opt/lanman` and grows as it is used. Therefore, it is important to set aside space for its growth (see Chapter 5). Information pertaining to each domain name is kept in `/var/opt/lanman/domains/`*domainname*. This includes the administrator and guest account information.

Changes to the SAM database that are to be replicated to domain controllers reside in `/var/opt/lanman/datafiles/chglog.lmx`.

Domain-independent SAM objects, such as SID to UNIX user name mappings reside in `/var/opt/lanman/datafiles/lsa`.

The samcheck command (/opt/lanman/sbin/samcheck) is supplied in the PC NetLink software to dump the data of the SAM database. See Appendix C for the man page of this command A summary of the samcheck command is listed in TABLE 2-5.

TABLE 2-5 Commands for Displaying SAM Database Information

Command	Operation
samcheck -a	Dumps the accounts database
samcheck -b	Dumps the built-in database
samcheck -l	Dumps the lsa database
samcheck -c	Dumps the change log

The PC NetLink Server Directory Structure

Tables TABLE 2-6 through TABLE 2-13 list the package names and contents for the PC NetLink Server directory structure.

TABLE 2-6 NetBIOS Installation Package (SUNWlznb)

Package	Contents
/opt/SUNWlznb/sbin	Control daemon (nbdaemon) and the utilities used to configure it
/opt/SUNWlznb/man	Man pages for the utilities
/kernel/drv/nbx	The NetBIOS driver
/etc/opt/SUNWlznb	Directory for configuration files
/var/opt/SUNWlznb	Directory for persistent configuration data
/etc/init.d/netbios	Initialization script
/etc/rc0.d/K20netbios	Symbolic Link to /etc/init.d/netbios
/etc/rc1.d/K20netbios	Symbolic Link to /etc/init.d/netbios
/etc/rc2.d/S98netbios	Symbolic Link to /etc/init.d/netbios

TABLE 2-7 PC NetLink 1.1 Installation Package (`SUNWlzs`, `SUNWlzsr`)

Package	Contents
`/opt/lanman/bin`	User commands and utilities
`/opt/lanman/sbin`	Administration commands and utilities
`/opt/lanman/lib`	Daemons, shared libraries, and scripts that are for internal use only
`/opt/lanman/msgfiles`	Help files (`.hlp`) used by the net command, a port of Windows NT's net
`/opt/lanman/shares`	Message DLLs (Microsoft-style dynamically linked libraries) used by the net command
`/var/opt/lanman`	Directory where the persistent datafiles are maintained (BLOB files such as Registry, SAM, and ACL) (Moved to SUNWlxsr for V 1.1)
`/etc/opt/lanman/` `lanman.ini`	A configuration file available to users with the same format as Microsoft's `lanman.ini`. Its format is documented in the Admin Docs. (Moved to SUNWlxsr for V 1.1)
`/etc/init.d/ms_srv`	Initialization script
`/etc/rc0.d/K19ms_srv`	Startup script
`/etc/rc0.d/K19ms_srv`	Startup script
`/etc/rc2.d/K19ms_srv`	Startup script
`/etc/rc3.d/S99ms_srv`	Startup script
`/etc/rcS.d/K19ms_srv`	Startup script

TABLE 2-8 PC NetLink Server Manager Install Packages (`SUNWlzac`, `SUNWlzas`)

Package	Contents
`/opt/lanman/lib/java`	The server classes and "common" classes
`/opt/lanman/lib/scripts`	The scripts invoked by the Java server application and used to configure the PC NetLink Server
`/etc/init.d/slsadmin`	Initialization script
`/etc/rc0.d/K19`	Symbolic Link to `/etc/init.d/slsadmin`
`/etc/rc1.d/K19`	Symbolic Link to `/etc/init.d/slsadmin`
`/etc/rc3.d/S99`	Symbolic Link to `/etc/init.d/slsadmin`

TABLE 2-9   PC NetLink Server Client Installation Package (`SUNWizag`)

Package	Contents
`/opt/lanman/lib/locale/XXX/html`	Documentation for use of the SLS Manager (XXX = Locale)
`/opt/lanman/lib/images`	Images (.gif) used by the client gui
`/opt/lanman/lib/java`	Client Java classes
`/opt/lanman/sbin/slsmgr`	Client Java SLS Manager application

TABLE 2-10   PC NetLink Man Pages Package (`SUNWlzm`)

Package	Contents
`/opt/lanman/man/man1`	User command man pages
`/opt/lanman/man/man1m`	Administration command man pages

TABLE 2-11   PC NetLink Server Documentation Package (`SUNWlzd`)

Package	Contents
`/opt/lanman/lib/locale/XXX/html/admindoc`	The .htm and .gif files that comprise the administration guide (XXX = Locale)

TABLE 2-12   Windows NT Server Tools Package (`SUNWizst`)

Package	Contents

`/opt/lanman/shares/astools/win95`
`/opt/lanman/shares/astools/winnt.40`
`/opt/lanman/shares/astools/winnt.351`
`/opt/lanman/shares/astools/windows`
	These directories contain the Windows NT server tools (Microsoft binaries) for the client operating systems Windows 95, NT 4.0, NT 3.51, and Windows 3.11. The `astools` directory is shared so that clients can access these subdirectories over the network. The clients can either install these binaries on the local system or run them remotely from this share.

TABLE 2-13   Windows TCP Stack Package (`SUNWlzcl`) Contents

Package	Contents

`/opt/lanman/shares/msclient/tcp32wfw`
`/opt/lanman/shares/msclient/update.wfw`
`/opt/lanman/bin/makeclients`
	The Microsoft TCP stack for Windows 3.11 (WFW) and Microsoft's update to the TCP stack. The `makeclients` script copies the `tcp32wfw` and `update.wfw` directories to diskettes which can be used to install TCP on Windows 3.11 clients. Alternatively, a client which already has a TCP stack can be used to copy these directories from the `msclients` share to local diskettes

How PC NetLink Software Supports Windows NT File Systems

Just as Solaris operating environment shares (or exports) UNIX file system (UFS) volumes through the NFS™ file system, a PC NetLink server can share the same volume by a different protocol. Windows NT shares a Windows NT file system (NTFS) by these same protocols. A PC client sees no difference between shares on either system. Full functionality for Windows NT ACLs and MS-DOS file attributes are maintained. Because the UFS does not have native support for Windows NT ACLs or MS-DOS attributes, the PC NetLink software must perform a bit of magic to support these extensions of the file system.

How PC NetLink Software Supports MS-DOS Attributes

To support MS-DOS attributes, the PC NetLink software utilizes UNIX groups to store the three bits of information needed to store the system, archive, and hidden attributes. The Read/Only attribute is supported by standard UNIX permissions. An `/etc/group` file after a typical Solaris PC NetLink software installation is shown in

FIGURE 2-9. Note that groups 92–99 have been used to define groups DOS---- where ---- defines the attributes represented by that group. While in this case 92–99 group IDs were utilized for this purpose, the PC NetLink software installation will use other unused group IDs on the system if the group has already been defined. This normally causes no problems because the PC NetLink software maintains the files for the users. Using unused groups normally causes no problems when accessing the files from UNIX

```
root::0:root
other::1:
bin::2:root,bin,daemon
sys::3:root,bin,sys,adm
adm::4:root,adm,daemon
uucp::5:root,uucp
mail::6:root
tty::7:root,tty,adm
lp::8:root,lp,adm
nuucp::9:root,nuucp
staff::10:
daemon::12:root,daemon
sysadmin::14:
nobody::60001:
noaccess::60002:
nogroup::65534:
DOS----::99:lanman
DOS-a--::98:lanman
DOS--s-::97:lanman
DOS---h::96:lanman
DOS-as-::95:lanman
DOS-a-h::94:lanman
DOS--sh::93:lanman
DOS-ash::92:lanman
lmxsrvgid::91:
```

FIGURE 2-9 Typical /etc/group File After a PC NetLink Installation

To help illustrate this point, an MS-DOS batch file that produces every possible combination of the four MS-DOS attribute bits for 16 files were used to change the attributes of files on a volume shared by a PC NetLink server. The batch file is shown in CODE EXAMPLE 2-1.

CODE EXAMPLE 2-1   Batch File Used to Change MS-DOS File Attributes

```
REM Make sure all files are set to default.
attrib -a -r -h -s *.*
REM set individual MSDOS attribute bits
attrib +a +s +h +r allon
attrib -a -s -h -r alloff
REM Attributes one at a time
attrib +a a
attrib +h h
attrib +s s
attrib +r r
REM attributes two at a time
attrib +a +r a_r
attrib +a +h a_h
attrib +a +s a_s
attrib +h +s h_s
attrib +h +r h_r
attrib +r +s r_s
REM attributes three at a time
attrib +a +h +r a_h_r
attrib +a +h +s a_h_s
attrib +a +s +r a_s_r
attrib +h +s +r h_s_r
```

After the execution of the batchfile in a Windows 95 MS-DOS window, the MS-DOS `dir /v /a` command returns the output shown in FIGURE 2-10. Note the archive (A), system (S), hidden (H), and read only (R) attributes change exactly as expected.

```
  I:\don\SLStest> dir /v /a
Volume in drive I is WGS40-03
Directory of I:\don\SLStest
   File Name        Size      Allocated      Modified       Accessed   Attrib
      .            <DIR>                   01-21-99 10:44a  01-21-99      D
      ..           <DIR>                   01-21-99  9:41a  01-21-99      D
   attrtest bat      507                   01-21-99 10:45a  01-21-99
   allon               0                   01-21-99 10:41a  01-21-99    RHS  A
   alloff              0                   01-21-99 10:41a  01-21-99
   a                   0                   01-21-99 10:41a  01-21-99         A
   h                   0                   01-21-99 10:41a  01-21-99     H
   r                   0                   01-21-99 10:41a  01-21-99     R
   s                   0                   01-21-99 10:41a  01-21-99      S
   a_r                 0                   01-21-99 10:42a  01-21-99     R   A
   a_h                 0                   01-21-99 10:42a  01-21-99     H   A
   a_s                 0                   01-21-99 10:42a  01-21-99      S  A
   h_s                 0                   01-21-99 10:42a  01-21-99     HS
   h_r                 0                   01-21-99 10:42a  01-21-99     RH
   r_s                 0                   01-21-99 10:42a  01-21-99     R S
   a_h_r               0                   01-21-99 10:42a  01-21-99     RH  A
   a_h_s               0                   01-21-99 10:42a  01-21-99     HS  A
   a_s_r               0                   01-21-99 10:42a  01-21-99     R S A
   h_s_r               0                   01-21-99 10:42a  01-21-99     RHS
        17 file(s)          507 bytes
         2 dir(s)    364,052,480 bytes free
                   1,999,405,056 bytes total disk space,   81% in use
  I:\don\SLStest>
```

FIGURE 2-10 Output of the MS-DOS dir /v /a Command

In contrast, the UNIX ls command gives the result shown in FIGURE 2-11. Notice that the UNIX file permissions were changed (to "-r--r--r--" (or 444)) only when the MS-DOS read-only attribute was changed. The rest of the MS-DOS attributes change the group ID of the file with a different group representing every possible combination of the system, hidden, and archive bits.

```
wgs40-03 127 =>ls -l
total 2
-rw-r--r--    1 don        DOS-a--           0 Jan 21 10:41 a
-rw-r--r--    1 don        DOS-a-h           0 Jan 21 10:42 a_h
-r--r--r--    1 don        DOS-a-h           0 Jan 21 10:42 a_h_r
-rw-r--r--    1 don        DOS-ash           0 Jan 21 10:42 a_h_s
-r--r--r--    1 don        DOS-a--           0 Jan 21 10:42 a_r
-rw-r--r--    1 don        DOS-as-           0 Jan 21 10:42 a_s
-r--r--r--    1 don        DOS-as-           0 Jan 21 10:42 a_s_r
-rw-r--r--    1 don        DOS----           0 Jan 21 10:41 alloff
-r--r--r--    1 don        DOS-ash           0 Jan 21 10:41 allon
-rw-rw-r--    1 don        DOS----         507 Jan 21 10:45 attrtest.bat
-rw-r--r--    1 don        DOS---h           0 Jan 21 10:41 h
-r--r--r--    1 don        DOS---h           0 Jan 21 10:42 h_r
-rw-r--r--    1 don        DOS--sh           0 Jan 21 10:42 h_s
-r--r--r--    1 don        DOS--sh           0 Jan 21 10:42 h_s_r
-r--r--r--    1 don        DOS----           0 Jan 21 10:41 r
-r--r--r--    1 don        DOS--s-           0 Jan 21 10:42 r_s
-rw-r--r--    1 don        DOS--s-           0 Jan 21 10:41 s
arab64
wgs40-03 128 =>
```

FIGURE 2-11 Output of the UNIX ls Command

Also, remember the archive bit is normally set by default by the PC NetLink software every time a new file is created. Setting the archive bit signifies the file needs to be archived or backed up.

During installation, the PC NetLink installation software decides which group IDs will represent these MS-DOS attributes states. The choice of group IDs is not guaranteed to be the same from one PC NetLink installation to the next.

How PC NetLink Software Supports Windows NT ACLs

The PC NetLink software does not support Windows NT ACLs using Solaris POSIX-based ACLs. Unfortunately, POSIX ACLs do not map well to Windows NT style ACLs. Instead, the PC NetLink software uses a private database that normally resides in the /var/opt/lanman/datafiles/acl file. As users on PC clients use ACLs to access a PC NetLink server based file, the PC NetLink software will maintain a separate database that defines the ACL for each directory and file.

By default, ACLs are supported at the directory level only to save space in the database. As files are created in a directory, they take on the ACL of that directory. However, if a file is assigned an ACL that differs from its parent directory, the PC NetLink software will insert a separate file ACL entry into the database.

Maintaining a separate database for ACLs allows the PC NetLink software to support ACLs when files are being accessed by only one PC NetLink server. Because the directory and file ACL database used to support the system message block (SMB) or common internet file system (CIFS) protocol supported by the PC NetLink software exists only on the PC NetLink server where the access to the file has been made, avoid situations that allow the access of the same file from two different PC NetLink servers at the same time.

Native file system access from one Solaris system to another is supported via Solaris's own NFS protocol. If a local file system on a Solaris server A were mounted from NFS by two Solaris servers B and C running the PC NetLink software, then multiple PC NetLink servers (B and C) could access the same file on server A using the native NFS protocol. If this file is accessed by one user via the PC NetLink software on server B and by another user via the PC NetLink software on server C, the ACL database on both servers can easily get out of sync. A more restrictive ACL on the file set by one user using the PC NetLink software on server B would not be seen by the PC NetLink software running on server C and the restriction would *not* be enforced.

If ACL functionality is used by a user community, it should never be allowed to support access to files from two different PC NetLink servers at the same time or security problems can occur. Instead, make sure only one PC NetLink server is used to support access to any one file system.

If the data to be accessed is read-only, or ACL support is not required, accessing the same Solaris supported NFS from multiple PC NetLink servers may be desirable.

## CHAPTER 3

Tuning a Solaris Server to Use PC NetLink Software

This chapter discusses the parameters needed to tune a Solaris server to be used as a PC NetLink server.

Supporting Microsoft NT network functionality on Solaris using the PC NetLink software has many benefits. Solaris servers scale to very high levels with a multitude of Redundancy, Accessibility, and Serviceability (RAS) capabilities. When installing the PC NetLink software it is always important to consider tuning the Solaris server so the PC NetLink software can benefit fully from these features.

For many small server installations, a simple installation of the PC NetLink software provides a high performing, fully functional product. On large server configurations, however, some Solaris parameters must be modified to take full advantage of the system and scale as expected.

Before Installing the PC NetLink Software

Be sure your system meets the requirements for installing the PC NetLink software listed in the "PC NetLink Requirements" section in Chapter 1.

The Java Development Kit

The PC NetLink Server Manager software requires the use of the Java Runtime Environment (JRE) that comes with a specific version of the Java Development Kit (JDK). If you do not have JDK on your system, or if you have an incompatible version, the installation asks if you want to install the JDK from the Solaris PC

NetLink product CD-ROM. In this case, if you refuse to install the JDK, the PC NetLink software installation cannot proceed. The JRE JDK requirements are listed in TABLE 3-1.

TABLE 3-1   Requirements for the PC NetLink Server Manager

PC NetLink Server Manager Component	JRE of the JDK Required
PC NetLink Server Manager Client on a Windows 95, Windows 98, or Windows NT 4.0	JRE from JDK 1.1.7
PC NetLink Server Manager Client on a SPARC Solaris Client	JRE from JDK 1.1.6
PC NetLink Server Manager Server daemon on Solaris SPARC	JRE from JDK 1.1.6

The PC NetLink Server Manager does not run with the Java JDK 2.0. Both JDKs (Java JDK 1.1.X and Java JDK 2.0) can, however, coexist on the same server at the same time. System administrators need not worry about downgrading the Java JDK version by installing the PC NetLink Server Manager and its required JDK.

Under normal installations of the PC NetLink software, where JDK components have never been installed before, the JDK version details need not be a concern. The installation procedures for the individual PC NetLink Server Manager components are automatically installed and configured with the correct JRE from the appropriate JDK. If, during the installation of the PC NetLink Server Manager software, it is determined that the incorrect version of the JRE or JDK has previously been installed on the Solaris server, the installation software will give you the option of updating the JDK on the server, or attempting to continue the installation without updating the JDK. While using another version of the JDK may work fine, it will not be a supported installation.

In most cases there is no problem upgrading the JDK. If existing software components use an older version of the JDK, determine if the existing installed software can work with the JDK 1.1.6 JRE. If previously installed software requires an alternate version of the JDK, installing two versions on the same server is an option and the installation of the PC NetLink software will handle this situation.

It may be acceptable to use the PC NetLink software without the benefit of the PC NetLink Server Manager by using the command-line interface alone. The PC NetLink Server Manager supports all its functionality by running the same command-line executables you would use from a shell to perform its functions.

The PC NetLink software requires only the Java JRE to run the PC NetLink Server Manager GUI. Normal PC client-server services do not require the Java JRE for file, print, authentication, and non-PC NetLink server administration. Only if you expect to manage the PC NetLink software via a PC client do you need to install the JRE components.

After you upgrade or install the JDK, you must reboot your system to use the PC NetLink Server Manager software.

The `/opt/lanman` Directory

You may need to know the specifics of the `/opt` directory. TABLE 3-2 lists the disk space required in `/opt` for each version of the PC NetLink software.

TABLE 3-2   PC NetLink `/opt` Requirements

Package	Memory Requirement for Version 1.0 US	Memory Requirement for Version 1.0 Global	Memory Requirement for Version 1.1
SUNWlzac	296	374	372
SUNWlzag	5362	8468	5232
SUNWlzas	790	1520	922
SUNWlzcl	7010	7012	4996
SUNWlzd	1746	12030	1416
SUNWlzm	202	202	98
SUNWlznb	1370	1370	1214
SUNWlzs	26642	39662	20416
SUNWlzsr	NA	NA	122
SUNWlzst	28218	69004	62468
Total	71636 or 69.95 Mbytes	139642 or 136.36 Mbytes	97256 or 94.95 MB

Disk Space Requirements for `/var/opt/lanman/datafiles`

The databases that the PC NetLink software creates and maintains in the `/var/opt/lanman/datafiles` directory can grow considerably as the server is used. Both the user accounts in the SAM database and ACL database that stores the ACL file and directory information require space on the server. The SAM database is reasonably straightforward to plan for, as we will see. However, planning the ACL database is more difficult because of following reasons:

■ Access Control Lists are variable length.

- The ACL refers to a directory or file that in itself creates a variable length record that defines the Solaris path of the directory or file.
- Some user communities use ACLs heavily, others hardly use them at all.

A good rule of thumb is to allocate 1 Kbyte of space to store each ACL. As the database grows, the PC NetLink software will, by default, store an ACL for each directory created by the user. Files in the directory are given the same ACL as that of the directory they occupy even though no ACL is associated specifically with the file. If a user community is expected to create 100 directories per user for 500 users, initially allocate 100 * 500 * 1 Kbytes, or approximately 50 Mbytes.

Note – Plan for 1 Kbyte of disk space in `/var/opt/lanman` for each ACL your PC NetLink server supports.

If file ACLs are placed directly to files as well as the directories they are in, the ACL database can grow even faster.

SAM database records are easier to plan for. Several real SAM databases have been measured and a good rule of thumb is to plan for 4 Kbytes for each user account you plan to include in the domain for which the PC NetLink server will be a domain controller. Copies created during the normal operation can double the required space as it reaches a high water mark to perform some operations.

Note – Plan 4 Kbytes of disk space in `/var/opt/lanman/datafiles` for each user account to be placed into the SAM database. Because normal operation can create up to three instances of the database, multiply your disk requirement by three.

While this may be more disk space than you will ever need, it is important that the PC NetLink software never run out of disk space in `/var/opt/lanman/datafiles`. A domain of 5000 users requires 5000 * 4 Kbytes = 19.53 Mbytes of disk space to store one instance of the SAM database. To calculate the high water mark required during normal operation, multiply by two. The final disk space needed to support SAM database operation is ~40 Mbytes.

The ACL and SAM database disk space requirements in `/var/opt/lanman/datafiles` are only two of the databases found there. Other databases, such the registry (~200 Kbytes), require space, but the ACL and SAM databases require the most space once the server is in use.

After the server has been used for a month or so, review the disk space utilization in the `/var/opt/lanman/datafiles` directory to see if the calculations used to plan the disk space hold true. Heavy use of ACLs can force the ACL database to grow quickly, and it is the database to focus on the most. Develop your own rule of thumb for the amount of disk space your user environment requires.

Planning for High Availability and Performance

If possible, place the `/var/opt/lanman/datafiles` directory on a redundant, high-performing disk subsystem. This usually means allocating space on a hardware RAID 5, or a software RAID 0+1 disk volume and placing a symbolic link in the `/var/opt/lanman` directory pointing to the `datafiles` directory on the RAID device.

The databases in the `/var/opt/lanman` are critical to the operation of the PC NetLink software. A redundant RAID environment helps ensure that a one-disk failure will not bring down the server and lose the database that may have taken months to create.

Under normal operation, when the server has enough memory to cache most of the PC NetLink software databases, disk performance of the databases in the `/var/opt/lanman/datafiles` directory should not be a major bottleneck. However, if the server becomes starved for memory, and the ACL and SAM databases become large, the disk performance required to access these databases can become a bottleneck. Placing `/var/opt/lanman/datafiles` on a high-performing disk subsystem is the best way to avoid this situation. Again, hardware RAID 5 or software RAID 0+1 provide the highest performing redundant disk subsystem for the PC NetLink software to work with.

Saving Disk Space

Not all the PC NetLink Server packages are required on every PC NetLink server (see TABLE 2-1). If you have limited disk space and must reduce disk requirements, you can place less commonly used PC NetLink software packages on just one server of a multiserver site.

For example, to save space and consolidate the locations where certain PC administration software is located, you can place the `SUNWlzst` (PC NetLink Server Tools) package on just one server. This package contains the Win32 and Win16 Windows NT Server Administration tools that are used only on PC clients from which you want to administer a PC NetLink server. Installing this package on just one server, or no server if it is not needed, is an option.

The descriptions of each package listed in TABLE 2-1 will help you minimize the system disk space requirements of the PC NetLink server. With today's larger disk drives, performing a full installation is ideal. You can use the `pkgrm` command later to free up space if you decide certain packages are not required.

Moving PC NetLink Installation Directories

On busy production servers with small /opt or /var/opt disk partitions, or on servers with a large number of packages installed, the disk space requirements may exceed the available disk space. In such a situation, you can install the software quickly without the time consuming requirement of repartitioning the disk subsystem to enlarge the /opt or /var/opt directories. Unfortunately, the PC NetLink 1.0 and 1.1 installation procedure does not allow the packages to be installed into an alternative directory.

A common UNIX technique is to use symbolic links to force the packages to install into an alternate directory and still allow the standard installations to work. All standard paths used by the software and expected by the system administrators and support personnel will still be in place. The following procedure lets you install the PC NetLink software into alternative location.

Note – This procedure has a number of manual operations. A mistake may require you to start over. Try it only when finding additional space in /opt or /var/opt is not possible. Practice the procedure on a non-production server before trying it on a production server.

▼ To Install in a Directory Other than /opt

1. **Before installing the PC NetLink software, locate a disk partition local on the server that is large enough to contain the PC NetLink software packages.**

2. **Create a directory on this partition to contain the PC NetLink software packages. Change the protection of the directory to 777 with the** chmod **command so anything can write into it.**

3. **In this new directory, create directories that match the package names of the PC NetLink software packages. See the list of packages in** TABLE 2-1.

4. **In the** /opt **directory, create symbolic links that point to the directories created in Step 3.**

5. **Install the PC NetLink software as you would normally, via the instructions that came with the product.**

   As the files are installed into the directories, the symbolic links automatically redirect the creation of the package files into the desired directory.

Note – While it may be possible to use symbolic links to install the PC NetLink software into an NFS-mounted server on another system, it is extremely problematic, and may make it impossible to support the PC NetLink software for all network configurations. Placing files that the PC NetLink server routinely needs on another server can easily cause availability, performance, security, and compatibility problems and make the system overly dependent on other servers.

After the PC NetLink Software Is Installed

The PC NetLink Registry Changes

Occasionally, changes made to the PC NetLink registry from the default values may require manual changes to Solaris software, for example, when the VCDistribution registry value is changed to force higher numbers of lmx.srv processes. The VCDistribution registry table (discussed fully in Chapter 4) specifies the distribution of sessions (PC clients) each lmx.srv will support. If the number of lmx.srv processes is increased by changing this table, eventually the amount of shared memory allocated by Solaris software at boot time will be exceeded. Edit the /etc/system file to allocate more shared memory. See Chapter 4 for more details.

If the default configuration of the PC NetLink server is changed using the PC NetLink registry or lanman.ini file, changes to Solaris resources may be affected in ways that are not obvious. When changing registry and lanman.ini values, pay close attention to the PC NetLink manuals and Release Notes to see what possible Solaris configuration options might change as well.

PC NetLink Database Directory Location and Performance

As was discussed in Chapter 2, the PC NetLink software supports Windows NT ACLs and other Windows NT-related information databases found in the /var/opt/lanman/databases directory. For this reason, sharing this directory is not possible, and it should never be placed on a non-local file partition.

With regard to performance, under extreme conditions, if the PC NetLink software is placed in an environment where the PC NetLink databases are updated frequently by the creation of many directories or specific file ACLs from many PC clients simultaneously, the location of this database might become a bottleneck to PC NetLink performance. If you suspect this is happening, you can increase the performance of the system by moving the database in `/var/opt/lanman/datafiles` to a higher performing disk subsystem.

An even more important reason to move these files to a RAID device is to take advantage of the redundancy inherent in RAID 0+1 and RAID 5 volumes. To decrease the chances of the PC NetLink databases being lost due to a single disk failure, move the data files to a RAID 0+1, RAID 5, or any disk subsystem that supplies a redundant environment.

In summary, there are 3 good reasons to move the `/var/opt/lanman/datafiles` directory to a RAID disk subsystem. These reasons are:

- Higher Capacity: The `/var/opt/lanman/datafiles` directory may be on a file structure that does not have the needed space to support the growing databases that the PC NetLink software requires.
- Redundancy: The databases in `/var/opt/lanman/datafiles` are extremely important to maintain PC NetLink operation. RAID 0+1 and RAID 5 (among others) offer redundancy that will allow these database to survive a one-disk failure.
- Performance: Under low memory or high demand situations the performance of the `/var/opt/lanman/datafiles` databases can limit the performance of the PC NetLink software.

In addition to placing the data files on the RAID volume, schedule periodic backups of the databases. The PC NetLink documentation and Chapter 10 of this book list backup procedures.

If you move the data files to a RAID volume after the PC NetLink software is installed on a working server, take all standard precautions so that you can return the database to its prior state if you decide to move back.

Also, use the PC NetLink Server Manager to back up the database files before attempting this procedure. Consider making these changes only if you are experienced. If possible, practice the procedure on a non-production server before attempting it on a production server.

▼ To Move the Database Directory to RAID Disk Subsystems

1. **Plan a time during off hours to bring down the PC NetLink server for routine maintenance.**

2. **Become superuser.**

3. Fully stop the PC NetLink server using the following command or use the PC NetLink Server Manager (/opt/lanman/sbin/slsmgr).

```
# /opt/lanman/bin/net stop server
```

4. Back up all the PC NetLink data files involved in the change using the PC NetLink Server Manager.

5. Choose a new location for database files on a redundant RAID disk subsystem.

This example uses the directory datafiles on the disk subsystem mounted on raid1.

```
# cp -r /var/opt/lanman/datafiles /raid1
```

6. Keep the current /var/opt/lanman/datafiles directory fully intact by renaming the directory. (If the procedure fails, you will still have the original.)

```
# mv /var/opt/lanman/datafiles /var/opt/lanman/datafiles.before
```

7. Create a symbolic link to the new directory created in Step 5.

```
# cd /var/opt/lanman
# ln -s /raid1/lanman/datafiles
```

8. Restart the server using the PC NetLink Server Manager or use the following command:

```
# /opt/lanman/bin/net start server
```

9. Test the server to ensure that everything is working.

Storage Subsystems

This section focuses on storage issues when setting up a PC NetLink server for a specific purpose. Let's first look at the features of the Solaris operating environment that can improve performance.

Solaris File Operations

Solaris software has many features that optimize access to files during the execution of the PC NetLink software. Because the PC NetLink software executes primarily in user space, it automatically takes advantage of all the functionality and performance-enhancing techniques offered by the Solaris operating environment. In the Solaris operating environment, all file read and write operations are supported by the in-memory page mechanism. The Solaris operating environment will use all unused memory as a read cache for any file the PC NetLink software has open. If your system has enough memory, all the data files that the PC NetLink software has read for the user can reside completely in memory. This pertains only to read data; write file operations are flushed to disk often. See the Preface of this book for web sites where you can find papers on the Solaris memory system.

First, a quick look at most of the popular single-volume disk storage systems available to the Sun Enterprise 450 Workgroup server.

Simple SCSI Drives

The Sun Enterprise 450 supports 20 Ultra Wide SCSI drives within the server itself. These disk drives are attached to SCSI controllers by way of five Ultra Wide SCSI paths that have four drives each. A fully configured Sun Enterprise 450 has three dual-ported SCSI controllers that are placed on three of the system's six separate PCI buses. Limiting each of the multiple SCSI paths on the multiple PCI buses to just four drives makes the Sun Enterprise 450 capable of handling almost any I/O-intensive, disk-focused application.

Individual SCSI drives configured as simple UFS files systems to store data and user home directories is still common at many sites, but current technology and the lower costs of disk drives allow a better solution. If you use individual drives, keep in mind some of the drawbacks of using simple drive UFS volumes with the PC NetLink software:

- Single-drive SCSI UFS volumes have limited performance. Benchmarks show that you will be lucky to get 2.5 Mbytes/second of throughput. While one PC client accessing files via the PC NetLink software is not likely to saturate one SCSI-based PC NetLink share, two to five PC clients can easily saturate a drive if they all request file access at the same time.

- Simple SCSI UFS volumes offer no redundancy. Even with Mean Time Between Failure (MTBF) specifications for each drive of 1,000,000 hours, an organization with 100 drives will experience a disk failure within 417 days during which one user's data will likely will be lost.

- Simple SCSI UFS volumes have lower capacity. Today's large capacity drives make this less of an issue, but for large databases, the drive size can limit the size of the database.

Software or hardware RAID disk subsystems are the clear choice for minimizing these two drawbacks of using simple SCSI drives as NFS volumes.

RAID Support

The only way to get both high performance and robust PC NetLink Server support is to use Redundant Array of Inexpensive Disks (RAID). While not required, making RAID a part of every PC NetLink server solution maximizes the redundancy, availability, and serviceability (RAS) benefits of using Sun Enterprise servers. It is the only way to offer full functionality of the server if a single disk failure occurs.

Sun systems and Solaris software support a variety of RAID environments. Two software RAID solutions (DiskSuite and Veritas), as well as a variety of hardware RAID solutions (A1000, A3000, SRC/P), enable you to take simple SCSI or FC-AL drives and configure to offer enhanced redundancy and performance. A full discussion of RAID technology is not appropriate here. Instead, the following sections discuss how RAID environments relate to the PC NetLink software and how they might be used to offer solutions on the network, as well as the pros and cons for each RAID type with the PC NetLink software.

Hardware RAID

Sun offers a variety of hardware RAID solutions that can match a variety of performance and capacity requirements. Hardware RAID volumes provide the highest performance and reliability. The obvious gain in using hardware RAID is that the processors of the server are no longer required to support the RAID environment and thus are free to handle other tasks. In addition, hardware RAID controllers usually have battery-backed-up, persistent storage cache that enables them to cache write operations without committing the data to disk. This cache allows write operations to be completed without delay, increasing performance considerably for write operations, and still guaranteeing the data will reach the disk in the event of a power failure.

To illustrate the performance difference between a simple SCSI drive and a hardware RAID 5 volume, three benchmarks were performed using Ziff-Davis NetBench 6. (See Appendix A for the benchmark setup used.) For these benchmarks, a Sun Enterprise 450 server (4x400MHz processors, 1 Gbyte memory) was configured with a Sun StorEdge™ SRC/P PCI Hardware RAID card. In one benchmark a four-disk RAID 5 volume was used as the target for the benchmark, and in the second benchmark an eight-disk RAID 5 volume was the target. These benchmarks were charted along with a benchmark of the same system with one SCSI drive as the target for the benchmark. FIGURE 3-1 shows the results.

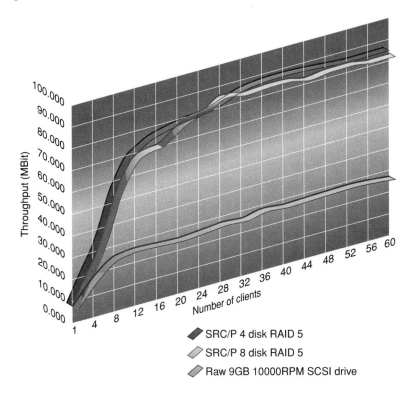

FIGURE 3-1 NetBench 6 Results of StorEdge SRC/P PCI RAID 5 vs. SCSI Drive

The RAID volumes' throughput is three times better than the throughput of a raw SCSI drive. However, the four-disk RAID 5 performs at the same level as the eight-disk RAID 5. The on-card persistent memory allows these two RAID volumes to have the same performance.

Hardware RAID solutions usually include management software that enables you to set up RAID on a device that appears to the Solaris operating environment as a simple SCSI device. As reads and writes are requested using the SCSI (or FC-AL) bus, a SCSI device in the form of a controller takes the requests and supports the operation in a full RAID fashion. Typically, all RAID environments (RAID 0, 0+1, 5) are supported. For fully redundant systems, some hardware RAID solutions support two SCSI controllers on the server accessing the hardware RAID device, using two different ports to allow for full redundancy at the SCSI controller and SCSI cable level. While the two SCSI controllers are working well, you get double the bandwidth through the dual cable configuration. If the driver detects that a SCSI controller or cable has failed, it backs off to a standard one controller/cable configuration.

Hardware RAID volumes are the highest performing single volumes that the PC NetLink software can support. For this reason, hardware RAID is the best solution where single volumes will be used extensively, such as in a database. Especially in high demand environments, hardware RAID solutions off-load considerable processing from the main CPUs when implementing RAID 5 parity.

However, if the PC NetLink software is used to support home directories or a similar disk environment where random reads and writes are made to a variety of volumes, a software RAID solution might be more cost-effective and still deliver performance and redundancy.

Software RAID

User home directories can be supported with software RAID. The Sun 4 processors Sun Enterprise 450 workgroup server has 20 internal drives that work well with either of the two supported RAID software solutions.

RAID Software

Sun has two forms of RAID software: Solaris DiskSuite software and Veritas™ RAID software. Either of these software environments works well with the PC NetLink software. Following is a comparison of the two software environments to help you choose.

Advantages of DiskSuite Over Veritas Software

- Depending on the configuration, boot time checks can be 20 to 40 minutes faster using DiskSuite. On the tested configuration, the volumes under DiskSuite had boot time of 5 to 6 minutes, whereas volumes under Veritas had a boot time of 20 minutes. The variation depends on the number of configured objects in the Veritas database. Newer versions of Veritas and DiskSuite may improve boot time.

- No initial disk setup time—disks can be used immediately. Adding a disk under Veritas control with a private region of 20 Mbytes takes 30 seconds per disk. If the private region is larger or the `nconfig` parameter for the disk group is higher, it takes even more time.

- Metadevice (volume) creation time is much less. Under DiskSuite `metainit` (initializing metadevice/volume) takes a few seconds. Under Veritas, depending on the Private Region in the disks and the `nconfig` parameter, volume creation can take from a few seconds to 10 minutes. Thus, depending on the situation, adding a large number of volumes under Veritas can take hours.

- Default kaio size is 1 Mbyte in DiskSuite. For Veritas, the parameter must be set in the `/etc/system - set vol_maxio = 2048`.

Advantages of Veritas Over DiskSuite Software

- Under Veritas software, any number of volumes can reside on one disk. Under DiskSuite software, the number of volumes that can reside on one disk is limited to the VTOC size—7 for SPARC machines and 14 for x86 machines.

- Creating a volume (metadevice) is much simpler under Veritas software. It can be as simple as giving the disk names and letting the software determine the partition sizes on different disks.

- Veritas software does not require pre-created slices (VTOC) on disks. Pre-creating slices is cumbersome and is the only factor that can potentially deter people from using DiskSuite software on large systems.

- If controller numbers change, Veritas software requires no action, but under DiskSuite software, the `md.tab` file must be regenerated manually, which can take a long time. In such cases, when the machine is booted, the metadevice actually comes up without checking if the partitions have the correct content, and that can potentially corrupt data.

- Default number of volumes is 128 and the default number of metasets is four in DiskSuite software. Entries for `nmd=XXX` and `md nsets=YYY` have to be changed in `/kernel/drv/md.conf` and a `boot -r` is necessary.

RAID 0

RAID 0 stripes or concatenates individual drives into one large drive. When set up correctly, RAID 0 volumes are the fastest RAID volumes available on either hardware or software RAID configurations. A four-disk RAID 0 volume that is supported by four SCSI paths on four separate SCSI controllers can benefit from four times the SCSI bandwidth. A large file copy operation will execute considerably faster because four drives can be reading or writing simultaneously.

A significant drawback of RAID 0 is that there is no redundancy. If any drive in a RAID 0 volume fails, the complete volume is lost.

Consider using RAID 0 volumes only for fast, redundant, READ ONLY, local storage for utility, or application executables. If you are setting up the volume to act as a shared directory of read-only information that is easily restorable from elsewhere, then RAID 0 may be an acceptable solution. However, if minimum down time is a paramount goal, the time required to restore a RAID 0 may make it unacceptable.

One possible use would be as an application server, which is a duplicate of other application servers elsewhere on the network. If the volume were to lose a disk, users could be redirected to other servers during the time the volume is being restored. The resulting loss in performance that occurs because the files are no longer local to the subnet may be an acceptable price for a normally high-performing RAID 0 volume.

Disk drive MTBF specifications are much higher than five or ten years ago, which means they are considerably more robust. Use of RAID 0 drives, however, lowers the volume's MTBF, making the volume less reliable because the MTBF of the volume is equal to the MTBF of each drive divided by the number of drives in the volume. If a typical SCSI drive has an MTBF of 1,000,000 hours, the MTBF of a six-disk RAID 0 volume would be 1/6 of this value or 166,666 hours. While individual MTBF of one volume of 166,666 hours (19 years) seems like a long time, additional volumes make the MTBF for the total system lower still. A system with ten six-disk RAID 0 volumes would have an MTBF of 16,666 hours, or just 1.9 years. Life is too short to be taking this kind of risk with real data.

RAID 1

RAID 1 supports disk mirroring. Each SCSI or FC-AL drive is mirrored by another disk. This form of RAID allows for full redundancy, but does not add any performance gain over that of a RAW disk, and capacity is limited to the size of the disk being mirrored. Pure RAID 1 is rare these days because the same disk drivers can be better used in a RAID 1+0.

RAID 1+0

As with RAID 1, RAID 1+0 uses mirrors to offer redundancy, but instead of mirroring simple disk volumes, RAID 0 volumes are mirrored. This gives the added benefits of performance and volume capacity that RAID 0 offers. For these reasons, RAID 1+0 is typically the highest performing solution for software RAID environments. While the disk capacity of the disk subsystem is half that of the raw disk capacity, minimal CPU resources are used in supporting this RAID environment.

Disk drive prices have fallen steadily over the last few years while disk drive capacity has risen. These trends make RAID 1+0 volumes even more attractive as the highest-performing, high-reliability volumes for use on systems with software RAID environments.

RAID 5

For systems with hardware RAID solutions, RAID 5 solutions give you good performance, at maximum capacity for RAID, without loading the system CPUs to perform parity calculations.

RAID 5 offers the ability to produce volumes with reasonable performance and maximum disk capacity, while still maintaining redundancy. To accomplish this task, RAID 5 volumes are organized so that parity is distributed on a stripe throughout the volume. The storage needed to maintain the parity will consume one drive's worth of capacity. The parity contains all the information needed to reproduce any disk that fails in the RAID 5 volume. In a six-disk RAID 5 volume, one drive's worth of capacity is used to store the parity. The volume has a capacity of five disks that make up the volume.

In software RAID 5, these benefits come at the cost of consuming CPU resources. For this reason, using RAID 5 on servers where other services (email, database web hosting) are supported must be carefully considered. A busy PC NetLink server supporting hundreds of users with RAID 5 volumes can consume considerable CPU resources to generate and maintain the parity of the volume.

While software RAID 5 volumes are generally faster than raw SCSI or FC-AL volumes, their performance is usually only a fraction of that obtainable by a RAID 1+0 volume. If the user community is not expected to use the PC NetLink server heavily, consider using software RAID 5. For higher-load environments, consider using RAID 1+0.

Use of hardware RAID 5 volumes is another matter. Because hardware RAID controllers support the RAID 5 environment completely within the controller itself, there is little, if any, penalty for using RAID 5. Many hardware RAID controllers are even tuned for RAID 5 performance.

RAID 6 or (5+0)

Only if large volumes and storage capacity efficiency are absolutely required should you consider making large (more than 8 disks) simple RAID 5 volumes. The reason you should avoid using a large number of drives in a RAID 5 (or any RAID for that matter) is to minimize the amount of time you are vulnerable to a second disk failure.

If larger volumes are required, use RAID 5+0 (also known as parity groups or RAID 6). This form of RAID adds additional parity that can reduce the risk that a second disk failure will destroy the volume.

Reducing the Risk of a Secondary Disk Failure

Even with redundant RAID volumes there are times when the volume is vulnerable to a second disk failure. This occurs between the time the first disk fails and the time the replacement disk is rebuilt with the data from the original failed drive. You want to minimize this time as much as possible. First let's look at the risk.

MTBF for a Second Disk Failure

Disk drives have become quite large—9GB, 18GB, and larger, over the last few years. When placed into RAID 5 volumes, the size of the total volume becomes extremely large. Losing this amount of data to a second disk failure can be a nightmare.

Fortunately, the mean time between failure (MTBF) for individual drives has also increased over the years, making the risk of having large capacity acceptable. The MTBF of a typical drive shipped by Sun is 1,000,000 hours. These MTBF values are statistical in nature and can lead to a false sense of security. When disks are placed into a RAID environment, the MTBF of the RAID environment becomes:

Total RAID MTBF = (MTBF of 1 Disk)/(Number of disks in the RAID volume)

Redundant RAID environments allow you to continue through the first failure, but the MTBF to the second failure is the same equation with one less drive. If a drive fails in a 12-disk RAID 5 environment consisting of 1,000,000 MTBF drives, you are left with 11 drives. The MTBF of this now non-redundant environment is 90,909 hours or 10.3 years. The clock for this MTBF started at the same time as the MTBF of the first drive failure. If the failure goes unnoticed for long periods of time, even this seemingly long MBTF means a second error can occur, causing full loss of the volume.

There are several steps you can take to reduce the time a RAID volume is vulnerable to a second disk failure.

When Volumes Are Susceptible to a Second Failure

Part of the time the RAID volume is susceptible to a second disk failure cannot be avoided. This is the time the hardware or software RAID environment takes to rebuild the data that was on the original failed drive. This period can vary from a few minutes to several hours. It is difficult to predict the exact time required to rebuild a RAID volume on an active system. It depends on the size of the drive, the amount of data that was on the failed drive, and the activity of the system during the rebuild period.

RAID environments will attempt to rebuild the disk data as quickly as possible, but if it is doing the rebuild while the RAID volume is being used by the system, the rebuild operation can be lengthened considerably. By default, some RAID environments make the rebuild operation a lower priority than normal operation. A heavily used system can have exceptionally long rebuild times. In addition, the system will have degraded performance because the RAID environment needs to synthesize the data lost from the failed drive for every read operation to the disk.

In addition to the unavoidable parity rebuild time, the other vulnerable time for the RAID volume is the time it takes the RAID environment to see a new replacement to start the rebuild process. This can be from zero seconds to several months if the disk failure is not noticed.

Assigning a Hot Spare Drive

Assigning a hot spare drive effectively reduces the chances of a second drive failure. A hot spare allows the RAID environment to start rebuilding a RAID volume as soon as a drive failure is detected. If a Hot Spare is *not* allocated, the RAID volume can be working without redundancy for a dangerously long time before you can detect failure, allocate a replacement drive of the correct size, and install it into the system. The time it takes to install a replacement disk is typically many times the rebuild time, increasing the risk of second disk failure.

Having a spare disk allocated (by way of the RAID environment management software) allows rebuilding of the failed disk data to start immediately, eliminating the human response requirement.

To reduce the chance of a second disk failure destroying the RAID volume, assign at least one spare drive to RAID environment and make sure you a have a procedure to detect and replace failed drives as soon as possible. If policies are hard to enforce, assign two drives as spares.

Disk Technology

Most hardware RAID solutions do not allow you to choose the type of disk drive to use with the hardware RAID subsystem. The most common hardware solution is either an external box that connects to the server with one or two SCSI cables or an internal RAID solution that supports RAID directly on the SCSI controller of the system.

Software RAID, on the other hand, is implemented by using either SCSI or FC-AL drives. The choice of which type to use is usually dictated by the type of server you plan to use. For example, the workgroup server Sun Enterprise 450 has 20 internal Ultra Wide SCSI drives supported by five separate SCSI paths on three dual-ported SCSI controllers. Many user communities can, and do, exceed the capacity of the internal drives. Additional capacity is possible with externally connected drives.

Typical SCSI and FC-AL drives are based on the same disk drive mechanics and primary drive electronics. While an FC-AL bus can transfer data at one-gigabit speeds compared to 40 Mbytes for most SCSI buses, the internal transfer rate of approximately 10 Mbytes/second for both these drives limits what you can expect from each drive.

SCSI Drives

SCSI bus speed and capacity have grown over the years. Original SCSI controllers and drives supported a mere 5 Mbytes/second, with eight devices and a cable length of six meters. Fast SCSI doubled the speed of the bus to 10 Mbytes/second. The cable length shortened to three meters. Addition of a wide SCSI bus doubled the number of bits that could travel down the bus at one time, giving 20 Mbytes/second. It also doubled the number of possible SCSI devices to 16. Ultra SCSI doubles the clock rate again, giving 20 Mbytes/second for a standard width SCSI and 40 Mbytes/second for a wide SCSI.

Ultra Wide SCSI drives are standard today with Ultra II/Wide SCSI coming around the bend with 80 Mbytes/second bus speeds. Both the Sun Enterprise 450 and the Sun Enterprise 250 Sun workgroup servers use internal Ultra Wide SCSI (also known as SCSI-3) drives.

Capacity has also increased over the years. Typical drive configurations include 2-, 4-, 9-, and 18-Gbyte disk drives. The Sun Enterprise 450, for example, can have 20x9-Gbyte drives installed internally, for a maximum capacity of 180 Gbytes of non-RAID disk capacity.

A major contributing factor to transfer speed of the drive is the rotational speed of the drive itself. The faster the disk spins, the faster the bits of one track can be read. Typical server drives spin at 7200 RPM, but 10,000 RPM drives are becoming more prevalent.

When It Is Best to Use SCSI

SCSI drives are the best solution when:

- SCSI is an inherent part of the server design. Both the Sun Enterprise 250 and the Sun Enterprise 450 have SCSI buses and drives installed inside the server itself. The systems were designed for SCSI disk solutions.

- The needed capacity of the system stays well within the limits of the number of SCSI buses, controllers, and drives that can be installed inside and external to the system. While Ultra Wide SCSI allows for 15 drives to be placed on the bus, it rarely exceeds 12 because of cable length and signal quality issues. Also, even four SCSI drives with their 10 Mbyte/second internal transfer rates can almost fully saturate a 40 Mbyte/second Ultra Wide SCSI bus. If the SCSI drives will be part of highly active RAID volumes, it is best to keep the limit to four or six drives per SCSI bus.

- Cable length from the server does not need to exceed the three-meter limit.

- Cost is the primary concern. A SCSI disk subsystem is almost always less expensive than a FC-AL storage solution.

Fibre Channel Arbitrated Loop

Fibre Channel Arbitrated Loop (FC-AL) is a standard that interconnects drives using a fiber optic cable. Each disk subsystem, typically in an external box, is connected to the server by a bi-directional one gigabit (100 Mbyte) cable that transfers a form of the SCSI-like protocol. Many FC-AL disk subsystems offer two fiber loops, which offer redundancy and can potentially double the bandwidth. The Sun StorEdge A5000 FC-AL array can sustain 180 Mbytes/second over a dual channel. In addition to the higher speed, the fiber cable can be up to 1000 to 2000 meters long and can address up to 126 drives. While the FC-AL operates at one-gigabit speeds, individual drives are still limited to much lower speeds, primarily because of mechanical limitations such as disk head movement speeds and rotational latency.

When to Consider FC-AL Drives

The following are some of the reasons for implementing an FC-AL solution:

- Performance—FC-AL arrays of drives can obtain extremely high levels of performance with only one controller on the server.
- Capacity—FC-AL disk arrays can address 126 drives on one controller.
- Flexibility—Unlike SCSI, which has a maximum distance of three meters between the drive and the controller, FC-AL disk arrays can have up to 10 kilometers between drive and controller. This means that FC-AL drives can be placed even in nearby buildings, if necessary.

Comparing Disk Storage Performance

For many customers, performance is the primary consideration in determining which server to purchase. Because most computer vendors, including Sun, purchase SCSI drives from the same vendors, the raw disk performance of the these drives is usually fixed for one SCSI type. However, computer vendors add value by using layering technologies such as RAID and file caching to make raw disk subsystems handle data at higher speeds than the raw disk speed might imply.

To compare the relative performance of the file systems, NetBench, a benchmark written by Ziff-Davis, was utilized. Appendix A provides a brief description of the benchmark, defines the benchmark configuration, and explains the methodology used in providing performance information included in this book. Refer to the Ziff-Davis documentation for a full description of the benchmark.

FIGURE 3-2 shows relative performance of the various disk subsystems available to the Sun Enterprise 450 workgroup server.

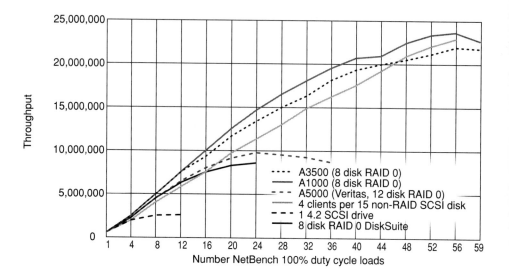

FIGURE 3-2 Relative Disk Subsystem Performance

FIGURE 3-2 shows relative throughput of six different disk subsystems when an ever-increasing load of 100 percent duty cycle clients are placed on the same server with the same network infrastructure. It is useful for comparing relative disk subsystem performance and shows the maximum throughput that can be measured on each single volume of that disk subsystem type. The "4 clients per 15 non-RAID SCSI disk" benchmark configuration is a departure from the other curves. Instead of one volume being tested, 15 volumes of raw (non-RAID) SCSI drives were used. FIGURE 3-2 shows how much bandwidth can be measured if you distribute the benchmark load across many volumes instead of just one. Some observations:

- As expected, the highest performing, single volume storage solutions were the Sun StorEdge A1000 and A3500 hardware RAID solutions.

- One reason the Sun StorEdge A3500 subsystem is slower than the Sun StorEdge A1000 subsystem in this comparison is that the StorEdge A3500 uses 7200 RPM drives, while the Sun StorEdge A1000 subsystem uses 10000 RPM drives.

- The "1 4.2 (Mbyte) SCSI drive" performance hits a maximum at approximately 3 Mbytes/second. A good hardware RAID solution allows a performance approximately 10 times that of a volume created on a single drive. Note that the benchmark throttles at approximately four 100 percent duty-cycle NetBench loads (equivalent to 20–50 users). After the benchmark tested 12 of these clients, the disk became so saturated with requests, many clients timed out, due to the Windows 95 45-second timeouts, forcing the benchmark to stop. During this test the CPUs in the system were extremely underutilized. Any server will saturate in this way when a disk subsystem is saturated.

- The "8-disk RAID 0 DiskSuite" curve saturated, but at a much higher level. When saturated, it too can cause PC clients to time out due to long response times. The difference in performance between the eight-disk software RAID 0 solution (DiskSuite) and the eight-disk hardware RAID 0 solution is approximately 2.5 times. This difference is primarily due to persistent storage in the form of battery backup RAM on the hardware controller. This RAM acts as a cache that allows write operations to complete as fast as the data can get into the controller. If the power is lost on the system, the battery ensures the data will be written to the disk as soon as the power is restored.

- The "4 clients per 15 non-RAID SCSI disk" solution shows what happens when the 60 PCs used in the benchmark are assigned to 20 different volumes instead of just one. Distributing the benchmark load across additional SCSI paths, PCI buses, and disk bandwidth as the test proceeds better utilizes the system as a whole. The curve is the most linear of the six and continues to show signs of scaling at the end of the test.

CPU

Sun Enterprise servers are designed for maximum throughput as multiple processors are added to the system. The servers scale extremely well as you add CPUs to the system. The upper-end performance of the system also improves almost linearly as you move from slower to faster CPUs. Technologies such as crossbar switching and a 1.6 Gbyte/sec. UPA interconnect enable this scaling to be almost linear. The following chart illustrates the performance increase as you move from 300-MHz processors to 400-MHz processors on the same Sun Enterprise 450 four-processor system.

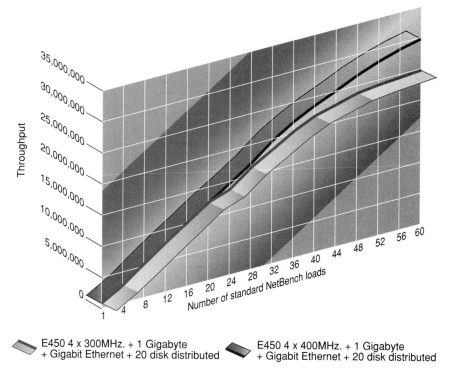

FIGURE 3-3   300-MHz Processors Compared to 400-MHz Processors

FIGURE 3-3 illustrates the following points:

- As expected, a faster CPU scales better than a slower CPU.

- In this benchmark, 1 to 20 100 percent duty cycle NetBench loads created the same load on the server. This shows that in this range, both the 4x300 MHz and 4x400 MHz processors were capable of delivering everything the PCs demanded in the benchmark. There is no significant difference between 300 MHz and 400 MHz CPUs.

- As the benchmark scaled to approximately 48 100 percent duty cycle NetBench loads, the 4x300 MHz processors curve became saturated and delivered only minimal additional throughput, while the 4x400 MHz processors continued to contribute significantly to the throughput.

- If the test had used more than 60 PCs, it might have been possible to see almost linear scalability. Adding 33 percent more CPU speed from 300MHz to 400 MHz produces approximately 33 percent more throughput— 25 Mbytes/second to 33 Mbytes/second.

The PC NetLink software is designed to scale well on multiprocessor configurations. Much work has gone into the PC NetLink software to improve the performance, the interprocess communication, and the NetBIOS layer.

NetBIOS Layer and Multi-Processors Servers

The NetBIOS layer is installed to support the network calls that are made from PC clients to and from the PC NetLink environment. The NetBIOS layer is multi-threaded, and runs on top of the Solaris TCP/IP network layer. Solaris software assigns multiple CPUs to threads that pass through this code and the code will maintain Mutual Exclusion locks (mutexes) to protect the integrity of NetBIOS data regions. These mutexes are the only places the threads working their way through the NetBIOS layer can delay.

## CHAPTER 4

PC NetLink Tuning Parameters

A PC NetLink server maps Windows NT server functionality to the Solaris operating environment. Several aspects of the architecture are tunable and can impact performance. As with all performance-related tuning, features that can enable faster performance in the area of file operations may come at the expense of memory and other parameters.

For the best performance with the least impact on the server, always use the most recent version of the Solaris PC NetLink software. Even the differences between the versions 1.0 and 1.1 of the PC NetLink software have resulted in environments that require fewer memory resources for comparable performance.

Reasons to Tune PC NetLink

Most PC NetLink software installations do not require changes to parameters to get good performance. If the PC NetLink software is routinely placed into performance-related situations outside the norm, or if it is required to share a server as part of a server consolidation, you will want to use the options offered in this chapter. Chapter 7 discusses resource management during server consolidation.

Usually, you tune a system to maximize or minimize one or a number of system parameters. For PC NetLink software, you may want to tune parameters in the following areas:

- Performance:
  - How fast can you support one user?
  - How fast can you support many users?
- Resources:
  - What are the minimum CPU resources needed to support a level of performance?
  - How much memory will be consumed to meet a certain level of performance?
  - How much disk throughput can be maintained?

- What is the least amount of network bandwidth that can be consumed to meet a certain level of performance?

This chapter focuses on maximizing PC NetLink software performance, highlighting any necessary tradeoffs in system resources to improve the performance. Tuning a system to meet performance requirements for one service will almost always have some effect on other services.

Before You Start

Hundreds of parameters can be changed in the Solaris PC NetLink product. Not all of these parameters deal exclusively with performance. As with Microsoft Windows NT, on which the PC NetLink software source code was based, changing parameters that control PC NetLink operations can cause the product to cease functioning. Be sure to back up these databases before you try performance tuning.

Before changing any parameter within the PC NetLink product, pay close attention to the following issues:

- Only experienced system administrators should attempt to change the PC NetLink Registry or control files. If you have not had experience changing Microsoft Windows NT registry, practice on a non-production server. Only after you have fully tested the change should you consider deploying the change on a production server.

- Back up any file you plan to change. The PC NetLink software includes a command that will load a default registry if you want to start with a fresh registry. (See the regload man page in Appendix C.) See Chapter 10 for instructions on backing up the files that control the PC NetLink software operations. To back-up the registry, copy all the files starting with registry in /var/opt/lanman/datafiles to a different directory (for example, cp /var/opt/lanman/datafiles/registry* /regbackup). Note that the content of the registry is not always just one file. Anytime it stores a record of 4 Kbytes or larger, the registry creates a new file to hold that record separately. Therefore, there may be several files in /var/opt/lanman/datafile directory that make up a valid registry. Use the command /opt/lanman/sbin/regcheck -C to check the state of the registry to ensure you have a valid registry. The regcheck command makes sure the registry data is intact. The actual data in the registry could still be in a state that would cause problems with the PC NetLink software.

- Most of the changes made to the PC NetLink Registry and the lanman.ini file require a shutdown and restart of the PC NetLink server processes before the changes will take effect. While Solaris software does not need to be rebooted, the stop and start procedure for the PC NetLink software takes time and will make the PC Netlink services unavailable. For this reason, try to test changes on an experimental server before trying them on a production server. Make changes only after they have been tested thoroughly. Make changes to a production server only during scheduled down time or at off hours when no one is using the server.

- The PC NetLink software is tuned to handle most customer situations well. For most customer environments, the motto "If it ain't broke, don't fix it!" applies. Few tuning parameters will give you more than 5 to 15 percent gain in performance unless the system is starved for resources, or you have an unusual load you want to place on the PC NetLink server. The benefit may be more in the resources used to obtain a certain level of performance.

PC NetLink Control Files

Outside of the SAM and ACL databases, the PC NetLink software parameters reside in three locations:

- PC NetLink memory default values
- The PC NetLink registry
- The lanman.ini file

Following is a brief discussion of each of these configuration areas, along with some procedures for working with them.

PC NetLink Memory Default Values

Many PC NetLink software operation parameters are set within the executable code itself and may not manifest themselves in the registry, the lanman.ini file, or any other file. These values are usually set within a data segment of the executables. As the PC NetLink software starts up, it checks these default values against values set in the registry or lanman.ini file. If a value in the registry is different from the default value in the executable, it will update the value in memory with the value from the registry.

This can lead to confusion if you are trying to find the default value for a parameter and you don't find the entry listed in the registry or the lanman.ini file. Because the new value will, in most cases, not be looked at until the PC NetLink software restarts its server code, the value in the freshly updated registry may be different from the value in memory and the one by which it is operating. The PC NetLink software must be up and running to change registry values. To avoid confusion, find a time when no one is using the server, change the parameters in the registry, or lanman.ini file, then stop and start the PC NetLink server. Following this procedure will minimize the time when there are differences between the registry and the working values.

The PC NetLink Registry

Most of the parameters that control the PC NetLink software operation are contained in the PC NetLink registry. This registry is equivalent in function to the Windows NT registry, but the user should be wary of attempting to use any Windows NT registry techniques that work on Windows NT servers. The PC NetLink software and Windows NT software architectures are significantly different, and Windows NT specific tuning techniques are likely to cause the PC NetLink software to stop working, if they do anything at all.

The SAM database, the ACL database, and the system shares are *not* part of the registry, so reloading the registry with the `regload` command will not overwrite databases and system settings that are not directly related to the registry.

From a Windows NT 4.0 server on the network, you can use the `regedt32` tool to remotely access the values defined in the registry. Using this tool requires that the PC NetLink software be running for you to gain access to the registry in this way. You can also use the Solaris executable supplied with the PC NetLink software (`/opt/lanman/sbin/regconfig`) to inspect and change these values. This tool allows you to change the registry even when the PC NetLink software is stopped.

The files that include the registry database are located in `/var/opt/lanman/datafiles`. To avoid any possibility of the registry being updated while you are trying to back it up, shut down the PC NetLink server before copying files.

Creating a Registry Change Script File

Developing procedures to log changes to the registry should be a fundamental part of system maintenance, especially when multiple system administrators are maintaining the same system, or if you are maintaining several servers.

A well-defined registry recovery procedure should be part of any server recovery plan. This will allow system administrators to reinstate the server to a predefined state with minimum downtime.

The key to maintaining change control of the registry is to create and maintain one script file that has all the registry changes for that server. The script file should contain every command necessary to update the registry from the state, following the initial installation, to the final state of your desired environment. It is vital to add comment lines, with dates, to identify the reason for each change.

The script shown in CODE EXAMPLE 4-1 performs the changes to make sure that any version of the PC NetLink software is running with improved PC NetLink 1.1 registry values which minimize memory requirements. This script will update the registry using the PC NetLink software command: `regconfig`. The value will be read back from each entry as confirmation that the change did take place.

If you want to set up many servers the same way, you can execute this script to ensure the PC NetLink software is set up exactly the same way on all the servers. After changing many registry values, you can force the registry back to the default settings by using the `/opt/lanman/sbin/regload` command if necessary. Then you can use the script file to return the PC NetLink software back to a known state.

Note – Collect all registry changes in one master script so you have documented the changes and can reset them if necessary

---

CODE EXAMPLE 4-1   Example Registry Script File - `registry.changes`

```
#! /bin/sh -u
# Solaris PC NetLink Registry change script
# Place ALL changes to registry here. Follow each change
# With a readback of the value from the registry
#
echo The following Solaris PC NetLink registry entries
echo have been set to the values listed
echo
##################
#
# 1/10/2000 - The following registry change will ensure Solaris PC NetLink is running
# with the latest V1.1 recommended values that control lmx.srv  process spawning
# Default value for Version 1.1
#
/opt/lanman/sbin/regconfig \
SYSTEM/CurrentControlSet/Services/AdvancedServer/ProcessParameters \
VCDistribution REG_MULTI_SZ \
1,5,50"
"500,6,65"
"700,8,80"
"1000,10,100
#
# Follow up change with a readback of value from registry
#
echo VCDistribution
/opt/lanman/sbin/regconfig \
SYSTEM/CurrentControlSet/Services/AdvancedServer/ProcessParameters \
VCDistribution
echo
##################
#
# 1/10/200 This variable controls the number of trusted relationships
# that Solaris PC NetLink will support at one time.
# Default value for Version 1.1
#
/opt/lanman/sbin/regconfig \
SYSTEM/CurrentControlSet/Services/AdvancedServer/ProcessParameters \
NumCLIENT_SESSION REG_DWORD 10
#
# Follow up change with a readback of value from registry
#
echo NumCLIENT_SESSION
/opt/lanman/sbin/regconfig \
SYSTEM/CurrentControlSet/Services/AdvancedServer/ProcessParameters \
NumCLIENT_SESSION
echo
##################
#
# Place next registry change here
#
```

Script Notes

- The "\" character forces the shell to continue the command on the next line.
- The quotes (") may appear unbalanced, when in fact they are balanced. The quotes force a new line within the entry of a command. (If you are viewing this section online you can copy and paste the script into your script editor)

- Note that the only difference between using the `regconfig` command to set a registry value and reading back a registry value is including the registry value type and value in the command line.

- You must become superuser to execute the script.

CODE EXAMPLE 4-2 shows the execution of the `registry.changes` script.

CODE EXAMPLE 4-2 Example of Executing the `registry.changes` Script

```
sys1# ./registry.changes
The following Solaris PC NetLink registry entries
have been set to the values listed

VCDistribution
1,5,50
500,6,65
700,8,80
1000,10,100

NumCLIENT_SESSION
10

sys1#
```

Determining Changes Made to the Registry

Occasionally, you may need to find out what changes have been made to the registry. If you do not have one master registry change script, the state of the registry may be difficult to track.

The command `regcheck  -D` dumps out the registry in excruciating detail. It is possible, but not recommended, to use this ASCII representation of the registry with the Solaris `diff` command to show changes that have been made to a registry. Unfortunately, the `diff` output does not align well if there have been even a few changes, and it makes sorting out the differences extremely difficult.

A more manageable solution involves using tools from both Windows NT 4.0 on a PC and the `diff` command on the Solaris operating environment. A description of the procedure follows.

▼ To View Changes to a PC NetLink Server Registry

1. **Install and configure your PC NetLink software on a Solaris system.**

2. **Before making any manual changes to the PC NetLink registry, use the Windows NT 4.0** `regedt32.exe` **tool on a Windows NT 4.0 server system to dump the registry from the Windows NT machine to an ASCII file on the PC NetLink server. The steps to perform this are:**

   a. **From the Windows NT 4.0 server machine, map a network drive to the PC NetLink machine. This drive is where you will place the ASCII representations of the registry.**

   b. **From the Windows NT 4.0 server machine enter the** `regedt32` **command in the /Start/Run window. You must work in an account that has administrator privileges on both machines.**

   c. **Type the name of your PC NetLink server in the window that comes up after you select the /Registry/Select_Computer Menu entry.**

   d. **Use the /Registry/Save Subtree As menu selection to save the registry to a file on the PC NetLink machine. Name the file** `originalreg.txt` **to identify it as the reference "no change" registry ASCII dump.**

3. **After making changes to the PC NetLink registry, you can repeat the procedure to create a second file. Name it** `changedreg.txt`.

4. **On the PC NetLink server,** `cd` **to the directory where you placed the ASCII files of the registry.**

5. **Use the command** `diff -C 3 originalreg.txt changedreg.txt` **to see the differences between the two files.**

   FIGURE 4-1 shows the output generated after one change is made to the registry. In this example, the parameter `SYSTEM/CurrentControlSet/Services/LanmanServer/ AutoDisconnect` was changed from 10 to 20. The `diff` output shows the value was 10 (Hex 0xa), and was changed to 20 (Hex 0x14).

```
#Using a Windows NT 4.0 Server, dump the registry to a file called originalreg.txt
#Change the registry with the regconfig command. The "\" below continues the line
#
eelab1#./regconfig parameter SYSTEM/CurrentControlSet/Services/LanmanServer\
/Parameters AutoDisconnect REG_DWORD 20
#
#Using an Windows NT 4.0 Server, dump the registry to a file called changedreg.txt
#
eelab1# diff -C 2  changedreg.txt originalreg.txt
*** changedreg.txt       Wed Aug 11 16:54:47 1999
--- originalreg.txt      Wed Aug 11 16:52:02 1999
**************
*** 2149,2153 ****
  Key Name:              SYSTEM\CurrentControlSet\Services\LanmanServer\Parameters
  Class Name:            GenericClass
! Last Write Time:       8/11/99 - 4:50 PM
  Value 0
    Name:                AccessAlert
--- 2149,2153 ----
  Key Name:              SYSTEM\CurrentControlSet\Services\LanmanServer\Parameters
  Class Name:            GenericClass
! Last Write Time:       8/11/99 - 4:20 PM
  Value 0
    Name:                AccessAlert
**************
*** 2158,2162 ****
    Name:                AutoDisconnect
    Type:                REG_DWORD
!   Data:                0x14

  Value 2
--- 2158,2162 ----
    Name:                AutoDisconnect
    Type:                REG_DWORD
!   Data:                0xa

  Value 2
```

FIGURE 4-1   Example of `diff` Output Showing Registry Change

The `lanman.ini` File

The `lanman.ini` file parameters are rooted in years of legacy code from some of the first network-aware PCs. This file is located in the `/etc/opt/lanman` directory and can be edited using a standard text editor, such as vi, if necessary. If a parameter is *not* present in the `lanman.ini` file, its default value will be used. The default values are defined in the PC NetLink software executables. You can view them using the `/opt/lanman/sbin/srvconfig` command.

> **Note** – Use the `/opt/lanman/sbin/srvconfig -p` command to display the current settings of `lanman.ini` controllable server parameters.

Before changing any of the parameters in the `lanman.ini` file, it is useful to understand the relationship between the `lanman.ini` file entries and server defaults.

Every server parameter has a default setting. Use the `srvconfig` utility to display and edit default settings. The `srvconfig` utility resides in the `/var/opt/lanman/bin` directory.

You can edit the `lanman.ini` file and set parameters to values other than the defaults. The value assigned to any parameter in the `lanman.ini` file always supersedes the default value for that parameter.

Use the following procedure to edit the `lanman.ini` file.

▼ To Change a Parameter in the `lanman.ini` File

1. **Use the `srvconfig` command to display default settings for the server parameters (not visible in the default `lanman.ini` file).**

   ```
   # /var/opt/lanman/srvconfig -p | more
   ```

2. **Use a text editor such as vi to edit the `lanman.ini` file.**

3. **To add a section heading to the file, use the `srvconfig -s` command:**

   ```
   # /var/opt/lanman/srvconfig -s "section.parameter=value"
   ```

4. **Add a `parameter=value` pair to the appropriate section of the `lanman.ini` file.**

5. **After you edit the file, stop and restart the server for the new values to take effect. Schedule this step for times when no user is using the system.**

   As with the registry changes, collect all the `lanman.ini` changes and place them into one script file that can edit a default `lanman.ini` file. Use the script file to document the changes you make over time. For more information about the `srvconfig` command, see its man page in Appendix C.

   TABLE 4-1 describes `lanman.ini` parameters:

TABLE 4-1   Common `lanman.ini` File Parameters

[Section] Parameter	Description
[Server] maxclients	Identifies the maximum number of simultaneous client sessions that the server must support. This number is set by default to a number that is equal to the PC NetLink user license installed on the server computer.
[Workstation] domain	The name of the domain that includes the server. Values: any name of up to 15 characters, including letters, numbers, and the following characters: ! # $ % & ( ) - . ^ _ { } ~ ; default: domain
[Lmxserver] country	The country code for server-generated messages. Values: Country Code Country Code Asia 099 Latin America 003 Australia 061 Netherlands 031 Belgium 032 Norway 047 Canada 002 Portugal 351 Denmark 045 Spain 034 Finland 358 Sweden 046 France 033 Switzerland 041 Germany 049 United Kingdom 044 Italy 039 United States 001 Japan 081 Value set by installation for locale
[Lmxserver] listenqlen	Maximum number of client connection requests outstanding. If the server supports numerous clients that all attempt to connect to the server simultaneously, and some get refused, you should raise the value of this parameter. Only applicable if the listenname= parameter is being used. Values: 1—unlimited; default—3
[Lmxserver] netmsgwait	The interval, in seconds, that the server waits for a response when it sends a message that requires one. Values: 0—unlimited; default—30
[Lmxserver] nativelm	An additional field in the session setup request/response. Default—)

Tuning Strategies

The PC NetLink software performance tuning that yields the greatest increased performance is the spawning of the `lmx.srv` processes. Because the PC NetLink software supports PC clients by spawning multiple `lmx.srv` processes, more processes allow more system processors to be involved in supporting the load of the system. The tradeoff is the amount of memory consumed and the CPU overhead in the mutual exclusion locks (mutexes) needed to support the interprocess communication these processes require.

Let us look first at the algorithm and the parameters that control the generation of lmx.srv processes.

lmx.srv Process Spawning Algorithm

If you install and configure the PC NetLink 1.0 software and then map network drives from users' Windows 95 systems, you will see a new lmx.srv process spawned for every 5 users (10 users with version 1.1). As additional users establish connections to the server, more and more lmx.srv processes are spawned until they reach the limit of 100 (20 for version 1.1) processes.

Two memory parameters maintained by the lmx.srv process control the algorithm that governs this behavior. They are originally set by the following algorithm, after which they remain fixed for the duration of the session. Note that at certain times some of the parameters may be ignored, based on decisions made within the algorithm.

Parameters Used to Spawn lmx.srv Processes

A multistep process controlled by several parameters determines the maximum lmx.srv processes that will be spawned. We will first list the parameters that the algorithm uses, and then look at the algorithm itself.

Here is a list of the parameters used by the algorithm to spawn lmx.srv processes:

- Maxclients

  This value can be set within the /etc/opt/lanman/lanman.ini file to control the total number of PCs that can be connected. If there is no value in the lanman.ini file, a default value in the code itself will be used. In versions 1.0 and 1.1, this value is 1000 clients.

- VCDistribution

  This is what exists in the PC NetLink registry. The table is made up of multiple lines with three numbers separated by commas.
  - 1,2,10
  - 500,3,13
  - 700,4,16
  - 1000,5,20

The values in the default table for the PC NetLink 1.0 software are listed in TABLE 4-2:

TABLE 4-2 VCDistribution Table for PC NetLink 1.0

Number of Clients Supported by Proc Parameters	MinVirtual Clients per lmx.srv Process	Max Virtual Clients per lmx.srv Process
1	2	10
500	3	13
700	4	16
1000	5	20

For the Solaris PC NetLink Global 1.0 and version 1.1 software, the default values are:

- 1,5,50
- 500,6,65
- 700,8,80
- 1000,10,100

They are shown in TABLE 4-3.

TABLE 4-3 VCDistribution Table for the PC NetLink 1.1 software

Number of Clients Supported by the Proc Parameters	MinVirtual Circuits per lmx.srv Process	Max Virtual Circuits per lmx.srv Process
1	5	50
500	6	65
700	8	80
1000	10	100

In each set of numbers, the first number specifies the number of clients the remaining two refer to. The second number in the line represents the minimum number of virtual circuits each lmx.srv process supports. The third number is the maximum number of virtual circuits each lmx.srv process supports before another process can be spawned. To view the setting on your system, become root and issue the following command:

```
# regconfig SYSTEM/CurrentControlSet/Services/AdvancedServer\
/ProcessParameters VCDistribution
```

The table represents ranges of values that will be used once, and only once, per session. Using the version 1.1 table values, if maxclients is set in lanman.ini to be between 1 and 500, the values 5 and 50 will be used for MinVCPerProc and MaxVCPerProc. If maxclients were set somewhere between 500 and 700 for these parameters, the values in the second line of the VCDistribution table would be used, and so forth.

If the lanman.ini maxclient default value of 1000 is not changed, the other values in the table should match the 1000 entry.

- MinVCPerProc

By default this value is zero, which means the algorithm will use the second parameter in the VCDistribution table. If this parameter is set to nonzero, it will override the second parameter in the VCDistribution table. To view the value, use the following command:

```
# regconfig SYSTEM/CurrentControlSet/Services/AdvancedServer\
/ProcessParameters MinVCPerProc
```

The default value of this parameter is calculated by first determining the default value of Maxclients(1000) and then looking up the second value in the VCDistribution table. This would make the default value of 10 for the PC NetLink 1.1 software.

- MaxVCPerProc

This parameter, if nonzero, will override the third parameter in the VCDistribution table. As with MinVCPerProc, it is, by default, set to zero so the table will be used. This parameter sets the maximum number of connections each server process (lmx.srv) will allow. This value indirectly controls the maximum number of lmx.srv processes using a formula that will be explained in the following section.

```
# regconfig SYSTEM/CurrentControlSet/Services/AdvancedServer\
/ProcessParameters MaxVCPerProc
```

The default value of this parameter is calculated by first determining the default value of Maxclients(1000), then looking up the third value in the VCDistribution table. This would make the default value 100 for the PC NetLink 1.1.

- MaxProc

This parameter is calculated as the PC NetLink software initializes. It represents the maximum number of lmx.srv processes that can be spawned. The algorithm is explained in the following section.

Algorithm for Dynamically Determined Parameters

- Setting the parameter `maxclients`—As the PC NetLink software initializes, it reads the `/etc/opt/lanman/lanman.ini` file to see if the parameter `maxclients` has been set. By default, there is no entry for `maxclients` in the `lanman.ini` file and the `lmx.ctrl` process uses a fixed value within the code. This value is 1000 for both Solaris PC NetLink 1.0 and 1.1.

- Determining the value for the internal MinVCPerProc value—If the registry has a nonzero `MinVCPerProc` value, it will be used. If there is no registry value, or if the value is zero, the `VCDistribution` table will be used to determine the value. The `maxclients` value (determined in Step 1) will be used to look up the appropriate `MinVCPerProc` value to use with the VCDistribution table.

  For example, if `maxclients` is 1000 (the default for versions 1.0 and 1.1), the table entry starting with 1000 will be used. The default in version 1.1 for this value is 10.

- Determining the value for the `MaxVCPerProc` value—If the registry has a nonzero `MaxVCPerProc` value, it will be used. If there is no registry value or if the value is zero, the VCDistribution table will be used to determine the value. The `maxclients` value, again, is used to look up the appropriate `MaxVCPerProc` value to use.

  Default example: If `maxclients` is 1000 (the default for versions 1.0 and 1.1) the table entry starting with 1000 will be used. The default value for version 1.1 is 100.

  Manually set example: If the registry was set to a value of 20 for `MinVCPerProc`, the VCDistribution table would not be used and 20 would be the final value.

- Determining the value for `MaxProc`—The values for `MaxVCPerProc` and `MinVCPerProc` do not change while the PC NetLink software continues to run. To activate the new values, stop and restart the PC NetLink software using the `net stop server` and `net start server` commands.

  Once the values for `MaxClients` and `MaxVCPerProc` have been determined, the following formula is used to determine the `MaxProc` value:

  MaxProc = (MaxClients * 2 + 10) / MaxVCPerProc.

  Using the PC NetLink software version 1.0 defaults of `MaxClients` (1000) and `MaxVCPerProc` (20), `MaxProc` equals (1000 * 2 + 10) / 20, or 100 processes.

  Using the PC NetLink software version 1.1 defaults for `MaxClients` (1000) and `MaxVCPerProc` (100), `MaxProc` equals (1000 * 2 + 10) / 100, or 20 processes.

Defining a PC Connection

When a PC requires any service of the PC NetLink software, a connection or virtual circuit must be established. These connections can be transitory, as are some authentication requests, or they can be maintained for a long period, such as when a PC maintains a defined network-mapped drive. If a PC maintains several network-mapped drives to the same PC NetLink server, only one connection needs to be maintained.

Windows 95 and Windows 98 clients most often use a transient authentication connection, but require a persistent connection if they are network-mapped drives.

Windows NT 4.0, on the other hand, usually requires two connections. One is for authentication, which occurs more frequently, and another is for mapped drives.

Algorithm That Spawns the `lmx.srv` Processes

As PC clients make contact they require connections, or virtual circuits, with the PC NetLink server. The `lmx.ctrl` process receives these requests and processes them using the following rules:

1. If the total number of clients is equal to `maxclients`, the connection will be refused. For the PC NetLink software versions 1.0 and 1.1 the `maxclients` value is 1000.

2. If an `lmx.srv` process is not currently supporting a number of connections equal to or less than the internal value of `MinVCPerProc`, it will be assigned the new connection. At the start, there is always one `lmx.srv` process.

3. If the condition in item 2 is not met, a new `lmx.srv` process will be spawned as long as the total number of `lmx.srv` processes does not exceed `MaxProc`.

4. If the number of `lmx.srv` processes is already equal to `MaxProc`, the connection will be assigned to the `lmx.srv` process that has the fewest connections to support. The PC NetLink software continues to distribute the connections across the existing `lmx.srv` processes to balance the load.

5. If all the PC clients drop their connections to an `lmx.srv` process, that process will terminate.

Experimenting With `lmx.srv` Process Creation

If you are determined to study the effect of `lmx.srv` creation to minimize resource requirements or maximize performance, you may need to study what happens as you try out ideas for your environment.

The two scripts that follow illustrate what happens as the PC NetLink software is asked to support more and more connections.

To test a PC NetLink server at the maximum number of connections it will support, you either need to have 1000 PCs, or make a unique connection under programmatic control. The smbclient program from Samba allows you to establish an FTP-like connection to a PC NetLink server. This Solaris executable allows you to log on as a different user and maintain a connection. It can be used to simulate a massive number of connections from a Sun workstation to a PC NetLink server.

Using the smbclient tool (available at http://www.samba.org), you can stimulate the PC NetLink software and watch how it responds to new connections. To exercise a PC NetLink server in a more realistic situation, with a full SAM database, we will establish new accounts for every new connection access to the server as a different user. This means creating 1000 accounts, which you can easily do with the following Solaris script:

```
#!/bin/csh
set usernum=1
  while ($usernum < 1001)
  echo Setting up account for user$usernum
  /opt/lanman/bin/net user user$usernum  password /add
  @ usernum++
end
```

When executed as root on the PC NetLink server, this script will create 1000 accounts named user1 to user1000, all with "password" as the password.

Next, use the following script to launch as many sessions as necessary for your study, and monitor the number of lmx.srv processes that are spawned.

```
#!/bin/csh
set usernum=1
 while ($usernum < 1001)
 echo -n $usernum >>testserver.result
 /usr/local/samba/bin/smbclient //testlab/files1 password -U user$usernum&
 rsh testlab ps -eaf|grep lmx.srv|wc -l >>testserver.result
 @ usernum++
end
```

This script will spawn up to 1000 smbclient sessions, running them in the background. As it executes, it runs a ps -eaf command via rsh on the PC NetLink server.

Caution – Running this script will consume a vast amount of memory on the workstation. Each `smbclient` executable will continue to consume virtual memory until the script finishes or you run out of swap space, which can cause your system to freeze. Use the script only on a system that has significant swap space.

The results are sent to a file named `testserver.result`.

Using this script twice, once with the PC NetLink 1.0 software and again with the PC NetLink 1.1 software, and then importing the two data files into a spreadsheet and plotting them together, give the results shown in FIGURE 4-2.

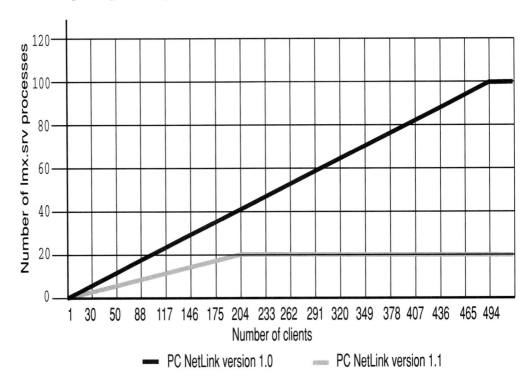

FIGURE 4-2 Number of Processes vs. Client Connections

The chart shows that as the number of client connections grows, so does the number of `lmx.srv` processes. In version 1.0, the slope of the line rises one `lmx.srv` process for every five connections, to a maximum of 100 processes. At that time clients can be added but no new `lmx.srv` processes will be created. In version 1.1 the slope is one process for every ten connections, to a maximum of 20 processes.

Version 1.0 spawns more processes faster and to a higher limit (100), while version 1.1 spawns fewer processes at a slower rate to a lower limit (20). The reason for this difference is twofold: memory and scaling.

Memory Required to Spawn `lmx.srv` Processes

The most important reason for changing the way `lmx.srv` processes are spawned between versions 1.0 and 1.1 is the cost of memory. Each `lmx.srv` process requires approximately 4 Mbytes of private memory. If you attach the maximum number of PC clients to a PC NetLink 1.0 server, the `lmx.srv` processes will use over 400 Mbytes of memory. If you have an active user community that requires services often, you need considerable memory just to hold the executables.

Any free physical memory is automatically used by Solaris software as file system read cache. This allows the operating environment to perform repetitive read operations on the same file very quickly. Therefore, you want to minimize the number of `lmx.srv` processes to allow for more read cache. You must determine the best balance between more processes and more free physical memory for read cache.

Scaling Limits

The PC NetLink 1.0 software scales to considerable levels. However, as you push the PC NetLink software to the limit, even a small overhead of inter-process communication can cause processes to slow down. Therefore, the number of processors the PC NetLink software can take advantage of is limited. However, the PC NetLink software is usually installed in an environment with only two to four processors, so there is little need to worry about this issue when all the processors are being fully utilized.

In large Sun Enterprise servers where 20 or more processors are used, the PC NetLink software can scale up to 12 processors when placed in an environment of loads that approximate that of the NetBench benchmark. The only manageable way to measure the scaling ability is to run benchmarks against a server with many CPUs. The `psradm` command allows you to turn off all processors except those you want, and perform the benchmark over and over with a different number of processors each time.

I ran benchmarks on a Sun Enterprise 5000 system. By configuring the system with three Gbytes of memory, using gigabit Ethernet, and distributing the benchmark load across as many disk drives as possible (20), I limited the performance differences to those caused by the number of processors. When I plotted the maximum values of each benchmark together, the results shown in FIGURE 4-3 emerged.

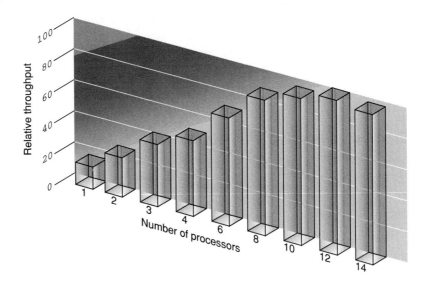

FIGURE 4-3 Relative Performance of the PC NetLink 1.1 vs. Number of Processors

The chart shows that the load generated by the PC NetLink 1.1 software does not gain in performance if more than 12 processors are used. This level is actually impressive when you consider that the typical large Windows NT server has only four processors.

The NetBench benchmark attempts to reproduce the traffic generated by PCs using office productivity applications. This profile of file operations tends to focus on small file operations. The opening and closing of many small files is one key area where lmx.srv processes must communicate with the other lmx.srv processes to ensure that locks are handled properly. This inter-process communication limits the scalability in this case. Environments where many larger files are used should actually scale better because there is more data being transferred and less opening and closing of files, thus reducing the inter-process communication bottleneck.

Note – Environments that read and write large files should scale further than environments where many smaller files are handled.

Guidelines for Producing the Fastest Possible System

If performance is the most important requirement of the system, use the following strategy to produce the fastest "general purpose" server:

1. Find a system with as many processors as possible. For versions 1.0 and 1.1 you need at least 15 processors. While the benchmark itself may not benefit from more than 12 processors, your environment might. Acquire processors with as much cache as possible.

2. Acquire as much memory as possible. The more memory you have, the more memory Solaris software will use as read cache.

3. Use multiple, fast network connections. The more network connections you have, the more processors will be involved in handling the interrupts from the network cards and the less conflict there will be for the network connection. Balance the load across as many connections as possible.

4. Distribute the load across as many disk subsystems as possible. You want to minimize the queue of I/O requests. If you have the Solaris 7 operating environment, use the logged file system. If you have the software RAID, use Veritas VFS driver, which does not use Solaris UFS.

5. If possible, use a disk subsystem with persistent storage. Many RAID controllers have battery-backed-up memory that allows them to return instantly after receiving a write request.

6. Increase the number of spawned lmx.srv processes so that initially there is one for every new connection. This ensures that each new client has a full lmx.srv process.

7. Decide on the upper limit of lmx.srv processes. You will need at least as many processes as there are processors in the system. Solaris software will balance the load and each process will be supported by a separate processor if they are fully saturated with requests. The default limit used by the PC NetLink 1.1 software is 20 to reduce memory consumption. Version 1.0 has a limit of 100. If memory is no object, this larger limit seems reasonable. To set these VCDistribution values in the registry, use the following command:

```
# regconfig SYSTEM/CurrentControlSet/Services/AdvancedServer\
/ProcessParameters VCDistribution REG_MULTI_SZ 1000,1,100
```

Note the "\" in the preceeding command allows you to continue the command on another line. Also remember the "20" in this table entry is used to calculate the MaxProc value. It does *not* represent MaxProc itself.

MaxProc = (MaxClients * 2 + 10) / MaxVCPerProc or (1000 * 2 + 10) / 20 = 100

Note – Ensure that at least one lmx.srv process is spawned for each processor in the system.

Other Registry Parameters

While many PC NetLink software parameters may be useful in your environment, there are far too many to discuss fully in this book. The registry parameters shown here are by no means the complete list of possible registry parameters. They have been chosen as those most likely to improve performance or solve problems caused by special user environments.

Not all the circumstances of changing these parameters from their default settings have been investigated. Therefore, it is critical that you do *not* make these changes without first trying them on a test system with no real users. Back up all PC NetLink software system files before proceeding. Changing these parameters is neither recommended nor supported by Sun. If the PC NetLink software stops working because of these changes, you may want to reload the registry with the regload command to reestablish a Sun-supported registry.

To change these values, use the Windows NT regedt32 tool. Remember to use regedt32, not regedit. Only regedt32 allows you to edit the PC NetLink software registry remotely. Also, remember that the account on the Windows NT 4.0 server system must have administrator privileges on the PC NetLink server as well as on the Windows NT 4.0 server to view and edit all parameters. Users who are not members of the Administrators group will see only a small subset of the parameters. By giving the Administrator account on both systems the same password, you avoid both mismatches in accounts and security problems. An example of a regedt32 screen is given in FIGURE 4-4.

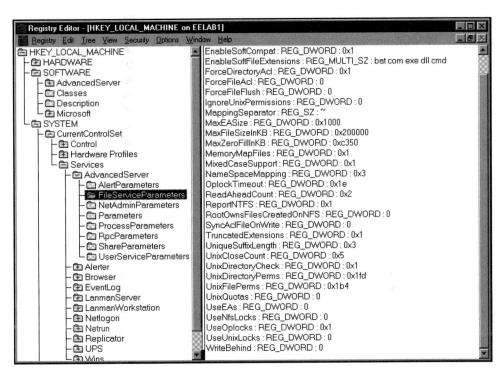

FIGURE 4-4 Sample `regedt32` Screen

The PC NetLink `regconfig` command executed as root on a Solaris command line
also allows you to view and change registry values, for example:

```
# regconfig SYSTEM\CurrentControlSet\Services\AdvancedServer\/
FileServiceParameters ForceDirectoryAclType REG_DWORD 1
```

Note – The "/" character is the command line continuation character.

You can set the registry parameters shown in TABLE 4-4 from
SYSTEM\CurrentControlSet\Services\AdvancedServer
\FileServiceParameter.

TABLE 4-4 File Service Registry Parameters

Registry Parameter	Type	Note
ForceDirectoryAcl	REG_DWORD	Determines whether the PC NetLink software will create an access control list for newly-created directories. If your PC client is creating many directories and you do NOT use ACLs, then it may save time to set this to 0. Default—1 (create new access control list)
MixedCaseSupport	REG_DWORD	Specifies whether mixed-case support is enabled on the server. Mixed-case support allows clients to access file names containing uppercase characters on the Solaris system. MixedCaseSupport is normally enabled (value=1). Setting this value to 0 may improve performance. Only recommended for personal use of a PC NetLink server. Default—1
KeepSpareServer	REG_DWORD	0 or 1—Specifies whether the server should have a spare lmx.srv process available for another client. New client connections are likely to be quicker if this key is enabled. Default— 1 (start lmx.srv process)
MaxVCPerProc	REG_DWORD	0–101—Discussed under KeepSpareServer. The maximum number of virtual circuits that each lmx.srv process should be able to handle. This limit normally is calculated on the fly by the PC NetLink software using the value of the VCDistribution registry key and the value of the maxclients parameter in the lanman.ini file. If the value of this key is non-zero, its value is used instead of the calculated value. Default—0 (Use value of VCDistribution key)
MinVCPerProc	REG_DWORD	Discussed under MaxVCPerProc. The minimum number of virtual circuits that each lmx.srv process should be able to handle. This limit normally is calculated on the fly by the PC NetLink software using the value of the VCDistribution registry key and the value of the maxclients parameter in the lanman.ini file. If this value is non-zero, its value is used instead of the calculated value. Default—0 (Use value of VCDistribution key)

TABLE 4-4   File Service Registry Parameters *(Continued)*

Registry Parameter	Type	Note
NumCLIENT_SESSION	REG_DWORD	5–128—Limits the number of trust relationships that a server can maintain with other domains. This figure should be at least one greater than the number of domains trusted by the server's domain. If you need to support more than five trusted domains, raise this value. Default—10
NumSERVER_SESSION	REG_DWORD	5–infinity—Limits the number of servers and Windows NT clients that can authenticate with the server. This figure should be large because it limits the number of Windows NT clients that can contact the server. On a primary domain controller, it must be at least the number of servers and Windows NT clients in the domain. Default—0x3e8 Hex

You can set the registry parameters from
`SYSTEM\CurrentControlSet\Services\AdvancedServer\RpcParameters` using
the values in TABLE 4-5..

TABLE 4-5   RPC Registry Parameters

Registry Parameter	Type	Note
BrowserMaxCalls	REG_DWORD	The maximum number of open browser sessions that an `lmx.srv` process can support simultaneously. Default—50
WkssvcMaxCalls	REG_DWORD	5–infinity—The maximum number of workstation sessions that an `lmx.srv` process can support simultaneously. If you wish `lmx.srv` processes to handle many client connections, increase this value. Default—50

You can set the following parameter in the registry from
SYSTEM\CurrentControlSet\Services\AdvancedServer\ShareParameters
using the values from TABLE 4-6.

TABLE 4-6   Share Registry Parameters

Registry Parameter	Type	Note
KeepAdministrativeShares	REG_DWORD	0 or 1—Specifies whether administrators are prevented from removing the ADMIN$ and IPC$ shared resources. If you have no need for these shared directories, change this value to 0. Default—1 (Prevented from removing shared resources)

Tuning Parameters When Upgrading PC NetLink Software

It is important to consider the state of the PC NetLink registry during upgrades. Many of the algorithms that define how the PC NetLink software works are based on variables maintained in the registry, as has been described earlier in this chapter. As Sun's engineers continue to work on the PC NetLink software, not only are the executables improved, but variables in the registry are updated to improve the way the algorithms operate on a typical server.

Between Solaris PC NetLink version 1.0, version 1.0 Global, and version 1.1, several registry settings were adjusted. These changes improve performance, reduce memory requirements for supporting most user communities, and increase the number of Windows NT domains that can be part of a trusted environment.

If you used Solaris PC NetLink 1.0, and upgraded to version 1.1, you probably upgraded to the new version without deleting the older versions of the registry and other PC NetLink software databases. Because the initialization program for the newer version detected an existing set of ACL, SAM, and registry databases, it would continue to use them. While this is a good way to maintain most of what was in the older databases, the new and improved settings for the registry database were not set. This is not usually a serious matter and no perceived issues are likely to surface.

For environments that must maximize performance and require that memory use be minimized, it is important to check these settings and make sure they are set to the up-to-date values. In extreme cases, availability of the system can be threatened when the older setting forces the software to use more memory than it needs. If memory is totally consumed, performance will drop dramatically and PC clients attempting to use the PC NetLink server may time-out while waiting to be serviced.

Checking for Older Settings in the Registry File

Two registry values should be updated when upgrading from version 1.0 to version 1.1. These values are not updated if an older registry exists at the time the new version of Solaris PC NetLink 1.1 is installed.

- VCDistribution—This registry table defines values used by the algorithm that controls the total number of lmx.srv processes and rate at which these processes are spawned in a system. The table is made up of multiple lines with three numbers separated by commas. The values in the default table for the PC NetLink 1.0 software are:

```
1,2,10
500,3,13
700,4,16
1000,5,20
```

The default values for version 1.0 global and version 1.1 are:

```
1,5,50
500,6,65
700,8,80
1000,10,100
```

To edit the registry over the network, you can view the registry with the Windows NT 4.0 regedt32 program. You can also use the PC NetLink command regconfig. To check the values used in your registry, use the following command:

```
# /opt/lanman/sbin/regconfig \
SYSTEM/CurrentControlSet/Services/AdvancedServer/
ProcessParameters \
VCDistribution
1,2,10
500,3,13
700,4,16
1000,5,20
```

Note in the above command, the "\" character is the line continuation character. This output shows the values for the PC NetLink 1.0 software settings. This server should be updated with new values. To set the values to the version 1.1 default settings, use the regconfig command with variable types and data. In the following example, the VCDistribution is set to reflect the values for version 1.1. You must use the "\" line continuation character to enter multiline data.

```
# /opt/lanman/sbin/regconfig \
SYSTEM/CurrentControlSet/Services/AdvancedServer/
ProcessParameters \
VCDistribution REG_MULTI_SZ \
1,5,50\
500,6,65\
700,8,80\
1000,10,100
```

Verify the data is set correctly by using the same command without type and data.

```
# /opt/lanman/sbin/regconfig \
SYSTEM/CurrentControlSet/Services/AdvancedServer/
ProcessParameters \
VCDistribution
1,5,50
500,6,65
700,8,80
1000,10,100
```

- NumCLIENT_SESSION—This variable controls the number of trusted relationships that the PC NetLink software will support at one time. The value for this variable should be at least one greater than the trusted domains you expect to support with the PC NetLink software. The PC NetLink version 1.1 value for this variable is 10.

The following command shows what happens if you look for the variable on an older registry. Because the older registry did not have a reference to the variable, you receive an error. In this case the software would use the default value of 5, which is built into the PC NetLink software.

```
# /opt/lanman/sbin/regconfig \
SYSTEM/CurrentControlSet/Services/AdvancedServer/
ProcessParameters \
NumCLIENT_SESSION
error reading value <NumCLIENT_SESSION>
#
```

To change the value to reflect the desired setting for version 1.1, use the following command. After making a change, always check to make sure the value was set correctly.

```
# /opt/lanman/sbin/regconfig \
SYSTEM/CurrentControlSet/Services/AdvancedServer/
ProcessParameters \
NumCLIENT_SESSION REG_DWORD 10
#
# /opt/lanman/sbin/regconfig \
SYSTEM/CurrentControlSet/Services/AdvancedServer/
ProcessParameters \
NumCLIENT_SESSION
10
#
```

The registry values can be changed only while the PC NetLink software is running, but will not be used by the software until the next time the PC NetLink software is restarted. If the server is part of a production environment, wait until no one is using the server before restarting the PC NetLink software.

If you find that these registry values did need to be updated, make sure you place the changes in a master registry control script for the server. See the section titled "Creating a Registry Change Script File" on page 80.

Removing All Traces of Solaris PC NetLink From a System

If you are removing the PC NetLink software from a server and you want to remove all accounts (SAM database) and ACL information, leaving no trace of the PC NetLink software and databases whatsoever, remove the /var/opt/lanman and /etc/opt/lanman directories after you run pkgrm. If there is any chance that you will want to run the PC NetLink software again on the server, back up these directories first or leave them intact.

Remember, removing these directories will remove the User Account (SAM) and ACL file databases, but *not* the files the ACLs refer to. Consider implications of the files created with ACL restrictions remaining on the server without software to enforce the ACL.

If you are moving the PC NetLink software to another server, you may be able to back up these directories and restore them to the new server if file shares are set up identically.

## CHAPTER 5

Sizing a Solaris PC NetLink Server

To help you determine the best sizing for your purposes, this chapter describes a specific example based on producing a home directory server. While this example may not apply directly to your use of the PC NetLink software, the benchmarks and methodology apply broadly enough to help you determine baseline sizing information for your use of the PC NetLink software.

Sizing Methodology

The first part of any sizing exercise is to develop a methodology that allows you to design a configuration that comes close to meeting your needs so you can start prototyping.

The following steps outline the methodology used to determine the server requirements:

1. **Determine the functional goals for the server.**

   Solaris PC NetLink functionality may be one of several services supported by the server. Here, we will focus only on goals defined for supporting the PC NetLink software. If other services are planned for your server, perform separate sizing exercises to determine the resources needed for the additional functionality, paying special attention to where multiple services may compete for the same resources.

2. **Determine the performance goals of the server.**

   For the example of a PC NetLink server supporting home directories, the goals are centered around the needs of the user community. In some cases, local policies and network infrastructure external to the server may limit what can be expected.

3. **Determine the loading characteristics on the server.**

   For the purpose of a home directory server, defining a typical end user lets us define as precisely as possible the average demand on the server. This step may be the most difficult one for which to acquire accurate information. Both throughput and peak load time must be determined during this step. Appendix B describes the typical end user used in this example.

4. **Determine the performance characteristics of the server.**

   Benchmarks were performed on a variety of the PC NetLink server configurations to determine the performance of each subsystem (CPU, disk, network) in supplying throughput to the server. These benchmarks were performed using an industry standard, which has been used for several years to determine the throughput for SMB servers (refer to `http://www/zdnet/com/zdbop`). Appendix A describes the benchmark environment and the benchmarks used to determine most of the server performance information presented in this chapter.

5. **Determine a baseline server configuration.**

   A baseline server configuration allows you to identify the resources within the system required for the PC NetLink software. The baseline server configuration accounts for all the resources needed to support the functionality and meet the performance demands.

6. **Determine the final system server configuration.**

   This takes into account requirements for the server beyond that of supporting the PC NetLink software. If the system is part of a multi-function server that will offer additional services not supported directly by the PC NetLink software, determine the resources required for these other services. Determine if any of the separate resources will collide on server subsystems. Later in this chapter, a sizing tool is described that will help determine the baseline system using the methodology, assumptions, and benchmarks presented here. You will need to make other time and cost trade-offs based on your specific server configuration.

7. **Prototype the server.**

   If the server is planned as part of a large roll-out of many similarly configured systems, prototyping a baseline configuration and trying it in a limited online test is essential. Skip this step only if the system is being configured to supply services for a limited community, and you have configured the server with some additional headroom to handle contingencies.

Home Directory Server Sizing Example

Sizing a server with capacity that will never be used can be as costly as sizing a server with inadequate capacity. A server should have enough capacity initially, or through upgrades, to serve the user community for the expected life of the server. The initial size of the server must take into account the current user community, as well as expected growth in both the user community and the services to be supported. Therefore, whenever you make a decision on how to size the server, err in the direction of providing additional capacity, if possible.

Note – The sizing information presented in this chapter should be used only as a starting point. Your "mileage" will almost always vary to some degree. Experiment and prototype server solutions to verify your assumptions. In large roll-outs where many servers are involved, prototyping your server is a prerequisite.

Understanding all the non-server external variables that can affect load is critical to correct server sizing. To determine the functional and performance goals, review the following list of external factors that might limit your configurations. The list highlights loading factors and bottlenecks that can exist outside the control of the server.

1. User community

   a. What type of user will be using the PC NetLink software?

   b. What percentage of time will users be performing file, printing, naming, or authentication operations that will impact the server?

   c. How many expert, intermediate, and beginner users will be using the server?

   d. How will users be using the server? As a home directory? As a common data R/O file server? As an application server?

   e. Will users work with documents locally on their own systems or directly in their server home directory? Will the applications autosave users' documents?

   f. What level of performance will users expect?

   g. When will users typically use their systems and for how long?

   h. Will users use Windows NT ACLs? Will they typically share files?

   i. What applications will access the PC NetLink server?

2. PC client

   a. What is the hardware configuration of the average PC that will use the server? Speed of the CPU? Memory? Local disk usage?

   b. What operating systems will the PC use?

3. Network infrastructure

   a. Is the typical network connection from the PC to the network 10/100 Mbit, switched, or hubbed?

   b. What possible network bottlenecks exist between the PC and the server?

   c. If multiple network connections to the server exist, is the load balanced?

4. Local policies

   a. What is the local policy for backing up the server?

   b. What is the local policy for users backing up documents on their PCs?

5. Other functions the server may be expected to support

   a. Will the server be an intranet web server?

   b. Will the system support a database?

   c. Will the system act as an email POP to IMAP server? Do the email server resources collide with the PC NetLink software?

   d. Will the server support home directories locally or on volumes on another server?

   e. Will the system be a PDC or BDC?

   f. What backup policies exist at the customer site?

Functional and Performance Goals

When setting goals, it is critical to know what you expect of the server. A home directory server is expected to support the load generated by end users as they perform their normal activities during an average work day.

Functional Goals

Functional goals for a file and print home directory server are reasonably simple to define: The system should allow file, print, and authentication services for the end users.

Before determining the performance goals of the system, keep an eye on what the system will be expected to support one or two years from now. You can forecast future trends by raising the demand of your typical end user or allowing for server expansion.

Trends With Conservative Requirements

Several trends make obvious the need for additional capacity so that the system you size for today's needs will also meet the needs of the future. These trends, in the areas of network infrastructure, usage patterns, and application demands, all help illustrate the need for planning servers that have additional capacity. Review the following list for any trend that could change the requirements of your server during its life expectancy:

- An experienced user demands more of a server than a beginner. As users become more savvy about how to use their system and learn how to solve more problems with their computers, they tend to use them more and to demand more disk space and throughput.

- Applications today make available functionality that even the beginner can use. This functionality consumes resources and places a higher demand on servers. These applications demand more of the server as they evolve. Specifically, office productivity application documents, such as those from Microsoft Office, have grown considerably over the years. An Excel spreadsheet that might have been 20 Kbytes several years ago may now be 100 Kbytes. Embedding large document object links (OLE) from other applications also increases document sizes. Email that was one to two kilobytes of simple text before, now can be 50 Kbytes with multimedia attachments.

- Servers are expected to support more than one function. One reliable server supporting two or three services can be a better solution than two or three servers supporting only one application each. This is especially true in the area of system administration. Purchasing and maintaining several systems, compared to supporting one system, is costly. Sun SPARC hardware and the Solaris operating environment can support multiple functions at one time. As long as the applications do not fight for the same resources, consolidating services is a desirable goal.

- Network infrastructure has opened bandwidth dramatically. In the past, slower, single-processor servers were sufficient to support simple 10BASE-T hubbed networks. The network would bottleneck easily, making it the limiting resource.

Today's network switching technologies deliver gigabits of full-duplex bandwidth through multiple connections. This improved network infrastructure allows PCs to place much heavier demands on the server.

- PCs and workstations have increased the load they can demand. Today's $1000 PC can produce a load that is 10 to 30 times that of a $3000 PC of just two or three years ago.

- The use of the Internet and intranets have increased the demand for performance.

These trends make it difficult to determine the future requirements of your server. Suffice it to say, the requirements of your server today will be a fraction of that required in one or two years. For that reason, we will make conservative estimates throughout our methodology, erring in the direction of more capacity whenever presented with two possibilities. The goal is to find a happy balance between the cost of the server today and the load it is expected to handle for its serviceable lifetime.

Unlike the Intel platform, Windows NT servers typically have one to four processors. Sun Workgroup and Enterprise servers can support from one to two processors as in the Sun Enterprise 250, or up to 64 processors as in the Sun Enterprise 10000. This makes sizing your server less critical because you can add processors as the load increases.

Performance Goals

Performance is in the eye of the beholder. Performance goals for a file and print server usually boil down to "make it fast enough so everyone doesn't complain about performance." Unfortunately, there is no metric that can easily identify this threshold. What we do know is that performance perception is based on latency. If an operation during a peak load time takes longer than it did in non-peak time, users perceive a performance problem. With such a semi-random load as a user's file services, you may have to study a subset of your user community in depth to fully understand where and when there are perceived performance problems.

Peak Loading Times

If you watch the server load during an average day, you will see several peak periods when users place the most demand on the server. (Chapter 8 offers some tools for monitoring these peak times.) At some sites, everyone walks into the building at 9:00 a.m. to start their day. There is a tremendous surge of demand on the server as everyone attempts to start at once, sometimes within a ten-minute period. At other sites, employees arrive and start using their system throughout the morning.

Peak loading times are, by definition, when your server is experiencing its highest load and where statistically it will experience most of its load. These periods can last from a few minutes to several hours. Just like rush hour on the highway, if everyone in a large network environment were to log in and start editing documents at exactly the same time, no reasonably-sized server or network infrastructure could handle the load. Luckily, statistics are in our favor and show that people use the server in a distributed fashion. In most sizing exercises, the peak loading time is the primary factor in determining the configuration of the server. If the server can meet its intended performance goals during the peak loading period, then performance at any other time will easily be met.

As with almost any server function, latency will usually remain acceptable, to within 20 percent of the fastest time measured, as long as you don't exceed 80 percent of the maximum possible throughput for any component involved in delivering the throughput. As the benchmarks show, PCs receive almost all the throughput they demand as long as the total throughput required by all PC clients does not remain near throughput saturation for moderate periods of time.

You will quickly realize in any sizing exercise that delivering reasonable peak-time service is the focus of your sizing efforts. Configure your system correctly, and your user community will experience few performance problems. Under-configure your system and your user community will not be happy. Over-configure the system and you may have spent too much.

What Is Your Average User?

To realistically size a PC NetLink server, you must define the load for your user community. Trying to track the file usage habits of everyone expected to use a home directory server is an impossible task. To make the task manageable, define a typical user. An average end user may not represent any particular person that uses the server. Many users will demand more of the servers, many will demand less. Define your typical user in terms of file types, file sizes, and when users are likely to use them. Appendix B defines the average end user load on the server. If your user environment does not match that of the average end user presented in Appendix B, apply the same methodology to determine the sizing information for your definition of an average user.

Note – To summarize the average end user definition, I estimated 40 Mbytes per user per day as the average load on the server. This load occurs between 9:30–10:00 a.m. and 2:30–3:00 p.m. (for a total of one hour) to account for peak loading. The storage capacity planned for each user is 100 Mbytes.

In the home directory sizing exercise, we force the full day's user load of 40 Mbytes per user into the server during the peak period. We also double our real throughput requirements to allow for growth, and to take into account trends that will continue to increase the size and quantity of files. These two conservative decisions should comfortably support the peak load the server must handle.

Our typical user community has a peak loading period of one hour. If in another sizing exercise this peak period were longer, let's say four hours, even a small server configuration could meet the demands of a large user community that is evenly distributed across a four-hour period. However, if the peak period is shortened to 15 minutes, maybe a Sun Enterprise 10000 could meet the demand. After reading the home directory sizing exercise, you can determine the loading characteristics of your user community and adjust your peak period accordingly.

Server Performance Characteristics

How Fast Will the PC NetLink Software Go?

Four primary services where performance is most important are printer services, authentication, WINS, and file services. The PC NetLink software testing environments showed that file operations affect the overall performance of the server by at least an order of magnitude more than other services. Therefore, if you size your server focusing on file operations as the primary area of concern, printing, authentication, and WINS services for the same user community should be easily handled by the same configuration.

File Services Sizing

Under normal conditions, file services demand the most resources while supporting home directories. The file service benchmark from NetBench was used by many implementors of the SMB (CIFS) protocol to measure the SMB performance of a server. See Appendix A for a brief description of NetBench and how it was used to determine throughput numbers. Appendix A includes a URL where you can see the benchmark, its full description, and its documentation.

After reading the NetBench description, you can determine if the load the benchmark produces closely mimics the file operations your environment might generate. If not, you can adjust your configuration to have more or less capacity.

Throughput Benchmarks

Before jumping into the subject of PC NetLink software performance throughput, let's take a look at a representative benchmark and see what information we can extract from the results. FIGURE 5-1 shows the throughput in Mbytes (Y axis) vs. the number of PC clients (X axis) running a NetBench DiskSuite test.

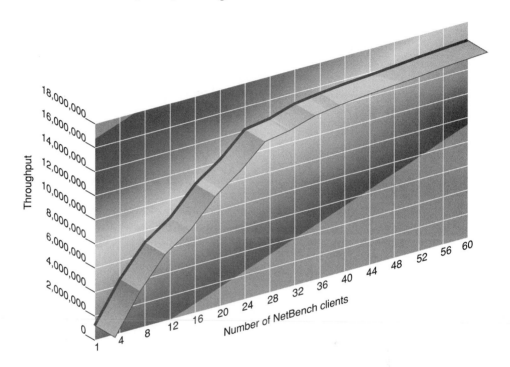

FIGURE 5-1   PC NetLink Server Throughput

This benchmark was run on a Sun Enterprise 450 with 4x400 MHz processors, one Gbyte of memory, performing the test through a Gbyte Ethernet interface. Each horizontal tick mark represents an additional four PC clients running the benchmark. Keep in mind that the load generated by each PC during each five-to-ten-minute interval is 10–100 times the load a real user would place on a server. At the beginning of the chart, on the left, the benchmark runs for approximately five minutes with only one PC client running the test. This first client shows the demand each client places on the server when it has full access to all the resources of the system. In this example, the one Pentium 200 MHz PC client demands and receives 1.152 Mbytes of file throughput in and out of the server. This throughput is measured by the NetBench client application.

Some of the throughput reported by the benchmark is real, over-the-wire throughput, and some is caused by opportunistic locking that can be established between SMB servers and clients. *Oplocks*, as they are called, are established to allow for PCs to perform client-side caching. When PCs establish a connection to a server via the SMB protocol, they will negotiate to determine the highest level of the SMB protocol they can both support. The current SMB protocol supported between most PCs and a PC NetLink server supports opportunistic locking. PC clients will automatically be granted an opportunistic lock if the server determines that no other PC client is accessing the file needed by the PC client making the request. As long as the lock exists, the PC client is allowed to cache the file locally, allowing for faster performance. The application running on the PC client will not be aware that this caching is occurring. Because the NetBench benchmark is designed to generate the same file operations that typical office applications perform, any gain caused by opportunistic locking would be reflected in real world use of opportunistic locks as well.

As the benchmark proceeds, four PCs are added to the benchmark to increase the load. Eventually, somewhere in the network or the server, a bottleneck is reached and the throughput no longer increases. This produces the characteristic knee in the curve (near 24 PC clients) as the benchmark approaches the maximum throughput the configuration allows. In a real world scenario, users attempting to use the server in the first part of the curve would see good to excellent performance as the server delivers additional throughput when additional PC clients place additional load on the system. Later on, after the system approaches and eventually reaches saturation, all the PC clients must share the maximum throughput the server can deliver. Latency times grow for file operations, eventually creating long delays, and all users would eventually experience poor performance.

The purpose of a good sizing exercise, with regard to file operations, is to ensure that the demand on the server remains below the knee of the curve most of the time during the peak period. Some saturation during extreme peak times is expected and cannot be avoided, due to the statistical loading of a typical user community.

One NetBench benchmark by itself can tell you some variable information. When two different server configurations are tested and the results compared, you get a great deal of additional information. For the remainder of this chapter, we will compare benchmarks of most configurable options and extract information so we can study the additional throughput each option offers. We will benchmark a particular server configuration, change one configurable component, then benchmark the system again. These side-by-side comparisons allow us to determine the additional throughput each sub-component offers. We will apply this technique first to a study of SPARC CPUs.

NetBench results are occasionally quoted by various sources to show how far a particular configuration can perform. Be aware that there are two types of benchmarks that companies may quote. One set of benchmarks results is the product of extensive performance tuning on the server, to the hindrance of all other operations of the system. This kind of benchmark may actually place file data at risk during power outages or abnormal terminations of the server to allow for faster file operations. Other benchmarks, like those presented here, are based on conservative settings of the product that allow for proper operation of the server for other services. They also allow for the most conservative settings that protect data from abnormal terminations of the server. We used only conservative benchmarks to develop recommended server configurations.

Sizing for CPUs

There are three factors to consider when configuring processors for a server: the CPU cache size, the number of processors, and the speed of the processor.

CPU Cache Size

Anytime a CPU attempts to access memory, the hardware attempts to access instructions or data from the local cache. If the access finds the instruction or data in the cache, the CPU proceeds quickly. If the item is not in cache, the hardware must go to regular physical memory, or worse, swap the data from disk to get the data. The larger cache size allows processors to run faster because there is a better chance the cache will contain the item being fetched.

If you are planning a PC NetLink software installation where the server will not be under a constant load, the size of cache may not play an important role in perceived performance. However, if you are planning a large server that will support hundreds or thousands of users, a large cache size allows the system, and every processor, to reach its full potential. It is best to acquire the largest cache size possible to obtain the maximum performance from every processor the server has installed. While Sun offers CPU modules that have different cache sizes, not all server configurations with the smaller cache sizes are officially supported by Sun. When planning server configurations where performance is crucial, always order CPUs with the largest cache possible.

Speed of the CPU

The speed at which the processors execute their instructions increases the performance almost linearly. Let's take a look at two benchmarks taken under identical conditions. FIGURE 5 2 shows a PC NetLink server's SMB performance on an Enterprise 450, using 300 MHz processors in one case and 400 MHz processors in the second curve.

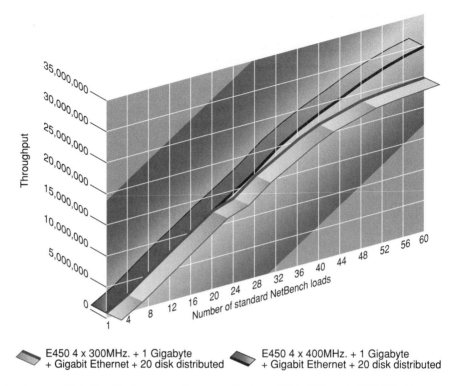

FIGURE 5-2 Relative Performance Between Systems With 300 and 400 MHz Processors

This benchmark was performed when all other resources that could possibly bottleneck the system were open to the maximum possible throughput. In this test, 20 individual SCSI drives were used to distribute the NetBench loading clients across as many SCSI controller and disk drives as the Enterprise 450 can support using internal storage. Using RAW SCSI drives in a real world scenario is not advisable because of the lack of redundancy and poor performance that each drive can deliver. For the purpose of benchmarks, using 20 SCSI drives allows us to build the test from fewer to more clients with an ever-increasing SCSI storage bandwidth. The number of drives, SCSI paths (four drives per path), and PCI buses used in the test, all increased as the test proceeded. The network used in both curves was a Gbyte Ethernet. This allowed considerably more bandwidth on the network side than the benchmark could use.

As the curves show, both servers can deliver essentially the same performance at the beginning of the test. Later, near 25 Mbytes/second, the 300 MHz processors level off while the 400 MHz system continues on to 30 Mbytes/second with the curve still rising when we ran out of PC clients. This shows almost linear scaling from 300 MHz to 400 MHz processors with an increase of approximately 25 percent. Benchmarks done on other systems also show close to linear scalability with other SPARC processors moving from slower to faster processors.

Later in the scaling exercise, you may determine that your server needs today can easily be met with the slower (and less expensive) 300 MHz processors. As the demand on the server increases with more users or more applications, you can always increase server performance by switching to faster processors or adding more processors.

Number of Processors

The PC NetLink software performance scales well on multiple processor configurations, but there are limits as was pointed out in Chapter . Benchmarks from two examples of multi-processor servers are shown in the following figure. FIGURE 5-3 compares 60 client-only executions of NetBench on one, two, three, and four 400 MHz processor configurations on a Sun Enterprise 450. FIGURE 5-4 shows comparative NetBench executions of 1, 2, 4, 6, 8, 10, 12, 14, 16, 18, and 20 processor configurations of a Sun Enterprise 6000 (20x250 MHz.)

In the first, each curve represents the throughput possible with one, two, three, and four processors running the PC NetLink software. Each processor module has four Mbytes of secondary cache.

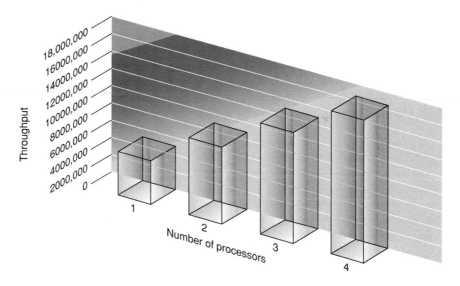

FIGURE 5-3   Comparative File Performance With 1 to 4 Processors

The detailed benchmark configuration used to acquire this data is described in Appendix A. Both network bandwidth (Gigabit Ethernet) and SCSI disk throughput (20 drives) were considerably below any saturation points, and were verified to have no significant limiting effects for these tests. In each test, 60 PC clients were running a 100 percent duty cycle NetBench benchmark Disk Mix test. This test will usually saturate any system. FIGURE 5-3 shows fairly good linearity as additional processors are used in the test. Later, this chart will be used to determine how many processors are required to support a specific number of users.

The Sun Enterprise 6000 was also benchmarked. This system was tested with a total of 20 250 MHz CPUs, three Gbytes of memory, 20 FC-AL drives, plus a one-gigabit Ethernet connection. As with the Enterprise 450, the benchmark tested a 60-client run of the Disk Mix test to extract a maximum throughput value for the Sun Enterprise 6000 with a specific number of CPUs active.

FIGURE 5-4 shows the highest level performance that can be achieved on a Sun Enterprise 6000 server with 250 MHz processors, using conservative settings. The full configurations for the servers tested are described in Appendix A. The Sun Enterprise 6000 was tested using 20 processors. Because we want to see how the product scales in a real-world scenario, it is important to bring up a difference between the NetBench benchmark and a real work environment.

The PC NetLink software spawns lmx.srv processes for every five connections made by PC clients to the server. Windows NT 4.0 workstations require two connections, and Windows 95 and Windows 98 require one connection. For the NetBench benchmark to utilize 20 processors, there must be 20 lmx.srv processes to take advantage of the 20 processors. Under a normal out-of-the-box configuration, the PC NetLink software would spawn only 12 lmx.srv processes and would not take full advantage of the benchmark. In the real world, hundreds of users would be needed to generate the equivalent load of a 60-client benchmark run. That scenario would have spawned many more lmx.srv processes and the server would utilize the processors as one would expect. For this reason, tuning parameters were adjusted in the PC NetLink software to spawn a lmx.srv process for every two PC clients. This allowed more lms.srv processes to be generated and allowed more processors to take part in the benchmark.

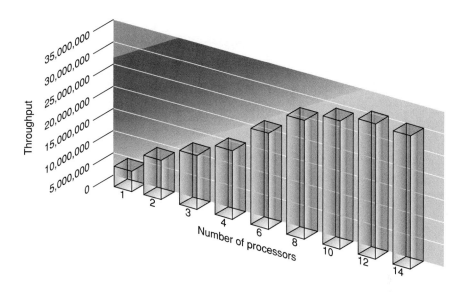

FIGURE 5-4 Throughput on an Enterprise 6000 Server for 1 to 14 Processors

Instead of the full NetBench curve being charted, only the data of the Benchmark MIX that places the maximum load (MIX 60) was plotted. As processors were enabled on the server, the same maximum load mix was rerun. The final result shows the maximum performance possible for the server as additional processors are added to the server. Here the chart shows the performance scales almost linearly until 8 to 12 processors. At that time, the PC NetLink software itself became the bottleneck. This scaling is more than sufficient for most configurations the PC NetLink software will be placed in. Additional throughput is possible by adjusting the PC NetLink registry parameters and making trade-offs.

The reasons the PC NetLink software can bottleneck vary. The PC NetLink software must provide Windows NT file services that are not directly supported by Solaris. Several parallel tasks must be performed to support these file operations. The PC NetLink software itself handles the Windows NT ACL database. Currently, no native Solaris functionality is used to support this ACL functionality. Every time a directory is referenced, a separate access to operate the ACL database must be made to support the correct security level. Typically, this ACL reference is out of memory, but frequent writes to disk must be made to keep the on-disk copy up to date.

Besides the ACL file access, additional file sharing and file lock management must also be supported outside the Solaris operating environment. The PC NetLink software can force Solaris locks and support the locks it is instructed by applications to place on files.

Many engineering avenues exist to increase the scalability of the PC NetLink software.

Network Connections

Planning a large server requires a network infrastructure that allows for the throughput you hope the server will deliver. PC clients today can consume considerable throughput. Older networks with 10BASE-T infrastructure will become saturated long before the simplest server configuration will be strained.

A NetBench benchmark forced through a 100 Mbit full-duplex connection shows a performance of 13 Mbytes/second. 100 Mbits/second is roughly 10 Mbytes/second. How can one 100 Mbit wire deliver 13 Mbytes/second? There are two explanations to this apparent paradox: First, the 100 Mbit Ethernet wire is a full-duplex connection that allows full 100 Mbit data rates both into and out of the server. The benchmark is designed to measure the throughput in and out of each client. Second, the opportunistic locks were also a factor.

Note – Each 100 Mbit full-duplex Ethernet can deliver 13 Mbytes of throughput as measured by NetBench.

When multiple 100 Mbit Ethernet interfaces are planned for a home directory server, be sure the load placed on the server is as balanced as possible. Also be sure that there are no bottlenecks elsewhere in the network infrastructure that will throttle the perceived performance under a heavy load. With unbalanced loading, some users will see good performance and others will see poor performance from the same server.

Use of today's sophisticated network switches can help both in detecting problems and allowing for quick reconfiguration if bottlenecks occur on a subnet. Upgrading to fiber-based gigabit Ethernet connections between the server and the switch will also eliminate the need to juggle users from one subnet to another to balance the load. Switches can route all the packets of multiple subnets into the gigabit connection with little need to worry about bandwidth limitation of older hubbed networks.

Memory Requirements

Determining the physical memory needed to support a PC NetLink server requires an understanding of the memory requirements of the whole system.

Solaris Memory Requirements

Tracking down every byte of physical memory used in even a small server configuration can be extremely difficult. For more information about the Solaris memory system and its requirements, refer to *Solaris Memory Sizing White Paper*

by Richard McDougall (http://www.sun.com/sun-on-net/performance/).
Sizing information and rules of thumb described in this paper are used to determine
both Solaris and UFS file cache requirements. In TABLE 5-1, we summarize memory
requirements for a medium-to-large server, using conservative values. Solaris
software always uses any excess memory for file read cache, which helps speed up
the file system.

TABLE 5-1   Memory Requirements for Solaris Components of a Medium-to-Large Server

Memory Requirement in Mbytes	Solaris Component
60	Large Kernel Size
10	System Process
15	System Libraries
27	Background processes
1	Solaris shared memory segment
113	Total fixed memory requirements

PC NetLink Process Memory Requirements

This section summarizes what is happening within the system and then looks at the
specifics of each memory requirement to support the operation.

The PC NetLink software executes primarily as a user process. Each lmx.srv
process typically serves several PC clients on the network. By default, the PC
NetLink 1.0 software initially allocates one lmx.srv process for every five PC client
connections (PC NetLink version 1.1 supports more clients per process to reduce the
memory requirements). Normally, you don't need to worry about the difference
between the number of connections and the number of PC clients, but to account for
all memory needed for a particular configuration, it is important to define the
difference as far as the PC NetLink software is concerned.

Each Windows NT 4.0 workstation client makes two connections to a server running
the PC NetLink software and each Windows 95 or Windows 98 PC client makes one
connection to the server. Windows NT 4.0 workstations need to maintain two
connections because one is used to handle authentication, and one is used for
normal SMB functionality. As additional PC clients establish a connection to the
server, the PC NetLink software will continue to spawn lmx.srv processes until a
maximum default limit of 101 processes are running. After 101 lmx.srv processes
are running, the normal five connections per lmx.srv process limit is raised,
allowing for up to 20 connections per process. As more PC clients are connected to
the system, the PC NetLink software reaches its final default limit of 1000 PC clients.
For Solaris PC NetLink Version 1.0, if all the PC clients are Windows NT machines
you will have established 2000 connections supported by 101 lmx.srv processes. If

all the PC clients are Windows 95 or 98 machines, you will have established 1000 connections on 101 `lmx.srv` processes. These details are not a concern unless the memory requirements on the system become a problem.

Now let's look at how the rules governing the PC NetLink software operations affect the memory requirements. Each `lmx.srv` process allocates memory of its own in addition to shared memory, which all the PC NetLink processes use as a common database for file descriptors, locks, and so on. We will establish a baseline memory requirement for PC NetLink software by looking at the memory requirements for each of its processes just after Solaris boots, and after only one Windows 95 PC has established a connection to the server. The memory allocated for the PC NetLink software and data are shown in TABLE 5-2.

TABLE 5-2 PC NetLink Processes Private Memory in Kbytes

Kbytes of Memory	Private Memory
4052	Amount of private memory for 1 `lmx.srv` process
1072	Amount of private memory for the `lmx.ctrl` process
1968	Amount of private memory for the `lmx.dmn` process
1928	Amount of private memory for the `lmx.alerter` process
1664	Amount of private memory for the `lmx.browser` process
2368	Starting shared memory
13052	**Total PC NetLink-specific memory required to boot**

Note – Allocate 4052 kbytes for each `lmx.srv` process spawned.

We use this value later to develop a rule of thumb for allocating physical memory for the number of PC clients you expect to support.

PC NetLink Shared Memory

Now we need to focus on the shared memory all PC NetLink processes will use to support the PC clients. By default, the PC NetLink software allocates 940K of shared memory. The most significant portion of shared memory is used to store `ustructs`, which are memory structures used to define open files and file locks. Inside the 940 Kbytes of shared physical memory, 15,000 `ustructs` are defined. Each file that is currently open will require two `ustructs` and each lock on a file will require one `ustruct`. Based on these defaults, 7,500 files (with no file locks) can be opened by the PC NetLink software at the same time. Again, these are default values for an out-of-the-box installation of the PC NetLink software.

The default PC NetLink software shared memory use is designed to closely match the default shared memory segment for Solaris software, which is one megabyte. The default shared memory parameters for Solaris and the PC NetLink software should handle almost every PC NetLink server configuration. However, if the server is to be used for multiple purposes and requires shared memory for reasons other than for the PC NetLink software, or the user community needs to open or lock many files, you will need to increase the number of file ustructs the PC NetLink software can support, and thus increase the size of the Solaris shared memory segment. Chapter 10 describes the procedure for increasing the size of the Solaris shared memory segment and increasing the number of file ustructs that the PC NetLink software can handle.

Note – 940 Kbytes of memory will be allocated by the PC NetLink software from the Solaris shared memory. Within this memory 15,000 ustructs are defined. Each file concurrently opened requires two ustructs. Each file lock requires one ustruct.

PC NetLink Mapped Files

The PC NetLink software must access several shared files during normal operation. These files are typically mapped into the process address space using a Solaris mmap call. All lmx.srv processes have the ACL database mapped into their address space. The mmap operation will, in effect, create a portion of memory that all lmx.srv processes will map into. This memory is allocated out of the physical memory in the same way as the file read cache. It is important that memory be allocated to allow a reasonable amount of the database to be in memory. If the server will be routinely pushed to peak levels, it is critical to allocate enough memory for this database to be resident as much as possible. If the system runs out of memory, and few pages of the database are allowed to be in memory, overall performance of the server will drop.

The ACL database will grow as users create directories via the PC NetLink software environment. The PC NetLink software will by default create ACL entries for directories only. The ACLs for files within the directory reflect the ACLs of the parent directory. If users place their own specific ACLs on files, they will force a file ACL to be placed on the file and additional space in the ACL database will be required. ACL database entries are not fixed. They vary in size because the ACL database entries contain the full path of the directory or file they refer to. Because the paths vary in size, the ACL database entries also vary in size.

Note – A typical directory ACL database entry is approximately 1 Kbyte. A file ACL database entry is typically 300 bytes.

If the user environment serviced by the PC NetLink software tends to create extremely long directory and file paths, the amount of memory of each ACL will be larger than that stated here and used in the sizing exercises. In these cases, allocate additional physical memory in sizing your server.

Read Cache

Solaris software will use all unallocated physical memory as file read cache. File read cache allows commonly accessed files to remain in memory to allow read operations to happen as quickly as possible. In contrast, file write operations are buffered to some extent, but are flushed reasonably quickly to disk to protect the data from any system outage that might occur. Meta data, in the form of directory and inode information, is always written to disk to maintain the correct state of the UFS file structure on disk.

A good rule of thumb developed in database server studies is to allocate at least two percent of the active database file (user files in a home directory server) to allow the system to benefit from the read cache. The key term here is active. In the following sizing exercise, we will use the files that are accessed in the peak period as the database size.

Another rule of thumb for determining the read cache physical memory allocation is to allocate an additional 10 percent of physical memory for read cache after sizing the system for all other purposes. To be conservative, in the following sizing exercise, we will use the larger of the two rules.

Tools and techniques for monitoring memory in Solaris software are covered in Chapter 8.

Note – Rule 1 for read cache allocation: Allocate an additional two percent of the size of all files allocated during the peak use of the system. Rule 2 for read cache allocation: Allocate an additional 10 percent of physical memory for read cache after sizing the system for all other purposes.

Storage Subsystem Requirements

The first area to bottleneck on most file servers is the disk subsystem. Configuring a server with fast CPUs and a gigabyte of memory contributes little to improving performance if most of the file disk I/O bottlenecks on the same disk subsystem. Other than having a shortage of memory, the disk subsystem is a primary cause of perceived slow performance from a server. Choosing and configuring the appropriate disk subsystem usually requires balancing the capacity requirements, RAS (Redundancy, Availability, Serviceability) features, performance, and cost. It is impossible to focus on just one of these factors without affecting the others. Chapter 3 discusses several tuning strategies for getting the most out a Solaris storage environment. Chapter 3 also summarizes the throughput you are likely to see with any one particular storage subsystem. Let us review a list of general and PC NetLink-specific considerations before determining the storage requirements for a server:

- Always use redundant environments (RAID 5, RAID 0+1) for read/write data whenever possible.

- Always back up read/write files.

- In environments with many PC NetLink servers, the PC NetLink software should support only the local disk subsystems of the server it is on. While it is possible and even desirable to access NFS-based storage volumes over the network from the PC NetLink software, in situations with only one PC NetLink server, the ACL operations can only be supported from the PC NetLink server where they were defined.

- If the ACL database is hyperactive because many directories are created by many users, or many individual file ACLs are established, moving the PC NetLink ACL database to the fastest disk subsystem possible may improve performance.

- In multifunctional servers, where the PC NetLink software will be only one of the services offered by the server, place the PC NetLink software support shares on their own storage volumes. Allocating separate volumes for separate purposes allows you to track resources used by each service.

- Place Solaris swap on its own volume if at all possible. If the disk is highly active, you can assume you don't have enough memory.

- In high throughput configurations, it is almost always better to use hardware RAID than software RAID. Software RAID environments are completely acceptable in environments where the load on the system does not routinely saturate the disk subsystem throughput or exhaust the CPU resource. However, if you expect the system to have peak periods where high throughput and low latency is critical, hardware RAID environments are a requirement. This is especially true when supporting RAID 5 environments where it is important that the CPU does not perform parity calculation, and the battery-backed-up persistent storage allows the disk subsystem to write cache much faster.

- When deploying a new home directory server, place individual home directories across as many volumes as possible to balance the load. Avoid filling up one volume with users before allocating space on remaining volumes.

- For home directories, hardware RAID 5 environments are usually best for several reasons. Hardware RAID 5 volumes give you the highest capacity possible with redundancy. Hardware support, either internally with a PCI RAID card or an external hardware RAID device such as the StorEdge A1000 allows for low latency because these devices contain battery-backed-up persistent storage that allows for write caching. In addition, the hardware RAID solutions have high-speed dedicated processors that perform parity calculation needed to support the RAID 5. This on-board processor off-loads work from the system processors.

- If a frequently used read-only database is to be supported with the PC NetLink software, RAID 0 volumes may be best to use. Assuming the database exists in some form elsewhere, RAID 0 volumes allow for highest performance. However, if no down time is allowed at all, even to restore a RAID 0 volume, a redundant RAID (RAID 5, 0+1) environment is required to eliminate a single point of failure and allow for 100 percent uptime.

- If a database must be made accessible, but is infrequently used, simple SCSI drives or even CD-ROMs may be all you need. Again if 100 percent uptime is a requirement, redundant RAID must be used.

- Use spare drives in all RAID environments to reduce the risk that a second disk failure will cause a failure of the volume.

Putting It All Together

We have looked at the performance characteristics of each subsystem of a PC NetLink server. It is now time to pull together what we have learned and apply it to our specific home directory server. While this specific example may not match your specific PC NetLink server needs, the methodology for determining the server configuration will apply to similar PC NetLink server configurations. By applying the methodology, you can determine your own baseline configuration. Specifically, we will determine the following requirements for our baseline configuration:

- Number and type of CPUs
- Number of Mbytes of memory
- Type, size, and number of disk subsystems
- Type and number of network connections

Sizing Exercise Assumptions and Requirements

There are literally hundreds of variables to consider when determining the components needed to support a server. The following list will set many of the variables and help narrow down the options for the list of server components we want:

- The file and print server of our PC NetLink server will support 400 users. Of these 400 users, 200 will be using Windows 98, and 200 will be using Windows NT Workstation 4.0.

- The average end user is defined in Appendix B. Specifically, the average end user (as defined by the example in Appendix B) requires 40 Mbytes of throughput per day. We will allocate 100 Mbytes of storage for each user. Office productivity applications will be installed locally on users' PCs, and they will save all their data files on the server to make sure they are backed up nightly.

- The mix of file types and the read/write characteristics of each user's file load will match the NetBench benchmark. The file operations produced by the NetBench benchmark were designed to reproduce the file operations of office applications, so this is a reasonable assumption.

- Each user will create on the average of 100 directories and force 300 separate file ACLs during their use of the server. This requirement is needed to help scale the memory required to hold the ACL database.

- All user directories will be placed on redundant storage volumes to eliminate a single point of failure and ensure 100 percent uptime.

- The network infrastructure is 100 Mbit full-duplex switched environment with each PC client on its own 100 Mbit switched port. The server will use one or more 100 Mbit full-duplex network connections attached to a network switch.

- We will plan for a peak period in the morning between 9:30–10:00 and a peak period in the afternoon between 1:30–2:00 for a total of 60 minutes of peak time.

- No more than 12 PC clients (three percent of our user community) will be demanding throughput at any time during the peak. Because it is statistically possible for many more or even all 400 users to attempt to access files at the same time, it is not cost effective to size a server based on these anomalous events.

- All 400 users will establish at least one connection to the server throughout the day.

- To allow for enough headroom, and to help define the theoretical load, we will plan for our server to support the complete user load within the peak period. While placing 100 percent of load into the peak is not a realistic requirement normally, it sets the theoretical performance we must expect from our server and allows for additional headroom during the peak.

- While additional server functionality will be considered for the server in the future, we will focus just on the resources needed to support the PC NetLink configuration.

- The server should be able to expand to service additional load if required, but still take up a reasonably small space.

- The server will have as few single points of failure as possible.

Determining the Throughput Requirements

The first thing to determine from the requirements is the number of Mbytes/second the user community will require. The requirements of 400 users at 40 Mbytes per user per day will be handled by the server during the peak period.

400 users * 40 Mbytes /day = 16,000 Mbytes of throughput will be required during the peak of 3600 seconds. The average load on the server during the peak period is 16,000 Mbytes/3600 seconds = 4.44 Mbytes/second. This throughput requirement sets the theoretical average demand the server must supply during the peak period.

Determining the CPU Requirements

Based on the benchmarks shown in FIGURE 5-3 and FIGURE 5-4, a Sun Enterprise 450 with even one processor might be able support this load. One of our goals is to have as few single points of failure as possible. This goal and the general goal of conservative sizing would make two 300 MHz or 400 MHz UltraSPARC™ processors the obvious decision for a Sun Enterprise 450 or larger server. Choosing 400 MHz UltraSPARC processors allows for even more growth and scalability if services other than file and print (email, web, and so on) are desired.

Choosing 400 MHz processors also will allow you to add additional processors for the longest time. The industry trend is that when newer faster processors are released, typically the older slower processor will be removed from the price list and no longer offered. It is not possible to mix different processor speeds, so attempting to upgrade a slower processor system to faster processors means upgrading all the processors if the older processors are no longer available. If you want to maintain the option to upgrade your server, choosing the fastest processors keeps this option available for the longest time.

Note – 2x400 MHz processors will be chosen for our sample file and print server baseline configuration.

Determining the Required Physical Memory

Memory is never wasted on a file and print server because the Solaris operating environment uses any free physical memory for read cache. This results in a faster system.

Our earlier look at Solaris memory requirements showed 113 Mbytes of memory as a reasonable amount for Solaris and all the normal backup processes. This is typically an upper limit requirement for memory, but because we may be planning other uses for the server, we will use this value.

Our earlier description of private memory required a baseline (for one user) of 12.74 Mbytes for the PC NetLink processes. Additional lmx.srv processes will be required to support 400 PC client connections. The PC NetLink software will by default spawn one lmx.srv process for every five PC connections until a default limit of 101 lmx.srv processes are spawned. Windows 98 PCs require one connection and Windows NT workstations require two connections. The number of lmx.srv processes spawned by the individual connections made to the PC NetLink software will be

((Windows 98 PCs) + (2 * Windows NT PCs)) / 5, in our case this is
(200 + (2 * 200))/5 = 120.

We have exceeded the limit of 101 lmx.srv processes, so the actual number of lms.srv processes that will be spawned if all 400 users establish a connection to the server will be 101.

The lmx.srv process requires 3.95 MBytes of private memory. The amount of private memory required to support the PC NetLink processes will be:

(baseline requirement) + (number of lms.srv processes * memory of each additional lmx.srv process).

12.74 Mbytes + (101 * (4052 Kbytes) = 412.4 Mbytes of memory.

Under medium-light loads, longer peaks allocating physical memory for all of these processes would not be required. Because we are asking the system to perform well during the peak time and because we agreed to make conservative decisions, we will allocate physical memory for this purpose.

The PC NetLink software maps the ACL database file into memory. Following our rule to be conservative, we will allocate physical memory to map this file into memory. Our requirement states that each user will create 100 directories and 300 specific file ACLs on the server. The disk file needed to hold this data will be approximately:

(400 users) * (100 * (avg. size of directory ACL) + 300 * (avg. size of file ACL)) or 400 * (100 * (1024 Bytes) + 300 * (300 Bytes)) = 73.4 Mbytes

Allocating enough memory for read cache is all that remains for us to determine. One rule of thumb allocates 10 percent more memory than that previously allocated. This rule suggests:

OS memory + process private memory + memory for ACL database

113 + 412.4 + 73.4 = 598.8 Mbytes

Ten percent of this value is 59.88 Mbytes additional memory.

An alternate rule of thumb for determining read cache is to allocate two percent of the size of the active database. The definition of the files to be read and written by our typical user is 15488 Kbytes of files. If these files (times 400 for 400 users) are our active database, the calculation looks like this:

.02 * (400 * 15488 Kbytes) = 121 Mbytes.

To be conservative we will choose the larger of the two values, which gives us a total physical memory requirement of:

OS Memory + Processes Memory + Shared data memory + Read Cache = Total

113 + 412.4 + 73.4 + 121 = 719.8 Mbytes

Later, we will raise or lower this baseline memory requirement to a real Sun supportable memory value you can order. For now, we will let the baseline configuration requirement stand.

Note – 719.8 Mbytes of physical memory will be chosen for our sample file and print server baseline configuration.

Determining the Storage Subsystems Requirements

The three governing requirements for choosing the storage subsystem for our example file and print server are redundancy, capacity, and performance.

To meet the redundancy requirement, a hardware supported RAID 5 storage subsystem is the most desirable. RAID 5 offers the highest capacity with redundancy that ensures no down time or data loss if one disk in the RAID configuration fails. If hardware RAID is not an option for the server you are considering, I recommend a software-based RAID 0+1 (mirrored striped) storage environment. Software-based RAID 5 relies on system CPU resources to perform the required RAID 5 parity calculation. While this may be acceptable in low to medium load environments, it would interfere with meeting throughput requirements during peak times. Software RAID 0+1 offers the speed and redundancy we want, but the down side is that it requires a full duplication of all data, doubling our disk requirements.

The hardware SRC/P PCI RAID card offers an extremely attractive RAID 5 solution for the workgroup server line of servers. For our example server we will choose it as our storage subsystem. The question that arises is how many of these subsystems are required to meet our capacity and performance requirements.

The capacity requirement for our example server is easy to determine. It is the number of users times the allocated disk space allowed to each user. This results in 400 users * 100Mbytes per user, or 40 Gbytes of storage.

The SRC/P RAID card inside a Sun Enterprise 450 server is configured to support four disks on each of the five Ultra-Wide SCSI buses the system supports. Either of these SCSI buses can be attached to one of the three SCSI paths the SRC/P PCI RAID card supports. How many disks will we need to include the RAID 5 volume and account for 40 Gbytes? The 5x9 Gbyte drives allow for 45 Gbytes. Allocating 10 percent for file system directories and overhead, this allows for ~40.5 Gbytes. With RAID 5 you must allocate an additional drive to store parity information for the volume. Just to meet the capacity requirement we will need a six-disk RAID 5. In the Sun Enterprise 450 server, this requires a system that supports three SCSI paths. One SCSI path will contain the system boot disk and must be on a non-PCI RAID controller. The other two SCSI paths will attach to the PCI RAID controller and support our six-disk RAID 5.

But what about performance? In the CPU portion of the sizing exercise, we determined we needed 4.44 Mbytes/sec. to meet our peak demand. The maximum performance for a PCI hardware-based eight-disk RAID 5 is 11.33 Mbytes/sec. Even though we have not benchmarked this exact RAID configuration, the six-disk RAID 5 PCI hardware-based disk system should easily deliver the bandwidth we require.

Note – A six-disk (9 Gbyte) PCI hardware RAID 5 storage subsystem is chosen for our sample file and print server baseline configuration

Determining Network Connection Requirements

The peak throughput requirement for our user community is 4.44 Mbytes/sec., but it would be nice if the network configuration would support the system configuration we have already decided upon. We have already decided the number of CPUs to be 2x400 MHz processors. Benchmarks of 2x400 MHz systems show a maximum throughput of 8.53 Mbytes/sec. Our six-disk RAID 5 disk subsystem should give us nearly 10 Mbytes/sec. Ignoring the network limitation for now, it appears that the CPU resource will be the limiting resource once our server configuration has been pushed to its maximum capability.

Benchmarks on systems with just one 100 Mbit full-duplex, switched wire show a maximum throughput of 12.98 Mbytes/sec. One 100 Mbit full-duplex connection could handle the load. Our requirement for as few single points of failures as possible forces us to two of these connections.

Note – Two 100 Mbit full-duplex connections are chosen for our sample file and print server baseline configuration.

We now have all the components needed to determine our baseline configuration These are summarized in TABLE 5-3..

TABLE 5-3   Baseline Sample Server Configuration Summary

Resource	Baseline Requirement
CPU	2x400 MHz UltraSPARC processors
Memory	719.8 Mbytes of memory
Storage subsystem	1x6 disk (9 Gbyte 10000 RPM) Sun StorEdge SRC/P Intelligent SCSI RAID PCI controller 1x1 disk (9 Gbyte 10000 RPM) System disk
Network	2x100 Mbit full duplex

We have defined a baseline server configuration. Now we can consider other functionality the server may be required to support. Email, web based applications, and databases could all be part of the same server configuration, but you must perform separate sizing exercises for each of these functional blocks and combine resource requirements. Use Chapter 7 to guide you to a resource management solution.

In this step, we will look at the resources we need to support our peak demand and see if any other trade-offs can be made based on requirements not dealt with in this chapter.

Following is a short list of these trade-offs:

- Our memory requirements of 719.8 Mbytes do not fit any standard memory configuration exactly. You can round up to the next standard configuration of one Gbyte or round down if you know the server will be over-configured. Typically 64, 128, 256, or 512 Mbytes options are offered for expansion. While mixing paired memory modules is allowed in server memory configurations, using the same kind of DIMMs takes advantage of interleaving. An example of this is in the Sun Enterprise 450 server, where four-way interleaving can be used if all eight slots are populated with the same DIMM type. For our example this would be 8x128 Mbytes DIMMs for one Gbyte of memory.

- If you are positive your system needs will never exceed a two-processor configuration, consider a two-processor server such as the Sun Enterprise 250. External storage may be required, because in the Sun Enterprise 250 a maximum of six drives can be configured within its enclosure. Our example configuration requires six drives for the RAID configuration alone. We still need another drive for the system drive. The trade-off may be made to use five disks initially and wait for larger drives that will inevitably be available.

- Besides the resources determined by this sizing exercise, additional resources and options may be needed, based on the server you choose. Redundant power supply options, server controller options, and other RAS options can also play an important part in your choice of a server.

- Review all assumptions and restrictions to see if they require more or less throughput than the baseline configuration has defined. Is the ratio of read file operations to write file operations similar to the NetBench benchmark? Are the file sizes similar? If your environment differs significantly, you may want to raise or lower the resource requirements of the configuration.

- If the server will be part of a consolidation effort, many trade-offs are possible when balancing the requirements of the other services that will be supported on the server. Extra CPU horsepower (like that needed to meet our redundancy requirement) can be utilized by other services on the server. Extra memory will always be used by Solaris software to speed up read file operations.

Prototyping Your Server

This can be the most important part of the sizing effort, especially if the server is going to be part of a multi-server deployment. In this step restrictions and problems not easily foreseen can be flushed out before they can affect real users. The benchmark used to acquire sizing limits for the PC NetLink software will not exactly match the load your specific user environment will generate. Prototyping is one of the only ways to determine how close it is. Following is a list of some things to look for.

- Does your network infrastructure support access to the server from all clients without bottlenecks? Network bottlenecks are a common cause of perceived slow performance. Bottlenecks do not become obvious until a significant load is placed on the server. Using the NetBench benchmark to do a limited test of several PC clients might help make obvious any problems. Also check to see the PC clients are routing to the server in the most efficient way.

- On servers where multiple services will be supported, it is critical that the various services do not collide on the same resources. While CPU and memory are allocated from one service to another by Solaris software, disk and network resources are usually fixed. Try to place each service on its own disk subsystem.

- During the prototype phase, try to place system swap on its own hard drive. While some activity on the swap partition is normal, constant activity means you are out of memory.

- If possible, benchmark the system to verify you are getting close to the throughput you are expecting for the peak.

- Use the various tools of the system (see Chapter 8) to monitor how the resources are being used in the server.

Sizing Spreadsheet Tool

Now that you understand the methodology for sizing a PC NetLink server and have followed one example, the next step is to combine all this information into a software tool that captures the logic of the methodology and allows you to change peak load demands and quickly determine a new baseline configuration. I have taken the information presented in this chapter and produced a spreadsheet that allows you to input five numbers, from which it determines a variety of baseline configurations that you can use to start the process of sizing a PC NetLink server.

You can download this spreadsheet sizing tool from a link on the Sun BluePrints web site (http://www.sun.com/blueprints.)

The web site includes a full description of the baseline configuration sizing spreadsheet. The PC NetLink Sizing Tool will be updated frequently, so check the web site for a updates. At this writing, the spreadsheet has the following inputs:

- Number of users you want to support (1 to 1000) via the PC NetLink software.
- Mbytes of IN/OUT traffic (1–100) caused by each user during peak period.
- Peak period in minutes.
- Disk requirements per user in Mbytes.

The output of the tool is a baseline server configuration:

- The number of 250 MHz, 300 MHz, or 400 MHz processors you will need.
- The amount of memory you will need.
- The number of 100 Mbit Ethernet connections you will need.
- The number of RAID 5 PCI hardware based volumes you will need, based on throughput and capacity

When using the Solaris the PC NetLink Sizing Tool, keep in mind the following:

- The spreadsheet attempts to define a baseline configuration that handles a user load during the peak.
- Consider network infrastructure, local policies, and individual user requirements when determining the final configuration.
- The sizing tool assumes the PC clients for the users will be Microsoft Windows NT 4.0 workstations.
- The sizing tool defines a baseline configuration for the PC NetLink file and print services only. Any additional functionality the server is expected to provide must be sized and configured separately.
- This baseline configuration is a starting point only. You will still need to work with a Sun sales representative, reseller, or sales engineer to determine a supportable server configuration you can order.
- No guarantees of performance are expressed or implied.
- The characteristic of the load comes close to that produced by the NetBench benchmark. This benchmark attempts to produce a load that mimics the file operations of office productivity tools. For a full explanation of the benchmark, see the Ziff-Davis web site at:
  http://www1.zdnet.com/zdbop/netbench/netbench.html
- The IN/OUT throughput traffic entered into the spreadsheet will be evenly distributed across the defined peak period.
- The sizing tool defines disk subsystems in the form of eight disk SRC/P PCI hardware RAID 5 disk subsystems. RAID 5 volumes using a smaller number of drives are possible but currently are not dealt with by the tool.
- The sizing tool takes into account both capacity and throughput when determining the number of RAID 5 volumes required.

- With the exception of the disk subsystem, the sizing tool does not take into account other RAS requirements. Any RAS-capable machine should have as few single points of failure as possible. This means every server should have:

  - At least two processors

  - One additional power supply more than you need for normal operation

  - At least two network connections

- When in doubt, always decide in a conservative direction that will define a system with more resources, not less.

## CHAPTER 6

Transitioning to a PC NetLink Server

PC NetLink servers are expected to transition into different types of network environments to:

- Support all or a portion of the functionality of an older Windows NT server
- Be the first server in a new satellite office network
- Replace or co-exist with other PC connectivity products compatible with the Solaris operating environment, such as SunLink PC™, Syntax Totalnet, or Samba.

This chapter focuses on the problems and solutions for making these transitions easier.

Installing a PC NetLink Server in a New Environment

If the server is being placed in a new network environment, the PC clients will require many network services. Following is a list of functions you might want to consider of your Solaris server in addition to the PC NetLink server functionality.

- Will the server support a name service? While the PC NetLink software supports Windows Internet Naming Service (WINS), other name services may need support. DNS is commonly used by PC clients to access intranet and Internet systems. NIS, while not the default name service preferred by Microsoft operating systems, must be considered if the server will be part of a larger network.

- Will the server act as a gateway? Layer III switches and routers reduce the need for servers to act as gateways to other networks. When multiple network interfaces are installed on a Solaris server, the server can act as a gateway. Refer to the Solaris documentation to administer this function.

- Will the server support the POP, IMAP mail protocols? If the server will be set up at a remote location that requires access to corporate intranets or the Internet, setting up the Solaris server as a POP or IMAP server may be required. Refer to Solaris documentation for instructions on how to support these functions.

- Will the server act as a firewall? If the PC NetLink server will act as the primary access point to the Internet, install firewall software on it to protect the network community. Set up the firewall software to restrict access to ports 137, 138, and 139 on the Internet side, making the PC NetLink server functionality unavailable on the Internet side of the firewall. For security and performance reasons, accessing PC NetLink server accessible files via the Internet directly is not recommended.

- Will the server act as a proxy server? If the server is used for web caching or is behind a firewall, the PC clients will need a proxy server to access the Internet. Solaris software can support these services. Several good proxy solutions are available from Sun and other vendors.

- Will the server act as Dynamic Host Configuration Protocol (DHCP) server? New networks, especially those with many PCs, can benefit greatly by supporting this protocol, which eliminates the need for manually configuring most of the network service options on PCs. Sun supports a DHCP service that runs independently of the PC NetLink software.

Solaris software can support all or any combination of these services simultaneously on the same server. If you expect to support large loads with any of these services, size the server so that it has enough Resources (CPUs, memory, disks, and network bandwidth) allocated for each service. Chapter 7 focuses on resource management techniques that can be applied with the PC NetLink software, and the other services running on the Solaris server, to allow each service to get the resources it needs without choking the others off. Another book in the BluePrint series, *Resource Management*, also deals with this subject in depth.

When installing the PC NetLink software on a server, it is best to get the Solaris operating environment and the network established before installing the PC NetLink software.

PC NetLink's User Account Synchronization Solution

Total, 100 percent seamless, one account, one password functionality is not yet fully integrated between the Solaris operating environment (or any UNIX operating system) and Windows NT 4.0 operating system. Solaris passwords are stored using a one-way algorithm that stores the password only in its encrypted form. For Solaris software to use the encrypted password, it challenges you for a password, performs the one-way encryption algorithm on the raw password, and then tests the stored encrypted password against the newly encrypted password. If they match, you must have known the real password.

Because of this fact and several other equally challenging issues, there is no simple way, with today's software, to take a Solaris /etc/passwd file, or NIS database and synchronize it with Windows NT domains.

The PC NetLink software includes several tools that allow for some automation in synchronizing accounts between Solaris and Windows NT domains. We will reference these tools in this chapter, but first some background.

PC NetLink Default Accounts

The PC NetLink 1.0 and 1.1 software creates four Solaris accounts (found in /etc/passwd) and nine Solaris groups (found in /etc/group) during its installation. These Solaris accounts and groups map the PC NetLink service accounts, privileged accounts, guest accounts, and user accounts from a Windows NT Domain to a Solaris name service. By default, the PC NetLink software maps all service accounts to lanman, all administrator accounts to lmxadmin, all user accounts to lmworld, and all guest accounts to lmxguest. The PC NetLink software creates nine Solaris groups when it is installed. Eight of these groups are used to implement the DOS file attributes discussed in Chapter 2. TABLE 6-1 lists the four Solaris accounts created during the PC NetLink software installation.

TABLE 6-1   Solaris Accounts Created During Installation

```
lanman:x:100:99:Advanced Server account:/var/opt/lanman:/bin/false
lmxadmin:x:101:99:Advanced Server Administrator:/usr/lmxadmin
mxguest:x:102:99:Advanced Server GUEST Login:/home/lmxguest:/bin/false
lmworld:x:103:99:Advanced Server World Login:/home/lmworld:/bin/false
```

By default, all accounts and services defined in the PC NetLink software access UNIX file systems by mapping to one of the Solaris-defined user accounts and groups. These special PC NetLink-mapped Solaris accounts are not intended to be real user accounts, and should not be logged into.

The PC NetLink mapuname Service

The PC NetLink software ships with the mapuname service, which maps a PC NetLink SAM user account to a new or existing Solaris user account. New PC NetLink-to-Solaris user account mappings occur on all hosts running the PC NetLink software.

To create real Solaris user accounts, or to reference existing Solaris user accounts, use the mapuname command to map a PC NetLink SAM user account to a new or existing Solaris user account, allowing a user in a Windows NT domain to be mapped onto a user in UNIX. For example, to map "johns" in UNIX to user "JohnSmith" in the Windows NT domain OFFICE_DOM, you would use the command:

```
mapuname -a OFFICE_DOM:JohnSmith johns
```

After this link is made, any files that JohnSmith creates from a Windows client and stores on the PC NetLink server system will be stored under the UNIX user name johns.

The PC NetLink-to-Solaris user account mapping is a virtual mapping, stored on the PC NetLink server, in the binary file /var/opt/lanman/datafiles/lsa. PC NetLink-to-Solaris account name mapping differences occur when there are long user names, duplicate user names, or special characters in a user name. The PC NetLink software requires only the Solaris user name and userid to complete a user account mapping. The Solaris password is not initially used and is assigned the value *LK* for all account mappings.

A PC NetLink user cannot log into a Solaris user account mapped only by the PC NetLink mapuname service. The entry in /etc/passwd uses /bin/false as the login shell. This entry in the passwd file disallows a login. By setting registry values with the PC NetLink Server Manager (/opt/lanman/sbin/slsmgr) and using the other account synchronization tools (password2sam, sam2passwd) these accounts can be created so that Solaris logins are allowed.

Enabling the mapuname service requires toggling the CreateUnixUser registry value, from zero to one, in the PC NetLink registry value HKEY_LOCAL_MACHINE. The CreateUnixUser registry path is:

```
\SYSTEM\CurrentControlSet\Services\AdvancedServer\UserServiceParameters
```

When you create a new user account using the Windows NT User Account Manager GUI, the PC NetLink software maps the new account to a Solaris user account in one of two ways:

- If the `mapuname` service cannot find its PC NetLink mapped account name in the Solaris name services (for example, `/etc/passwd`, NIS, NIS+), then the PC NetLink software creates a new Solaris account in `/etc/passwd` and `/etc/shadow` for each PC NetLink server defined in the Windows NT domain whose `CreateUnixUser` registry value is set to one.

- If the `mapuname` service finds its PC NetLink-mapped account name in the Solaris name services (for example, FILES, NIS, NIS+), then the PC NetLink software creates a virtual account mapping in its `lsa` database for each PC NetLink server defined in the Windows NT domain whose `CreateUnixUser` registry value is set to one.

If each PC NetLink server is running the same Solaris name service, then all PC NetLink-to-Solaris user account mappings will be identical for each PC NetLink server. Avoid using the PC NetLink software on Solaris servers that are not using the same name services, because the mapping of a Windows NT domain account to Solaris account can get confused. Following is an example that helps illustrate the problem.

A PC NetLink server A is running the NIS+ name service and the administrator creates a new PC NetLink user account called "joe". The `mapuname` service is enabled for all PC NetLink servers defined in the Windows NT domain. A PC NetLink server B is running the FILES name service and has a local UNIX account called "joe" in `/etc/passwd`. The PC NetLink server A will map the NIS+ "joe" account to the PC NetLink "joe" account. The PC NetLink server B will map the `/etc/passwd` "joe" account to the PC NetLink "joe" account. The problem is the NIS+ mapped "joe" account on server A may not be the same as the `/etc/passwd` mapped "joe" account on server B. In other words, the PC NetLink `mapuname` service cannot distinguish if the Solaris user account it is mapping is the same owner as the PC NetLink user account.

Note – To prevent account mapping mismatches, use the same Solaris name service for all PC NetLink servers.

If you create a new UNIX user account, `mapuname` will not automatically propagate it to the PC NetLink SAM database. If you delete a PC NetLink-mapped Solaris account, the PC NetLink user account will not have access to any UNIX file systems. To correct this problem, you can delete the PC NetLink and Solaris accounts and recreate them, or remap the PC NetLink user account to a new Solaris user account.

Installing PC NetLink Software Into Existing Environments

Except for the new environments, the PC NetLink software will be installed into basically two traditional environments. We will focus first on installing PC NetLink servers into PC-centric environments.

PC environments can have a variety of network protocols and services. PC clients may be in transition from Novell Netware or may be using Windows NT domain servers. We will assume the users have authentication accounts already established in the native PC environment.

Next, we will focus on a primarily Solaris or UNIX network environment where NFS is the primary file system used on the network, and NIS is the authentication and name service used.

What PC Clients Need in an Existing PC-centric Environment

All PCs that transition to Solaris PC NetLink servers have several common needs. While newer Microsoft operating systems include all the software needed to access the PC NetLink software, older environments may be missing some options.

Microsoft operating systems support several network transport protocols. These protocols allow the information to be moved from the PC client to the server and back without error. Use of these protocols also implies the naming mechanism by which the PC client will find the server. The typical transport protocols used are IPX/SPX, NetBEUI (not to be confused with NetBIOS), and TCP/IP. Microsoft operating systems support all three protocols. The one required to support PC client access to PC NetLink server functionality is TCP/IP. By default, Microsoft Windows 95 (and earlier) do not install this protocol. However, Windows 98 does. Because the TCP/IP protocol is the primary protocol needed to support Internet access, almost all PCs will have this protocol installed. If there is any doubt, make sure TCP/IP is installed before installing the PC NetLink software. If a PC client has a functioning web browser, the TCP/IP protocol is present. If the TCP/IP protocol is missing, you can install it using the network icon in the control panel for Windows 95, Windows 98, and Windows NT 4.0. Make sure you have your operating system CD-ROM media at hand.

For purposes of moving files during a transition from an older server to a PC NetLink server, all the standard transport protocols available with the Microsoft operating system can co-exist on the same PC client and be used simultaneously. If you are moving files from an older environment to the PC NetLink software and the protocols are installed, the procedure should work seamlessly.

Remember that if a transition procedure requires access to a system using the NetBEUI transport protocol, this protocol does not route to other subnets and will only work between two systems on the same subnet.

User Accounts in a PC-centric Environment

If you are installing the PC NetLink 1.0 or 1.1 software into a previously existing Windows NT domain where user accounts have already been established, the PC NetLink server can become a Backup Domain Controller (BDC) of the existing Windows NT domain. Making a PC NetLink server support existing Windows NT domain users is extremely easy. As soon as the PC NetLink server becomes a BDC member of the domain, the SAM database is duplicated from the master, and users can immediately access resources on the PC NetLink server.

While this is an acceptable way to use the PC NetLink software, it has a few drawbacks. One drawback is that files created on the Solaris system using the PC NetLink software will have lmworld ownership. Except with the PC NetLink software, there is no way to differentiate the ownership of the files. This can impact the way you back up the system. See Chapter 10 for procedures to help deal with this situation.

A better way to use the PC NetLink software is to create Solaris accounts. From the PC NetLink Server Manager(/opt/lanman/sbin/slsmgr) GUI tool, you can turn on an option that automatically creates restricted Solaris accounts. With this option turned on, files created with the PC NetLink software will have distinct ownership. This can aid in easily identifying the ownership of files from the Solaris side. Solaris-based backup tools can distinguish one user from another.

Note – When using the PC NetLink software in an environment where accounts have only existed as Windows NT domain accounts, use the PC NetLink Server Manager GUI (/opt/lanman/sbin/slsmgr) to turn on the option of creating Solaris accounts for Windows NT domain accounts.

Synchronizing Windows NT Accounts to Solaris Accounts

The PC NetLink software includes the `sam2passwd` utility that allows you to create Solaris accounts from Windows NT domain accounts. For this utility to work, the following assumptions must be made:

- Synchronization is from a Windows NT domain to a Solaris name service.
- A Windows NT domain exists and is available through the PC NetLink software.
- A Solaris name service may or may not exist on the PC NetLink server.
- Windows NT privileged accounts and service accounts will not be propagated.
- User accounts are managed on a Primary Domain Controller.
- The PC NetLink account passwords are RC4 encrypted or in clear text.
- The PC NetLink-mapped Solaris user accounts contain a default password.
- The PC NetLink software may or may not have access to a Solaris name service.

The `sam2passwd` executable uses a call to the PC NetLink software library routines, creates a local Solaris account, and makes a call to the `mapuname` executable that performs the final mapping of Windows NT domain accounts to Solaris accounts. You will have to move these accounts to NIS or NIS+ separately if you want them to be available on other servers.

The `sam2passwd` formats its output file as `/etc/passwd`. Each line in the output file represents one PC NetLink user account. Each user account entry contains seven fields (name, password, uid, gid, gecos, directory, and shell), separated by colons.

The normal use of the `sam2passwd` executable is to run the tool once, just after the initial installation of the PC NetLink software.

Running `sam2passwd` with no invocation parameters produces several output files. The `sam2passwd.passwd` output file is the `passwd` formatted file derived from the SAM database user accounts. The `sam2passwd.mapunames` output file is a Bourne shell script mapping the SAM user account names to Solaris account names. Execute the Bourne shell script once the entries in `sam2passwd.passwd` have been entered into a Solaris name service. The `sam2passwd.log` and `sam2passwd.errors` output files are log and error message files. Some `sam2passwd` invocation parameters override default values defined in the PC NetLink registry. In all cases, the PC NetLink registry parameters are assumed to be the default.

If you choose, you can delete PC NetLink user accounts from Solaris name services. When the `sam2passwd` application generates `/etc/passwd` entries from the SAM database, it will detect deleted PC NetLink user accounts and write these accounts to an output file called `sam2passwd.deleted`. You must remove the deleted PC NetLink user accounts from the Solaris name services.

Although the PC NetLink documentation does not list the command line switches supported by this tool, they are available in Appendix C or on-line through either the man pages or the -h switch. Use the following list as a reference.

```
# ./sam2passwd -h
Usage: ./sam2passwd [-f] [-i file] [-g gid] [-h] -l logon -p password
                    [-s shell] [-t directory path] [-u uid]
                    [-y password]
 -f                 List Solaris accounts deleted from NT
 -i file            Input file for -f option (/etc/passwd format)
 -g gid             Assign group id -g 10
 -h                 This message
 -l logon           Administrator logon
 -p password        Administrator password
 -s shell           Assign command shell -s /bin/csh
 -t directory path  Assign home directory path -t /export/home
 -u uid             Starting uid incrementing by one -u 1000
 -y password        Assign specific password or NULL for no password
```

The Administrator login and password are required for most operations.

You will normally use the sam2passwd tool in two cases:

- Run the sam2passwd tool just after creating a PDC (or becoming a BDC of a domain) and adding your initial list of users.
- After new users are added to the Windows NT domain from either the BDC or PDC, run the tool again. sam2passwd will skip creating /etc/passwd accounts whenever an account of the same name already exists. This allows you to easily add new accounts after the initial load.

The following section explains the passwd2sam command, which performs the reverse operation.

Installing PC NetLink Software in a Sun Environment

You may have used other SMB protocol PC interoperability products, such as Samba or SunLink PC (also shipped by Syntax as Totalnet). Transitioning from one of these environments to the PC NetLink software is reasonably straightforward.

During installation there is no conflict in the file structure when you install the PC NetLink software on a Solaris server that is running SunLink PC or Samba. However, before you attempt such an installation, you must disable SunLink PC or Samba because the PC NetLink software installation will experience errors if SunLink PC or Samba is running. To disable these services, see the instructions in TABLE 6-2.

If you are transitioning from a Solaris SunLink PC environment to the PC NetLink software, sometimes only the NetBEUI or IPX/SPX transport protocols will be installed on your clients. If this is the case, add the TCP/IP protocol to your PC client operating system. On Microsoft Windows 95, 98, and Windows NT 4.0 machines, you can do this with the Network icon in the Control Panel. For complete details, refer to the documentation for your operating system.

If you are transitioning from a Samba environment, your clients will have a TCP/IP stack, because like the PC NetLink software, Samba requires it.

If you determine that the NetBEUI and IPX/SPX protocols on your PC clients are no longer required, removing them may improve performance because fewer protocols are used in the chain of events that resolve host names.

Solaris Services That Use NetBIOS Over TCP/IP

The PC NetLink software supports network protocols using NetBIOS running on top of the TCP/IP layer. If you are not familiar with PC client protocols, do not confuse NetBIOS with NetBEUI (NetBIOS Extended User Interface), which is a non-routable transport protocol. The NetBIOS layer is based on the RFC1001 and RFC1002 NetBIOS protocol and is a standard networking protocol used primarily by PCs. This version of NetBIOS is sometimes referred to as RFCNB, for RFC NetBIOS. It is one layer below the Server Message Block (SMB) protocol used by Windows NT and the PC NetLink software network interface, and one layer above the TCP/IP transport protocol.

On a Solaris server running the PC NetLink software, the NetBIOS protocol is implemented in kernel space using the standard STREAMS framework. Unlike SunLink PC and Samba, where the NetBIOS support is implemented within the same user processes that support the SMB protocol, the NetBIOS layer in the PC NetLink software is implemented as a multithreaded kernel driver that is installed from a separate package during the PC NetLink software installation. This driver is loaded and unloaded independently by the /etc/init.d/netbios script.

The NetBIOS layer attaches to specific TCP/IP sockets on the system and responds to specific broadcasts to support NetBIOS naming requests. For this reason, only one NetBIOS layer can be active on a server at any given time. Neither SunLink PC nor Samba can support active NetBIOS functionality while the PC NetLink server is running.

Because of the potential conflicts on the NetBIOS level, you might think the best way to avoid problems is to fully uninstall the specific packages and to install and configure the new environment. However, this may not be a time-efficient approach. If during a transition procedure you need to switch back to the previous environment because of unforeseen problems, such as user account conflicts between NIS and the Windows NT domain, you will need to switch back as quickly as possible without losing valuable configuration information or wasting time in the installation process. The following section deals with these issues.

Supporting PC NetLink and SunLink PC on One Server

SunLink PC enables you to turn off the NetBIOS layer so you can support Appletalk and other non-NetBIOS related protocols. Simultaneous use of the PC NetLink software and these products is possible, but there is an important caveat: The PC NetLink software, SunLink PC, and Samba support protocols for locking and sharing of files through privately controlled databases and structures. These structures and databases are not shared between the PC NetLink software and the other environments. This can cause problems if files are shared among these environments.

For example, suppose a user on an Apple system tries to access a file on a Solaris server running SunLink PC, while another user on a Windows 95 system tries to access the same file through the PC NetLink software running on the same server, or by NFS on another server. The file sharing and locking protocols normally available to support the coordination within one environment will not work across both environments. While simultaneous attempts to access one file may be unlikely in most user communities, it can happen. Therefore, given the current architecture of these products, it is not possible to fully support both products on the same server at the same time. For this reason, Sun does not support these mixed configurations. If you find it necessary to use SunLink PC (with NETBIOS over TCP/IP turned off) at the same time as the PC NetLink software on the same server, and you experience a problem, it is best to disable the side that is *not* demonstrating a problem and see if the problem disappears. If the problem is solved in this manner, it is likely that the interaction between the two products is causing the problem. On the other hand, if you can duplicate the problem in this context, you have a legitimate issue that Sun can support.

Supporting PC NetLink and Samba on One Server

Samba is a popular GNU-licensed free software product that supports SMB using NetBIOS over TCP/IP. Sun does not officially support Samba. Like the PC NetLink software, Samba supports no other transport protocols than TCP/IP. There is no way for the PC NetLink software and Samba to run on the same system at the same time because they will both attempt to establish a NetBIOS layer for the system. However, they can be installed on the same system as long as only one of these products is actively running at any given time.

Supporting PC NetLink, SunLink PC, and Samba

If you are in the process of moving files from Samba or SunLink PC to a PC NetLink server, you may need to switch back and forth quickly between one environment and another to bridge security issues or for a variety of other reasons. While all three environments *cannot* be running and supporting NetBIOS over TCP/IP at the same time, they can be installed on the same server with only one enabled to run. Commands can be used to disable and enable the desired product while Solaris is running.

TABLE 6-2 shows the commands to turn on and off each of the products individually without rebooting, uninstalling, or reinstalling software. This information is provided to help you solve problems while you develop procedures to transition from older environments to a PC NetLink server.

TABLE 6-2 Commands To Disable and Enable Connectivity Products

Environment	To Turn Off the Environment	To Turn On the Environment
PC NetLink	su /opt/lanman/bin/net stop server /etc/init.d/netbios stop	su /etc/init.d/netbios start /opt/lanman/bin/net start server
SunLink PC or Syntax Totalnet 5.1, 5.2, 5.3	su /opt/totalnet/sbin/tnshut	su /opt/totalnet/sbin/tnstart
Samba	su /usr/local/samba/bin/killsamba (see script below)	su /usr/local/samba/bin/smbd -D /usr/local/samba/bin/nmbd -D

The killsamba script referred to in the previous chart is shown following:

```
#!/bin/sh -x
list=`ps -ef | grep smbd | grep -v grep | nawk '{print $2}'`
kill $list
list=`ps -ef | grep nmbd | grep -v grep | nawk '{print $2}'`
kill $list
```

The Samba software changes often. Check your version of Samba for the possibility of a more preferred mechanism for turning the Samba software off. Use the preceeding procedures only during a transitional phase of moving users from one environment to another. Never stop one environment and start another on a production server. Users using the server during such a transition may lose files that are opened.

Note – Never switch between SMB environments on an active production system serving real users.

/etc/init.d Start-up Scripts

The PC NetLink software, current versions of SunLink PC, and Samba add scripts to the /etc/init.d directory when they are installed. These scripts initialize and start the product at system boot time. Make sure that only one of these scripts remains in /etc/init.d to assure that only one NetBIOS environment starts at boot time.

The Samba script is /etc/init.d/samba. For SunLink PC or Syntax Totalnet, the script is /etc/init.d/TAS. For the PC NetLink software, there are two scripts: The script to start the NetBIOS interface is /etc/init.d/netbios, and the script to start the PC NetLink server is /etc/init.d/ms_srv.

Determining Which SMB Service Is on a Server

When you try to diagnose a problem on a Solaris server supporting the SMB protocol, it may be difficult to determine what server you need to work with and what software is supporting the SMB protocol. You can determine the server by using the Network Neighborhood icon on the Windows 95, Windows 98, or Windows NT desktop. Once you select the server in the Network Neighborhood, pull down the File menu and select Properties. The Comment field usually indicates the system type. If the PC NetLink software is running, "SunLink Server" or "PC NetLink Server" is shown at the beginning of the Comment field. If Samba is running, the Samba version is displayed, and so forth.

If you are logged onto the server, the best way to determine which environment is running is to use the ps command. To determine if the PC NetLink software is running, look for any process that starts with lmx. For Samba, look for smbd processes. For example, to see if the PC NetLink software is running, use the following command:

```
# ps -ef | grep lmx
```

The output will look similar to the following:

```
# ps -ef | grep lmx
   root  3757     1  0  Aug 18 ?         0:00 lmx.alerter
   root  3780  3688  0  Aug 18 ?         0:28 lmx.srv -s 4
   root  3688     1  0  Aug 18 ?         0:03 lmx.ctrl
   root  3753     1  0  Aug 18 ?         0:01 lmx.dmn
   root  3761     1  0  Aug 18 ?         0:02 lmx.browser
   root  3779  3688  0  Aug 18 ?         3:01 lmx.srv -s 3
   root 12410 12406  0 12:20:06 pts/15   0:00 grep lmx
```

User Accounts in a Solaris Environment

In a Solaris environment, NIS, NIS+, or /etc/passwd accounts have already been established. The goal is to give users a Windows NT domain account in addition to the Solaris access they already have. Here the passwd2sam executable is used to establish and maintain the initial accounts. As with the sam2passwd tool, the passwd2sam tool will skip over any accounts that are already part of the SAM database. Therefore, you can run the passwd2sam tool after adding new accounts to Solaris to allow users access to PC NetLink server functionality as well.

The input file format for passwd2sam is the /etc/passwd file format. The passwd2sam application supports two modes of operation. The first mode is to bulk load all Solaris name service user accounts into the PC NetLink SAM database. The second mode is to create an input file of Solaris user accounts (for example, /etc/passwd), and then use this input file to create new accounts (for example, passwd2sam -f input.file) into the PC NetLink SAM database.

As new Solaris accounts are created, you can use the command to synchronize the user account and password between a Solaris name service and a PC NetLink SAM database.

An example of the output generated by the -h command follows.

```
# ./passwd2sam -h
Usage: ./passwd2sam [-fh] [-i file] -l logon [-m connect] [-n local path]
                    [-o file] -p password [-r file] [-s logon script]
                    [-u user profile] [-y password]

 -f                  Disable NT accounts deleted from Solaris
 -h                  This message
 -i file             Input file to add users (/etc/passwd format)
 -l logon            Administrator logon
 -m connect          Global home directory -m H:\\\\SERVER\\USERS\\%USERNAME%
 -n local path       Local home directory -n C:\\USERS\\%USERNAME%
 -o file             Output file of added users (/etc/passwd format)
 -p password         Administrator password
 -r file             Input file of users to delete (/etc/passwd format)
 -s logon script     Logon script name -s NETLOGON.CMD
 -u user profile     User profile path -u \\\\SERVER\\PROFILES\\%USERNAME%
 -y password         Assign specific password or NULL for no password
```

Running the passw2sam command requires the administrator's account and password.

Setting up a Home Directory Server in a Sun Environment

If you have been using Solaris or UNIX servers to serve files by NFS, you can use the PC NetLink software to make these same files available to PC clients without adding and administering NFS PC client software. There are basically two approaches to doing this. Each approach has its pros and cons and you will need to determine the best practice solution for your environment.

Installing PC NetLink on all NFS Home Directory Servers

The PC NetLink software supports dynamic home directory shares that allow home directories to be established whenever a user logs on to a PC client. Some configuration is necessary. With the PC NetLink software, several options exist for sharing home directories.

The first approach to supporting user home directories for both NFS and SMB protocols is to install the PC NetLink software on all servers where users have home directories established. The pros for using this technique are:

- Each server is capable of supporting both NFS and SMB protocols.

- The network is used only once to transfer the files from the server to client. This is in contrast to the alternative method.

- This is the highest performing solution.

The cons are:

- The PC NetLink software must be installed on each server. Administration can be minimized by making each server a BDC of one PDC where all the account information is maintained.

- Older Sun servers may not support all PC NetLink server functionality.

Installing the PC NetLink Software on One Server

The second approach to supporting home directories is to install the PC NetLink software on only one server that is strategically close to home directory servers that already exist. The basic steps in setting up this environment are:

1. On a centrally located Solaris server, install the PC NetLink software and establish PC NetLink accounts for all the users who will have home directories accessible by PC clients.

2. Define a directory somewhere on the Solaris server where the PC NetLink software will share the home directories. A popular location for this is /export/home (as root, mkdir /export/home). If you will be the only one who can control the directory, protect the directory so that all can read and execute, but not write. (as root, chmod 755 /export/home). The 777 designation allows users to create and maintain their own home directory share.

Note – Using the automounter /home directory will not generally work for sharing home directories using the PC NetLink software 1.x because the PC NetLink software file operations will not always stimulate the automounter to initially mount, and maintain the mount, of the user's home directory.

---

3. Using Solaris symbolic links, create a symbolic link to each user's home directory using /home (preferred) or /net automounter locations (for example, ln. -s /home/don). The reason to create a symbolic link using the automounter's /home is that if a user's home directory is moved from one server to another, the symbolic link need not change. The /home automounter directory can automatically locate the user's home directory using NIS. /net can be used

in the symbolic link (for example, /net/homedir1/files1/don), but it will require a change if the user's home directory moves to another files system or server.

Note – Unlike using the automounter /home directory directly, using symbolic links will always stimulate the automounter so that every file operation will force the mount to occur if it is not already established.

---

4. Share the directory with the PC NetLink software (example:
   net share homedirs=c:/export/home).

5. Instruct users to define a network drive (or use the dynamic share creation that follows) to point to the PC NetLink directory you just created and shared. Users can browse their home directory and access their files from the mapped drive on their PC client.

The pros are:

- Only one PC NetLink server need be installed and maintained.

- Solaris automounter /home symbolic links will find the user's home directory even if the user's home directory is moved to another server.

- Not just home directories, but any NFS volume can be shared from the server using this technique.

The cons of using this technique are:

- Except for those users that have home directories on the server, the network will be used twice for all file operations to a user's home directory, once for the access from the PC client to the PC NetLink server, and again when the PC NetLink software accesses the home directory server using NFS.

  This method may be acceptable for casual use of files in home directories. However, if the load builds, remember you are consuming twice the network bandwidth. This method will have the least performance of the two.

- No two PC NetLink servers should ever access the same NFS directory at the same time if files are to be shared or locked. The locking established by one PC NetLink server will not transfer to other PC NetLink servers, and file corruption can result.

User Profiles

The PC NetLink software, like Windows NT 4.0, allows Windows NT Workstations (Windows 95 and 98 if enabled) to store a Windows NT 4.0-style User Profile that is used to save the state of the user's Windows environment. In addition, user profiles allow the PC client to automatically map the user's home directory and launch a script or DOS batch file to perform just about anything after the authentication has completed.

There are some differences in the paths used to launch scripts. The default path for the User Profile is `\winnt\system32\repl\import\scripts`. This script does not exist on PC NetLink servers. Instead, the default path used by the PC NetLink software is `/var/opt/lanman/repl/import/scripts`. If you want to use a login script, specify this path in the User Environment Profile window of the User Manager for Domains utility of Windows NT 4.0.

Login batch files launched at login can perform a variety of operations to set up the user's environment. One example is to map shares on servers with the `net use` command (`net use L: \\stsx\files1\data`).

Directory Synchronization

The PC NetLink 1.0 and 1.1 software cannot be installed and configured as a Windows NT member server. This means that all PC NetLink servers must be installed as Primary Domain Controllers (PDC) or Backup Domain Controllers (BDC). Installing many BDCs can affect system performance during PDC to BDCs replication of SAM databases, which increases processing time and network bandwidth.

Trusted Relationships

An alternative to making a PC NetLink server a BDC of an existing PDC is to make the server a PDC of a new domain and then use trusted relationships to allow the servers of the new domain to access the resources on the domain you want to use.

The benefit of using a trusted relationship is that no BDC-PDC synchronization traffic needs be done. The downside to this setup is the PC NetLink server must use another server in the trusted domain for all the authentication that is needed.

`passwd2sam` Account Synchronization

The most problematic issue with `passwd2sam` account synchronization is security. Read access to a Solaris name service is both a policy and a configuration decision established by a company. In cases where NIS or NIS+ password map read access is unavailable, you have two options:

- Create a `passwd` file containing Solaris user accounts and insert it into `passwd2sam` using the `-i` parameter.
- Enter Solaris user accounts using the Windows NT User Account Manager.

`sam2passwd` Account Synchronization

The most problematic issue with `sam2passwd` account synchronization is that the tool does not automatically move the new accounts to the NIS or NIS+ database. You must perform the second step of creating accounts in the name service from the file of accounts the `sam2passwd` tool has created.

The `sam2passwd` application generates `sam2passwd.mapunames`, a Bourne shell script, containing PC NetLink user accounts mapped to Solaris user accounts. You can run the Bourne shell script once the PC NetLink user accounts have been inserted into a Solaris name service. There is no error checking, so you must resolve duplicate account names or other problems in NIS or NIS+ name services.

Migration Procedures

Migrating from a Windows NT server to a PC NetLink server across an enterprise can take considerable time and planning. Following are procedures to help you plan and implement your migration.

Installing the PC NetLink Software

If you are setting up a new PC NetLink server to join an existing Windows NT domain, the following procedures outline all the steps necessary for installing PC NetLink 1.0 or 1.1 software.

Requirements

Make sure your server meets the requirements for the version of PC NetLink you plan on installing. The requirements for versions 1.0 and 1.1 are listed in Chapter 1.

Conflicts

Make sure no other program that uses a NetBIOS stack is running on the Solaris-based computer where you will install the PC NetLink software. You *must* uninstall or stop these products from running. See "Supporting PC NetLink, SunLink PC, and Samba" on page 150 for detailed information.

Recommendations

For best performance and functionality, install the PC NetLink software on the systems that have the local resources you want to share within the network, such as files and printers. It is better to implement home directories locally on UFS than to have user directories accessed over NFS files.

Windows Requirements

Make sure your PC clients meet the requirements listed in the Preface.

Preparing for Installation

For a successful installation you need the following information:
- Name of the domain you are joining.
- IP address for the Primary Domain Controller.
- Name and password for the system administrator.
- IP address for the primary and secondary WINS server (if any).

▼ To Install the PC NetLink Software

The instructions and manuals that are delivered with the Solaris PC NetLink product cover installation very well. For those who do not have the manuals handy and wish to review the procedures for installing the PC NetLink software, the following procedures will help you familiarize and plan your migration.

1. Login as root.

2. Insert the Solaris PC NetLink CD-ROM.

3. At the command line type the following to run the installation script:

```
# /cdrom/cdrom0/install
```

4. Choose option 3, Install server software and PC NetLink Manager. Type 3 and press Enter.

▼ To Install JDK

1. The installation script detects that you do not have JDK 1.1.6 installed on your system, and asks if you want to install it now. Press Enter to accept the default (yes).

2. When the patch installation completes, you will see the message, "Please note that the Solaris 2.6 patches will not take effect until the next system reboot." Do *not* reboot now.

3. Press Enter to continue when the installation script removes any older version of JDK that was installed with the Solaris operating environment.

4. Press Enter to continue when the message "Installed the Solaris Java Development Kit (Production version 1.1.6, NOT the Reference Release 1.1.6)." appears.

▼ To Install PC NetLink Server Manager

It might take a few minutes for the PC NetLink software installation to complete. Notice that if you have canceled any previous PC NetLink software installation, the installation script might detect it and display "Remove the previously installed PC NetLink packages?" If so, just press Enter to continue.

1. When the PC NetLink software installation is finished, press Enter to continue. If the script goes back to the menu choice, choose 4 (Exit) and press Enter.

2. Reboot the system using the `init 6` command.

Note – If you already have the JDK 1.1.6 installed properly and rebooted the system after the JDK 1.1.6 installation, installing the PC NetLink software does not require rebooting.

---

3. At the login, enter root and your password. Press Enter. The PC NetLink services will start automatically.

4. **Open a terminal. Type** /opt/lanman/bin/net computer **and press Enter.**

   This enables you to pre-set domain name (sunlink_server01_dom) with your new PC NetLink server listed as Primary Domain Controller. Notice that sunlink_server01_dom domain name contains sunlink_server01 which is your server computer name.

   Note – You can edit your /.profile and /export/.profile so your path will include the PC NetLink server commands.
   PATH=$PATH:/opt/lanman/bin:/opt/lanman/sbin; export PATH

   ---

5. **Before you join an existing domain (PDC), you must change the administrator password to the same password as the PDC you want to join. Open a terminal and type the following:**

   ```
   # /opt/lanman/bin/net password \\sunlink_server01 administrator
   password production01_password
   ```

   In this case, the administrator password on the PC NetLink server is password. The existing Windows NT server PDC password is production01_password. If successful you'll see: The command completed successfully.

6. **Join the existing Windows NT domain. As an example, we assumed the Windows NT domain name to be** production01_dom.

   ```
   # /opt/lanman/sbin/joindomain
   ```

7. **Press Enter.**

   This message is displayed:

   ```
   The SunLink Server configuration utility (joindomain) allows you
   to specify the server name, the domain name, and the servers. Do
   you want to continue [y/n]? y
   ```

8. **Press** y **and then Enter.**

   The following question will be displayed:

   ```
   The joindomain utility cannot continue when the server is
   running. Do you want to stop the server and continue [y/n]? y
   ```

9. **Press y and then Enter.**

   This will stop all PC NetLink server services. Wait for a few seconds for this next question:

   ```
   The current name of this server is (sunlink_server01). Would you
   like to change this name now [y/n]? n
   ```

10. **Press n and then Enter.**

    You don't need to change your server name (or computer name).

    The following message is displayed:

    ```
    This server is configured as a primary domain controller. Would
    you like to change the role of this server to backup [y/n]? y
    ```

11. **Press y and then Enter.**

    You want to change the role of the PC NetLink server from a PDC to BDC, joining an existing domain where a Windows NT server is a PDC.

    Read the instructions and answer the question:

    ```
    Enter the name of the primary domain controller:
    ```

    Assume that the existing Windows NT server name is `production_nt01`. Enter it and press Enter.

    The following prompt will appear:

    ```
    Enter the name of an administrator account on (production_nt01)
    or press Enter to select administrator.
    ```

    Press Enter unless you want to change your administrator name from the default (administrator).

12. **Enter** `production01_password`, **which is the password of the Windows NT server administrator/primary domain password. Press Enter.**

13. **The system will ask you to re-enter your password. Repeat your password and press Enter.**

    You'll see the following:

    ```
    Contacting the server (production_nt01) ... Success
    Confirm choices:      servername : SUNLINK_SERVER01
                          role       : backup
                          domain     : PRODUCTION01_DOM
                          primary    : PRODUCTION_NT01
    Is this correct [y/n]? y
    ```

14. **Press Enter to confirm that this is the correct information. You'll see the following message:**

    ```
    Creating SunLink Server accounts database. Do you want to start
    the server now [y/n]? y
    ```

15. **Press Enter to restart the PC NetLink server services. There is no need to reboot.**

    A few instructions will be displayed, read them for your information. Your PC NetLink server is now part of the production01_dom domain.

16. **Enter /opt/lanman/bin/net computer and press Enter. You will see the following message:**

    ```
    These computers belong to domain PRODUCTION01_DOM:
    Computer Type
    ----------------------------------------------------------
    SUNLINK_SERVER01 Backup
    PRODUCTION_NT01 Primary
    WINDOWS_CLIENT01 Workstation
    The command completed successfully.
    ```

17. **To verify that the PC NetLink server system successfully joined the existing Windows NT domain, go to the Windows NT server and do the following: Start ->Programs->Administrative Tools->Server Manager.**

    You should be able to see "SUNLINK_SERVER01" listed as "Windows NT Backup."

Migrating a Windows NT Server to a PC NetLink Server

Because each Windows NT server migration is unique, one general solution is difficult to implement. Following are several options you may find useful when moving files from Windows NT to a PC NetLink server.

▼ To Move Files From a Windows NT to a PC NetLink Server

1. **Install the PC NetLink software on the Solaris server.**

2. **Use the** `joindomain` **command to set the PC NetLink server to be a backup domain controller (BDC) of the Windows NT server.**

   (This will automatically copy the SAM database.)

3. **Use directory replication between the servers on the same domain to copy the logon scripts.**

4. **Use one of the following methods to copy the files:**

   - XCOPY and PermCopy

   a. **Type the following command to copy files from a Windows NT to a PC NetLink server:** `xcopy *.* j: /s.`

      where `j:= net share<New User Directory>`

      The `xcopy` command copies the files, making entries only on the ACL database for the directories. The `xcopy` command is very fast and the ACL database does not grow excessively. The problem with this method is that the file permissions are lost because the copied ACLs for the directories are:

      - Full Control for Administrator, Creator Owner.
      - Change for Everyone and Server Operator.

   b. **Copy Share permissions for every share by using the permcopy command on the Windows NT server:**

```
c:\ permcopy\\<Source NT Computer> <ShareName> \\<Dest Cascade Comp> <NewShareName>
where in most cases, ShareName = NewShareName
```

   c. **Use Windows NT Explorer to build directory permissions on directories on the PC NetLink server.**

Note – When setting directory permissions on Windows NT Explorer, the option "Replace permissions on existing files," is selected by default. If this option is selected, an ACL entry for each file will be created. Make sure to unselect this option if you want to have the same permissions on the subdirectories. Instead, select the "Replace permissions on subdirectories" option to keep an ACL database as small as possible.

- Scopy and PermCopy

a. Enter the following command to copy files:

```
Scopy *.* j: /s or /o
```

where j:= net share on new directory for user data such as c:/export/lanman. The /s option copies subdirectories. The /o (that's the letter "O") copies file permissions.

Note that it makes no difference whether or not you use /o to copy files to a PC NetLink server because you will always get an ACL entry for every file copied. The /s option is enough to copy all the files and permissions.

b. Reduce the size of the ACL database created from the previous command.

You must compress the ACL database before allowing users to use the server. This may take a long time if many files were copied. Shrink the ACL database using the following commands:

```
# /etc/init.d/ms_srv stop
# /opt/lanman/sbin/blobadm -A -q
# /etc/init.d/ms_srv start
```

c. Copy share permissions for every share using Permcopy on the Windows NT server. At the DOS prompt, enter:

```
C:\ Permcopy \\source\share \\destination\share
```

where *source* is the Windows NT server and *destination* is the name of the PC NetLink server.

While this procedure is slower—taking twice as long as xcopy to copy the same number of files—the ACL information is accurate, making this process more desirable. Also, when you reduce the ACL database size, even if you delete all the copied files, the ACL database will not be reduced to a size close to its original size before files were copied.

- Directory replication

While this is the fastest method of doing this migration, both the PC Netlink 1.0 and 1.1 software had a bug that would restrict their use. This bug has been fixed and a patch generated for it. Check Sun Service for the availability of this patch. (See the Preface for patch information.)

Setting Up System Policies

Being able to control resources, users, and rights is important in a network. Because you need ways to control how end users use their computer, what programs they run, and even how their desktop looks, it is important to understand how to set up and configure system policies.

The objective of this section is to provide you with a simple, easy way to set up system policies for a Windows NT domain. It is also designed so that you can understand the basic concepts of system policies and how they are applied.

Microsoft System Policies

System policies allow you to increase the security of a Windows NT network. This will work on any computer running Windows NT Server, Windows NT Workstation, or Windows 95 or 98. With system policies you can define two things:

- The desktop options for a Windows user or group. Examples are:
  - Type of wallpaper
  - Programs they can run
  - Type of shell they can have
- The computers settings. Examples are:
  - Removing the last login name from the login screen
  - Number of login attempts
  - Auto-disconnect

For system policies to work well, directory replication must be working first. You can have system policies without replication, but you will have to manually copy the policies file to the PDC and all the BDCs. Once replication is working you can start configuring policies.

▼ To Configure System Policies

1. **Open the Systems Policy Editor, which is in the Administration Tools (Common) menu.**

2. **Choose File --> New Policy**

   You should get a screen with two icons: Default User and Default Computer.

3. **To create policies go to:**
   Edit --> Add Computer
   Edit --> Add Group
   Edit --> Add User

4. **Use the browse box to choose a computer, group, or user, when the system asks you for a name.**

5. **Double-click on the icon and a new menu will appear.**

6. **Choose the policies you want. Click on OK.**

7. **When you have finished choosing the policies, save the file as** `NTconfig.pol`. **This is your policy file.**

   To create policies for Windows 95/98 workstations, the system policies will have to get created in a Windows 95 or 98 machine. Name the file `Config.pol` and save it in the `\NETLOGON` directory.

8. **To make the policies active, copy the policy file into the** `\Netlogon` **folder of the PDC.**

   Note – In Windows NT the `\Netlogon` directory is in `\Winnt\System32\Repl\imports\Scripts`. On the PC NetLink server the `\Netlogon` directory is in `/var/opt/lanman/repl/import/scripts`

   If the replication is implemented, you will only have to put this on the PDC and let it be copied. If replication is not working, then this will have to be done by hand.

9. **If replication is implemented and running, wait 5 to 10 minutes for the policies to take effect.**

10. **To test if the policies are working, log in on a workstation that has some policies defined or log in as a user with policies.**

▼ To Set Up Windows NT File Shares Using PC NetLink

1. Create a directory on Solaris that you want to be shared, using the PC NetLink software.

Any Solaris directory can be shared on any file system. Solaris UFS file systems mounted to Solaris directories at boot time or by the `mount` command are the most commonly shared. Use the `df` command to see the Solaris UFS files systems that have been mounted.

```
# df
/                  (/dev/dsk/c0t0d0s0 ): 1591138 blocks    399433 files
/proc              (/proc            ):       0 blocks      1885 files
/dev/fd            (fd               ):       0 blocks         0 files
/tmp               (swap             ):  451824 blocks     19130 files
/files1            (/dev/dsk/c1t2d0s2 ):   44130 blocks   3783980 files
/files2            (/dev/dsk/c0t1d0s2 ): 1575488 blocks    973889 files
```

You can share full UFS file structures, or you can share individual directories.

2. Set up the Solaris permissions.

This enables the PC NetLink server to access the directory. If the directory was owned by the Solaris `root` account, and had 700 permissions on it, it would be inaccessible to the PC NetLink software.

This sets up the username for the directory owner, the DOS group permissions, and the directory permissions. For general access permissions use the following commands:

```
# chown lmxadmin:DOS---- directory-name
# chmod 775 directory-name
```

If the share is to be owned by a specific user and that user is already mapped using mapuname, substitute the UNIX username for lmxadmin.

3. Set up the Windows NT permissions.

Use a Windows NT system and mount the share that contains the directory you are going to share. For example, to set Windows NT permissions for a Solaris directory /newshare, mount the share that contains the directory /newshare, in this case, the root share C$. If the directory was /export/lanman/newshare, you could either mount C$ or "USERS."

Note – The "$" character in Windows NT share names has special significance. A trailing "$" on a share name means that the share will not be seen when browsing from the Network Neighborhood. The root directory is not set up as a visible share because it is not normally necessary for users to see it. Its high permission disallows viewing it. In the same way, a user's home directory share might normally be set up with a trailing "$". Imagine how unwieldy the share listing would be for a system with 2000 users if each user's home directory share were listed in one directory. Instead /export/home/mikeb is shared as MIKEB$. Only mikeb needs to use that share so it doesn't need to be listed. The share will still exist, it just cannot be browsed.

Once the parent directory share has been mounted from Windows Explorer, right-click on the directory to be shared. Select Properties and the Security tab. From here you can set the file permissions. Typical permissions are

- Domain Administrators—Full Control
- World—Read
- Specific owners of the directory—Full Control

It is also possible to change the ownership of the directory, but this is not simple. It involves either logging in as that user and taking ownership or using the xcacls program from the Windows NT Resource Kit.

4. **Execute the PC NetLink command to share the directory.**

You can use either of two commands: lmshare -a or net share. The lmshare command is typically found to be easier.

a. **To use lmshare, you need three pieces of information: the sharename, the directory to share, and a description.**

For example, to create a share called TSHARE of /export/lanman/testshare, the lmshare session would be similar to the following:

```
# lmshare -a
For those fields that are not mandatory and that you do not want
to enter anything, just press Return.

Sharename? TSHARE
Type (d|p|c|i)? [d]
Local path? /export/lanman/testshare
Remark? Test Share
Permissions(rwcxdaps)? [rwcxda]
Maximum users? [unlimited]
Password?
TSHARE added
```

Note that most of the options have been given a default value. See the man pages for lmshare, or use the lmshare command with no options for more details.

b. **To use the** `net share` **command with the same example as above, type the following:**

```
# net share tshare=c:/export/lanman/testshare /remark:"Test Share"
tshare was shared successfully.
```

Note the syntax of the `net share` command is somewhat odd. You must use `C:` to represent the root of the Solaris system and then the UNIX style path delimiter, forward slash (/), for the rest of the definition of the share.

Deleting a Share

● **To remove a share, use either the** `net share` **command:**

```
# net share tshare /delete
tshare was deleted successfully.
```

or the `lmshare -d` **command:**

```
# lmshare -d tshare
tshare deleted
```

Note – If users merely have mapped drives pointing to the share, the command will complete without prompting you. However, if users have files open on the shared mapped drive, you will be warned and given the option to complete the command or not. Be careful not to delete a share while a user has an active file open.

If files are open, the output for the `net share` command is similar to the following:

```
# ./net share files1 /delete
Users have open files on files1.  Continuing the operation will
force the files
closed.
Do you want to continue this operation? (Y/N) [N]: n
#
```

## CHAPTER 7

Server Consolidation and Resource Management

The push to consolidate workloads and servers onto fewer systems creates new demands on system and performance management. The data center is full of systems, many of which are lightly used. Data center planners are reluctant to place multiple applications on operating environments less stable than Solaris. In addition to the system administration headaches of managing multiple systems, there is less and less physical space to accommodate more systems.

It can be a nightmare to manage so many small server systems. Each has its own custom setup, and unlike desktop machines, it is hard to automate a cloned installation process. How can you reduce the system administration overhead by combining many small servers into a few big ones? How can you add a new application to an existing system and continue to manage the system effectively without impacting its level of service?

This chapter looks at a range of tools that allow you to consolidate servers.The first part of the chapter provides an overview of the most common resource management tools for the Solaris operating environment. The latter part of the chapter features a specific PC NetLink resource management example using Solaris Resource Manager.

When you want to place multiple network services on the same system, the first concern is how to manage the resources effectively. No single network service or application should be allowed to dominate the resources of a server unless that is the expressed policy of the system planner. At times, all network services (file, print, email, web, and so on) should run at equal priority levels without any server application choking off another. At other times, one application (such as database applications) may need to have the highest priority and should be allowed to receive more resources for completing tasks. This chapter shows how the PC NetLink software works with several resource management products available on the Solaris system to accomplish a variety of server consolidations.

Single-Function Server Consolidation

A single-function consolidation uses one server to replace several servers performing one operation. With the PC NetLink software, this applies to supporting file services, Windows NT domain authentication, WINS services, and PDC/BDC operations. For example, a company might decide to take five older single- or dual-processor Pentium 133 MHz class Windows NT servers and consolidate them to one Sun Enterprise 450 Solaris PC NetLink server.

Although such a consolidation can be desirable, the planner must understand the load each preconsolidated server was under and apply this information to the methodology for sizing the new server. If the peak bandwidth requirements exceed what the planned server is capable of delivering, then you must decrease the number of servers to be consolidated, increase the number of target servers, or give the servers more resources to meet the demand.

In many cases, attempting to perform a single-function consolidation will reroute the traffic through longer paths on the network. You must check the network infrastructure to ensure that it can handle the increased bandwidth traffic.

In single-function consolidations, where demands of a network service on multiple servers are redirected to one server, the goal is to meet the load of a new, larger, community of users. Advanced resource management techniques may not be necessary, and the controls specific to PC NetLink through the registry may be the only area where resource management tuning is needed.

Multifunction Server Consolidation

Multifunction server consolidation places the functionality of several different servers, performing different operations (such as file, print, email, authentication, and web services), on one server. If there are enough processors to distribute the load, and there are no collisions on other resources such as disk subsystems and network connections, Solaris and SPARC systems scale well to support this kind of consolidation. Often servers are not busy and other services and applications can be running to take advantage of the available resources.

A possible problem with multifunction server consolidation, however, is the possibility that several services will require the same resources at the same instant. How do you manage the priorities of allocating the resources? If left alone, Solaris software will attempt to distribute the resources (primarily CPU and memory) fairly. Unfortunately, Solaris software cannot know the business and user priorities of the system without some form of resource management. Solaris software runs a batch process that is intended to run at a low priority at the same level as interactive applications that should be run at high priority.

Sizing the Complete System

Before attempting a multifunction consolidation, be sure the system can meet the requirements of the peak loads it is expected to handle.

Complete a sizing exercise to determine what system resources will be required to support the PC NetLink software portion of the planned server. Chapter 5 covers this topic in detail.

When sizing a multifunction consolidation, keep the following in mind:

- Allocate at least 10 to 20 percent more resources to allow enough expansion for other functional blocks without dramatically affecting their performance.

- Know when the peak demand occurs for each application or network service. If they appear at the same time, clearly more resources will be needed by the server. If you are relatively certain the services will be staggered, then fewer resources will be needed. Acquire enough memory for each function to perform well simultaneously if necessary. Err in the direction of more memory. The Solaris operating environment will always put additional memory to use as file read cache.

- For purposes of resource management, analysis, and troubleshooting, assign different disk subsystems to the various functions to be supported. Many performance-related problems are bottlenecks on disk subsystems. If two server functions need to use the same disk subsystem, it can be difficult to determine which application or function is at fault.

- If possible, place the swap partition on its own disk drive as well as its own RAID partition—if RAID disk subsystems are being used on the system.

- As with any sizing activity, prototype the system if possible.

- If you are attempting to restrict the resources of the PC NetLink software to ensure resources are available for other applications, it is possible to restrain the PC NetLink performance to the point where extremely long delays may occur at users' PCs. However, the PC NetLink software can be throttled down to extremely low levels before this occurs. This condition may cause PC clients to time-out as they try to perform a PC NetLink function. Usually, simply retrying the operation will allow the PC client to proceed. If too many of these instances occur, users have a legitimate right to complain. If the PC NetLink server becomes starved for resources routinely, consider either increasing the resources allowed to the PC NetLink server or restricting the number of users who can gain access to the system.

Resource Management

Resource management allows controlled allocation of resources to different applications as required to meet service levels and performance goals. In multi-function consolidations, where many services (file, print, email, web support, database, and so on) are being placed on the same server, it is critical to have tools and techniques that allow the separate services to share the same system without interfering with one another's resources. Sometimes managing these resources can be as simple as allocating a separate disk subsystem to one resource and another separate disk subsystem to a different service. However, resources like CPU and memory are not as easy to split between the various services. Without tools to prevent it, one service can dominate the server and make it difficult or impossible for other services to meet a minimum level of performance.

Up to this point, we have looked at the PC NetLink software on servers where it is the only or the primary network service offered by the server. In this chapter we will focus on the tools for the PC NetLink software designed to share the resources of a system with other services and applications.

Sun provides a base-level operating environment with many facilities, as well as several unbundled products that extend its capability. How can you tell what combinations of products work together to solve your business problems?

The following sections introduce you to some resource management techniques and tools, and highlight how the PC NetLink software participates in each of these resource management mechanisms. Another book in the BluePrint series, *Resource Management*, deals with this topic in much greater detail.

In December 1998, Sun introduced a flexible resource management package for the Solaris operating environment, the Solaris Resource Manager™. Solaris Resource Manager provides the ability to allocate and control major system resources. It also implements administrative policies that govern which resources different users can access, and more specifically, what level of resource consumption each user is permitted.

With regard to the PC NetLink software, you will usually approach resource management in two basic ways:

- PC NetLink performance is a priority. For example, if you are using the PC NetLink software as a home directory server for a user community, you want to be sure other services and applications running on the server do not interfere with it.

- PC NetLink performance is of secondary importance on the server. For example, if the PC NetLink software has been installed on a database server to offer reports to users on PC clients, it must be allocated only a small amount of resources so that it does not interfere with the higher-priority database applications on the system.

In either case, you can use resource management tools and techniques to control the PC NetLink services, other applications running on the server, or both. You can also use a combination of tools to accomplish what you want.

Service Level Agreements

Computer systems provide a service to their end users. System managers are responsible for the quality of this service. System and application vendors provide a range of components that can be used to construct a service. A service must be available when it is needed and must have acceptable performance characteristics.

Service Level Management involves interactions among end users, system managers, vendors, and computer systems. Although these interactions are commonly captured with a Service Level Agreement (SLA) between the system managers and the end users, in reality many additional interactions and assumptions are not often captured formally. Guaranteeing that the end user will always see a certain level of performance can be a difficult or impossible task. A 1000-user community, all demanding services at the exact same instant, will exhaust the resources of even the largest server and network infrastructure. A business decision must be made to find ways of off-loading demand during the peak. Possibilities include upgrading the overloaded server, distributing the load across more servers, or just living with the high-demand peaks.

With respect to the PC NetLink software, an SLA might best be based on the peak load anticipated by sizing the server. Sizing a PC NetLink server (see Chapter 5) requires picking a peak time and load in Mbytes/sec. Benchmarks help determine what resources are needed to meet this peak period. Resource management tools allow you to make certain these resources are available during the peak time.

Measurements

Making measurements to determine if the server is meeting the expected service level may be difficult. Many times you may not know you have a performance issue until a user complains about slow response. How do you know the server is meeting its expected level of performance? Chapter 8 specifically deals with monitoring a PC NetLink servers.

There are several situations where users on the same server may experience completely different levels of performance. While one user may be getting good to acceptable performance, another may be receiving poor performance. A short list is presented here for you to review if you do encounter such a situation.

- Are the two users on different subnets where significantly different network traffic can account for the difference in performance? Confused route tables can also account for poor performance. Network bottlenecks, where the routing from the client to the server needs a higher speed network to route through a lower speed network are common. Problems like this may not be perceptible until the bottleneck has reached saturation. Using `tracert` or `ping` on the PC clients might show a significant difference in paths and latency.

- Are the two users using two different disk subsystems where one is heavily used and the other is lightly used? All the sizing information presented in Chapter 5 assumes the user load will be balanced across all disk subsystems. Use the command `iostat -txc`, or the other tools mentioned in Chapter 8 to see if the loads on your disk subsystems are balanced.

- Are many highly active users sharing the same `lmx.srv` process? On rare occasions many busy users can share the same `lmx.srv` process. Because of this, users of the heavily used process may experience poor performance, while other users in less used `lmx.srv` processes see good performance. Use the `/opt/lanman/sbin/lmstat -c` command to see if busy PC clients are sharing the `lmx.srv` process.

Resource Management Techniques and Tools

This section lists each tool or technique you can apply to servers where you must manage resources (CPU, memory, disk, network).

Managing Resources With the PC NetLink Software

The PC NetLink software has several areas that can limit how the server resources are used. If PC NetLink performance is the highest priority, the PC NetLink software parameters can be changed to force the PC NetLink software to spawn more `lmx.srv` processes and allow fewer users per process. While this can demand more memory of the system, it also allows additional performance because there is less contention for the processes assigned to PC clients and more processors can become involved. Benchmarks show that a 10 to 15 percent increase in performance can be obtained by forcing the PC NetLink software to use more processes to support the user community at the expense of using more memory. For most installations, the added demand of memory to support these additional processes may be considered too costly to pay for increased performance, especially on a server where other services are running at the same time.

If you want to allocate only minimal resources to the PC NetLink software in favor of the server's more important database function, there are several techniques for handling this.

- First consider limiting the total number of users that can access the server at any one time using the PC NetLink software. To do this, change the value `maxclients` in the `/etc/opt/lanman/lanman.ini` with the `/opt/lanman/sbin/srvconfig` command. To read the value of the `maxclients` variable, use the following command:

```
# /opt/lanman/sbin/srvconfig -g server,maxclients
```

To set the value to 30 clients, for example, use the same command with the `-s` switch, as shown in the following example:

```
# /opt/lanman/sbin/srvconfig -s server,maxclients 30
```

- Forcing the PC NetLink software to limit the number of `lmx.srv` processes spawned also limits the number of processors involved in handling the PC Netlink server requests. In a multiprocessor system, this technique limits the number of processors involved in supporting the PC NetLink software. For example, if you adjust the registry parameters to force the PC NetLink software to spawn only two `lmx.srv` processes, only two processors in the system can be involved in supporting the PC NetLink software. Solaris Resource Manager might be a better tool to perform this function, especially if more than just the PC NetLink software and one additional service are on the server. See Chapter 4 for details on adjusting these parameters.

If your servers support many applications, you may be tempted to spawn multiple instances of the PC NetLink server to solve a variety of resource issues. Unfortunately, unless your server is a Sun Enterprise 10000, only one instance of the PC NetLink 1.0 or 1.1 software can be running on one server at a time. One reason is that the current NetBIOS layer needs to respond for just one PC NetLink server environment.

Another more important issue concerns support for the file structure and ACLs. Only one instance of the PC NetLink software can support the ACL database for any given file or directory on the system. If there are two instances of the PC NetLink software you will have two sets of ACLS for the same file. This issue also makes supporting mounted file systems from multiple PC NetLink servers problematic. If two PC NetLink servers attempt to access the same NFS mounted file on a third system, there will be no sharing of ACL information. While nothing in the PC NetLink software prevents you from doing this, ensure that only one PC NetLink server supports any writable file systems. With read only files systems, where any ACL data will not change, there is no need for concern.

Accounting and Charge Back

The resources consumed by each user or work load can be accumulated into an accounting system so that projects can be charged in proportion to the resources they consume. This technique can put the responsibility of using resources on a system via the PC NetLink software, and perhaps other services, onto the users themselves. The more they use, they more they are charged.

If you are using the PC NetLink software with Windows NT domain accounts alone and users do not have Solaris accounts, a useful alternative to setting up Solaris accounting for users is to monitor the PC NetLink software processes. Thus, you could monitor the PC NetLink software activities for a user community, focusing on the resources of the service instead of just individuals.

Base Solaris Software

The Solaris operating environment includes several features that provide control over certain types of resources. Some features, such as nice(1) and processor sets, are part of the basic Solaris software and allow a limited form of resource management.

The nice(1) command permits users to manipulate program execution priority. Unless superuser privilege is invoked, this command only permits the user to lower the priority. This can be a useful feature (for example, when a user starts a low-priority batch job from an interactive login session), but it relies on the cooperation of the user. Depending on requirements, you can use the nice command to temporarily solve a resource management issue. With regard to the PC NetLink software, using the nice command to solve resource management issues would be difficult to implement. Solaris Resource Manager enforces administrative policies, even without the cooperation of the user, and manages the resources automatically.

Processor Sets

Processor sets were introduced in the Solaris 2.6 operating environment. This feature enables you to divide multiprocessor systems into logical groups and permits users to launch processes into those groups. The advantage with this setup is that work loads running in one processor set are protected from CPU activity taking place in any other processor set. In some ways, this is similar to what Solaris Resource Manager does, but the two features operate on a completely different basis. Processor sets control only CPU activity. The control is at a relatively coarse-grained hardware level, because processors can belong to only one processor set at a time. Especially in the case of relatively small systems, the granularity can be quite high: on a four-processor system, the minimum resource that can be assigned is 25 percent of the system.

When using the PC NetLink software with processor sets, you need to know the process IDs (PIDs) of the `lms.srv` processes and use the `psrset` command to assign them, and perhaps other PC NetLink processes, to processor sets. Manipulating current startup scripts or creating new scripts can automate the use of processor sets and the PC NetLink software to some degree. If you want processor-level resource management granularity and if the PC NetLink software is requiring excessive CPU resources from the system, processor sets may solve your problem. Refer to the Solaris documentation on processor sets and the `psrset` command for further information on how to apply this to the PC NetLink processes. However, I recommend Solaris Resource Manager for most CPU-based resource management issues.

Dynamic System Domains

The Sun Enterprise 10000 has a feature called dynamic system domains (DSDs), which enables you to logically divide a single system rack into one or more independent systems, each running its own copy of Solaris software. (Do not confuse Enterprise 10000 DSDs with Windows NT domains.) For example, a system with 32 CPUs on eight system boards might be operated as one system with 16 CPUs, and two other systems with eight CPUs each. In this configuration, three copies of Solaris software would run independently of each other. The DSD feature also permits controlled movement of resources into and out of each of the Solaris images, thus creating a relatively coarse-grained facility for managing physical resources. (The minimum unit of inter-domain allocation is an entire system board.)

Dynamic Reconfiguration

The dynamic reconfiguration feature of Sun Enterprise servers enables users to dynamically add and delete system boards, which contain hardware resources such as processors, memory, and I/O devices. A dynamic reconfiguration operation on memory has no impact on Solaris Resource Manager memory-limit checking.

Sun Enterprise 10000 DSDs offer some interesting possibilities for the PC NetLink software installations. A Sun Enterprise 10000 can be set up with eight Enterprise 10000 DSDs, each with eight processors (for a total of 64 processors). In this configuration, a PC NetLink PDC can be set up in one of these Sun Enterprise 10000 DSDs, with seven BDCs set up in the remaining Sun Enterprise 10000 DSDs. While this configuration would rarely be needed, it's nice to know that these systems can scale to this level if necessary.

A more realistic use of the PC NetLink software and Sun Enterprise 10000 DSDs is an environment where a corporate information service group wants to place its Windows NT PDC on a highly reliable and available system. The Sun Enterprise 10000 has the most RAS features of any Sun Enterprise server. Only one or two processors need to be assigned to the Sun Enterprise 10000 DSD supporting the PC

Netlink PDC, while the other services to be supported by the Sun Enterprise 10000 can run in separate DSDs, making them completely independent of any resource required by the PC NetLink software.

Solaris Bandwidth Manager Software

Solaris Bandwidth Manager software provides the means to manage network resources to provide Quality of Service (QoS) to network users. At this writing, Solaris Bandwidth Manager is available only with the Enterprise server and ISP. server versions of Solaris software. The current version of the product is Bandwidth Manager 1.5. The previous version of the product was known as Bandwidth Allocator 1.0.

Solaris Bandwidth Manager software allows network traffic to be allocated to separate classes of service so that urgent traffic gets higher priority than less important traffic. Different classes of service can be guaranteed a portion of the network bandwidth, leading to more predictable network loads and overall system behavior. Service Level Agreements can be defined and translated into Bandwidth Manager software controls and policies. Tools and APIs provide the interface to monitoring, billing, and accounting options.

Since almost all network links are shared by more than one user or application, the available bandwidth has to be shared. Bandwidth management tools enable you to manage how it is shared.

If a network link is continuously congested, the link needs to be upgraded to provide greater capacity. In many cases, however, the average load on a link is within the link capacity, and the link is congested only temporarily. Temporary congestion that occurs during peaks in network use at particular times of the day or following a particular event, are predictable. Other causes of temporary congestion, such as the transfer of a large file, are not possible to predict.

Solaris Bandwidth Manager software enables you to manage the bandwidth used by IP traffic. It does this by allocating traffic to a class based on the application type, source and destination address, URL group, or a combination, then assigning individual limits for each class. With respect to the PC NetLink software, the following examples illustrate how you can allocate bandwidth using Bandwidth Manager software:

- NFS file traffic to the engineering department must have at least 50 percent of the link.
- Traffic for a high bandwidth image scanner could be allocated 25 percent of the link to ensure no data loss occurs.
- PC NetLink traffic in general could be limited to 25 percent of the link, allowing for equally important web pages on the server to be accessed.

Some types of traffic, for example interactive traffic generated when using `telnet` or `rlogin`, need a quick response time. Solaris Bandwidth Manager software lets you assign a higher priority to that traffic. Traffic that does not require a quick response time, such as a file transfer using FTP, can be assigned a lower priority.

By balancing the bandwidth allocated to different types of network traffic and the relative priorities, you can optimize your network performance. Solaris Bandwidth Manager software also allows you to monitor the performance of your network, and it has interfaces for third-party billing applications.

You can control the amount of resources consumed by the PC NetLink file and print operations indirectly by throttling the amount of network bandwidth on TCP port 139, which is the NetBIOS Session socket. The Solaris Bandwidth Manager product provides the means to do this.

First assess the network interfaces that need to be controlled. If clients come in over several network interfaces, all of these interfaces will have to be brought under control by the Solaris Bandwidth Manager software.

When defining interfaces in the Solaris Bandwidth Manager software, you must specify whether incoming or outgoing traffic needs to be managed. In the case of the SMB protocol that the PC NetLink software supports, network traffic could go in both directions (reads and writes). In the Solaris Bandwidth Manager software configuration, this would appear as follows:

```
interface hme0_in
rate      100000000 /* (bits/sec) */
activate  yes

interface hme_out
rate       100000000
activate   yes
```

Next, correctly define the service you want to manage. You need to define a class for handling the SMB (file and print) traffic.

```
service smb_tcp
protocol tcp
ports 139, *
ports *, 139
```

Put in place a filter that can categorize network traffic in SMB (PC NetLink) and non-SMB traffic:

```
filter  SMB_out
src
type      host
address  servername
dst
type      subnet
mask      255.255.255.0
address  129.146.121.0
service  SMB_udp, SMB_tcp
```

The filter in the previous example is for managing outgoing SMB traffic to the 129.146.121.0 network. You can leave out the destination part to manage SMB traffic to all clients from wherever they come.

Create another smb_in filter for SMB traffic in the opposite direction. Only the src and dst parts need to be reversed (not shown here). Last, create a class that will allocate a specific bandwidth to this.

```
class managed_nfs
interface      hme_out
bandwidth      10
max_bandwidth  10
priority        2
filter         smb_out
e
```

This class sets a bandwidth of 10 percent of the available bandwidth (10 Mbytes in case of fast Ethernet). Control the maximum bandwidth by setting an upper bound to the CPU resources that the PC NetLink software consumes on the host. The key variable is max_bandwidth. It specifies an upper limit to the consumed bandwidth. You can even set the bandwidth variable to 0, but this could cause the SMB protocol to be starved for bandwidth if other types of traffic are being managed. This could also cause PCs to time out their requests to the server.

The priority variable is less important. It will be a factor if other types of traffic are being managed. Generally, higher priorities will have lower average latencies, because the scheduler gives them higher priority if it has the choice (within the bandwidth limitations that were configured).

Throttling the bandwidth obviously manages the network access to the server, but what of the other resources that the PC NetLink software needs to support this managed bandwidth? Generally speaking, the more activity demanded by the PC clients, the more CPU and memory resources that will be required as well. Solaris software automatically brings into physical memory what it needs to support the PC client. If the traffic is managed to restrict the PC NetLink traffic, the CPUs will have less to do and will be available for other processes running on the system. It would be advantageous to have enough memory for the lmx.srv process to remain in memory, so that when traffic does need to be handled, the CPUs go to work immediately without paging or swapping the required memory back into physical memory.

Alas, Solaris Bandwidth Manager software is not free in terms of its use of resources. To implement what it does, it inserts a streams module that filters all the traffic flowing through the network connections configured to be used with Solaris Bandwidth Manager. This overhead varies, depending on the sophistication of the filter.

Solaris Resource Manager Software

Solaris Resource Manager software is the Sun resource management extension for the Solaris operating environment, and should be used when more advanced resource management and control is required. It is especially useful when placing the PC NetLink software on servers where many services are to be supported.

You can use Solaris Resource Manager software in two ways: one as a way to control other applications and workloads from interfering with the PC NetLink software, and the other as a way to control the PC NetLink software from interfering with other workloads.

We will first look at how Solaris Resource Manager software accomplishes its role of managing the resources. Then, we will do a brief overview of the Solaris Resource Manager software functionality. Finally, we will show some examples of how the PC NetLink software can be controlled by Solaris Resource Manager software.

To cover Solaris Resource Manager software fully requires a great deal more explanation than can be offered here. Refer to the *Resource Management* BluePrint or to the Solaris Resource Manager documentation itself for more information.

Note – Throughout the discussion of Solaris Resource Manager, the term "user" applies to a Solaris user identified in /etc/passwd or NIS. Do not confuse this term as being a user known to the PC NetLink Windows NT domain.

To see how Solaris Resource Manager differs from the base Solaris resource control, consider how two applications or workloads can be consolidated onto a single system using processor sets to manage the CPU resource. Processor sets allow you to allocate ten processors to workload A and eight processors to workload B. Although this would provide processor limits for each workload, resources could be wasted if one of the workloads is not using all of its share of the processors because the spare CPU cannot be used by any other workload.

Solaris Resource Manager Overview

Solaris Resource Manager provides the following advantages over base Solaris resource control:

- Better utilization of system resources
- Dynamic control of system resources
- More flexible resource allocation policies
- Finer grained control over resources
- Decayed usage of resources
- Accounting data for resource usage
- Solaris Resource Manager functions

Because the PC NetLink software may be installed on a server where many different applications are competing for the same resources, it is difficult to say what is the best way to use Solaris Resource Manager with the PC NetLink software. Once the PC NetLink software begins execution within the Solaris Resource Manager environment, some experimentation may be required to tune your system. Some of the experimental benchmarks performed later in this chapter should aid you in determining a good starting point. First, let us briefly review all of the capabilities of the product.

Solaris Resource Manager Policies

Solaris Resource Manager software is built around a fundamental addition to the Solaris kernel called an lnode (limit node). These lnodes correspond to UNIX UIDs, and may represent individual users, groups of users, applications, and special requirements. The lnodes are indexed by UID and used to record resource allocations policies and accrued resource usage data by processes at the user, group of users, and application levels. Users will retain the same UID they normally use in Solaris. User groups, applications, and any other grouping require that new UIDs be created to represent these entities.

Hierarchical Structure

The Solaris Resource Manager management model organizes lnodes into a hierarchical structure called the scheduling tree. The scheduling tree is organized by UID: Each lnode references the UID of its lnode parent in the tree. Each sub-tree of the scheduling tree is called a scheduling group, and the user at the root of a scheduling group is the group's header. The root user is the group header of the entire scheduling tree.

A group header can be delegated the ability to manage resource policies within the group. The lnodes are initially created by parsing the /etc/passwd file. An lnode administration command (limadm(1MSRM)) creates additional lnodes after the installation of Solaris Resource Manager and assigns lnodes to parents.

The scheduling tree data is stored in a flat file database, which can be modified as required.

Though UIDs used by lnodes do not have to correspond to a system account, with an entry in the system password map, it is best to create a system account for the UID of every lnode. For non-leaf lnodes (those with subordinate lnodes below them in the hierarchy), it may be that the account associated with that lnode is purely administrative and no one ever logs into it. However, it can also be the lnode of a real user who does log in to run processes attached to this non-leaf lnode.

Note that Solaris Resource Manager scheduling groups and group headers have nothing to do with the system groups defined in the /etc/group database. Each node of the scheduling tree, including group headers, corresponds to a real system user with a unique UID.

Hierarchical Limits

If a hierarchical limit is assigned to a group header in an lnode tree (scheduling group), then it applies to the usage of that user plus the total usage of all members of the scheduling group. This allows limits to be placed on entire groups, as well as on individual members. Resources are allocated to the group header, who can allocate them to users or groups of users that belong to the same group.

In the most simple use of Solaris Resource Manager software, consider the scenario where you are attempting to allocate CPU time for two CPU-intensive processes that are the only two active processes in a system. With Solaris Resource Manager software, you can assign one share of the CPU resources to process A and four shares to process B, creating a total of five shares. Process A would receive 20 percent of the available CPU resource, and process B would receive 80 percent. If either process were to pause or stop, the other process would be allowed additional CPU resources if requested.

After we look at the full functionality of Solaris Resource Manager software, we will cover a slightly more complex example to make the use of shares absolutely clear.

Controls Available With Solaris Resource Manager

Solaris Resource Manager software provides control of the following system resources:

- CPU (rate of processor) usage
- virtual memory, number of processes
- number of logins
- terminal connect-time

For the PC NetLink software, we will focus only on CPU allocation.

Solaris Resource Manager software keeps track of each lnode's usage of each resource. For all resources except CPU, users may be assigned hard limits on their resource usages. A hard limit will cause resource consumption attempts to fail when the limit is reached. Hard limits are directly enforced by either the kernel or whatever software is responsible for managing the respective resource. A limit value of zero indicates no limit. All limit attributes of the root lnode should be left set to zero.

Solaris Resource Manager software progressively decays past usage so that only the most recent usage is significant. The system administrator sets a half-life parameter that controls the rate of decay. A long half-life favors even usage—typical of longer batch jobs—while a short half-life favors interactive users.

The CPU resource is controlled using the Solaris Resource Manager SHR scheduler. Users are dynamically allocated CPU time in proportion to the number of shares they possess (analogous to shares in a company), and in inverse proportion to their recent usage. The important feature of the SHR scheduler is that while it manages the scheduling of individual threads (technically, in Solaris software, the scheduled entity is a lightweight process (LWP)), it also portions CPU resources among users.

Each user also has a set of flags, which are boolean-like variables used to enable or disable selective system privileges, for example, login. Flags can be set individually per user or inherited from a parent lnode.

The usages, limits, and flags of a user can be read by any user, but can be altered only by users who have administrative powers.

CPU Resource Management

The primary advantage of the Solaris Resource Manager scheduler over the standard Solaris scheduler is that it schedules users or applications rather than individual processes. Every process associated with an lnode is subject to a set of limits. For the simple case of one user running a single active process, this is the same as subjecting each process to the limits listed in the corresponding lnode. When more than one process is attached to an lnode, as when members of a group each run multiple processes, all of the processes are collectively subject to the listed limits. This means that users or applications cannot consume CPU at a greater rate than their entitlements allow, regardless of how many concurrent processes they run. The method for assigning entitlements as a number of shares is simple and understandable, and the effect of changing a user's shares is predictable.

The allocation of the renewable CPU service is controlled using a fair-share scheduler. Each lnode is assigned a number of CPU shares, analogous to shares in a company. The processes associated with each lnode are allocated CPU resources in proportion to the total number of outstanding active shares, where active means that the lnode has running processes attached. Only active lnodes are considered for an allocation of the resource, as only they have active processes running and need CPU time. As a process consumes CPU ticks, the CPU usage attribute of its lnode increases.

The scheduler regularly adjusts the priorities of all processes to force the relative ratios of CPU usages to converge on the relative ratios of CPU shares for all active lnodes at their respective levels. In this way, users can expect to receive at least their entitlements of CPU service in the long run, regardless of the behavior of other users. The scheduler is hierarchical, because it also ensures that groups receive their group entitlement independently of the behavior of the members.

Solaris Resource Manager software is a long-term scheduler. It ensures that all users and applications receive a fair share over the course of the scheduler term. This means that when a light user starts to request the CPU, that user will receive commensurately more resource than heavy users until their comparative usages are in line with their relative fair-share allocation. The more you use over your entitlement now, the less you will receive in the future.

Solaris Resource Manager software has a decay period you set, that forgets about past usage. The decay model is one of half-life decay, where 50 percent of the resource decays away within one half-life. This ensures that steady, even users are not penalized by short-term, process-intensive users. The half-life decay period sets the responsiveness or terms of the scheduler. The default value is 120 seconds. Shorter values tend to provide more even response across the system, at the expense of slightly reduced accuracy in computing and maintaining system-wide resource allocation. Regardless of administrative settings, the scheduler tries to prevent marooning (resource starvation) and ensure reasonable behavior, even in extreme situations.

Solaris Resource Manager software will not waste CPU availability. No matter how low a user's allocation, that user will be given all the available CPU if there are no competing users. One of the consequences of this is that users may notice performance that is less smooth than they are used to. If a user with a very low effective share is running an interactive process without any competition, it will appear to run quickly. However, as soon as another user with a greater effective share demands some CPU time, it will be given to that user in preference to the first user, so the first user will notice a marked job slowdown. Nevertheless, Solaris Resource Manager software goes to some lengths to ensure that legitimate users are not marooned and unable to do any work. All processes scheduled by Solaris Resource Manager software (except those with a maximum `nice` value) are allocated CPU regularly by the scheduler. There is also logic to prevent a new user that has just logged on from being given an arithmetically "fair" but excessively large proportion of the CPU to the detriment of existing users.

Processes

With respect to Solaris Resource Manager, every process is attached to an lnode. The init process is always attached to the root lnode. When processes are created by the `fork(2)` system call, they are attached to the same lnode as their parent. Processes may be reattached to any lnode using a Solaris Resource Manager system call, given sufficient privilege. Privileges are set by root or by users with the administrative permissions.

Example of Using Solaris Resource Manager Shares

To further illustrate the concepts Solaris Resource Manager uses, consider the more complex situation illustrated in FIGURE 7-1. This diagram shows two basic types of workloads to be controlled, namely users and applications. To allow users faster interactive response time, they were allocated more resources when needed. In the boxes that represent these workloads, users are given four shares and applications are given one share. In turn, specific users and applications are given shares below each workload category. Mark gets 60 shares, Chuck gets 20 shares under users, and `/usr/bin/app1` gets four shares and `/usr/bin/app2` gets one share under the applications workload. The shares allocated below the users and applications level are allocated within the context of the hierarchy. In the example, Mark and Chuck get 60 and 20 shares (of 80 total shares) allocated under the users' portion of the hierarchy. These shares are numerically evaluated only within the context of the users' portion of the tree. In turn, the applications app1 and app2 get four and one shares (of a total of five shares) respectively.

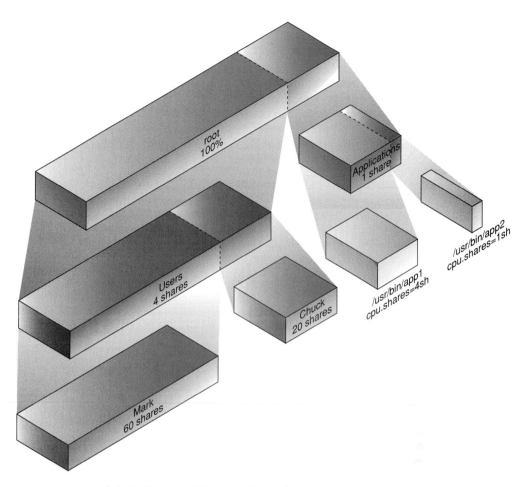

FIGURE 7-1 Solaris Resource Manager Hierarchy Example

Let's study the example in a situation where all nodes of the hierarchy are attempting to use 100 percent of the CPU. If the processes for Mark, the processes for Chuck, app1, and app2 all become 100 percent CPU intensive, Solaris Resource Manager would allocate the following amount of CPU resources:

- Mark gets 60 shares of 80 total shares (60/80) for users. The category users is allocated four of five shares (4/5) of the system resources. Mark gets 60/80 of 4/5 of the CPU. This is 60 percent of the system CPU (lucky Mark!).

- Chuck gets 20 shares of 80 total shares (20/80) for users. Chuck gets 20/80 of 4/5 of the CPU. This is 20 percent of the system CPU.

- app1 gets four shares of five total shares (4/5) for applications. The category applications is allocated 1 of 5 shares (1/5) of the system resources. app1 gets 4/5 of 1/5 of the CPU. This is 16 percent of the system CPU.

- app2 gets one shares of five total shares (1/5) for applications.
  app2 gets 1/5 of 1/5 of the CPU. This is four percent of the system CPU.

At times, it may be difficult to see Solaris Resource Manager working because it performs its magic only when many processes are requesting resources at a high level for a considerable period of time. At other times, when only one process is resource intensive, you will see the process get nearly 100 percent of the available resources because other processes in the hierarchy are inactive. In our example, if no other competing process was running and app2, the lowest priority batch-type process, required many hours to execute, it would consume 100 percent of the system. Under high-load situations, it can receive as little as 4 percent of the system.

To implement the hierarchy within Solaris Resource Manager, each user and application is given a UID in the /etc/passwd file. In the case of the users, they already have a UID, so no special additions to /etc/passwd are required.

Note that in the example, the users are running applications in the Solaris environment. They are not users known to the PC NetLink domain.

The applications may or may not be associated with a specific UID. If a process normally runs as root, let's say, then a unique place holder UID would have to be created for Solaris Resource Manager to associate the application to an lnode. This UID is used only by Solaris Resource Manager to create the lnode hierarchy it uses to allocate resource shares. Applications would still run as root if that is the way they normally work.

The work load categories Users and Applications also must have unique entries in the /etc/passwd file even though Solaris itself might never use these passwd entries.

Using PC NetLink With Solaris Resource Manager

With an understanding of Solaris Resource Manager, we can now look at how the PC NetLink software can be used when other workloads are being controlled by Solaris Resource Manager. There are two fundamental ways the PC NetLink software can function inside a system where Solaris Resource Manager is being used. The first way is to let Solaris Resource Manager control everything but the PC NetLink software. If the resources consumed by the PC NetLink software are not significant compared to other workloads, leaving the PC NetLink software out of the Solaris Resource Manager hierarchy will allow it to work as a peer with all the Solaris Resource Manager controlled processes. Using other resource management techniques, like changing the PC NetLink registry to spawn fewer processes, may be an easier way to restrict its use.

The second way to have the PC NetLink software function with Solaris Resource Manager is to have it participate within the Solaris Resource Manager hierarchy. Determining the best approach would be driven by controlling the PC NetLink software in context with the other applications running in the system. The goal is to get all the PC NetLink software processes scheduled by the Solaris Resource Manager scheduler. The general approach for doing this is outlined in the following steps:

▼ To Run PC NetLink Processes Within Solaris Resource Manager

1. **Define or use the already established** /etc/passwd **entries that will be used by Solaris Resource Manager software to define lnodes.**

   Using the PC NetLink software defined lmxadmin entry already in the /etc/passwd file is fine for the purpose of Solaris Resource Manager lnode hierarchy definitions.

2. **Use the** /usr/srm/sbin/limadm **command to place the** lmxadmin **user in the appropriate spot in the Solaris Resource Manager hierarchy.**

   This will be different for each server configuration. Try to place the PC NetLink software at the same level as other important applications you want to control. The amount of shares you give the PC NetLink software will depend on server (CPUs and memory), the number of users, and how busy the users are.

3. **Stop the PC Netlink software execution as root, using the following command:**

   ```
   /opt/lanman/bin/net stop server
   ```

4. **In the** /etc/init.d **directory, from which the PC NetLink software is started at boot time, edit the** ms_srv **script to use the** /usr/srm/bin/srmuser **command to start the PC NetLink software processes.**

   Note that the process will still execute as root, but will be attached to the lnode lmxadmin. All PC NetLink commands will use the /etc/init.d/ms_srv script to start or stop the PC NetLink services.

   ```
   Original /etc/init.d/ms_srv code segment:
   . . .
   else
       cd `dirname $LMXCTRL_PATH` && $LMXCTRL_NAME < $DEV_NULL_PATH
   fi
   . . .

   New /etc/init.d/ms_srv code segment:
   . . .
   else
       cd `dirname $LMXCTRL_PATH` && /usr/srm/bin/srmuser lmxadmin \
       $LMXCTRL_NAME < $DEV_NULL_PATH
   fi
   . . .
   ```

When editing the file, search for LMXCTRL.

All PC NetLink lmx.* processes are forked by lmx.ctrl which, after the edit, will be under the Solaris Resource Manager control. Starting and stopping processes from server manager does *not* break the Solaris Resource Manager control. This addition to the PC NetLink software startup command line will start the lmx.ctrl process running as root, using the lnode of lmxadmin.

5. **Restart the PC NetLink server using the** /opt/lanman/bin/net start server **command. This command will in turn execute the** /etc/init.d **script you just edited. The PC NetLink software will now be scheduled by way of the Solaris Resource Manager scheduling class.**

6. **Determine the best way to allocate shares for the PC NetLink processes.**

This will be different for each application and work load mix. The data presented in the next section should help you determine what shares to allocate to the PC NetLink software.

Remember that in the previous procedure users refers to Solaris users as defined by /etc/passwd or NIS. The PC NetLink software as it supports requests for a user does so with an lms.srv process that runs as root. There is no easy way to control the PC NetLink software with Solaris Resource Manager to allow individual users to have more resources allocated to them over other users using the PC NetLink software.

Solaris Resource Management and PC NetLink Throughput

To determine what reasonable levels of CPU shares should be allocated to the PC NetLink software, an experiment was setup to benchmark the software throughput as it was given fewer and fewer shares. In this experiment the following server configuration was used:

- Sun Enterprise 450 (4x300 MHz Processors), 4 Gbytes Memory.
- /tmp was shared via the PC NetLink software and was used as the file system for the NetBench benchmark. This eliminated the possibility that a disk subsystem could be the bottleneck for the benchmark.
- One 100 Mbit Ethernet connection was used for this experiment. This was not enough network bandwidth to allow the CPUs to saturate, but was adequate to derive the information we need.
- Thirty 300 MHz PCs were used to run the benchmark, all PCs were attached to a network switch using full duplex 100 Mbit connections to a network switch.
- Four 100 percent CPU duty-cycle processes (for a four-processor system) were used to consume 100 percent of the CPU resource.

- The NetBench benchmark (see Appendix A) was configured to test all 30 PCs with no wait time to allow for maximum potential load.

To measure performance differences caused by using Solaris Resource Manager, you must have a competing application that will attempt to consume CPU time. For this experiment, the following command was used to consume CPU resources.

```
# srmuser acctsrvr dd if=/dev/zero of=/dev/null &
```

This launches a Solaris dd command under the lnode group acctsrvr (explained later). This dd command moves an infinite stream of zeros (0x00) (/dev/zero) to the bit bucket (/dev/null), as fast as possible. After executing one of these commands on an otherwise idle system, you will see one CPU show 0 percent idle time when viewing the mpstat command. To consume 100 percent of the CPU time for all processors, you will need to run one of the commands for each of the processors on the system. Solaris will do the job of distributing the processes across all processors and the mpstat command will report something like this (the idle time is the last column on the right):

```
# mpstat
CPU minf mjf xcal  intr ithr  csw icsw migr smtx  srw syscl  usr sys  wt idl
  0    0   0  171   654    0 1401  650    8  867    0 61700   35  65   0   0
  1    0   0   63   402    4  510  253    6 4769    0 68027   32  68   0   0
  2    0   0    0  2722 2675  190   91    5  579    0 56246   25  75   0   0
  3    0   0 1038   488    0 1158  482   11 2338    0 50320   31  69   0   0
```

Now that we have something that can compete for resources with the PC NetLink software, we need to create a Solaris Resource Manager lnode tree from which we can allocate CPU resource shares between the competing resources (the four dd commands) and the PC NetLink processes. An lnode tree was created where both the PC NetLink processes and our CPU consuming processes are part of a group called srvgroup. Branching off from srvgroup are our two competing lnodes lmxadmin and acctsrvr. For this test, user and system processes remain inactive and will not compete for resources. The lnode tree is shown in FIGURE 7-2.

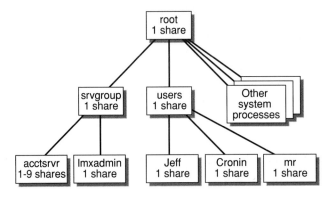

FIGURE 7-2 lnode Tree Used in Solaris Resource Manager PC NetLink Test

Another way of viewing the lnode tree is by use of the Solaris Resource Manager `limreport` command. The lnode tree can reconstructed from the output of this command. FIGURE 7-3 shows the output of the `limreport` command for our test environment:

```
# limreport flag.real "%s \t %s \t %i \n" lname sgroupname
cpu.shares
root            1s
daemon    root    1s
bin       root    1s
sys       root    1s
adm       root    1s
lp        root    1s
smtp            1s
uucp      root    1s
nuucp     root    1s
listen    root    1s
lanman    root    1s
lmxadmin        servgrp         1s
srmidle         root    0s
srmlost         root    1s
srmother        root    1s
jeff      users   1s
cronin    users   1s
mr        users   1s
servgrp         root    10s
acctsrvr        servgrp         8s
users     root    1s
```

FIGURE 7-3 `limreport` Command for the PC NetLink Solaris Resource Manager Test

The flag.real parameter selects only those UIDs that have mapped lnodes.

Each of the lnodes required an /etc/passwd entry even though the processes were running under the root or some other account. The /etc/passwd entries for the lnodes used in the test are shown in FIGURE 7-4.:

```
. . . standard system /etc/passwd entries not shown . . .

lanman:x:100:13:SunLink Server account:/opt/lanman:/bin/false
lmxadmin:x:92780:13:SunLink Server Administrator:/var/opt/lanman/lmxadmin:/bin/sh
lmxguest:x:92781:13:SunLink Server GUEST Login:/home/lmxguest:/bin/false
lmworld:x:92782:13:SunLink Server World Login:/home/lmworld:/bin/false
srmidle:x:41:1:SRM idle user:/:/bin/false
srmlost:x:42:1:SRM lost user:/:/bin/false
srmother:x:43:1:SRM other user:/:/bin/false
jeff:x:50:10::/export/home/logullo:/bin/ksh
cronin:x:51:10::/export/home/kevin:/bin/ksh
mr:x:53:10::/export/home/mr:/bin/ksh
servgrp:x:44:10::/:/bin/sh
acctsrvr:x:45:10::/:/bin/sh
users:x:46:10::/:/bin/sh
```

FIGURE 7-4 /etc/passwd Entries Used by Solaris Resource Manager to Define lnodes

The specific change made to the system to incorporate the PC NetLink processes (processes starting with lmx) was a simple edit made to the /etc/init.d/ms_srv file that starts the PC NetLink environment at boot time. To edit the file, search for the entry LMXCRTL.

The differences in the file before and after the edit are as follows:

```
Before the Edit
     cd `dirname $LMXCTRL_PATH` && $LMXCTRL_NAME < $DEV_NULL_PATH

After the Edit

   cd `dirname $LMXCTRL_PATH` && /usr/srm/bin/srmuser lmxadmin \
                   $LMXCTRL_NAME < $DEV_NULL_PATH
```

This change to the file causes the system to launch the lmx.ctrl process within the Solaris Resource Manager framework under the lmxadmin lnode. Keep in mind that the processes will run as root but will be in the Solaris Resource Manager hierarchy as lmxadmin. All processes that are spawned by lmx.ctrl will also fall within the Solaris Resource Manager hierarchy as lmxadmin, allowing them all to be controlled as one entity.

The next step was to assign shares to the two competing processes. Initially we gave each lnode one share, using the limadm command.

```
# limadm set cpu.shares=1 acctsrvr
# limadm set cpu.shares=1 lmxadmin
```

We have assigned acctsvr and lmxadmin one share each. They both fall under the servgrp lnode in the Solaris Resource Manager hierarchy, so they will initially get 1/2 of whatever shares the servgrp lnode is allocated. Because this system is performing no significant function other than the two we want to control, we can start running a benchmark and see how the allocation of shares changes the throughput. TABLE 7-1 shows the measured results under the various settings of Solaris Resource Manager shares. Using this particular NetBench test forces all 30 PCs in the test to place a full load on the server. This normally would give us a throughput much higher than that first measured, but because of the one 100 Mbit Ethernet connection, we are limited to the bandwidth of the connection.

TABLE 7-1   Effect of Load on Throughput

NetBench Maximum Throughput	Setting of PC NetLink / acctsrvr(100% load)
10,346,435	1 / 1 No processes but PC NetLink running (Maximum possible, in this server configuration)
8,670,323	1 / 1 With 4 CPU dd command loads
6,712,454	1 / 2 With 4 CPU dd command loads
5,479,512	1 / 3 With 4 CPU dd command loads
5,006,338	1 / 4 With 4 CPU dd command loads
4,657,473	1 / 5 With 4 CPU dd command loads
4,409,744	1 / 6 With 4 CPU dd command loads
4,135,639	1 / 7 With 4 CPU dd command loads
3,693,225	1 / 8 With 4 CPU dd command loads
3,533,888	1 / 9 With 4 CPU dd command loads

As we give the competing process more and more shares, the PC NetLink software receives a smaller and smaller percentage of the CPU resources, and thus its maximum throughput performance decreases (see FIGURE 7-5.)

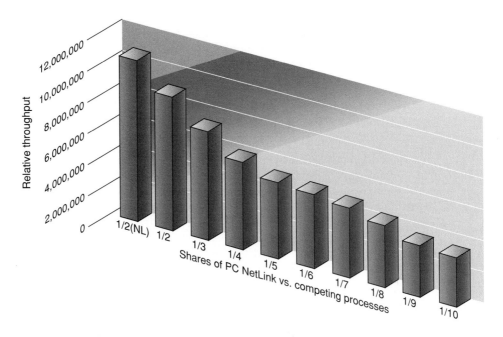

FIGURE 7-5   Relative Performance of PC NetLink as Shares are Reallocated

The first entry of the chart (labeled 1/2(NL)) shows the performance of this system when no competing processes were running. Because the system was using only one 100 Mbit full-duplex connection, the maximum throughput was gated by the network connection, and we see just over 10 Mbytes/sec. The CPU utilization was measured to be 60 percent for this data sample. When the four dd CPU loads were turned on to consume every remaining CPU cycle, and the PC NetLink processes were allocated their one share (50 percent of the CPU resources), the throughput dropped just as it should. As more shares are allocated to the CPU loading processes (the dd command) the throughput continues to drop further and further, allocating more CPU resources to the artificial load and less to the PC NetLink processes.

In a real-world setting you could launch web servers, email servers, or any other server processes into the Solaris Resource Manager hierarchy with the PC NetLink software, and the other processes it competes with for resources would never be given more than their allocated shares when all are actively consuming resources. Remember, you will not easily see Solaris Resource Manager work unless all the processes it controls are actively seeking resources. If some processes are not using their shares and are placing themselves in the idle state, the other processes with greater demands will be allowed to consume the resources that they otherwise could not use.

Note – Seeing Solaris Resource Manager work is sometimes difficult unless you perform tests like the one shown here, where you can guarantee CPU loads that will consume the full system.

In this test the PC NetLink software, or the PC clients that were running the NetBench benchmark, never became so starved for resources that it caused the benchmark to time-out and fail.

Continuing the test, from 1/10 to 1/20, 1/40, 1/60, 1/80, and 1/100 shares, we see something we might not expect (see FIGURE 7-6.) We would expect the benchmark throughput to continue to get lower until it starves the PC clients to the point where time-outs occur. We would also expect the curve to approach zero.

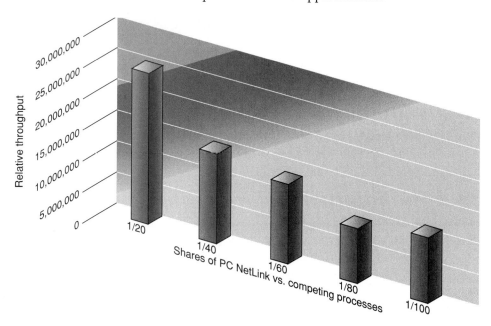

FIGURE 7-6 Solaris Resource Manager Controls PC NetLink Shares to 1/100

Instead we see the benchmark settle at a line of approximately 1 Mbytes/sec. What accounts for this additional throughput is SMB opportunistic locking that allows the PC clients to cache files locally. As the PC clients operate on files that they are caching, the benchmark continues to show throughput as these locally cached files are accessed. The really significant point to be made here is that even when the PC NetLink software is allocated only one percent of a four-CPU server, with 99 percent of the CPU resources being consumed by other processes, it continues to function. None of the 30 PC clients failed to finish the benchmark under these extreme conditions.

With Solaris Resource Manager, you can give the PC NetLink software as little as one of 100 shares, and while the performance will be slow, it will be reliable. In the this test, the Solaris /tmp directory was used as the test file system that the PC NetLink software shared. This was done to make sure no disk waits could place the PC NetLink processes in an I/O wait state. As long as the file server load is distributed across as many file subsystems as possible you will see similar results.

Other Possible Resource Management Techniques

There are alternatives to solving the resource management issues by means other than using Solaris programmatic methods. While improving performance is usually the goal of most installations, there may be times when restricting the performance between a client and a server is desirable.

Limiting Users Who Can Access PC NetLink Servers

One of the easiest ways to limit the use of the PC NetLink servers is to restrict the number of users it can support concurrently. Use the maxclients variable to set the maximum number of PC clients the PC NetLink server will support. The default value of this variable (if no maxclients value is defined in lanman.ini) is 1000, which is the maximum number of concurrently active PC clients supported by the PC NetLink software 1.0.

By lowering the value of maxclients you can limit the impact of the PC NetLink software on a server. If you want to restrict the PC NetLink software activity so that users are allowed only occasional access to the server, you can set maxclients to 25, or even less, to guarantee a limited impact on the server.

Restricting PC Clients to Low Bandwidth Devices

For environments that consume a great deal of throughput, you may want to throttle the bandwidth available to a PC client, if a series of automated procedures impacts the performance of interactive users. In situations where there is no demand to finish the automated procedure at the expense of users, you may want to restrict the throughput of the automated procedures. You can either place all the data files for the automated procedures on a slow disk drive, or force the PC client to access the server via a 10 Mbit network connection. Both of these techniques limit the ceiling of performance that can be demanded from the server because of the hardware limitations placed on the connection by demand.

You will want to have a redundant storage system (RAID) for most environments. Using a slow, single, non-redundant drive is not an option for any R/W file system. If the data is read only, or can be replaced easily if the drive goes bad, a slow disk may be an acceptable solution for throttling performance.

Throttling the Network

If you have several PCs doing automated procedures, and you want to limit the throughput they can demand, place them on a 10 Mbit or 100 Mbit hub where all the PCs must share the same common connection to the server. Even if the PCs saturate the network connection, the maximum throughput they can demand is ~1 Mbyte/sec. (more if you include opportunistically locked files).

Server Use Policies

For some cooperative user environments, where the PC NetLink software has been installed, many resource management problems can be avoided by simply scheduling times when users are requested not to use the server. Servers at many customer sites are used heavily to process payroll, end-of-quarter financial information, or regularly-scheduled software builds for engineers. In situations like these, it may be acceptable to ask the user community to avoid using the server during the one day per month, or afternoon per week, when the server must be dedicated to one task. If the server is not being used to support their home directory, this is not usually a problem. If you are using Solaris Resource Manager software, you only need to change the shares allocated between the PC NetLink processes and other applications running on the server to implement this policy. The Solaris Resource Manager performance data presented earlier shows the PC NetLink software is capable of supporting a community of users, albeit slowly, even when allocated less than five percent of the CPU resource.

Use the `/opt/lanman/bin/net session` command to show who is attached to the server and the number of files they have opened. As a courtesy, or perhaps a way to avoid career-limiting moves, run a script several minutes before shutting down the server and notify users with open files to close their applications. Following is an example of the use of this command:

```
# ./net session

Computer                User name           Client Type         Opens Idle time
-------------------------------------------------------------------------------
\\EELAB1~X              ADMINISTRATOR       NT LANMAN 1.0        1     00:00:00
\\EELAB1~X              ADMINISTRATOR       NT LANMAN 1.0        0     00:00:00
\\PS4300                LAB                 NT LANMAN 1.0        1     00:05:00
The command completed successfully.
```

Controlling Resources Used by One User

Unfortunately, it is difficult to control requests from individual PC clients for the PC NetLink resources. It is usually impossible for one PC client to completely choke a server. Occasionally, when gigabytes of data must be moved between servers, one connection may require constant demand on the PC NetLink resources. Only if several users are doing this type of operation would it be desirable to lower the priority of one connection to the PC NetLink software. A problem with lowering the priority of a single `lms.srv` process is that the process may be supporting other PC clients.

It is important to detect what users are routinely demanding significant amounts of throughput. Chapter 8 offers several scripts that will help you determine the PC NetLink resources users are accessing.

Network Switches and the IEEE 802.1p Standard

A technique similar to using Solaris Bandwidth Manager is to use network switches that support the network traffic prioritization. The IEEE 802.1p standard was developed recently, and network switch manufacturers are now implementing this standard. This standard allows you to prioritize traffic using filter techniques that help ensure a quality of service (QoS) through the network. Use of switches that support this standard can increase or decrease the priority of the PC NetLink related traffic.

To implement this capability in a switch, there must be a way for the switch or router to prioritize the TCP traffic on socket 139 and UDP traffic on sockets 138 and 139 for the server where the prioritization is being applied.

## CHAPTER 8

Monitoring the Resources Used by PC NetLink Software

This chapter covers the various tools that allow you to monitor and refine how your network environment affects the server. It shows you ways to answer the following questions:

- How much CPU is the PC NetLink software using?
- What devices have been saturated to the point where the PC NetLink software cannot deliver additional throughput?
- How much memory is the PC NetLink software using?
- Which users of the PC NetLink software are demanding the most resources?

We will use a variety of tools to answer these questions, highlighting how you can plan your system better so that monitoring will be easier once the system is in production.

We will not cover each tool or technique to its full extent, but will instead focus on the PC NetLink specifics only. See the Preface of this book for references where these topics are discussed fully.

Tools for Monitoring PC NetLink Resource Utilization

If you have used or administered Solaris systems for any length of time, you are probably familiar with many of the Solaris commands presented here. We will highlight the data items to focus on when you are using these commands. While there are GUI-based applications available to monitor Sun servers, the traditional commands are still used widely, and their output has been used for years to monitor systems. You can count on these tools being available on all Solaris systems.

Another good reason for focusing on the use of the traditional command-line tools is that they can be easily combined with the PC NetLink software commands to derive information that will be more informative for tracking down sources of problems.

In addition to the tools available with Solaris software, we will look at several other tools that are not shipped with the Solaris operating environment.

Tools for Monitoring Disk Subsystems

On a well-configured server, the resource that is most likely to bottleneck and accounts for most performance issues is the disk subsystem. For this reason we look at monitoring tools first.

Unfortunately, there is no one-step command that can show disk statistics in the form of PC NetLink shares. Performing this operation is a three-step procedure. We will first show the manual commands necessary for determining which PC NetLink share is the bottleneck, then we will look at a script that will simplify the process into one easier command.

If you experience a performance problem and suspect that a disk subsystem is saturated, you can determine the specific PC NetLink share by using the following steps:

▼ To Find a Saturated Disk

1. **To determine which disk is busy, use the Solaris** `iostat` **command.**

2. **Use the** `df` **command to determine which UNIX directory the disk drive is mounted to.**

   Note that there may be another step added here if a software RAID environment like Veritas or Solaris Disk Suite is being used. You will want to determine what software RAID volume the saturated disk(s) are members of.

3. **Use the PC NetLink command** `/opt/lanman/bin/net share` **to determine the share that is exporting the UNIX mount point.**

   Let's look at each of the steps in detail.

iostat Command

The Solaris iostat command is usually the first Solaris native tool for monitoring disk subsystem resources. It creates I/O activity reports for a variety of terminal, tape, and disk devices. Following is an example of the simplest form of the command:

```
iostat
          tty          fd0           sd0           sd1           sd2          cpu
   tin tout kps tps serv kps tps serv kps tps serv kps tps serv us sy wt id
     0    0   0   0    0   0   0    5   1   0   20   0   0    5  0  0  0 100
```

The iostat command has several options that will make viewing its output easier to interpret. Consult the man page for the full list. On a large server, where there will be many disk subsystems, the simple form of the iostat command will only show a few disk subsystems and label their names created as symbolic links. Many people find the default names it reports to be less useful than the disk names more commonly used with mounting and formatting drives. To obtain the cXtYdZ disk names use the -n switch. If you use multiple partitions on the same hard drive, use the -p switch as well. It is easier to match these names to the mounted file structures reported by the df command. To print statistics for all the disks, use the -x switch.

The first time you use the iostat command it reports statistics since the system was rebooted. This is usually not useful for showing current activity, so you will want to have iostat print at least two reports, one after the other to see the current state (over the last 1 second) of the system.

Following is an example output of using all of these switches:

```
# system6 85 =>iostat -xn 1 2
                            extended device statistics
    r/s    w/s    kr/s     kw/s wait actv wsvc_t  asvc_t   %w   %b device
    0.0    0.0    0.0      0.0  0.0  0.0    0.0     0.0    0    0 fd0
    0.0    0.2    0.1      1.2  0.0  0.0    0.0    38.2    0    0 c0t0d0
    0.0    0.0    0.1      0.1  0.0  0.0    0.0    38.4    0    0 c0t1d0
    0.0    0.0    0.0      0.1  0.0  0.0  609.7   101.5    0    0 c0t2d0
    0.0    0.0    0.0      0.0  0.0  0.0    0.0   106.9    0    0 c0t6d0
                            extended device statistics
    r/s    w/s    kr/s     kw/s wait actv wsvc_t  asvc_t   %w   %b device
    0.0    0.0    0.0      0.0  0.0  0.0    0.0     0.0    0    0 fd0
    0.0    0.0    0.0      0.0  0.0  0.0    0.0     0.0    0    0 c0t0d0
    0.0    0.0    0.0      0.0  0.0  0.0    0.0     0.0    0    0 c0t1d0
   11.1   45.2  388.0   1512.7 46.2  8.0  820.1   142.1  100  100 c0t2d0
    0.0    0.0    0.0      0.0  0.0  0.0    0.0     0.0    0    0 c0t6d0
```

If the PC NetLink software appears to be giving slow performance to users and the CPU resources are *not* saturated, disk subsystem saturation is the limiting factor a majority of the times. In the preceeding example output, the second set of statistics for the c0t2d0 disk show a disk under considerable strain. The statistics show the requests for the disk are waiting 100 percent of the time (%w), the disk is 100 percent busy (%b), the queue of transactions waiting for service is 46. If users are accessing this disk using the PC NetLink software, there will be considerable performance issues. Statistically, during peak times on a typical day, many users trying to access the same application at the same time can cause a momentary saturation of the drive. Usually this will not cause significant delays and will be transient in nature. You will want to track down disk saturations that last for several minutes. You may want to determine if the saturation occurs at the same time during a typical day.

If Veritas or Solaris DiskSuite software RAID environments are being used to support larger or faster disk volumes, you will want to use the tools supplied with these products to determine what volumes the busy disks belong to.

Hardware RAID environments like the StorEdge SRC/P (PCI RAID card) produce disk subsystems that appear in the iostat command as single entities.

After you detect a busy disk subsystem, the next step is to determine what is causing the disk to be so busy.

Identifying Users Causing Disk Saturation

When a disk subsystem is saturated for a long period of time, you must determine which applications of which users are causing the saturation. Other users using the same disk subsystem will experience slow performance if the saturation is allowed to remain.

Many PC applications, such as full-text indexing engines that allow fast searching of user content, will do nothing but access files in large directory trees. These types of applications typically are scheduled to run every day and can run for several hours. Be sure they are scheduled to run on off hours. If several users were to use these types of applications during peak times, performance would suffer.

It is important to know whose application is causing problems if chronic performance problems are to be eliminated. You can ask the user to run problem applications at off hours, or you can move that user's files to a disk subsystem where other users will not be effected.

Unfortunately, there is no single command that will derive this information simply. The PC NetLink /opt/lanman/bin/net session command will tell you which PC clients are accessing the system, but you must use the command again with the PC client as a parameter to see which shares the PC client is using. If there are hundreds of users using the server, searching the output can be very tedious. FIGURE 8-1 and FIGURE 8-2 are examples of the command with and without the parameter.

```
eelab# /opt/lanman/bin/net session

Computer              User name          Client Type        Opens Idle time
----------------------------------------------------------------------------
\\CON-AIR~X           ADMINISTRATOR      NT LANMAN 1.0      1     00:00:00
\\CON-AIR~X           ADMINISTRATOR      NT LANMAN 1.0      0     00:04:00
\\EEPC01              LAB                NT LANMAN 1.0      1     00:00:00
\\EEPC02              LAB                NT LANMAN 1.0      1     00:00:00
\\EEPC03              LAB                NT LANMAN 1.0      1     00:00:00
\\EEPC56              LAB                NT LANMAN 1.0      0     00:00:00
\\EEPC57              LAB                NT LANMAN 1.0      1     00:00:00
\\EEPC58              LAB                NT LANMAN 1.0      0     00:00:00
\\EEPC59              LAB                NT LANMAN 1.0      0     00:00:00
\\EEPC60              LAB                NT LANMAN 1.0      1     00:00:00
\\EEPC61              LAB                NT LANMAN 1.0      1     00:00:00
The command completed successfully.
```

FIGURE 8-1   Example Output of the net session Command

The first use of the net session command (FIGURE 8-1) shows all the PC clients currently using the server.

```
eelab# /opt/lanman/bin/net session \\EEPC01
User name       LAB
Computer        EEPC01
Guest logon     No
Client type     NT LANMAN 1.0
Sess time       00:42:00
Idle time       00:00:00


Share name      Type    # Opens
----------------------------------------------------------------------------
FILES1          Disk    1
The command completed successfully.
```

FIGURE 8-2   Example Output of net session With Client Name as Parameter

The second use of the command (FIGURE 8-2) shows a query to the server, using a PC client name as a parameter. The output tells you the user ("LAB" in this case), the shares currently being used, and the number of open files. If we could determine all the users that had files open on share FILES1, we would have a good idea which applications of which users might be causing the problem.

Using a Script to Identify Users Causing Disk Saturation

With a little Solaris scripting, you can use the Solaris commands and the PC NetLink commands to create the command you want. CODE EXAMPLE 8-1 is a script that will show you all users, clients, and the number of open files for any PC NetLink share. Once you know which PC NetLink share is saturated, you can use this script to track down users who may have applications contributing to the saturation.

CODE EXAMPLE 8-1   share2user Script to Determine Users Accessing a Share

```
#!/bin/sh
# Copyright(C) Sun Microsystems
# Don DeVitt
#
# Use PC NetLink tools to determine users using a share
# Usage: share2user <Share Name>
# Where <Share Name> is the name of a PC NEtLink share
# Currently the script does NOT do a lowercase to uppercase translation
#
if test "$1" <> ""
 then
  TARGET=$1
  for CLIENT in `/opt/lanman/sbin/lmstat -c|grep vcnum=0|awk '{print $1}'`
   do
     VALUE=`/opt/lanman/bin/net session \\\\$CLIENT|tail +10|tail -r|\
          tail +2|grep $TARGET|awk '{print "with " $3 " File(s) open"}'`
     ACNT=`/opt/lanman/bin/net session|grep $CLIENT|\
          awk '{print substr($0,24,15)}'`
 # Don't print anything if the PC Client is not using
     if test "$VALUE" <> ""
     then
       echo User $ACNT on PC Client $CLIENT has $TARGET as a network drive $VALUE
     fi
   done
 else
    echo Usage share2user PCSHARE  Example: share2user FILES1
fi
```

FIGURE 8-3 is an example output of the share2user script.

```
eelab# share2user FILES1
User LAB on PC Client EEPC07 has FILES1 as a network drive with 0 File(s) open
User LAB on PC Client EEPC22 has FILES1 as a network drive with 0 File(s) open
User LAB on PC Client EEPC42 has FILES1 as a network drive with 0 File(s) open
User LAB on PC Client EEPC01 has FILES1 as a network drive with 1 File(s) open
User LAB on PC Client EEPC36 has FILES1 as a network drive with 0 File(s) open
User LAB on PC Client EEPC24 has FILES1 as a network drive with 0 File(s) open
User LAB on PC Client EEPC09 has FILES1 as a network drive with 1 File(s) open
User LAB on PC Client EEPC30 has FILES1 as a network drive with 0 File(s) open
```

FIGURE 8-3   Example Output of share2user Script

Here the same user "LAB" on two different PC clients (EEPC01 and EEPC09) has files open. If FILES1 were experiencing chronic performance problems, the applications on these two PCs should be looked at to determine what they are running.

Remember that the script and the commands it uses all show information based on a snapshot of the system. Use the script repeatedly to discern any pattern that makes it easier to determine which PC clients are placing the heaviest load on the server.

You can modify the script, to automatically email share-related information such as capacity limits or performance issues to users. You could also alter it to hide the users with no (0) files open on the PC NetLink shared volume to help narrow the list further.

Tools for Monitoring CPU Resources

When a user community places a heavy load on a server, it can demand considerable CPU resources. Solaris software has many commands to collect and display information on CPU resources. As with the disk resources, once you determine you have a CPU resource problem, you need to know which applications, on which PC client, used by which user, are demanding the most from the server. The manual method for making this determination follows.

▼ To Identify Precise Source of Resource Problems

1. **Determine if the server's CPUs are saturated by using the Solaris** `mpstat` **command.**

2. **Use the Solaris** `ps` **command to monitor the** `lmx.srv` **processes.**

   Thus you can determine which PC NetLink processes are active.

3. **Use the** `lmstat` **command to track down the PC client and user being serviced by the process consuming the resource.**

   Again, a script can reduce the effort in tracking down PC clients and applications that are causing performance issues.

   First, we will look at each command and see what part each plays in narrowing the possible CPU consumers.

mpstat Command

Use mpstat as the first tool to monitor CPU utilization. Following is an example mpstat command.

```
CPU minf mjf xcal   intr ithr   csw icsw migr smtx   srw syscl   usr sys  wt idl
  0    0   0 1413    363    0   936  359   44 1536     0 14259    49  50   1   0
  1    0   0 1779    877    0  2615  871   89 1433     0 12372    42  44  14   0
  2    0   0 1314   1680  329 2454  880   93 1493     0 12346    46  46   6   2
  3    0   0 2289   3808 3725  660  244   48 1141     0 10270    40  56   3   1
```

Note that mpstat first prints the average values (not shown here) since the system was booted. This example mpstat output is of a four-processor Sun Enterprise 450 system. The system is quite busy and very close to saturation, with little of the CPU in the wait (wt) or idle (idl) state.

With respect to the PC NetLink software, the things to keep in mind when viewing mpstat output are:

- If the server seems to deliver poor performance, check the CPU utilization times (the last four entries on the right). If usr plus sys is greater than 90 percent for each CPU, you may indeed have reached the CPU processing limit of you server. If the idl column is not close to 0 percent, then additional CPU resources are not being used and you need to investigate the disk subsystem or network next. Considerable time in the wt column usually means a disk subsystem is saturated.

- In a heavily loaded system, the interrupts (the intr column) for the network cards should be distributed across the various processors. If you have only one network connection, the interrupts traffic will be associated with only one processor. Interrupts from the disk subsystem would be the other major contributor to interrupts, and on a multiprocessor system should be seen on another processor.

After looking at the mpstat command output to determine your CPU utilization, use the Solaris ps command to determine if a PC NetLink process is the source of the CPU consumption. The lms.srv processes consume the most CPU resources assigned to support a number of PC clients. Chapter 4 explains how lmx.srv processes are spawned as PC clients make requests of the server.

Following is the output of a ps command of a server. Use the grep filter to see only the lmx.srv processes.

```
system1 46 =>ps -eaf|grep lmx.srv
    root 13134 13079  0   Aug 25 ?        2:18 lmx.srv -s 1
    don 22030 22004  0 13:48:07 pts/11    0:00 grep lmx.srv
    root 25926 13079  0   Aug 25 ?        4:47 lmx.srv -s 2
```

In a busy server that is serving hundreds of users, this command will show up to 20 processes for the PC NetLink 1.1 software or up to 100 processes for the PC NetLink 1.0 software.

If a CPU is at full utilization and repetitive use of the ps command can't account for the CPU time, the CPU is being consumed elsewhere. If an lmx.srv process is accumulating CPU time at a considerable rate, next find out which PC clients are requesting the I/O. One PC client cannot usually consume 100 percent of even the slowest SPARC processor. It usually takes several extremely active PC clients to accomplish this state.

lmstat Command

Use the /opt/lanman/sbin/lmstat -c command to determine which PC client is attached to which lmx.srv process. Following is a example of the output from this command:

```
# ./lmstat -c
Shared memory initialization time: Tue Aug 24 10:37:24 1999
Lmx.ctrl's current time:           Mon Sep  6 14:26:28 1999
Server statistics last cleared:    Tue Aug 24 10:37:24 1999
Shared memory size:                940444 bytes

Clients:
     UNAGI (nwnum=0, vcnum=0) on 563
     FUTOMAKI (nwnum=0, vcnum=0) on 563
     EELAB4 (nwnum=0, vcnum=0) on 563
     EELAB1~X (nwnum=0, vcnum=1) on 563
```

In this lightly used system, all the PC clients are supported by one lmx.srv process with process ID (PID) of 563. On a heavily used server, this command would show a line for every PC client that is maintaining a mapped drive. With hundreds of users, it would take some time to track down all the users associated with a particular process ID. While this command does supply the PC client-to-process ID association, it does not supply the user ID, which would be more helpful.

To see the user account each PC client supports, use the
/opt/lanman/bin/net session command. Following is an example of this
output:

```
# /opt/lanman/bin/net session
Computer                  User name            Client Type          Opens  Idle time
----------------------------------------------------------------------------------
\\BACALL                  LHUTCHIN             NT LANMAN 1.0        10     00:02:00
\\BRIGHTOJR               DMAHONEY             NT LANMAN 1.0        0      02D 18H 02M
\\CHOCOLATE               JELVEHG              NT LANMAN 1.0        2      02D 18H 38M
\\DARUSH                  MIKETEH              NT LANMAN 1.0        0      05D 19H 06M
\\LST57188                REINDEER             NT LANMAN 1.0        0      18D 18H 23M
\\MOET-PC                 BMUNROE              NT LANMAN 1.0        0      00:27:00
\\NIFTY                                        NT LANMAN 1.0        0      05D 22H 26M
\\PETER                   PCB                  NT LANMAN 1.0        0      01:14:00
\\PINOCHIO                REINDEER             NT LANMAN 1.0        10     00:02:00
\\RATTTOP                 RCRERIE              NT LANMAN 1.0        0      00:38:00
\\SHIMMY~X                                     NT LANMAN 1.0        0      00:02:00
\\SHIMMY~X                                     NT LANMAN 1.0        0      00:42:00
\\SUSWARE                                      NT LANMAN 1.0        0      00:08:00
\\THELONIOUS                                   NT LANMAN 1.0        0      00:08:00
\\THELONIOUS                                   NT LANMAN 1.0        0      00:08:00
\\UNAGI                   DON                  NT LANMAN 1.0        0      00:35:00
\\WGS-EB                  YKUMAR               NT LANMAN 1.0        0      04D 19H 23M
\\WGS40-03~X              ADMINISTRATOR        NT LANMAN 1.0        1      00:00:00
\\WGS40-03~X              ADMINISTRATOR        NT LANMAN 1.0        0      10D 23H 27M
\\WGS40-03~X              ADMINISTRATOR        NT LANMAN 1.0        0      00:02:00
\\WGS40-102~X                                  NT LANMAN 1.0        0      17D 16H 20M
\\WGS40-13                                     NT LANMAN 1.0        0      00:02:00
\\WGS40-13                                     NT LANMAN 1.0        0      00:03:00
The command completed successfully.
```

This command shows the PC client and user account association, but it doesn't show
the lmx.srv processes the PC client and user are supported by. The idle time helps
show how long users have been inactive. Suffice it to say those with long idle times
can't be the cause of a PC NetLink-related performance problem.

Using a Script to Determine Users Serviced by `lmx.srv` Process

UNIX scripts again come to the rescue to help narrow down which users, on which PC clients, are using the `lmx.srv` process that is consuming considerable CPU resource. CODE EXAMPLE 8-2 is alisting of the script followed by an example of it's use.

CODE EXAMPLE 8-2   `lmx2user` Script to Determine User Serviced by `lmx.srv` Process

```
#!/bin/sh
# Copyright(C) Sun Microsystems
# Don DeVitt
#
# Use ps, lmstat, and net session to determine user being
# serviced by a specific lmx.srv process
# Usage: lmx2user [PID]
# If PID specified then only users for specific lmx.srv process are
# determined. If no PID specified then print out all users for all
# lmx.srv processes.
#
if test "$1" <> ""
 then
  PID=$1
  for CLIENT in `/opt/lanman/sbin/lmstat -c|grep $PID|awk '{print $1}'`
   do
    ACNT=`/opt/lanman/bin/net session|grep $CLIENT|awk '{print
substr($0,24,15)}'`
      echo lmx.srv process $PID servicing \"$ACNT\" on Client $CLIENT
   done
 else
  for PID in `ps -e |grep lmx.srv|awk '{print $1}'`
   do
    for CLIENT in `/opt/lanman/sbin/lmstat -c|grep $PID|awk '{print $1}'`
     do
      ACNT=`/opt/lanman/bin/net session|grep $CLIENT|awk '{print
substr($0,24,15)}'`
      echo lmx.srv process $PID servicing \"$ACNT\" on Client $CLIENT
     done
   done
fi
```

The script can be used in two way. When used without a parameter it prints out all users on all PC clients for all `lmx.srv` processes (see FIGURE 8-4.) When used with a process ID parameter, it prints out only the users being supported by a specific `lmx.srv` process (see FIGURE 8-5.)

```
# ./lmx2user
lmx.srv process 13134 servicing " " on Client NIFTY
lmx.srv process 13134 servicing "MIKETEH " on Client DARUSH
lmx.srv process 13134 servicing " " on Client WGS40-102~X
lmx.srv process 13134 servicing " " on Client THELONIOUS
lmx.srv process 13134 servicing "REINDEER " on Client LST57188
lmx.srv process 13134 servicing " " on Client SHIMMY~X
lmx.srv process 13134 servicing "ADMINISTRATOR ADMINISTRATOR
               ADMINISTRATOR " on Client WGS40-03~X
lmx.srv process 15538 servicing "DON " on Client UNAGI
lmx.srv process 15538 servicing " " on Client WGS40-13
lmx.srv process 15538 servicing " " on Client SUSWARE
lmx.srv process 15538 servicing " " on Client WGS40-13
lmx.srv process 15538 servicing "PCB " on Client PETER
lmx.srv process 15538 servicing "DMAHONEY " on Client BRIGHTOJR
lmx.srv process 15538 servicing " " on Client SHIMMY~X
lmx.srv process 15538 servicing "BMUNROE " on Client MOET-PC
lmx.srv process 25926 servicing " " on Client THELONIOUS
lmx.srv process 25926 servicing "REINDEER " on Client PINOCHIO
lmx.srv process 25926 servicing "LHUTCHIN " on Client BACALL
lmx.srv process 25926 servicing "YKUMAR " on Client WGS-EB
lmx.srv process 25926 servicing "JELVEHG " on Client CHOCOLATE
lmx.srv process 25926 servicing "ADMINISTRATOR ADMINISTRATOR
          ADMINISTRATOR " on Client WGS40-03~X
lmx.srv process 25926 servicing "RCRERIE " on Client RATTTOP
lmx.srv process 25926 servicing "JSWEENEY " on Client MAYHEM
```

FIGURE 8-4 The lmx2user Script Without a Parameter

```
# ./lmx2user 13134
lmx.srv process 13134 servicing " " on Client NIFTY
lmx.srv process 13134 servicing "MIKETEH " on Client DARUSH
lmx.srv process 13134 servicing " " on Client WGS40-102~X
lmx.srv process 13134 servicing " " on Client THELONIOUS
lmx.srv process 13134 servicing "REINDEER " on Client LST57188
lmx.srv process 13134 servicing " " on Client SHIMMY~X
lmx.srv process 13134 servicing "ADMINISTRATOR ADMINISTRATOR
          ADMINISTRATOR " on Client WGS40-03~X
```

FIGURE 8-5 The lmx2user Script With a Process ID as a Parameter

The latter use of the script is most useful after you determine which lms.srv process is accumulating CPU time. Modification of the script can continue the analysis further by determining the number of files each PC client is using.

Monitoring Memory Resources

Lack of sufficient memory to support the PC NetLink software and all the Solaris functionality required will affect performance dramatically. The issue of allocating and monitoring memory resources becomes more difficult when viewed in the context of a server that is supporting several services (email, web, and so on) in addition to the PC NetLink functionality.

If a server runs out memory, it will stop swapping out inactive processes as it attempts to find memory for the various active processes. When the lack of memory becomes really serious, response times grow very quickly, making performance of the server unacceptably slow.

Swap Partition

Perhaps the best indicator of a lack of memory is a hyperactive swap partition. When setting up your system, place `swap` on its own disk subsystem. If this disk subsystem is abnormally active, you are probably running out of memory. Having a fast disk subsystem to support swap improves performance slightly, but there is no substitute for making sure sufficient memory is available to the system.

To monitor memory to a finer granularity requires tracking down the memory used by each process. Monitoring memory at this level for each PC NetLink process can be complex and may not solve memory related issues. But if you want to track down the memory used by processes, you can use the `/usr/proc/bin/pmap` command to list all the memory utilized by an `lmx.srv` process. Following is a example output of this command.

```
# /usr/proc/bin/pmap -x 5288
5288:    lmx.srv -s 2
Address   Kbytes Resident Shared Private Permissions         Mapped File
00010000    1024     840    608     232 read/exec           lmx.srv
0011E000      24      24      -      24 read/write/exec      lmx.srv
00124000     944     928      -     928 read/write/exec      [ heap ]
EDC00000     920     920      -     920 read/write/exec/shared   [shmid=0x0]
EE802000       8       8      -       8 read/write/exec      [ anon ]
EE904000       8       8      -       8 read/write/exec      [ anon ]
EEA06000       8       8      -       8 read/write/exec      [ anon ]
EEB08000       8       8      -       8 read/write/exec      [ anon ]
EEC0A000       8       8      -       8 read/write/exec      [ anon ]

. . . Many lines deleted . . .

EF71C000      16      16      8       8 read/write/exec      librpcapi.so.1
EF730000     336     336    336       - read/exec           libsam.so.1
EF792000      16      16      8       8 read/write/exec      libsam.so.1
EF796000       8       8      -       8 read/write/exec      [ anon ]
EF7A0000       8       8      8       - read/exec            libdl.so.1
EF7B0000       8       8      -       8 read/write/exec      [ anon ]
EF7C0000     120     120    120       - read/exec           ld.so.1
EF7EC000       8       8      8       - read/write/exec      ld.so.1
EFFD6000     168     168      -     168 read/write/exec      [ stack ]
--------  ------  ------  ------  ------
total Kb    7024    6608    3488    3120
```

Much of this pmap output was deleted to fit the page. The most important numbers are at the bottom. The private memory column and total memory represent the memory not shared and specific to the process being measured.

If you have a server where the PC NetLink memory utilization must be kept to an absolute minimum, the best way to accomplish this is to change the PC NetLink Registry values to force the PC NetLink software to spawn fewer lmx.srv processes. This means that each lmx.srv process will need to support more PC clients. On user environments where many users maintain inactive mapped drives, this may be an acceptable solution.

While this may help solve a memory problem, you might create a performance problem as too few processes are supporting too many active PC clients. If this kind of manipulation is attempted, it is always important to have at least as many lmx.srv processes as there are processors in the server.

Sun Enterprise SyMON

Sun Enterprise SyMON was developed by the server software organization in Sun Computer Systems to act as a user interface to the hardware features they created. It is also a powerful and extensible system and network monitoring platform that is being picked up by other groups at Sun as a platform that can be extended to manage other products. Solstice Simon 1.x was a Motif-based system monitor for a single machine. Sun Enterprise SyMON 2.0 is a Java-based monitor with multiple user consoles that can monitor multiple systems, using the secure extensions to Simple Network Management Protocol (SNMP) version 2 to communicate over the network.

SyMON and PC NetLink

Sun Enterprise SyMON is good at monitoring large and complex hardware configurations with many systems. It has a great deal of knowledge about possible hardware error conditions embedded in it. SyMON is too extensive a product to explain in full detail here, but with regard to the PC NetLink software, SyMON is probably best used to monitor the system for resource or performance-related issues of the complete server. SyMON can notify you of performance-related problems in terms that will be familiar to Solaris system administrators. Once SyMON shows you have a performance or resource problem, either by way of alarms or its configuration browser, you can track down the source of the problem with the scripts presented earlier in this chapter.

The SE Toolkit

The SE Toolkit (SE stands for systems engineer) is a tool for measuring and monitoring the resources of a server. It is based on a C language interpreter that is extended to make available all the Solaris measurement interfaces in an easy form. All the code that takes particular metrics and processes them is provided as C source code to run on the interpreter, so that it is easy to trace back and see where data comes from and how it is processed. You can then write your own programs to obtain the same data. The SE Toolkit was jointly developed by Richard Pettit and Adrian Cockcroft as a "spare time" activity since 1993. Richard worked at Sun but is currently at Resolute Software, and Adrian is one of the authors of the *Resource Management* BluePrint. The SE Toolkit can be downloaded from `http://www.sun.com/sun-on-net/performance/se3`.

While the SE Toolkit is an extremely useful tool, it is *not* supported by Sun.

Monitoring Traffic With External Methods

Most modern network switches offer a variety of ways to determine loading statistics about the network ports they support. At a minimum, these switches offer commands from a telnet login session to generate ASCII data. The best way to utilize this information is through an SNMP interface, which can be accessed using external software to monitor traffic over a period of time. FIGURE 8-6 shows an HTML page from software known as Multi-Router Traffic Grapher (MRTG). MRTG is available under the GNU General Public License. The charts produced from this software show when peak periods occur on your network, and allow you to determine if network bottlenecks are a source of problems.

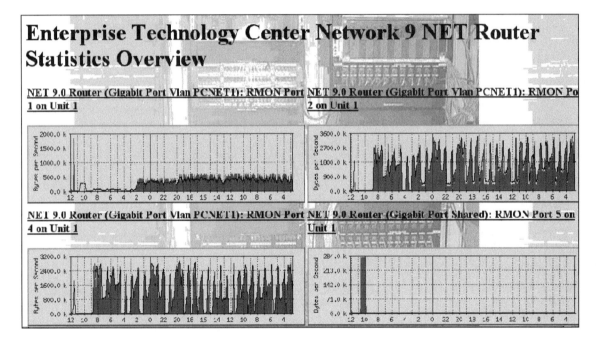

FIGURE 8-6 MRTG Graphs

Many network switch vendors offer similar tools for monitoring the network traffic.

## CHAPTER 9

Printing With PC NetLink

Printing in a workgroup environment is evolving toward intelligent network-based printers that talk directly to PC clients. This can often be done without server intervention. Microsoft Windows printer support now allows PCs to print directly to UNIX print spoolers.

This chapter will first briefly list several possible ways PC clients can print, whether the solution requires the PC NetLink software or not. It will then focus on instances where the PC NetLink software can be part of the solution.

Supporting PC-style printing on a Solaris server for typical workgroup PostScript and HPPCL printers is reasonably straightforward. If you can select the printer to use with the PC NetLink software, a good PostScript printer is best.

Getting the PC NetLink software to work with the hundreds of other kinds of printers is not always straightforward. All the mechanisms necessary for supporting the PC-style printing are not always available. The PC NetLink software relies heavily on standard Solaris functionality for supporting print functions from the PC NetLink software.

Another key aspect of printing support is that the PC NetLink software must see the Solaris spool directory to support all the functionality expected by users of PC clients. If the PC NetLink software does not have direct access to these spool directories, it cannot offer the status and control functionality that the PC software and users expect. This requirement forces the limitation that only printers directly hooked up to the Solaris server where the PC NetLink software is installed, or printers being spooled by software running on the server, are supported by the PC NetLink 1.0 and 1.1 software.

Because printing mechanisms have changed substantially with each major release of Solaris software, older versions of Solaris software may provide limited support. This chapter looks at issues and concerns with printing, and gives pointers and rules for setting up your printer.

Printing Overview

Sun is very conservative when it says it supports a printer configuration. Support means the printer configuration has been tried and tested. The hundreds of printers and various Microsoft drivers make it impossible for Sun to try and test all printer configurations.

This chapter offers several options so you can produce a solution that fits your needs. If you require that all printing be fully supported by Sun, be sure you meet the requirements for your version of the PC NetLink software.

It is important to follow closely the instructions listed here and make sure all required patches are installed. Pay close attention to the release notes where other current PC NetLink software printing issues and workarounds are listed.

PC Windows Printing

In the PC world, applications print using standard Microsoft Windows APIs. The Windows libraries in turn make calls to the printer driver, which converts the graphics device interface (GDI) calls it receives, translates them to the appropriate language, and sends them along to either a parallel port driver to be printed locally, or through network interfaces to be printed remotely. The actual byte stream is produced by the PC client software (application + Windows + drivers). It is up to the network interface on the client, the server, and any other layers to deliver this byte stream to the printer without corruption.

In most workgroup settings, the only standard added value a printer server provides is to manage the queue of printer jobs and place banner pages between print jobs as they are sent to the printer.

Types of Printers

There are hundreds of printers on the market today. For the purposes of this chapter, we will look at three types of printers:

- High-level language printers (PostScript and PCL)—This type of printer is most commonly found on Solaris and UNIX servers today. These printers receive byte streams of printer jobs that are representations of the pages to be printed in the PostScript or PCL language. These types of printers are capable of considerable processing, and can off-load a great deal of the work of printing a document. If you were to actually view the byte stream going to a PostScript printer, you would recognize programming language commands.

- Image printers—These low-cost printers are matched to Windows drivers that create a raster of the page image and then send very low-level bit images to the printer. This kind of printer is typically sold to work with PCs directly, but they can also be used with servers. In some cases, only the PC clients can produce meaningful output for these printers because most Solaris applications are not designed to produce output for image printers.

- Simple ASCII printers—These printers print nothing but ASCII characters. They receive a byte stream of ASCII and print it one character at a time. Printers in this category usually print the characters in a non-graphical, mechanical way. Their speeds range from very slow matrix printers to very fast line printers.

Each of these printer types requires a different level of support when you use them with the PC NetLink software.

Typical PC Printing Spooling Configurations

- **The printer is spooled by Solaris software directly on the server where the PC NetLink software is installed.**

  This is the preferred way for the PC NetLink software to support printing for PC clients. In this case, the printer is attached directly to the parallel port of the server, or a network printer is spooled to by the Solaris server.

- **The printer is attached to a server where the PC NetLink software is not installed.**

  In this situation a printer is attached directly to a Solaris parallel printer port and Solaris controls the printing. The PC Netlink software unfortunately cannot work with printers that are remotely spooled on other Solaris servers. The reason is that the PC NetLink software requires direct access to the spool directory of the printer to control the print queue and provide status information. In this situation, your options are:

  - Install the PC NetLink software on the server where the printer is attached.

  - If possible, move the printer to the server where the PC NetLink software is installed.

  - If Windows NT clients are being used, both Windows NT 3.5 and 4.0 machines are capable of talking directly to UNIX servers without the PC NetLink software. You will need to set up a printer on Windows NT that supports TCP/IP printing. The following URL points to instructions for setting up a TCP/IP-based printer on your Windows NT machine:
    `http://msdn.microsoft.com/library/winresource/dnwinnt/S771E.HTM`

- **A network printer is spooled on a remote Solaris machine.**

In this situation, a non-PC NetLink server spools to the printer directly attached to the network. Because the PC NetLink software cannot gain access directly to the Solaris spool directory, it cannot supply back to the PC clients the needed information to control and monitor the queue. While the remote server queue cannot be used, your printer may allow you to set up an alternative spool directory that can talk to the same printer.

- **The printer is attached directly to the PC.**

  All PCs today are shipped with parallel ports. For home, small office environments, or when the user requires private or dedicated access to a printer, this may be the best solution. There are hundreds of low-cost printers on the market that fit this need. The disadvantage of this approach is the cost of purchasing, maintaining, and managing individual printers. For a large workgroup, this clearly is not acceptable.

How the PC NetLink Software Prints

To help you understand what the PC NetLink software printer configuration is doing, following is a quick description of how the PC NetLink software handles print requests.

When a PC client requests a print operation, the PC NetLink software role is to support the printer-related SMB protocol for the PC client. While the PC client generates printer output, the PC Netlink software sends the output to a file. Whether the output is PostScript, PCL, ASCII, or some proprietary bit image data, the PC NetLink software produces the file without any alteration to the data whatsoever. When the PC client stops producing the printer output, the PC NetLink software uses standard Solaris calls to spool the file to the printer.

Later, as requests for status come in from PC clients, the PC NetLink software uses Solaris calls to check the spool directory to see how the print job is going. If a request is made to cancel the print job, standard Solaris tools are used to cancel the print job.

Getting the printer to work well with Solaris is fundamental to obtaining smooth operation with the PC NetLink software.

Owner of Print Jobs

The PC NetLink software print jobs must be submitted by root. The Solaris printing subsystem has no concept of account mapping between Solaris and Windows. If you use a Solaris `lpq`, or some other Solaris print query command to view the jobs in the queue, you will see they are owned by the Solaris root account.

Print jobs submitted by Windows-based clients will have the correct Windows domain user account name attached to them when viewed from the Windows printer manager. They will also have the correct name of the user on the banner page.

The only simple way to guarantee that the print job has a Solaris account name associated with the job is to print the job to a PostScript file, then print the PostScript file using the Solaris `lp` command while logged on as the Solaris user.

Configuring a Printer for Use With PC NetLink Software

Refer to the *PC NetLink System Administration Guide* and the *PC NetLink Release Notes* that are shipped with Solaris PC NetLink 1.0 and 1.1 for instructions on how to get your printer to work with the PC NetLink software. There are several important printer issues and workarounds dealing with parallel ports, Windows problems, and patches you may need. Following is a list of things to keep in mind before starting your printer installation.

Printing Configuration Issues

- Use IEEE 1284-certified printer cables to attach printers to Solaris servers directly. Data can be corrupted in electrically noisy environments, especially with long cable lengths. Even though you may have seen a non-IEEE cable work with one printer and server combination, it is no guarantee that a different printer (with less tolerance for noise) will work. You can reduce the possibility of this problem by using IEEE 1284 cables.

- Not all parallel ports on Sun servers are the same. Use only the newer `/dev/ecpp0` parallel ports available on the supported server configurations. The `/dev/bpp0` printer driver is problematic. While bringing up printing support on a Sun Ultra 2, I was able to get reliable support for the HP IIISi printer using the

/dev/bpp0 Solaris driver, but the Canon BJP4000 printer would not work with the same /dev/bpp0 driver. When I moved the printer to a server with a /dev/ecpp0 port and applied patch #106235-03, all worked.

- If you are installing a printer using any parallel port on Solaris 2.6, make sure you install Solaris 2.6 patch 106235-04 or later. The patch is available from http://sunsolve.sun.com. Without this patch, the printer output may be corrupted.

- Use the PC NetLink Server Manager to define the Solaris printer to be used with the PC NetLink software. Using admintool or other Solaris administration tools to define the printer can be problematic and may not accomplish all the steps needed to get full support. If a printer is already installed on a Solaris server, it is best to redefine the printer with the PC NetLink Server Manager (/opt/lanman/sbin/slsmgr).

- Only printers that are connected directly to the PC NetLink server using a parallel port or a direct network connection can be supported with the PC NetLink software. The PC NetLink software requires direct access to the printer spool directory to provide status information to the PC clients. Printers spooled by other Solaris servers do not allow direct access to printer spool directories, so the PC NetLink software has no way to control the queue or offer status information.

- If the printer you are configuring is not a PostScript or PCL printer, it is important to turn off the production of the banner pages. By default, the PC NetLink Server Manager will configure printer spools that will generate banner pages. These banner pages may corrupt the output going to the printer.

- Before upgrading from the PC NetLink software 1.0 to the PC NetLink software 1.1, you must move the /opt/lanman/shares/asu/system32/drivers directory to /opt/lanman/shares/asu/drivers before you upgrade to any later version of the product (1.0 global or 1.1 domestic). If you do not move the directory, the upgrade installation will fail and delete all saved information from the original installation. This problem occurs because the location of the PRINT$ share directory was changed between 1.0 domestic and 1.0 global.

The path /opt/lanman/shares/asu/system32/drivers in 1.0 global and later versions is now a symbolic link, and installation will fail if a directory is found with the same name. When installation fails, all installed packages are removed, and all data (including the upgrade data) is removed. The workaround is to move the directory /opt/lanman/shares/asu/system32/drivers to /opt/lanman/shares/asu/drivers *before* performing the upgrade.

```
# net stop server
# mv /opt/lanman/shares/asu/system32/drivers /opt/lanman/shares/asu/drivers
# /cdrom/cdrom0/install
```

Setting Up Printers

You must complete two major steps to add a printer to a PC NetLink server. First you have to add the printer to the Solaris operating environment using the PC NetLink Server Manager (slsmgr), and then to the Windows NT network using a Windows NT server or workstation.

A PC NetLink server will handle printers in only two ways:

- Attaching them directly into the PC NetLink server.
- Using the printer via a network connection.

Both methods are described in the following sections.

▼ To Attach a Printer Directly to the PC NetLink Server

In this example, assume that the printer is already attached to the system. Complete the following steps:

1. **Open the PC NetLink Server Manager using the root account:**

```
# /opt/lanman/sbin/slsmgr &
```

2. **Authenticate by putting in the name of the PC NetLink server with the printer and the Solaris root password.**

   Once authenticated, the left side of the window will read as follows:

```
o Name of Server
- Information
- Services
- Events
- Tasks
- Policies
```

3. **Double-click on Tasks.**

4. **Double-click on Install Solaris Printer.**

   A new window will be displayed, asking the name of the new printer.

5. **Choose a name.**

This will be the name of the Solaris printing queue.

Note – The name of the printer cannot exceed 14 characters, and can be composed of letters (lowercase, uppercase, or mixed), numerals, or an underline. The printer name will be checked against all printer queues that already exist.

- If it's a new queue, continue with the next step.
- If the queue already exists, you will be asked to change the original configuration.

6. **Select OK to make the printer use the configuration that already exists. Select CANCEL to return to choosing the name of the printer.**

7. **In the next window, select Local Printer.**

8. **Specify the port to which the printer is attached. Select either Parallel Port or Other, and specify the port.**

9. **Specify the type of printer. Select either Generic PostScript printer or Other.**

If you select Other, specify hplaserjet for PCL printers or RAW for non-PostScript non-PCL printers. Note that RAW or PCL printers are *not* supported on Solaris 2.5.1 software.

10. **Click on Finish.**

The printer should produce a test page indicating that everything worked correctly.

▼ To Use a Network Printer

1. **Follow Steps 1 through 5 of the previous procedure.**

2. **Select the Network Printer.**

3. **Type the name of the printer or its IP address.**

By default the name will be the same as the one typed in Step 5 of the previous procedure.

Note – If the printer name cannot be resolved by Files, NIS, or DNS, then the printer won't work. If this is the case, use the IP address.

---

4. **Continue with Steps 8 and 9 of the previous procedure.**

▼ To Define the Printer From a Windows NT System (Required)

This procedure must be performed on a Windows NT 4.0 system. Windows 95 and 98 systems cannot be used to define printer shares. However, they can use the printer after it has been defined.

1. **At a Windows NT server or workstation, log in to the domain as Administrator.**

2. **Go to Network Neighborhood and open the PC NetLink Server system.**

3. **Open the printers folder.**

4. **Double-click on Add Printer.**

   The Add Printer Wizard is displayed.

5. **Select the Remote print server box and click Next.**

   Do *not* choose the box that says Network printer server.

6. **Select the port for the configured printer in the PC NetLink Server Manager (this is the same as the queue name) and click Next.**

7. **Select the type of printer.**

   If the printer is not on the options, click on Have Disk and supply the drivers.

8. **Type the name of the printer.**

   This is the name by which the printer will be known. This name must be different from the name given in Step 5 of "To Attach a Printer Directly to the PC NetLink Server" on page 225.

   Note – The name must not be longer than 31 characters or some applications may not work correctly.

   ---

9. **Check Shared, and leave the shared name as it appears.**

10. **Select the type of clients that will have access to the printer and then click Next.**

    Select the drivers for the selected clients. If none are selected, only the Windows NT 4.0 drivers will be supplied.

11. **Click on Finish.**

    The printer should produce a Windows NT Printer Test Page Printer box.

▼ To Install the Printer on the Local Client

The valid clients are Windows NT 4.0, 3.51 server and work stations, Windows 3.11, 95, and 98.

1. **From any valid client, go to the Network Neighborhood, select the server that is sharing the printer and find the Printer Share Name that you created earlier. Right-click on it.**

2. **Click on Install from the menu.**

   If you loaded the corresponding drivers that match this client type, the drivers will be installed from the PC NetLink server. If you didn't load all the different client drivers, you will be asked to select the printer.

3. **Select the type of printer.**

   If the printer is not on the options list, click on Have Disk and supply the drivers, or get the latest drivers from the internet.

4. **After the drivers are loaded, select Print Test Page.**

5. **Click on Finish.**

   The printer should produce a test page.

6. **Press F5 to see the new local printer.**

   The client is now ready to print.

Configuring Printer Pooling

Pooling printers increases printer throughput and availability. Pooling can also be used to consolidate printers. Among the many different ways to configure printer pooling, the following are the most frequently used:

- One logical printer attached to two or more physical printers.
- Two logical printers attached to one physical printer.

To configure printer pooling, follow the same steps that you follow to configure any Solaris PC NetLink printer:

1. Configure a Solaris printer.

2. Set the Solaris printer as a Solaris PC NetLink shared printer.

3. Connect the print clients to the newly defined printer.

Pooling One Logical Printer Attached to Multiple Physical Printers

This printer pooling mechanism allows you to balance the load of the logical printer queue among two or more identical physical printers. Only one logical printer is shared to the users, but the print jobs are printed on the next available physical printer.

▼ To Configure One Logical Printer for Multiple Physical Printers

1. **Using the PC NetLink Server Manager (`slsmgr`), install one Solaris printer for each physical printer available.**

2. **Give a different name to each printer.**

   For additional instructions, see "To Attach a Printer Directly to the PC NetLink Server" on page 225.

3. **From a Microsoft Windows NT Workstation, use Network Neighborhood to open the Solaris PC NetLink server you are using as the Solaris print server.**

4. **Open the Printers folder.**

5. **Use the Add Printer wizard to define the Solaris PC NetLink shared printer.**

6. **Select `Remote Print Server \\`*ServerName* and then click Next.**

7. **Select Enable Printer Pooling.**

8. **From the Available Port list, select every Solaris printer that will participate in the pool, and then click Next.**

9. **Add the appropriate printer driver.**

10. **Assign a name to the logical printer.**

11. **Select Shared and the type of clients (Windows 95, Windows NT, and so on) that will use the printer, and assign the shared printer a name (by default, this name is the same as the logical printer name), and then click Next.**

12. **(Optional) Select No if you don't want a test page.**

13. **Select Finish.**

▼ To Connect PC Clients to a Newly Defined Printer

● **Use the Add Printer wizard on each client and select Network Printer. Then connect the new printer to the PC NetLink shared printer defined above.**

▼ To Attach Two Logical Printers to One Physical Printer

This printer pooling mechanism enables different clients to print to the same printer using different priorities and different times.

1. Using the PC NetLink Server Manager (`slsmgr`), install the Solaris printer for the physical printer available.

2. Configure the printer with highest priority:

   a. From a Windows NT Workstation, use Network Neighborhood to open the Solaris PC NetLink server that you are using as the Solaris print server.

   b. Open the Printers folder.

   c. Use the Add Printer wizard to define the PC NetLink server shared printer.

   d. Select `Remote Print Server` *ServerName* and then click Next.

   e. From the Available Port list, select the Solaris printer defined in Step 1, and then click Next.

   f. Add the appropriate printer driver.

   g. Assign a name to the logical printer with highest priority.

   h. Select Shared and the type of clients (Windows 95, Windows NT, and so on) that will use the printer, and assign the shared printer a name (by default, this name is the same as the logical printer name), and then click Next.

   i. Select No if you don't want a test page (Optional).

   j. Select Finish.

   k. Right-click on the new printer and select Properties.

   l. Select the Scheduling tab and designate that the highest priority of this printer is the time when the logical printer will use the physical printer.

   m. Click OK to finish.

3. Configure the printer with lowest priority:

   a. From a Windows NT Workstation, use Network Neighborhood to open the Solaris PC NetLink server that you are using as the Solaris print server.

   b. Open the Printers folder.

   c. Use the Add Printer wizard to define the Solaris PC NetLink shared printer.

   d. Select `Remote Print Server` *ServerName* and then click Next.

e. From the Available Port list, select the Solaris printer defined in Step 1, then click Next.

f. Add the appropriate printer driver.

   (Use the one that is already installed).

g. Assign a name to the logical printer with lowest priority.

h. Select Shared and the type of clients (Windows 95, Windows NT, and so on) that will use the printer and assign the shared printer a name (by default, this name is the same as the logical printer name).

i. Click Next.

j. Select No if you don't want a test page (Optional).

k. Select Finish.

l. Right-click on the new printer and select Properties.

m. Select the Scheduling tab and designate that the lowest priority of this printer is the time when the logical printer will use the physical printer.

n. Click OK to finish.

4. To connect the print clients to the new defined printers, use the Add Printer wizard on each client and select Network Printer.

5. Connect the new printer to one of the printers defined above in accordance with the client's priority on the printers.

Solving Banner Page Problems

The Microsoft Windows feature that enables you to configure special .SEP files to create "separator" pages for various network printers was implemented using Solaris printer banner pages. These Solaris generated banner pages convey both system and user information.

The Solaris printer banner pages that separate print jobs include four lines:

- First line—Solaris host name and root as owner
- Second line—Sender's Windows NT user name and client PC's name
- Third line—Date
- Fourth line—Printer job name

If your printing devices furnish their own banner pages in addition to the Solaris banner pages, you can create a custom lp/model file to turn off the Solaris banner pages. Use one of the following sets of instructions, depending on whether the printer is local (attached directly to a PC NetLink Server computer) or a network printer.

▼ To Turn Off Banners on a Local PC NetLink Printer

1. **From the PC NetLink Server Solaris command line, change to the /usr/lib/lp/model directory.**

```
system% cd /usr/lib/lp/model
```

In that directory are two files, standard and netstandard. The file named standard controls the banner setup on your local printer.

2. **Create a copy of the standard file under a different name** (standard_nb **in the examples that follow) to serve as the foundation for the new custom file.**

```
system% cp standard standard_nb
```

3. **Using a text editor, open the** standard_nb **file for editing, and find the following string:**
nobanner="no"

4. **Edit the** nobanner="no" **string to become the following:**
nobanner="yes"

5. **Save the** standard_nb **file, and quit the text editor.**

6. **Enter the following command, replacing** *printername* **with the actual printer name:**

```
system% lpadmin -p printername -m standard_nb
```

▼ To Turn Off Banners on a Network PC NetLink Printer

1. **From the PC NetLink Server Solaris command line, change to the** /usr/lib/lp/model **directory.**

```
system% cd /usr/lib/lp/model
```

In that directory are two files, standard and netstandard. The file named netstandard controls the banner setup on your local printer.

2. Create a copy of the **netstandard** file under a different name (netstandard_nb in the examples that follow) to serve as the foundation for the new custom file.

```
system% cp netstandard netstandard_nb
```

3. Using a text editor, open the netstandard_nb file for editing.

4. In the netstandard_nb file, find the following string:
   nobanner="no"

5. Edit the nobanner="no" string to become the following:
   nobanner="yes"

6. Save the netstandard_nb file and quit the text editor.

7. Enter the following command, replacing *printername* with the actual printer name:

```
system% lpadmin -p printername -m netstandard_nb
```

## CHAPTER 10

PC NetLink Setup Maintenance and Troubleshooting Procedures

This chapter describes many of the procedures and commands necessary to set up and maintain a PC NetLink server. Other procedures have been discussed in previous chapters specific to the material of those chapters. (For example, Chapter 6 deals with procedures for transitioning from Windows NT environments to the PC NetLink Software, and Chapter 9 has many procedures dealing with setting up printers.)

These procedures meet the majority of system administration needs for enabling the PC NetLink software to work in a variety of environments. In addition, the documentation shipped with the PC NetLink software is an excellent source for procedural information.

A complete set of the manpages for all the PC NetLink commands is available in Appendix C. A full listing of the help documentation available from the `net help` command is also included in Appendix C.

Backing Up Files

Every PC NetLink server should have a procedure to back up user and system files daily. Standard daily, weekly, and monthly procedures should be set up before anyone is allowed to use the system. Producing a high availability (HA) system with RAID disk subsystems that will protect the data with redundancy is no substitute for nightly backups. It is common for users to accidentally delete documents that they then want restored. The following sections discuss some of the PC NetLink-specific issues that you must be aware of in planning your backup procedures.

The PC NetLink software architecture (see Chapter 2) implements several Windows NT style file attributes (namely, Windows NT ACL, ownership, and protection) using separate databases. These databases can make backing up the file data with their ownership and attributes problematic.

The PC NetLink software can be set up to map Windows NT Domain user accounts to Solaris accounts. If there is no association between these accounts, the PC NetLink software will assign the ownership of the files it creates and manipulates for Windows NT accounts as lmxworld. Let's illustrate what happens for a specific case.

A Windows NT domain user account, jsmith is set up on a PC NetLink-supported domain. There is no account association between the Windows NT domain account for jsmith and any Solaris user account. Because the jsmith account is set up within the PC NetLink software environment only, the user has only the privileges allowed it by the jsmith account with the PC NetLink environment and other Windows NT-style servers, within the Windows NT domain. As the user writes files into a file structure on the PC NetLink server, the files are placed into the Solaris environment with the default PC NetLink user account lmworld. A typical Solaris ls command of files written by the PC NetLink software for the Windows NT domain account jsmith would look similar to the output shown here.

```
-rw-rw-r--    1 lmworld   DOS-a--     11776 Aug 24 16:37 test.doc
drwxrwxr-x    3 lmworld   DOS----       512 Aug  9 13:43 vnc
-rw-rw-r--    1 lmworld   DOS-a--     93768 Jul 25  1998 WRSHD95.HTM
-rw-rw-r--    1 lmworld   DOS-a--      3045 Feb 28  1999 wrshReadme.1st
```

In this ls output we see the file names on the right and we see that the files have been written using the account lmworld. The Solaris group used for these files reflects the PC NetLink software use of Solaris groups to represent DOS file attributes. All the other Windows NT file attributes associated with these files (User account, ACLs, and so on) are stored within the PC NetLink software databases found in /var/opt/lanman/datafiles. The separation of the ownership and attributes in the PC NetLink database from the data file itself in the Solaris file structure can make backups with Solaris tools problematic. At the time of this writing, work is being done to develop a backup program that deals with this problem, but there is no Solaris backup program that can back up and restore both the file data and its Windows NT attributes as one entity.

Standard Solaris backup tools allow you to back up the data files without a problem. The issue is with the file ownership and its attributes. The Solaris backup tools also allow you to back up the full PC NetLink database separately, but there is no way to extract one file and its attributes alone without restoring the whole database. Restoring the whole PC NetLink database to restore the attributes of just one file would erase the attribute and ownership changes made to all files between the back up and the restore and is clearly *not* something you should do.

The following sections discuss some options for setting up, backing up, and restoring the PC NetLink software database files.

Using Solaris Accounts in Backups

When setting up the PC NetLink software, Solaris accounts can be associated with Windows NT domain accounts. If this association exists for an account, the files will be written and updated by the PC NetLink software using the Solaris account User Identification (UIDs). This allows the standard Solaris backup programs to clearly identify the owner of the files. You can use these backup programs, and the identity of the owner of each file will be stored with the file and will be available during the restore.

There is still the issue of ACL attributes. The Solaris account name allows us to identify the user, but any ACL related attributes placed on the file must be re-established once the file is restored. Simply restoring the file with standard Solaris-based backup programs will restore the data, but the PC NetLink software will not have any ACLs associated with the file.

To make sure that high enough security is maintained during the restore process, it would be best to place any restored files into a highly protected area that only system administrator and the owner can access. Once the file has been restored to this directory, the files can then be moved to the desired location and any needed ACLs can be reapplied.

Backup Conventions

Whether or not Solaris accounts are used, knowing where the files are located may be sufficient for you to restore these files for users without losing the user account association during the restore procedure. A simple convention can reduce security issues when restoring files.

As is typical with most home directory servers, user home directories are placed in the root of the file structure. The Solaris and the PC NetLink supported path identifies the owner of files by the user directory they were originally in. If a Solaris file structure named /users1 was set up to store home directories for accounts jsmith, hjames, and tjones, the file paths to the user home directories would be /users1/jsmith, /users1/jsmith, and /users1/tjones. The files and directories found below /users1/jsmith would belong to the account jsmith. This simple convention should be sufficient for a majority of the restore operations needed by most sites. Even with this convention, any ACL-based attributes that were placed on the original files would need to be re-established by the user. It would be wise to force user-only access to the files as soon as they are restored. The user could then re-establish any ACLs that were originally on the files before the backup was performed.

Using Windows NT-based Backup Programs

If you do not use Solaris accounts, and the conventions offered above are insufficient to meet your security requirements, you can use a Windows NT-based backup and restore program running on a Windows NT server to back up files with all the ownership and attributes information. To back up the files, the Windows NT server, which must be a member of the same domain, can map a share on the PC NetLink server and back up the files over the network. This technique consumes network bandwidth, but it allows you to save the data files and their Windows NT-style attributes so that you can restore them later. If you set your backup procedure to run at night, consumption of network bandwidth may not be an issue.

Backing Up the PC NetLink Databases

It is equally important to back up the files the PC NetLink software uses to maintain the Access Control List (ACL), the Security Accounts Manager (SAM), and the Registry. These files, with the exception of the WINS database, are located in the /var/opt/lanman/datafiles directory. Normally, the files in this directory are the only files that change as you change the PC NetLink settings. Another file you may want to save, if you have manually changed it, is the lanman.ini file. This small file is located in the /etc/opt/lanman directory.

For most servers, backing up the databases in the /var/opt/lanman/datafiles directory is best done by using the PC NetLink Server Manager program (/opt/lanman/sbin/slsmgr). This tool takes necessary precautions before performing the backup. The PC NetLink data files are constantly being changed as the PC NetLink software supports users. For this reason, simply copying the files to a directory may not save them in a state that can be restored later. The PC NetLink software must be shut down to back up these files. The PC NetLink Server Manager GUI performs all the necessary functions for backing up the data files, including shutting down and restarting the PC NetLink software.

Because the following backup procedure requires that you shut down the PC Netlink services (but not the Solaris operating environment), you must schedule a time when users will not be using the server. All users must close their files. To insure users are given adequate time to perform this task, it is best to send email to the user community about the planned interruption in service.

In addition to backing up the PC NetLink databases, during scheduled down time you may want to perform other needed maintenance of the database files. One such procedure compacts the ACL database by removing unneeded entries.

▼ To Back Up PC NetLink Server Databases

Note – Plan your backup procedure to occur at off hours. You may also want to include other PC NetLink routine maintenance procedures that require the PC NetLink software to be stopped.

---

1. **Notify users that the PC NetLink server will be off line for several minutes at a specified time.**

2. **Just before performing the backup procedure, use the `/opt/lanman/bin/net session` command to see if any user files are open.**

3. **Once you are sure you are cleared to proceed, login as root and start the PC NetLink Server Manager (`/opt/lanman/sbin/slsmgr`) program.**

4. **From the displayed window, choose the PC NetLink server you want to back up or restore.**

5. **Enter the password for the administration account on the server (usually the root account).**

6. **From the five icons that appear, select Tasks.**

7. **From the four tasks that appear, select the Backup and Restore the Database icon. The following window will appear.**

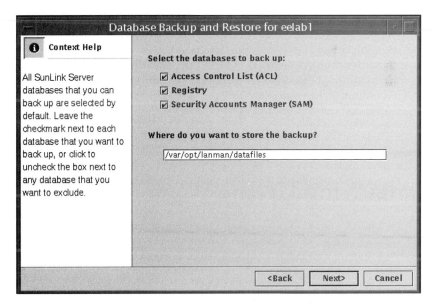

8. **You have the option to save any of the three databases. Save all databases at the same time to maintain consistency among them.**

9. **If the PC NetLink software is running, a window with the "Allow Database Backup and Restore to stop the processes" message is displayed. Select the check box, and click on the Finish button.**

The following window appears, showing you the status of the procedure. It may take several minutes to complete the full operation.

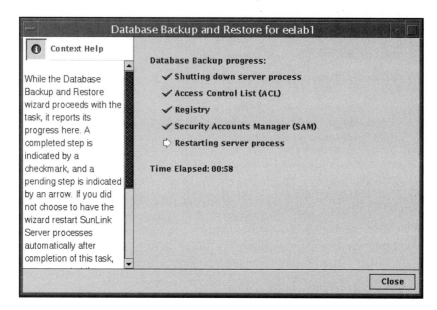

10. **Click the Close button once the procedure has completed.**

It is important to back up the database regularly. Also, back up the database before and after changes are made to it. Changes occur after many users have been added to the domain that the PC NetLink software supports. The database also grows when many files and directories are added to the server using the PC NetLink software.

Backing Up the WINS Database

If your PC NetLink server supports the Windows Internet Name Service (WINS) functionality, you must back up the WINS database regularly. Use the /opt/lanman/sbin/winsadm executable to perform this operation. By default, this tool creates only one backup in the /var/opt/lanman/wins directory. Copy or place on tape the wins_bak file, if you want to keep more than one backup.

In FIGURE 10-1, the /opt/lanman/sbin/winsadm tool is used to back up the WINS database. As the help output states, you can back up the database while the WINS PC NetLink service is running, but you must stop the PC NetLink WINS services to restore, dump, or compact the WINS database.

```
eelab1# ./winsadm
Usage: ./winsadm [ -b | -r | -c | -d ]
        -b       Backup WINS local database
        -r       Restore WINS local database
        -c       Compact WINS local database
        -d       Dump WINS local database

    WINS server must be stopped if -r, -c or -d is specified.

eelab1# ./winsadm -b
Backup request has been submitted to WINS server for further processing.

eelab1# ./winsadm -r
WINS database can not be restored while WINS server is running.
```

FIGURE 10-1 Help Output for the winsadmin Tool

Maintaining the PC NetLink Databases

Like Windows NT itself, the PC NetLink software maintains several databases to maintain the state of the server. PC Netlink settings, user accounts, the access control lists (ACL) database, and the WINS database are all maintained as separate files. They should be backed up regularly.

Upgrading PC NetLink 1.0 to 1.1

If you have installed a printer driver in the PRINT$ share of a PC Netlink 1.0 domestic installation, you *must* move the /opt/lanman/shares/asu/system32/drivers directory to /opt/lanman/shares/asu/drivers before you upgrade to any later version of the product (1.0 global, version 1.1, or later). If you do not move the directory, the upgrade installation will fail and delete all saved information from the original installation.

Managing the ACL Database

The ACL database grows naturally as more data is stored on the system and more subdirectories are created. It can also happen accidentally, and possibly catastrophically, because of human error.

The ACL database will grow dramatically if an administrator or user inadvertently sets file ACLs recursively. In this case, every file within a directory and all its subdirectories will generate an entry in the ACL database that is approximately 300 bytes in length. In a worst-case scenario of a 30 gigabyte share with 45,000 subdirectories, the following would happen:

- Original ACL database: 45000 @   1 Kbyte =   44 Mbyte
- New ACL database: 45000 @   1 Kbyte =   44 Mbyte
    750000 @   300 bytes =   214 Mbyte
    258 Mbyte

If the system is only sized to cope with a much smaller ACL file, the new ACL file, which needs to be maintained in memory, will have a significant effect on system performance. This situation can be recovered as discussed in the following examples.

It is also possible for the ACL database to become stale. This happens when data is created on a Solaris PC NetLink share by a client, but is removed by a Solaris user or process without using the PC NetLink software. In this case, the PC NetLink software behaves as though the data still exist, so it will not touch the ACL. The ACL, however, now refers to a non-existent file. When this happens, you must prune the database.

The ACL database, as well as the SAM, and registry database can be "cleaned up" using the PC NetLink Server manager (/opt/lanman/sbin/slsmgr). Look for the Database Cleanup accessible from the Tasks icon of the tool.

The operation performed in the background by this selection executes a pruning process using the /opt/lanman/sbin/acladm -P command.

It is also possible to remove ACLs using the rmacl command. Unfortunately, the ACL database never shrinks unless you take the server offline and force it to do so. If it gets too large, it is checkpointed and recreated as a larger version of itself. If you delete ACLs in the database, the database doesn't shrink back to its previous size. It does, however, leave gaps that can be filled by new ACLs. It will maintain what is known as a high water mark until you shrink it manually.

Deleting ACLs and Shrinking the Database

The following are different ways to delete ACLs and a way to shrink the database. Bear in mind that the first two methods can be done while the PC NetLink software is running. The third method, which physically reduces the size of the database, must be done while the PC NetLink software is offline and not available to users.

- **Deletion method 1**—Periodically run the `acladm -y -P` command to prune the database. ACL entries can be left dangling if a file or directory is deleted by a non-Microsoft client. The best option here is to put the command into a `cron` job. Using `crontab` to do this is acceptable because the pruning operation can be performed while the server is running.

- **Deletion method 2**—If someone has created file ACLs, you can use the following command to delete the ACLs. The following command will remove the ACLs from a directory called `/my-nt-share` by traversing the directory with the Solaris find command:

```
# find /my-nt-share -type f -exec /opt/lanman/sbin/rmacl {} \;
```

- **Shrinking the ACL file**—You must periodically shrink the ACL database to remove wasted space in the database. This procedure requires you stop the PC NetLink software and perform the procedure during scheduled down time. To shrink the ACL database, enter the following commands:

```
# /etc/init.d/ms_srv stop
# /opt/lamnan/sbin/blobadm -A -q
# /etc/init.d/ms_srv start
```

Bear in mind that a very large ACL file could take some time to shrink, so make sure you have sufficient time to complete the procedure.

Setting Up Alerts and Security Auditing

Two of the most useful administrative features available to a PC NetLink server are the Windows NT Alert service and the Auditing service.

Set up the Alert service by way of Windows NT Server Manager to notify you (or any Windows NT-connected machine that you specify) whenever specific events occur. Set a threshold value, and the Alert service generates an alert whenever the actual value exceeds or falls below the threshold. You can set alerts to be triggered, for example, based on the number of server sessions or on a specified throughput level. You can have the alerts stored in a dedicated log or even sent immediately and directly to your machine.

Auditing is a key security service that you can use, for example, to monitor users who are accessing files or directories on a PC NetLink server. Almost any action performed by a user can be audited. This service is not enabled by default under Windows NT.

▼ To Set Up Alerts

1. **Make sure the Alert service is running on the PC NetLink server.**

   Using the PC NetLink Server Manager (`/opt/lanman/sbin/slsmgr`), log on to the PC NetLink server, then double-click the Services icon.

   If the state of the Alert service is not Running, use the Action menu to start the service.

2. **On a Windows NT server, start Performance Monitor.**

   From the Start button, select Program->Administrative Tools->Performance Monitor.

3. **In the Performance Monitor, select View->Alerts.**

4. **In the Alerts sheet, select Edit ->Add to Alerts. Use the following guidelines:**

   a. **Computer—Choose the PC NetLink server**

   b. **Counter—Pick one; for example, Bytes Total/sec. (For details about the Counter, click Explain.)**

   c. **Alert If —Set the over/under value.**

5. **View Alerts in the Alert Log.**

▼ To Save Alert Settings

- **From the File menu, select Save Alert Settings.**

▼ To Use Saved Settings

- **From the File menu, choose Open.**

▼ To Set Up Security Auditing

> **Note –** The following instructions assume that the user has "Managing Auditing and Security Log rights."

1. **In Network Neighborhood, highlight a PC NetLink file or folder.**

2. **Under Properties, select Security->Auditing.**

3. **In the File Auditing sheet, select Add, then pick an option (for example, Everyone).**

4. **Choose an event in the Security Log to audit (for example, Read, Write, View audited events).**

▼ To View the Security Log

1. **In Event Viewer, select Log->Computer, and select the PC NetLink Server.**

2. **Select the Security log.**

Installing PC NetLink for Different Locales

Use the following procedure for the PC NetLink Global 1.0 or 1.1 software.

To make PC NetLink software work with different versions of Windows NT Server, you must perform additional steps in the PC NetLink software installation process.

▼ To Enable Internationalized Versions PC NetLink

1. **Use the** `locale` **command to make sure that your Solaris environment supports the locale you want the PC NetLink software to support.**

   a. **To see all available locales, use the following command on your Solaris server:**

   ```
   # locale -a
   ```

   b. **If you do not find the locale that you want to install for the PC NetLink software, use Solaris** `admintool` **to add the locale to your Solaris system.**

2. **Edit the** `/etc/default/init` **file, which is a system-wide configuration file, to include the locale that you require.**

   This file sets all required environment variables for the processes forked by `init(1M)`, including `lmx.ctrl` (which is started in `/etc/rc3.d/ms_srv` through `init`).

3. **Restart the server (if applicable).**

   If `lmx.ctrl` is already running, you must restart the PC NetLink server. Use either the PC NetLink GUI (`slsmgr`) or the `/etc/init.d/ms_srv` command.

Setting Up System Policies

Being able to control resources, users, and rights is very important in a network. Because you need ways to control how end users will use their computers, the programs they run, and even the way the desktop looks, it is important to understand how to set up and configure system policies.

System policies are a way for you to increase the security of a Windows NT network. This will work on any computer running Windows NT Server, Windows NT Workstation, or Windows 95/98 software. With system policies you can define two things:

1. **The desktop options for a Windows user or group.**

   Examples of these options include type of background, type of shell, and programs that the user can run.

2. **The computer settings.**

Examples of these settings are removing the last login name from the login screen, number of login attempts, and auto-disconnect.

For system policies to work properly, you must first get directory replication working (see "To Set Up Directory Replication" on page 248). You can have system policies without replication, but you will have to manually copy the policies file to the PDC and all the BDCs. Once replication is working you can start configuring policies.

▼ To Configure System Policies

1. **Open the Systems Policy Editor, which is in the Administration Tools (Common) menu.**

2. **Choose File->New Policy.**

   A screen with two icons: Default User and Default Computer is displayed.

3. **Select the Edit->Add Computer-> Add Group->Add User.**

4. **When prompted for a name, use the browse box to choose a computer, group, or user.**

5. **Double-click on the icon.**

   A new menu displays.

6. **Choose the policies you want and click on OK.**

7. **When you have finished choosing the policies, save the file as** `NTconfig.pol`.

   This is your policy file.

8. **To make the policies active, copy this file into the** `\Netlogon` **folder of the PDC.**

Note – In Windows NT, the `\Netlogon` directory is in `\Winnt\System32\Repl\imports\Scripts`. In PC NetLink, the `\Netlogon` directory is in `/var/opt/lanman/repl/import/scripts`. If the replication is working, you only have to put this on the PDC and let it be copied. If replication is not working, you will have to manually copy the file.

---

9. **If replication is working, wait 5 to 10 minutes for the policies to take effect.**

10. **To test if the policies are working, log in on a workstation that has some policies defined or log in as a user with policies.**

The steps above describe how to create policies for Windows NT computers and users. To create policies for Windows 95 or 98 workstations, create the system policies on a Windows 95 or 98 machine, name the file `Config.pol`, and save it in the `\NETLOGON` directory.

Enforcing Solaris Disk Quotas in a PC NetLink Environment

Solaris disk quotas enable system administrators to control the size of UFS file systems by limiting the amount of disk space and the number of inodes (which roughly corresponds to the number of files) that individual users can acquire. For this reason, quotas are especially useful on file systems where user home directories reside.

One advantage of running your Windows NT network by way of a the PC NetLink server is that you can enforce Solaris file creation quotas even for Windows NT clients—provided that you have created a quota for the user's Solaris account and mapped the user's Windows NT account to his or her Solaris account. When the user has reached the file-creation limit specified by the quota, the PC NetLink server sends an error message to the user's client PC:

```
There is not enough free disk space
```

Note – If you are running the PC NetLink 1.1 software, install the PC NetLink jumbo patch 108274-02 for disk quotas to work properly. Contact your Sun representative for more information.

▼ To Set Up Directory Replication

Log on to NT server as Administrator and complete the following steps to achieve directory replication:

1. **Create a new user (`repladmin`) and add it to following groups:**
   - Domain users
   - Replicator
   - Backup Operator

2. Select User Manager for Domains->Policies ->User Rights->Show Advanced User Rights.

   a. From the Right option, select Log in as a Service.

   b. Click Add, then select Replicator Group.

3. Click Add again, then click OK.

4. From the Server Manager window, select the server you want to export the files from, then select Computer->Services.

   a. Select the Directory Replicator service-> Startup.

   b. Select Automatic, This Account.

   c. In This Account, type the name of the user account, for example, *DomainName*\repladmin, and the password.

   d. Close these dialog boxes.

   e. Restart the Directory Replicator service.

5. Double-click on the server you want to export the directory from.

   a. Click the Replication button to open a dialog box.

   b. Select Export Directories.

   c. In the From Path field, type the folder you want to export.

   Use the default path in most cases. Change it only if absolutely necessary.

   d. Click the Manage button to open a dialog box.

   Do not select Add Lock, which will temporarily or permanently prevent the subdirectories from being replicated.

   e. Enable Wait Until Stabilized.

   f. Enable Entire Subtree.

   g. Click OK to close the Manage Exported Directories dialog box.

   h. Close remaining dialog boxes.

Note – In the Directory Replication box, To List is blank by default. In this case, exported directories are automatically replicated in a local domain. Add a specific server only if absolutely necessary. In most cases, leave it blank.

---

6. **From the Server Manager tool, select the import computer and make sure that the Replicator service is started by the user** `repladmin` **command.**

   a. **Double-click on the import computer and click the Replication button.**

   b. **Select Import Directories.**

   Type the new path only if necessary. Make sure that Add Lock is not selected inside the Manage button. If selected, this will prevent it from importing. The From List field is usually blank because the computer imports from the local domain.

   c. **Click OK to close all the windows and initiate the replication process.**

Setting Up Directory Replication Between Different Domains

A server can play the following roles in directory replication:

- Export server
- Import server
- Both export server and import server

You must configure the server according to the role it will play. Place the files to be replicated on the export server in subdirectories under `C:\Winnt\System32\Repl\Export` on Windows NT servers or on `C:\var\opt\lanman\repl\export` on Solaris PC NetLink servers.

Each time you add or modify a file in these subdirectories, the export server sends an update message to the import servers. The Replicator service on the import servers then logs on to the export server as a service and retrieves the files. The replicated files are placed in the same subdirectories names under `C:\Winnt\System32\Repl\Import` (Windows NT systems) or `C:\var\opt\lanman\repl\import` (Solaris PC NetLink servers).

To achieve directory replication between servers on different domains, a trusted relationship must be defined between the two domains (see "To Set Up Trust Relationships" on page 259). The user who runs the Replicator service on the import domain has to be added to Replicator Local Group of the export server and also has to be able to perform the Log on as a Service operation on the export server.

▼ To Configure the Import Server

1. Log on to the import server as Administrator.

2. Open the User Manager tool and create a new user, `repladmin`, adding it to the following groups:

   - Domain Users
   - Backup Operator
   - Replicator

3. Assign a password to the `repladmin` account, setting the password to Never expire and Not to be Changed on Next Logon. Be sure no machine restrictions are set.

4. Still using the User Manager tool, add the export server's domain as a Trusting Domain:

   a. From the Policies menu, select Trust Relationship.

   b. Click the Add button to the right of Trusting Domains.

   c. In the window that appears, type the name of the Trusting (Export) Domain, password, and password confirmation.

   Note – Password and Confirm Password are used only at the time the trust relationship is set. You can leave them blank. You must use the same password when you configure the export server.

   ---

   d. Click OK.

5. In the Server Manager tool, select the Import Server->Computer->Services.

   a. Select the Directory Replicator service and click Startup.

   b. Select Automatic as the Startup Type.

   c. From the Logon As option, select This Account and type the name of the user account such as: `Import Domain Name\repladmin`. Then type the password of the `repladmin` user in the Password and Confirm Password fields.

   d. Close these dialog boxes. If the operation is successful, this will add `repladmin` to the Replicator Local Group on the import domain and will grant `repladmin` the Log on as a Service right on the import domain.

   e. Restart the Directory Replicator service by clicking the Start button.

6. **Still using the Server Manager Tool, double-click on the import server.**

   a. **Click the Replication button to open a dialog box.**

   b. **Select the Import Directories option.**

   c. **In the From Path field, type the path to the directory where you want to import the subdirectories.**

   In most cases, you should be able to use the default path of
   `C:\Winnt\system32\Repl\Import` on Windows NT or
   `C:\var\opt\lanman\repl\import` on Solaris PC NetLink servers.

   d. **Click the Add button below Import Directories, and type or select the export domain name or export server name.**

   e. **Click OK to close the Add window.**

   f. **Click OK to close all windows.**

Note – Verify that the directory you are importing files to has the correct Solaris permissions; otherwise the files won't be imported. To verify permissions, enter the following commands at the Solaris server:

```
# chmod 777 <dirtoexport>
# chown lmxadmin <dirtoexport>
# chgrp DOS---- <dirtoexport>
```

It is much easier if you create the directories to be exported from a client mapped to the share. They will automatically be given the attributes required by the PC NetLink software.

▼ To Configure the Export Server

1. **Log on to the export server as Administrator.**

2. **From the User Manager tool, create a new user, `repladmin`, and add it to the following groups:**
   - Domain Users
   - Backup Operator
   - Replicator

3. Assign a password to the `repladmin` account, setting the password to Never Expire and Not to be Changed on Next Logon.

4. Still using the User Manager tool, add the Import Server's domain as a Trusted Domain:

   a. From the Policies menu, select Trust Relationship.

   b. Click the Add button to the right of Trusted Domains.

   c. In the window that appears, type the name of the Trusted (import) Domain and password.

   You must use the same password that you used to configure the import server.

   d. Click OK.

5. From the User Manager tool on the export domain, add the `repladmin` account from the import domain to the Replicator Local Group.

   a. Double-click on the Replicator Group from the Group List at the bottom of the window.

   b. Click the Add button.

   c. In List Names From, select the import domain name.

   d. Double-click the `repladmin` user account.

   e. Click OK to close the Add window.

   f. Click OK to close the Group window.

6. From the User Manager pull-down menu, select Policies-->User Rights.

   a. Select Show Advanced User Rights.

   b. From the Right options list, select Log on as a Service.

   c. Click the Add button.

   d. From the new window that appears, select the Replicator group.

   e. Click the Add button.

   f. Click OK to close the User Rights window.

7. In the Server Manager tool, select the export server.

   a. From the Computer menu, select Services.

   b. Choose Startup from the Directory Replicator service menu.

   c. Select Startup Type as Automatic.

d. On the Logon As option, select **This Account** and type the name of the user account such as *Export Domain Name*\repladmin.

e. Type the password of the <repladmin> user in the **Password** and **Confirm Password** boxes.

f. Close these dialog boxes.

If the operation is successful, this will add repladmin to the Replicator Local Group on the export domain and will grant repladmin the Log on as a Service right on the export domain.

g. Click the **Start** button to restart the Directory Replicator service.

8. Still using Server Manager tool, double-click on the export server.

a. Click the **Replication** button to open a dialog box.

b. Select the **Export Directories** option.

c. In the From Path field, type the export path name.

In most cases, you can use the default path of C:\Winnt\System32\Repl\Export on Windows NT or C:\var\opt\lanman\repl\export on Solaris PC NetLink servers.

d. Click OK to close these dialog boxes.

9. Use the Server Manager tool to make sure that the Replicator service was started on both servers and initiate the replication process.

If you want to establish a two-way replication (both servers acting as import and export server), you have to establish a two-way trust relationship between the two domains. The repladmin users of both domains must be added to the Replicator Local Group in each domain, and the Replicator Local Group must be able to Log on as a Service in each domain.

▼ To Set Up Roaming Profiles

Follow this procedure for setting the Roaming Profile to obtain the same desktop setting when you log in from any of the Windows NT workstations.

1. Open User Manager for Domains.

2. Double-click on a user whose Profile has to be set as Roaming.

3. Click on the Profile button to open the User Environment Profile dialog box.

4. **Type the complete path to the user's home directory in the User Profile Path field to create a roaming profile.**

For example,

```
User Profile Path \\server name\shared dir\user's home dir
```

The user can create any required desktop settings. When the user logs out, a file named `ntuser.dat`, containing profile information, is created in the user's home directory.

Combining UNIX and Windows NT Permissions on the Server

The PC NetLink software stores files as standard UNIX files. Windows NT ACL information is held separately. To allow PC NetLink users to access the files on the Solaris file system, a combination of UNIX user names and groups are used.

Files created by a PC NetLink user are owned in one of four ways:

- `lmxadmin`—Any file created by Windows NT user Administrator
- `lmxguest`—Any file created by Windows NT user Guest
- `lmworld`—Any file created by a Windows NT user who does not have a username mapping
- `username`—Any valid UNIX username mapped to a Windows NT username

User names can be mapped with the `mapuname` command, which allows a user in a Windows NT domain to be mapped to a user in UNIX. For example, to map `johns` in UNIX to user `JohnSmith` in the Windows NT domain `OFFICE_DOM`, you would use the command:

```
# mapuname -a OFFICE_DOM:JohnSmith johns
```

After this, any files that `JohnSmith` creates from a Windows client and stores on the PC NetLink server will be stored under the UNIX user name `johns`.

The PC NetLink software also has some special groups defined. These are: `DOS----`, `DOS-a--`, `DOS--s-`, `DOS---h`, `DOS-as-`, `DOS-a-h`, `DOS--sh`, `DOS-ash`. These are the same as DOS archive, hidden, and system attributes.

▼ To Set Up File Shares With Solaris PC NetLink

Setting up a share for the PC NetLink software is not quite so straightforward. It is a four-stage process:

1. **Create the directory on Solaris.**

   Any Solaris directory can be shared via a PC NetLink share. Frequently the directory you want to share with the PC NetLink software will be the mount point Solaris has used to mount a disk subsystem. The Solaris `df` command will show these mount points and Solaris paths to consider first in creating a share.

2. **Set up the Solaris permissions.**

   This stage is necessary so that the PC NetLink Server can access the directory. If the directory were owned by root and had 700 permissions on it, it would be inaccessible. This stage involves setting up the user name for the owner of the directory, the DOS group permissions, and the directory permissions. To set general access permissions for a share, do the following:

   ```
   # chown lmxadmin:DOS---- directory-name
   # chmod 775 directory-name
   ```

   If the share will be owned by a specific user who is already mapped to a UNIX user name, then use the UNIX user name in place of `lmxadmin`.

3. **Set up the Windows NT permissions.**

   To do this you must use a Windows NT system and mount the share that contains the directory you want to share. For example, to set the Windows NT permissions for a Solaris directory `/newshare`, you must mount the share that contains the directory `/newshare`, in this case, the root share C$. If the directory is `/export/lanman/newshare`, you could either mount C$ or USERS.

   Note – The "$" character in Windows NT share names has special significance. A trailing "$" on a share name means that the share will not be seen when browsing from the Network Neighborhood. The root directory is not set up as a visible share because normally it is not necessary to see it. In the same way, a user's home directory share will normally be set up with a trailing "$." Imagine how unwieldy the share listing would be for a system with 2000 users if each user's home directory share was listed. Instead `/export/home/mikeb` is shared as MIKEB$. Only `mikeb` needs to use that share, so it doesn't need to be listed.

Once the parent directory share has been mounted, open Windows Explorer and right-click on the directory to be shared. Select Properties and the Security tab. From here you can set the file permissions. Typical permissions could be:

- Domain Administrators—Full Control
- World—Read
- JohnSmith—Full Control

It would also be possible to change the ownership of the directory, but this is not simple. It involves either logging in as that user and taking ownership, or using the xcacls program from the Windows NT Resource Kit.

4. **Share the directory.**

Two commands can be used here: lmshare -a or net share. To use lmshare you need three pieces of information: the sharename, the directory to share, and a description. For example, to create a share called TSHARE of /export/lanman/testshare, the lmshare session would be as follows:

```
# lmshare -a
For those fields that are not mandatory and that you do not want
to enter anything, just press Return.
Sharename? TSHARE
Type (d|p|c|i)? d
Local path? /export/lanman/testshare
Remark? Test Share
Permissions(rwcxdaps)? rwcxda
Maximum users? unlimited
Password?
TSHARE added
```

Note – Most of the options have been given a default value. See the man pages for lmshare for more details.

Another way to set up a share is with the net share command. Using the same example as above, the net share command would be:

```
# net share tshare=c:/export/lanman/testshare /remark:"Test Share"
tshare was shared successfully.
```

Listing the successful share with `net share` will give the results:

```
# /opt/lanman/bin/net share
Share name Resource Remark
--------------------------------------------------------
TSHARE C:\export\lanman\testshare Test Share
```

▼ To Remove a PC NetLink File Share

- **You can use either net share or lmshare -d commands.**

```
# net share tshare /delete
tshare was deleted successfully.
```

or

```
# lmshare -d tshare
tshare deleted
```

Joining a Domain as a BDC to PDC in Another Subnet

When you need to have your PC NetLink server become a backup domain controller (BDC) to a primary domain controller (PDC) in different subnet, the PC Netlink server must resolve the NetBIOS name of the PDC. There are two ways of doing this, depending on whether a WINS server exists in the PDC's domain.

If a WINS Server Exists

If a WINS server exists in the PDC's domain and is registered on this WINS server, you must also register the PC NetLink server on this same WINS server. In this way, the PC NetLink server can resolve the PDC's NetBIOS name.

▼ To Register the PC NetLink Server in the WINS Database

1. Restart the PC NetLink server by entering the following commands:

```
system% winsconf -p IP address of WINS server
system% net stop server
system% net start server
```

2. Use the `joindomain` **command to join the PC NetLink server to the domain.**

If a WINS Server Does Not Exist

If a WINS server does not exist in the PDC's domain, use the following procedure to resolve the NetBIOS name.

▼ To Resolve the NetBIOS Name When No WINS Server Exists

1. Enter the following commands (shown in boldface).

Note that you should type the second command on one line; also note that you type the name of the PDC in *uppercase* letters, and you type the IP address in *reverse* order:

```
system% cd /opt/SUNWlznb/sbin
system%./nbns_adm -a -N UPPERCASE NAME of PDC -A \
                     reverse IP address-P TCP
```

2. Use the `joindomain` **command to join the PC NetLink server to the domain.**

▼ To Set Up Trust Relationships

If Domain A requires access to resources of Domain B, then Domain B has to trust A. This involves two steps:

1. Go to a Windows NT Server (PDC or BDC) in Domain A and do the following:

   a. Open User Manager. Start->Programs->Administrative Tools ->User Manager for Domains.

b. Use pull-down menu. Policies ->Trust Relationships.

This will open a dialog window with two boxes, top one for Trusted and bottom one for Trusting domains.

c. Add Trusting Domain name (B) in the lower box.

During this process it will ask for a password. Enter any password.

2. **Go to a Windows NT Server (PDC or BDC) in Domain B and follow the same procedure:**

a. Open User Manager. Start->Programs->Administrative Tools -> User Manager for Domains.

b. Use pull-down menu. Policies -> Trust Relationships.

This will open a dialog window with two boxes, top one for Trusted and bottom one for Trusting domains.

c. Add Trusted Domain name (A) in the top box.

Issue the same password entered in Step 1.

Now the users of the Domain A can start accessing the resources of the Domain B.

Note – Before doing this, make sure that the WINS servers in both the domains are partners. Otherwise, you may get the following error message while adding Trusted Domain in the dialog box:
`"Could not find Domain Controller for this Domain"`

Setting Up User Accounts

The procedure for setting up user accounts depends on what users accounts existed before you started using the PC NetLink software.

▼ To Set Up Accounts for Preexisting Solaris Users

1. **Open `slsmgr` GUI and create a mapping between UNIX and PC NetLink Server users.**

a. Go to Policies->User Account Mapping and enable the following items:
   - Map new PC NetLink Server accounts to Solaris accounts
   - Use existing account when user names match

2. **Create a directory under which all the users' home directories will reside, such as the following:**

```
# mkdir /export/home
```

3. **Change the permission of this directory to 755.**

```
# chmod 755 /export/home
```

4. **Share this directory using the following command:**

```
# net share HOME_DIR=c:/export/home /REMARK:"Users Home Dir"
```

Where *HOME_DIR* is the share name that will appear on Windows NT, 95, or 98 machines. You can choose any name.

5. **If all user directories are on the local PC NetLink server under** /home, **create a link for these users under the** /export/home directory. **For example, if a user name is** xyz, **you would do the following:**

```
# cd /export/home
# ln -s /home/xyz
```

Note – If users' home directories are on the remote machine, mount these directories under /export/home on the PC NetLink server. Refer to the *UNIX System Administration Manual* for details about mounting.

---

6. **Create the corresponding PC NetLink server user** xyz.

```
# net user xyz password /passwordreq:yes /passwordexp:no /
fullname:"Test User" /add
```

Where *password* is any password you wish to assign for user xyz. Type the command net help user to find more options.

7. **User xyz is by default a member of a group called Domain Users.**

If you want to add the users xyz and abc to the local Administrator group, type the following command:

```
# net localgroup administrators xyz abc /add
```

Type the net help localgroup command for more options.

8. **Map the PC NetLink server user name with the Solaris user name.**

If you have already completed Step 1 of this procedure and if the PC NetLink Server user account name and Solaris user account name are the same, skip this step.

```
# mapuname -a DOMAIN NAME:PC NetLink user name  Solaris User Name
```

Now you can log in from Windows NT/95/98 clients as xyz and browse the Network Neighborhood to write files on to the PC NetLink server system.

Copying User Accounts From Windows NT to UNIX

If user accounts already exist in Windows NT and you want to create these accounts in UNIX, use the sam2passwd utility. This creates a file similar to the format of /etc/passwd. Following is the syntax of the command:

```
sam2passwd -g<group-id> -l administrator -p <password> -s /bin/
csh -t <path to user's home dir> -u <starting uid> -y <password>
```

For this example, we'll use the following information:

Administrator password: secret
Temporary password to be set for all the users: changeme
Group ID for all the users: 10
Path to users' home directory: /export/home
Starting UID: 300
Login Shell Account: /bin/csh

▼ To Copy User Accounts

1. **To create users from Windows NT to UNIX, type the following:**

```
# sam2passwd -g 10 -l administrator -p secret -s /bin/csh -t
/export/home -u 300 -y changeme
```

This creates the `/var/opt/lanman/dirsync/sam2passwd.passwd` file.

Note – Instead of `changeme`, you can set no password by supplying NULL to the `-y` option.

---

2. **Append this file to** `/etc/passwd` **file and run the** `pwconv` **command to create entries in the** `inetc/shadow` **file for these additional users.**

3. **Create the directories for additional users in the** `/export/home` **directory and change ownership of the user directories accordingly.**

   For example, if the user name is `xyz`, type the following command:

```
# chmod 755 xyz
# mkdir xyz
# chown xyz xyz
```

Copying User Accounts From UNIX to Windows NT

If user accounts already exist in UNIX and you need to create these accounts on the PC NetLink Server, use the `passwd2sam` utility:

```
passwd2sam -i /etc/passwd -l administrator -p admin passwd -y passwd
```

where *passwd* can be the same for all users or set to NULL. If you need to pick all the users from NIS, do not use the `-i` option which takes the user account only from specified file (`/etc/passwd`).

Upgrading the PC NetLink Software

When you transition from PC Netlink 1.0 to the 1.1 version, you must move several PC NetLink software installation directories to avoid loosing previous printer setup information.

The path `/opt/lanman/shares/asu/system32/drivers` in the 1.0 global and later versions is now a symbolic link, and installation will fail if a directory is found with the same name. When installation fails, all installed packages are removed, and all data (including the upgrade data) is removed. This can result in loss of setup data.

The workaround to avoid the problem is to move the directory now associated with the symbolic link.

● **Move the** `/opt/lanman/shares/asu/system32/drivers` **to** `/opt/lanman/shares/asu/drivers` **before performing the upgrade.**

```
# net stop server
# mv /opt/lanman/shares/asu/system32/drivers \
        /opt/lanman/shares/asu/drivers
# /cdrom/cdrom0/install
```

The "\" character is the line continuation character.

Troubleshooting Browsing Procedures

Browsing networks to find servers you are looking for is not always guaranteed to work even on the best maintained network. Browsing relies on the existence of a master browser, which is selected by an election process. In certain conditions even Windows 95 or 98 clients can win this election.

Browsing reliability is also hindered by issues in support of the protocol with Windows NT as well as the PC NetLink software. One issue deals with browsing Windows NT domain master browser that has multiple network interfaces (also know as being multihomed). Search the Microsoft Knowledgebase (`http://search.support.microsoft.com`) for Q133241 for a more complete explanation of this problem. To briefly summarize this issue, all Windows NT servers (this includes PC NetLink servers) that have multiple network connections maintain separate lists of servers for each network interface they are supporting.

Because the browse master server doesn't know if the client making a request has access to both networks the server is attached to, it only offers the list that exists for the subnet the client has made the browse request for. In situations like this, the client will not see a complete list of the servers it may have access to.

In this situation, it may be best to disallow servers with multiple network connections from becoming a master browser if other equally qualified servers that can perform the function are on the subnet.

To disallow a PC NetLink server from becoming a domain master browser, set the Registry Value `MainTainServerList` to "NO".

Techniques for Troubleshooting Browsing

To diagnose browser-related problems that may or may not be related to the Solaris PC NetLink product, use the following tools:

- `nbtstat -a`—This utility exists on Windows operating systems to help monitor NBT NetBIOS over TCP/IP statistics. The `-a` switch lists the system name table.

- `lmhosts`—This file exists on Windows 95 and 98 machines (`\windows`) as well as Windows NT (`\WINNT\system32\drivers\etc`). This file contains host-to-IP address entries used by the system to access NetBIOS over TCP/IP systems. Make sure the information within these files is correct. Under normal operation, where a name server is used to resolve name-to-IP address, you do not need this file.

- `nbms_adm`—This utility, supplied with the PC NetLink software, enables you display the current NetBIOS cache contents. It also enables you to clear the cache if entries become stale.

- `browmon`—This GUI utility, available with the Windows NT Resource Kit, enables you to monitor the status of browsers

File Service Benchmark Methodology

During development of this book, four key areas of PC NetLink software performance were studied. These areas affect the most common uses of the PC NetLink software: file service (CIFS/SMB) performance, printer service performance, PC client authentication operations, and naming services (WINS). Clearly the most important of the four under normal conditions is the speed at which PC client users can perform file operations.

The purpose of this appendix is to explain how NetBench was used to measure and tune PC NetLink software performance, and to explain how the benchmark is used to derive performance and scaling information.

NetBench 5.01 Benchmark

The NetBench 5.01 benchmark measures the performance of a server's file I/O operations by placing an ever-increasing load of PC client requests on the server being tested. NetBench replicates real users using real productivity applications performing file operations (open, read, write, delete, lock, and so on). The benchmark traditionally uses 60 PC clients to perform a full execution of the benchmark. The full benchmark is described as a suite, with each test along a horizontal axis termed a mix. Users of the benchmark can derive valuable information by using even one PC client to perform the benchmark. During a typical mix, which takes approximately five minutes, a PC client can demand from 100 to 400 Mbytes of throughput through the server. This is considerably more than several users will demand of a server in a full day.

NetBench outputs an Excel spreadsheet that includes all the individual PC client loading data from the test and a chart displaying the throughput performance characteristics of the server. FIGURE A-1 shows an example of a NetBench benchmark result.

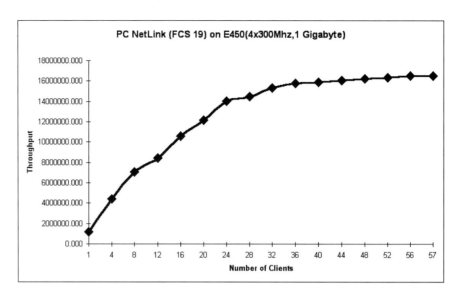

FIGURE A-1 Example NetBench Result

FIGURE A-1 shows the number of clients performing the NetBench benchmark on the horizontal scale and the resulting throughput in Mbytes/sec. for the server on the vertical scale. In FIGURE A-1 the server continues to deliver additional bandwidth demanded by the PC clients until about 24 loads. At that point a resource was exhausted and the benchmark levels off.

Key Points of NetBench

- NetBench tests everything from the PC client, through the network infrastructure, through the servers network interface layers and operating system, to the disk itself. If any hardware or software component changes, the resulting curve produced by the benchmark would also change.

- The NetBench benchmark (and in fact all Ziff Davis server benchmarks) can only be used to compare two servers, or two server configurations that have been tested in exactly the same laboratory environment. The same PC running the same desktop operating system must contact the server over the same network infrastructure.

- Unlike other server benchmarks, the NetBench benchmark produces no absolute benchmark number that can be published. Because it is nearly impossible to duplicate the hundreds of hardware and software configurable items on the PC clients, network infrastructure, and server configurations, it is not valid to compare results from two different laboratories and expect to see a true comparison. You must always test the two servers, or server configurations, in exactly the same environment to get a valid, nondistorted, comparable result.

NetBench Configuration

The NetBench benchmarks used to derive information in this book were performed in the Enterprise Technology Center (ETC) on the Burlington, Massachusetts, U.S., Campus of Sun Microsystems, using the following configuration:

1. 120 Micron 200 MHz Pentium MMX PCs configured as follows:

   a. 28 Windows 95 PCs (OEMR2) with 32 Mbytes of memory

   b. 90 Windows 95 PCs (OEMR2) with 64 Mbytes of memory.

   c. 1 Windows 98 PC with 32 Mbytes of memory

   d. 1 Windows NT 4.0 PC (SP3) with 64 Mbytes of memory

   All PCs had 3Com 3C509 PCI NIC controller configured to access the network switch in a 100 Mbit full duplex mode. All PCs had an Adaptec SCSI controller (not significant in NetBench testing).

2. Four Extreme Summit 2 Network switches configured to support 4 subnets. Interconnections between switches done with gigabit connections.

3. Sun Enterprise 450 server:

   a. 4x400 MHz UltraSparc CPU (4 Mbyte cache)

   b. 1–3 Gbytes of memory

   c. 20 4-Gbyte Seagate drives

   d. Gigabit Ethernet controller

   e. Sun Volume Manager (Veritas) or DiskSuite if stated

   f. StorEdge A1000, A3000 hardware RAID disk arrays

   g. Solaris 2.6 software (unless otherwise stated)

4. Sun Enterprise 6000 server

   a. 30x248 MHz UltraSPARC CPUs (4 Mbyte cache)

   b. 8 Gbytes of memory

   c. 53 FC-AL 4 Gbyte Seagate drives installed with StorEdge A5000 arrays

   d. Gigabit Ethernet controller

   e. Veritas, Sun Enterprise DiskSuite

   f. Solaris 2.6 software (unless otherwise stated)

FIGURE A-2 shows the typical NetBench configuration used to acquire results.

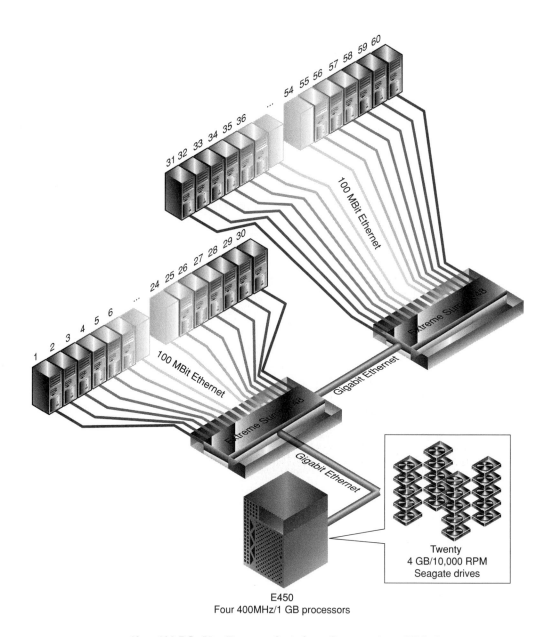

FIGURE A-2   60 to 120 PCs Use Extreme Switch to Communicate With Server

NetBench Suites

Number of Disk Drives Used

The NetBench suites, by default, test only one PC client network drive (F:). Including just one file structure in the benchmark usually saturates the disk subsystem quickly on most servers. While overloading disk subsystems is an interesting study, it is not a good way to exercise and test as many components as possible in the server and it does not test the system in a way that real servers are used. For this reason, unless the disk subsystem or RAID is the component being studied, all benchmarks used in this book spread the load of the NetBench benchmark across as many drives as would likely be found in a typical workgroup or enterprise server configuration. In the case of the Sun Enterprise 450, all 20 internal Ultra Wide SCSI drives (F: -Y:) were used to support the benchmark. Using this distributed load allowed the benchmark to better test the full capability of the server and avoided throttling the test to one overly saturated disk subsystem.

Time Required to Run NetBench Benchmark

The default NetBench benchmark can take more than two hours to perform a standard 60-client execution. NetBench was developed before fast network switches and fast PCs (120 MHz and above) were available. For this reason, the suites were designed to run for a length of time appropriate for 486-based PCs on 10 Mbit hubbed networks to acquire a valid result. When you execute NetBench on fast PCs (200 MHz Pentium systems in our case), and fast networks (100 Mbit full-duplex, switched connections), the benchmark only needs to run for a fraction of the original suite times to acquire valid results. The NetBench GUI lets you change the time required to execute each mix of the suite.

Our tests used the times listed in TABLE A-1 to perform the benchmark.

TABLE A-1   Time Allocated to Acquire NetBench Results

Client Mixes	Time Allocated for NetBench Results
1, 4, 8, 12	200 Seconds
16, 20, 24, 28	300 Seconds
32, 36, 40, 44	400 Seconds
48, 52, 56, 60	500 Seconds

Tests were performed between the default NetBench suites and the accelerated suites to ensure they produced equivalent results.

A Profile of an Average End User

Before you can size a PC NetLink server, you need an accurate profile of your average user. Some user communities comprise a multitude of different user types from a variety of separate organizations within the enterprise. In other environments, the user community is homogeneous, with users performing essentially the same, or similar, tasks, and their load on the file server is more easily predicted. This variability makes an absolute answer to the question "How many users will my PC NetLink server support?" impossible to predict precisely without full resource-intensive modeling of the environment.

To simplify the procedure, I have defined an average user for sizing purposes. The network file load of this average user may not actually reflect that of any one particular user, but it should reflect the total throughput load of all users, divided by the total number of users. Many user demands will fall below the load generated by this average user, many will be above. The goal is to find a definition that represents the average.

If the assumptions about your average user differ from those defined in this appendix, you can define your own using similar methodology. Your new average end user assumptions can then be applied to the procedures defined in Chapter 5 to determine new sizing information for your server.

Calculating the load that each PC will place on a file server is a difficult task because of the number of variables to be considered. Administration policies, network topology, individual work habits, and so on, all contribute to the user load.

In developing sizing information for this book, we assume the following:

- Users use the server as their primary document storage file system, their home directory, and as their print server.
- PC applications (for example, Microsoft Office) are installed locally on the client PC hard drives.
- Most are medium and light users of the server. Special consideration should be made for power users that can place considerable demands on the server.
- Usage patterns create peak loading times between 9:30–10:00 and 2:00–4:00, for a total peak loading time of 4 hours per day.

We know from historical data at some sites that users are 15 percent to 45 percent busy with respect to use of a server while they are actually using their clients. A light user of a system, such as someone reading a small amount of email, would be 15 percent busy. Someone who spends most of their time working on the computer word processing and manipulating spread sheet documents would be 45 percent busy. Even for users with a 45 percent duty cycle, the number and size of files required from a central server can vary dramatically. PCs today typically have the operating system and the applications installed on the local hard drive, primarily utilizing the file server to store user-authored documents for backup and sharing purposes. MS Office documents can be small documents, such as 10 Kbyte Microsoft Word memos, or large 1 to 2 Mbyte multimedia documents with significant multimedia content.

TABLE B-1 defines the file server use of our average user (average document size and MS Office applications) used to produce an initial estimate of bandwidth requirements between the PC client and file server.

TABLE B-1 Average File Server Use

Document Type, Size and Quantity	Space Required
8 Word documents @ 100 Kbytes per document. 5 saves per document edit session 8 * 100 KBytes * (1 Read + 5 Writes)	4800 Kbytes
3 Excel spreadsheet document edits @ 200 Kbytes per document. 5 saves per document edit session 3 * 200 Kbytes * (1 Read + 5 Writes)	3600 Kbytes
4 Powerpoint presentation edit @ 1 Mbyte 4 * 1 Mbyte * (1 Read + 1 Write))	8192 Kbytes
50 email messages @ 4.0 Kbytes (via file system) 50 * 4.0 Kbytes * (1 Read + 1 Write)	400 Kbytes
10 emails with 100 Kbyte attachments 10 * 100 Kbytes * (1 Read + 1 Write)	2000 Kbytes
5 * 200 Kbyte print jobs	1000 Kbytes
Total throughput requirements for the average end user today	19.52 Mbytes

Planning the requirements of a file server based on today's needs usually produces a server that does not meet the needs of tomorrow. Allocate additional throughput to ensure that the server has a useful life before it needs to be upgraded. Key factors for sizing a file server include new technologies that enable even novice users to manipulate documents with significant multimedia content. New Internet and intranet technologies also require significant bandwidth to the file servers. These new technologies keep raising the requirements for file servers.

Doubling our initial estimates of PC client load should easily handle these future requirements. Using 40 Mbytes of files read or written per day for each active user of the file server should give our average user the needed space as their PC clients make ever greater demands on the server.

Note – The average user demands 40 Mbytes per day of file operation from the PC NetLink server.

Thousands of different application programs write files to servers, some small and some large. You may want to define your own average user by including the file service requirements of other applications used at your location. Following is a short list of other possible files to take into account:

- The process of doing a Microsoft NT Domain login may cause the PC client to download a profile file that allows the user to have the same desktop environment on any system in the domain. This profile file can become quite large. 20 Mbyte profile files are possible.

- The use of technologies outside of file operations reduces the load on the file server; for example, using IMAP or POP protocols to access users' mail instead of using the file system to access file-based post office directories.

- Access to web browser-related files. All popular web browsers, when installed into a PC, establish caches and other user-related files, such as bookmark files, on the local PC and not on the server. Local policies may require rethinking the assumptions. Place any user-valued data files, such as address book, mail folders, and such on the server where backups are performed. RAID improves the redundancy of the file system. Browser cache files should be placed locally on the PCs for performance reasons.

- Using applications installed on the servers changes the load on the file system dramatically. In the past, the benefits of installing applications on servers and accessing the file executables through the network were primarily based on management and administration issues. Disk drive capacity and performance as well as CPU performance have risen dramatically, while many corporate networks, at the PC client level, have remained at 10 Mbits. The performance difference in executing PC applications locally instead of through the network can be dramatic. Software technologies have also improved enough to allow for the complete management of the PC operating systems and applications. For these reasons, it may be best to install the applications locally on the PC.

- The number of file operations can have as much to do with performance as the actual number of bytes in the file transferred. Applications that create and delete many small files and directories can result in slower performance than several large files because of the number of caches and buffers that must be flushed. If you suspect the PC NetLink software will be handling requests from PC applications that will be manipulating many small files, allocate additional resources. The Netbench benchmark attempts to simulate the file operations of typical office productivity.

Disk Capacity Needed

Many factors affect each user's disk capacity needs. Company policy, application demands, and end user needs are just a few of the factors involved in planning this resource. Picking a specific number is important to configure your initial server, but making sure you can add significantly more disk subsystem capacity is probably the most important factor.

The first assumption made in determining this number is that the end users will not be using the server to install applications. Microsoft Office can easily exceed 120 Mbytes of disk space in a full installation. Even if your network has 100 Mbit, full-duplex connections to every PC client, installing such applications on a common server would consume a great deal of network bandwidth and disk space. Even if the application is installed so that the files are shared by many users, the network bandwidth consumed by loading these executables and shared libraries would be prohibitive in most environments. At the time of this writing, it is difficult to find a commercially available PC that doesn't have at least a 3 to 5 Gbyte, fast EIDE, drive. Placing these large applications on the local disk drive is clearly the best way to keep the application running as fast as possible. Many new system administration techniques and products have also reduced the need to administer these kinds of applications from one directory. If you require this kind of application installation, you need to recalculate the per-user load and disk capacity using new average user assumptions.

A quick survey of home-directory servers supports planning for 100 Mbytes per user a as good starting point.

Note – 100 Mbytes of disk capacity is allocated for each end user in this example.

APPENDIX **C**

Man Pages and Help Files

PC NetLink includes the man pages listed in TABLE C-1. The table includes the man page command, the path to the man page, and a description of it.

TABLE C-1   PC NetLink Man Page Descriptions

Man Page	Path	Description
acladm	/opt/lanman/sbin	Creates, checks, prunes, fixes, and removes access control list information.
blobadm	/opt/lanman/sbin	Displays statistical information; checks, compresses, and configures a well-known or specified blobfile.
chacl	/opt/lanman/sbin	Changes access control entry.
delshmem	/opt/lanman/sbin	Deletes unused PC NetLink Server shared memory segments.
elfread	/opt/lanman/sbin	Use to view and clear the system, security, and application logs at the UNIX system console.
euctosjis	/opt/lanman/bin	Converts the encoding of characters from Extended UNIX Code (EUC) to a Shift-JIS (S-JIS) encoding.
joindomain	/opt/lanman/sbin	Use to configure a PC NetLink server computer in a new domain.
lanman.ini	/etc/opt/lanman /lanman.ini	Contains default startup parameter values.
lmat	/opt/lanman/sbin	Schedules commands or programs to run on a server at a specified time or date.

TABLE C-1   PC NetLink Man Page Descriptions

Man Page	Path	Description
lmshare	/opt/lanman/sbin	Manipulates a share file without server intervention.
lmshell	/opt/lanman/bin	Enables you to link to other servers on the network. It also enables you to use the net use command to view and manipulate files on other servers.
lmstat	/opt/lanman/sbin	Gets statistical information on the server's shared memory.
lsacl	/opt/lanman/sbin	Displays access control list information.
makeclients	/opt/lanman/bin	Use to produce installation diskettes for Microsoft Network Client software.
mapuname	/opt/lanman/sbin	Maps and unmaps PC NetLink Server user, global group, and local group names to and from UNIX system user names.
nbmem	/opt/SUNWlznb/sbin	Displays various internal structures used by the NetBIOS software.
nbns_adm	/opt/SUNWlznb/sbin	NetBIOS over TCP/IP name cache management utility.
nbutil	/opt/SUNWlznb/sbin	NetBIOS status and control utility.
net	/opt/lanman/bin	Use to perform administrative tasks at the PC NetLink Server console.
netevent	/opt/lanman/sbin	Sends an administrative or user alert to other computers.
passwd2sam	/var/opt/lanman/dirsync /passwd2sam	Adds or deletes Solaris user accounts in PC NetLink server.
rcgcheck	/opt/lanman/sbin	Enumerates all of the keys in the Registry, dumps the contents of the Registry, checks and repairs the Registry.
reconfig	/opt/lanman/sbin	Sets or queries Registry key information.

TABLE C-1   PC NetLink Man Page Descriptions

Man Page	Path	Description
regload	/opt/lanman/sbin	Initializes a Registry and, if necessary, creates it.
rmacl	/opt/lanman/sbin	Deletes an entry from the access control list.
sam2passwd	/var/opt/lanman/dirsync /sam2passwd	Creates a passwd file containing PC NetLink server user accounts to add into the Solaris name service.
samcheck	/opt/lanman/sbin	Checks, repairs, or dumps the PC NetLink Server account database.
setdomainname	/opt/lanman/sbin	Changes the name of a PC NetLink server domain.
setservername	/opt/lanman/sbin	Changes the name of a PC NetLink server.
sjistoeuc	/opt/lanman/bin	Converts the encoding of characters from Shift-JIS (S-JIS) encoding to Extended UNIX Code (EUC) encoding.
srvconfig	/opt/lanman/bin	Modifies the PC NetLink server lanman.ini configuration file.
ud	/opt/lanman/bin	Converts text files between DOS, UNIX, and Macintosh file formats.
winsadm	/opt/lanman/sbin	Administers the Windows Internet Name Service (WINS) at the PC NetLink Server command prompt.
winsconf	/opt/SUNWlznb/sbin	Use to configure WINS services.

The following sections provide the complete text for each of the man pages.

Man Pages

To access UNIX or Solaris man pages type the following:

```
hostname% man man page command
```

To access PC NetLink man pages, you must include the path name from TABLE C-1. So you would type the following:

```
hostname% path man man page command
```

Maintenance Commands   acladm(1m)

Name   acladm - creates, checks, prunes, fixes, and removes access control list (ACL) information.

Synopsis acladm [-C I -E I -N I -O I [-P I -S I -U] I -R] [-y I -n I -f] [-v]

Description The `acladm` command creates, checks, prunes, fixes, or removes access control list data. Creation of a new ACL data store will fail if it already exists. The check (-C) option traverses through the ACL data store to determine if there are any inconsistencies.

Options   -C   Checks and repairs the ACL data store. The command prompts the user before making repairs. Corrupt entries are either fixed or deleted. If the -y option is used, the command repairs the data store automatically.

              -E   Enumerates all objects which have ACLs assigned to them.

              -N   Creates a new ACL data store if one does not already exist.

              -O   Reinitializes the default ACLs for standard objects. This option does not affect any user-created ACLs.

              -S   Removes redundant access control entries (ACEs) from ACLs.

              -U   Removes ACEs of deleted or unknown users from ACLs.

              -P   Prunes (synchronizes) the ACL information with the physical data on the UNIX file system. This option removes any ACLs for objects (such as files) that no longer are present on the system.   Users are prompted regarding each ACL unless the -y option is used, in which case the command prunes every ACL automatically.

              -R   Removes completely an ACL data store. This command asks for confirmation unless the -y option is used, in which case the ACL store is removed automatically.

              -f   Only valid when used with the -C option. Corrupt entries are fixed in the ACL data store. No corrupt entries are deleted. User is not prompted, each ACL entry that can be fixed is fixed automatically.

              -y   When used with the -C, -P, or -R option, ACL store changes are made without prompting the user for input.

              -n   When used with the -C or -P option, no changes are made to the ACL store. The object name of each ACL entry that needs repair is displayed with the action (fix or delete) that will be applied when the -n option is not used.

Example   To check access control list information, type the following command:
              ```
              acladm -C
              ```

Name   blobadm - display statistical information; check, compress, and configure a well-known or specified blobfile.

Synopsis   blobadm [options] -A | -B | -C | -D domainname | -R | -F filename | -L

Description   The blobadm command displays information for a specified blobfile. It also can be used to check a blobfile, grow the data position of a blobfile, compress and remove extra free space of a blobfile, or to update key information. To understand the displayed information, the pages at the head of the blobfile contain control information, followed by the free block map, up to three hash tables, and the key table. This is followed by the data portion of a file which consists of a configurable number of pages. Each page is 4 KBytes and consists of 32 fragments, each 128 bytes. The well-known blobfiles are the ACL store, the BUILTIN accounts store, the change log, domain SAM database, the LSA store, and the Registry store.

Options   -A   Displays information about the ACL store.

          -B   Displays information about the BUILTIN accounts store.

          -C   Displays information about the change log.

          -D domainname   Displays information for the specified SAM domainname.

          -F filename   Displays information about the blobfile specified by filename.

          -L   Displays information about the LSA store.

          -R   Displays information about the Registry store.

          The following are valid options and may be specified for any of the blobfiles. If no options are specified, the file statistics are displayed by default.

          -b   Dumps a map of the fragments in use from the data portion of the blobfile. The offset of each page and the status of individual fragments within the page is denoted by an x in the corresponding field.

          -c   Checks the blobfile.

          -d #   Deletes key #, where # is the virtual key number. Use the -K option to obtain a list of key numbers in use.

          -G <pages>   Grows the blob data portion by <pages> number of pages.

          -h <id>   Displays information for the hash table identified by <id> in binary format. Valid values are 0, 1 or 2.

          -k #   Dumps detailed information about the virtual key # in binary format.

          -K   Dumps a list of the virtual key numbers in use.

-q   Compresses the blobfile, removing excess free space.

-s   Dumps a summary of blobfile statistics.

-S   Displays the number of records in use and the amount of space used by the records.

Examples   To obtain a summary of blobfile statistics for the ACL store, type the following command at the UNIX system console:

```
blobadm -s -A
```

Note   This command must be run as root.

Maintenance Commands   chacl(1m)

Name   chacl - Change Access Control Entry.

Synopsis   chacl [options] [objectname ... | -]

Description   The chacl command changes access control entry associated with the specified object(s).

Options   -a mask:SID[:success | :failure | :all] set audit ACE.

-A mask:SID[:success | :failure | :all] set alarm ACE.

-B mask:SID   Block/deny access ACE.

-d   Non-filesystem object behaves as a directory.

-D   Delete ACL for target filename.

-g SID   set primary group.

-G mask:SID   Grant access ACE.

-L logName   Execute changes as Unix user 'logname'.

-N   Setup for a new object.

-O Name   Write output to file 'name'.

-o SID   Set owner.

-U Name   Set subject to 'name'.

-v   Verbose mode.

At a Solaris console, to set the primary group for an ACL entry for object 'objectname', type the following:

```
chacl -g /home/foo/bar
```

To overwrite an existing ACL and grant access ACE, type the following:

```
find /home/foo/bar -prin | ./chacl -N -
G RWXASM:LocalSystem -
```

Maintenance Commands   delshmem(1m)

Name   **delshmem** - delete unused PC NetLink Server shared memory segments.

Synopsis   **delshmem**

Description   The delshmem command is used to delete unused shared memory segments left by PC NetLink Server processes. This command is useful for cleanup purposes in cases where a PC NetLink Server process terminates unexpectedly.

Notes   The server must be stopped before running this command. The command must be run as root. This command should not be used to stop the PC NetLink Software.

Maintenance Commands   elfread(1m)

Name   **elfread** - used to view and clear the system, security, and application logs at the UNIX system console.

Synopsis   **elfread [-od I -cy] logname**

Description   The elfread command is used to view and clear event logs at the UNIX system console. It is especially useful if the server fails to start. Note that the -d (display) and -c (clear) options are mutually exclusive.

Options   -o   Displays the log file contents listing the oldest event first.

-d   Displays additional details about log events. If neither the -o nor the -d option is specified, a summary of all events in the log is displayed using this command.

-c   Clears the entire content of the selected log.

-y   Used with the -c option to clear the log without prompting for confirmation.

logName   Specifies the type of log you wish to display. Acceptable entries using this command are system, security, and application.

Example   To view a summary of the system log in reverse chronological order, type the
following command:

```
elfread -o system
```

User Commands   euctosjis(1)

Name   euctosjis - converts the encoding of characters from Extended UNIX Code
(EUC) to a Shift-JIS (S-JIS) encoding.

Synopsis   **euctosjis [-aderzw] [file]**

Options   -a   If an input character has an invalid EUC encoding, the euctosjis
command aborts.

-e   If an input character has an invalid EUC encoding, conversion to S-JIS
cannot be performed for this character. However, the euctosjis command
continues its conversion process for all subsequent characters.

-d   All conversions from EUC to S-JIS are performed within the input file.

-r   Converts a UNIX system file to the DOS file format by converting every
new line to a carriage return followed by a new line. Additionally a
control-Z character is emitted as the last character in the file.

-z   Ignore or do not emit a control-Z at end of file.

-w   A wide character space is converted to two ASCII spaces.

Examples   To convert all the EUC encoded characters in file-e to S-JIS encoded characters
and redirect the output to file-s, type the following command:

```
euctosjis file-e file-s
```

To convert all the EUC encoded characters in datafile to SJIS encoding, type the
following command:

```
euctosjis -d datafile
```

See also   sjistoeuc

Maintenance Commands   joindomain(1m)

Name   **joindomain** - used to configure a PC NetLink Server computer into a new domain.

Synopsis   **joindomain**

Description   The `joindomain` command is used to configure a PC NetLink Server computer into a new domain. It can be used to change the role of the server. It is an interactive command and takes no arguments. Do not use this command to change the role of the server if you are not changing domains. Instead, use Server Manager to promote or demote a server.

If there is an error during processing or if you interrupt the command, it restores the server to the state it was in before you issued the command. If you are configuring a server as a backup domain controller, you need to supply the name of the primary domain controller, which must be running and connected to the network. You also are prompted for the name of an existing administrative account and password in the new domain. This permits the command to connect to the primary domain controller and to configure the server into the domain.

Example   If a server is a backup domain controller in the domain sales and you want to move it to be a backup domain controller in the domain finance, you can use the joindomain command. You also can use the joindomain command to change the role (primary or backup) of the server if you also are changing domains.

Warning   Using the `joindomain` command reinitializes the accounts database. Using it on a primary domain controller will destroy all of your account information, except for SID-to-UNIX account mappings. SID-to-UNIX mappings are preserved to allow the users to keep their mappings if a server moves to a domain which trusts the server's original domain. If these mappings are not needed, the administrator can remove them by issuing the command `mapuname -p`.

Note   If this server runs the Directory Replicator service, use Server Manager to verify that the service is configured correctly.

File Formats   lanman.ini(4)

Name   lanman.ini - configuration file for startup parameters.

Synopsis   /etc/opt/lanman/lanman.ini

Description   The `lanman.ini` file contains some default startup parameter values. Only parameters that have been changed to values other than their default values are added to the `lanman.ini` file.

To display and edit default settings, a utility program called `srvconfig` is provided in the `/opt/lanman/sbin` directory. You may edit the `lanman.ini` file to set the value of a parameter to something other than the default. First locate (or add) the appropriate section title in brackets. Then add the desired `parameter=value` entry.

Examples   The services that are started by default may be set by changing the value of the srvservices parameter in the server section.
```
[server]
srvservices=alerter,netlogon,browser,replicator,wins
```

See also   `srvconfig(1m)`

Maintenance Commands   lmat(1m)

Name   lmat - schedules commands or programs to run on a server at a specified time or date. (Note that there also exists an MS-DOS at command.)

Synopsis   **lmat [id] [/delete]**
lmat time [/every:date[,...] | /next:date [,...]] command

Description   Use the `lmat` command to run commands at regularly scheduled intervals. To display a list of scheduled commands, type lmat without options. Commands scheduled with the lmat utility run as background processes; no output is displayed at the server.

To redirect the output to a file, use the redirection symbol (>) and the full path name. If you redirect output to a file, enclose the command you are scheduling in quotation marks. Scheduled tasks are not lost if you stop the server, but the server must be running at the time the commands are scheduled to execute.

Options   id   An identification number assigned to a scheduled command time. Specifies the time when command is to run. It is expressed as hours:minutes in a 24-hour notation (00:00 [midnight] through 23:59). Command specifies the command that is to run on the PC NetLink Server. When the command requires a path name as an argument, use the absolute path name.

/delete   Cancels a scheduled command. If id is omitted, all scheduled commands on the server are canceled.

/every:date[,...]   Runs the command on each specified day(s) of the week or month. Specify date as one or more days of the week (M, T, W, Th, F, S, Su) or one or more days of the month (using numbers 1 through 31). Separate multiple date entries with a comma. If date is omitted, the current date is assumed.

/next:date[,...]   Runs the command on the next occurrence of the day. Specify date as one or more days of the week (M, T, W, Th, F, S, Su) or one or more days of the month (using numbers 1 through 31). Separate multiple date entries with a comma. If date is omitted, the current date is assumed.

Examples   To display a list of commands scheduled on the server, type the following command:

```
net admin \\servername /command lmat
```

To learn more about a command with the identification number 3, type the following command:

```
net admin \\servername /command lmat 3
```

To cancel all commands scheduled on a server, clear the lmat schedule by typing the following command:

```
net admin \\servername /command lmat /delete
```

Maintenance Commands   lmshare(1m)

Name   lmshare - manipulates a share file without server intervention.

Synopsis   **lmshare [options][sharename]**

Description The `lmshare` command manipulates the set of shared resources without server intervention. It performs a variety of operations, including adding a new share (with optional non-encryption password), deleting a share, setting the banner page, and setting a queue start time.

Options   -a [-e] [-i] fileNameAdds a new share. The -e option means that password encryption is already active. The -i option with a file name reads information from a file. Otherwise, standard input is read.

-b share   Sets the printer banner page.

-d shareName   Deletes share name.

-f sharename fldnumberGets a specific field from the share.

-g share   Sets queue start time (go).

-h share	Sets queue stop time (halt).
-l	Lists share.
-m share	Sets queue parameters.
-n	Creates a new share list.
-o shareName	Reshares an unshared print queue.
-p shareName	Modifies a printer command string.
-q queueName	Lists printer shares.
-r queueName	Sets printer preset sequence.
-s queueName	Sets printer postset sequence.
-v queueName	Debugging on; if required must be first option.

Examples   To add a new share, type the following command:

```
lmshare -a
```

To list shares, type the following command:

```
lmshare -l
```

To obtain a specific field from a share, for example field 2, type the following command:

```
lmshare -f share 2
```

User Commands   lmshell(1)

Name   **lmshell** - allows you to link to other servers on the network. It also allows you to use the net use command to view and manipulate files on other servers.

Synopsis   **lmshell [command][\;command]**

Description   The lmshell command is for PC NetLink Server administrators who are UNIX system users, but are more comfortable with DOS commands and naming conventions. To use the lmshell command you must be at the UNIX system prompt. When you type lmshell, the prompt you receive looks like the prompt you see on a MS-DOS computer (for example, C:\TMP); when you see this prompt, you can enter commands.

To display the commands that you can use in lmshell, type ? and press ENTER.

These commands operate similarly to their MS-DOS counterparts. The default drive for lmshell is C: which is the local UNIX system file system. You can use lmshell to test for connectivity. If you can use lmshell to access shared files, you can be sure that the server is functioning properly. Also you can use lmshell to type out files on other servers' share areas, to copy them to or from your server, and to connect to printers. When you are executing lmshell, the "look and feel" follows the MS-DOS command line. The lmshell command allows you to view and manipulate files on other server computers by using the net use command to:

- Link to shared directories in order to look at files or copy files to the local computer's hard disk.
- Link to shared printers and copy files to them for printing.

The lmshell command understands UNC (Universal Naming Convention) names. A UNC name is a syntax for accessing files and directories without using a net use command. For example, to type out the file foo in the share area tmp on the server ernie, type the following:

```
type \\ ernie\tmp\foo
```

You can specify commands to lmshell on the command line.

To type out foo in the preceeding example from the UNIX system prompt, you can type the following:

```
lmshell 'type \\ ernie\tmp\foo'
```

The drive letters and drive redirections exist only while you are in lmshell. They do not affect any other commands executing on the UNIX system server computer and they disappear when you exit lmshell. While you are in lmshell you can temporarily escape to the system shell by using the ! command. Again, drive letters and other redirections cannot be referenced outside lmshell, not even in a subshell started with the ! command.

The lmshell command is not a UNIX system shell, nor is it the actual MS-DOS operating system. It is only able to run the commands that are displayed when you type ? at the console prompt.

Example   To type out the file foo in the share area tmp on the server ernie, type the following:

```
net use e: \\ernie\tmp
e:
type foo
```

Maintenance Commands   lmstat(1m)

Name   mstat - gets statistical information on the server's shared memory.

Synopsis   lmstat [-acCfglnNrtuv] [-i file] [-o file] [-p pid] [-I inode]
                lmstat [-w pid] [-m size] [-d count]

Description The lmstat command looks through the PC NetLink Server's shared memory
                and prints out what it finds. It is most useful for debugging purposes. It can
                show information about clients, files, locks, counters, and ustruct free lists.

Options   -a   Shows all server statistics.

                -c   Shows the client computers connected to server processes.

                -C   Shows SMB and RPC counters.

                -f   Shows information about files.

                -g   Shows the current client license limit.

                -l   Shows the locks.

                -n   Shows the counters.

                -N   Shows the functions that are never called.

                -r   Repeats.

                -t   Shows the task information.

                -u   Shows the ustruct free list.

                -o file Outputs shared memory to file.

                -i file Inputs shared memory to file.

                -p pid Shows only data for process pid.

                -I inode   Shows data only for inode file.

                -w pidWatches system calls for process pid. This option is not valid on all
                        operating systems.

                -m size   Buffer size. Optional, used with -w.

                -d count   Displays count; optional, used with -w.

                -v   Displays the version of the PC NetLink Server.

Examples   To show everything from the shared memory, type the following command:
                    lmstat -a

                To show locks, type the following command:
                    lmstat -l

Maintenance Commands   lsacl(1m)

Name   lsacl - Display ACL (Access Control List) information.

Synopsis   lsacl [-loF] [-E | objectname ... | -]

Description   The lsacl command displays access control information associated with the specified object(s)/enumeration. The output of lsacl consists of two sections: the comments section and the ACL entries section.

The optional comments section may contain multiple lines. The object name (via -l option), owner, object owning group, audit and alarm (via -a or -l option). Each line of comment begins with a '%'.

Each ACE appears on a separate line. The ACE entry contains a line with four fields separated by a colon. The first field is either 'granted' or 'denied'. The second field shows inheritance. The third field shows the access masks for standard and specific rights. The fourth field shows the SID (Security ID). In case of any error, this command should exit with a standard error code.

Options   -E   This enumerates ALL ACLs in the system. If the 'objectname' is '-', a list of objects is read from standard input.

-F   Display all ACE flags.

-g   Display primary groups.

-l   Display long listing.

-M   Display meaning of mask abbreviations.

-o   Display owners, e.g.%owner:<domain>:<user>.

Example   At a Solaris console, to display the long listing of an ACL entry for object 'objectname', type the following:
```
lsacl -l /home/foo/bar
```

Maintenance Commands   makeclients(1m)

Name   **makeclients** - used to produce installation diskettes for Microsoft Network Client software.

Synopsis   **makeclients [-f] [-ddrive] [-Ddevice] clientpkg**

Description   The makeclients command generates installation diskettes for the Microsoft network clients. The utility prompts you for each diskette in the set of client disks, formats the diskette in MS-DOS format, and populates the diskette with the client software. This command can be used only on UNIX system computers that support MS-DOS formatted diskettes.

Options	-f	Disables formatting of the diskettes.
	-d	Specifies the drive number of the floppy drive. The default is 0. This option cannot be used if the -D option is used.
	-D	Specifies the floppy device. The default is /dev/rdiskette. This option cannot be used if the -d option is used.
	clientpkg	The name of the client software package for which you wish to produce disks. The only supported option is tcp32wfw.

Example To produce installation diskettes for the Windows for Work-group client, type:

```
makeclients tcp32wfw
```

Note The msclients package must be installed prior to using this command.

Maintenance Commands   mapuname(1m)

Name mapuname - maps and unmaps PC NetLink Server user, global group, and local group names to and from UNIX system user names.

Synopsis **mapuname [[-d] domain:object | UNIXusername]**
mapuname -a domain:object UNIXusername
mapuname -p

Description The mapuname command is used to map the name of a PC NetLink Server object (user, global group, or local group) to the name of a UNIX system user. After a PC NetLink Server object has been mapped to the name of a UNIX user on a UNIX system, whenever that PC NetLink Server object creates a file on that UNIX system, the UNIX system owner of that file will be that UNIX system user. By default, all but a small predefined set of PC NetLink Server objects are mapped implicitly to the UNIX system user lmworld. Any mappings created explicitly using the mapuname command override this default mapping. Without arguments, the mapuname command displays all explicit mappings that are maintained by the system. Given an argument domain:object, the mapuname command displays the UNIX user name to which the indicated PC NetLink Server object is mapped; the specified object must be defined in the local or in a trusted domain. Given an argument in the form UNIX-username, the mapuname command displays all PC NetLink Server objects which map to the indicated UNIX user name. It is possible to map multiple PC NetLink Server objects to a particular UNIX user name; however, each PC NetLink Server object maps to only one UNIX system user name. UNIX system user accounts also can be created and assigned automatically to PC NetLink user accounts. For information, see the *PC NetLink Server System Guide.*

-d   Deletes the specified mapping or mappings.

-a   Maps the specified PC NetLink user, global group, or local group in the local or in a trusted domain to the UNIX system user name on this computer. The specified PC NetLink user, global group, or local group must exist. The UNIX system user name does not need to exist at the time that the command is run.

-p   Purges all obsolete mappings of PC NetLink Server objects to UNIX system user names. A mapping is considered obsolete if either the PC NetLink server object being mapped or if the UNIX system user to which it is mapped does not exist.

Examples To map the PC NetLink Server user myname in the domain mydom to the UNIX system user uuname, type the following command at the UNIX system console where the UNIX system user uuname is defined:

```
mapuname -a mydom:myname uuname
```

To unmap the PC NetLink server user myname in the domain mydom, type the following command at the UNIX system console:

```
mapuname -d mydom:myname
```

To delete all mappings of PC NetLink Server mapuname.1m objects to the UNIX system user uuname, type the following command at the UNIX system console:

```
mapuname -d uuname
```

Maintenance Commands   nbmem(1M)

Name   nbmem - display internal NetBIOS structures.

Synopsis   **nbmem**

Description   Nbmem is intended for displaying various internal structures used by the NetBIOS software. The structures may be displayed in short format (which shows the flags and state) or full format (which shows the whole structure). The nbmem output is routed to STDOUT. The intention of this command is to collect debugging information to pass on to Sun support. Its output should not be interpreted by the user.

Usage   After the nbmem command is entered at the console, the nbmem program is started and the following prompt is given:

```
nbmem>
```

The following options may be entered at the nbmem> prompt:

acs   Displays the application control structures.

control   Displays the control structures.

links	Displays the link structures.
names	Displays the name structures.
sessions	Displays the session structures.
lana	Displays the local LAN adapter structures.
rnd	Displays the remote name directory structures.
check start	Checks if NetBIOS started.
command	Prints NetBIOS command table.
page	Outputs one page at a time.
no page	Outputs all information.
all	Dumps all the structures.
full	Specifies full listings for output.
short	Specifies short listings for output.
justify	Specifies left or right justification for names.
!	Allows user to enter shell commands.
args	Print arguments to this command.
help	Lists available nbmem options.
?	Lists available nbmem options.
quit	Exits nbmem program.

Examples   To display the acs structures:

```
nbmem
nbmem>acs
```

To specify full listings:

```
nbmem
nbmem>full
```

Files   /opt/SUNWlznb/sbin/nbmem

Maintenance Commands nbns_adm(1M)

Name nbns_adm - NetBIOS over TCP/IP name cache management utility.

Synopsis **nbns_adm - [options]**

Description nbns_adm is used to monitor and manage the NetBIOS name cache.

Options: [-p [-u char]]Print cache contents

[-i] Get cache info

[-c] Clear local cache

[-m] Get maximum cache size

[-a -N name -A addr -P protocol [-f hexbyte] [-l hexbyte] [-t type] [-u char]]

[-d -N name [-f hexbyte] [-l hexbyte] [-u char]]

[-g -N name [-f hexbyte] [-l hexbyte] [-u char]]

[-v name]   Verify name length

[-s size]   Set maximum cache size

Maintenance Commands nbutil(1M)

Name nbutil - NetBIOS status and control utility.

Synopsis **nbutil [-v] -N start | stop**
nbutil [-vt] [-a num] -s name | - | *
nbutil [-vt] [-a num] -n name | - | *
nbutil [-v] [-a num] -c name | - | *
nbutil [-vt] -f name

Description nbutil is the NetBIOS status and control utility. It is used to start and stop NetBIOS, and to provide status information including transmission statistics, the contents of name and session tables, and name-to-address mapping.

The -s, -n and -c commands require a local or remote NetBIOS name. A dash (-) or an asterisk (*) may be used as a shorthand notation to obtain information about the local system. Quote or escape the * to avoid interpretation by the shell. Name arguments are space filled and left justified before issuing the appropriate ioctl call.

Options -v   Verbose. The -v option enables verbose output.

-t   Null Terminated Name

-N Start | Stop   Start/Stop NetBIOS. Either the start or stop keyword must be provided with the -N command.

-a num   Adapter number. The -a option specifies the ppa (physical point of attachment) of the LAN adapter associated with a particular instance of a protocol provider. The default ppa used by nbutil is 0. The -a option is required for the -s, -n and -c commands if NetBIOS is configured to use multiple adapters (e.g., NetBEUI over two or more Token-Ring adapters), multiple transport protocols (e.g., NetBEUI and RFC 1001), or if a nondefault ppa value is used in a single adapter configuration.

-s name | - | *   Statistics. The -s command displays statistics for the system associated with the NetBIOS name, or for the local system if - or * is specified. The -a option is required if the remote system is not on the NetBIOS sub-network associated with ppa 0. The following status information is obtained:

Burn-In Addressœ	Since the NetBIOS subnetwork type cannot be determined by nbutil, the address is displayed in three forms. The first and second form are hexadecimal, reverse and normal byte order, respectively. They represent the MAC address for NetBEUI subnetworks. (The reverse format is provided to conform to NetBEUI addressing conventions.) The third form, 137-xx.xx.xx.xx, is for RFC 1001, and represents the NetBIOS Name Service port (137), followed by the IP address in dotted decimal notation. .
SW Level Number	This value is always 0x22FF, regardless of the network adapter type.
Reporting Time	This represents the elapsed time since NetBIOS was started.
Number of Transmitted/ Received Packets	The total number of session and datagram packets send to/from the NetBIOS link level provider: ILD (DLPI) for NetBEUI; TCP/UDP for RFC 1001.
Local Station Went Busy	For RFC 1001, this represents the number of times STREAMS reported a flow control condition (!canput(q)).
Free Cmd Blk - Maximum - Configured - Current	Maximum is the architected maximum number of Command Block structures the current release is capable of supporting. Configured is the maximum number of command blocks the system currently has configured. For the local system, this value is determined by the commands parameter in the NetBIOS space.c kernel configuration file. Current is the number of free command blocks currently available.

Pending Sessions - Maximum - Configured - Current	Maximum is the architected maximum number of sessions the current release is capable of supporting. Configured is the maximum number of sessions the system currently has configured. For the local system, this value is determined by the sessions parameter in the NetBIOS space.c kernel configuration file. Current is the number of sessions currently established.
Datagram Packet Size	The maximum datagram packet size that can be transmitted or received.
Session Data Packet Size	The maximum session packet size that can be transmitted or received. This value is determined by the NetBIOS link level provider (ILD or TCP).

-n name | - | *   Names. The -n command displays the following information from the NetBIOS name table:

Num	The corresponding table slot number for the name.
Name	The 16 character NetBIOS name. Non-printable characters are displayed as a period.
Type	The NetBIOS name type - group or unique.
Status	The NetBIOS name status, which can have the following values: Registered, Registering, Deregistered or Duplicate.

-c localname | - | * Connections. The -c command obtains the status of all sessions (connections) for a specific local name or all sessions for all local names. The session status for all local names is returned if - or * is specified for the localname parameter. The following information is obtained:

LSN	The local session number.
State	The local session state, which can have the following values: Listening, Calling, Active, Hanging Up, Closed, Aborted.
Local/Remote Name	The NetBIOS names associated with the session.
Outstanding xmits	The number of outstanding TLI send commands (t_snd).
Outstanding rcvs	The number of outstanding TLI receive commands (t_rcv).

-f Name   Find Name. The -f command performs the NetBIOS Find
                   Name function, which obtains the network address of the system or
                   systems that have name registered, and the name type (unique or
                   group).

Examples   To obtain the name table using a specific name:

```
$ nbutil -n nbtest-srv
```

Num	Name	Type	Status
1	DOPEY.SERVE	Unique	Registered
2	DOPEY.SERVE	Unique	Registered
3	LANGROUP	Group	Registered
4	nbtest-srv	Unique	Registered

Files   /opt/SUNWlznb/sbin/nbutil

See also   IBM Token Ring Network Technical Reference, Release 2.0 RFC 1001, RFC 1002

User Commands   net(1)

Name   **net** - used to perform administrative tasks at the PC NetLink Server console.
                  The following net commands can be used to administer the PC NetLink Server:

net access	**net accounts**	**net admin**
net auditing	**net browser**	**net computer**
net config	**net config**	**net continue server**
net device	**net file**	**et group**
net help	**net helpmsg**	**net localgroup**
net logoff	**net logon**	**net password**
net pause	**net perms**	**net print**
net session	**net share**	**net sid**
net start	**net statistics**	**net status**
net stop	**net time**	**net trust**
net user	**net version**	**net view**

Synopsis   **net**
                  net help
                  net help [command]
                  net [command] /help
                  net command /?
                  net help [command] /options

Description   Although the net command can be used to administer many aspects of the PC NetLink Server, the programs available in Windows NT Server Tools serve as the primary administrative interface. When you administer a server while you are working at the console, that server is called the local server. If you are administering a server from the command prompt of another server, the server being administered is called the remote server. Some network users may be designated as account operators, print operators, or server operators. These users have limited administrative or operator privileges that enable them to perform specific tasks. These privileges are sufficient to use the net command to administer a local server at the console.

However, if you intend to use the net admin command to administer a remote PC NetLink Server, you must be logged on to the PC NetLink Server as an Administrator with full administrative privilege. If you have different operators responsible for parts of your network and you do not want to assign administer most of the aspects of the remote server.

The net help command provides on-line information for all of the net commands that you can enter at the server command prompt. It provides command parameters, syntax, details about a command, and examples of the commands in use.

Examples   net   Names all of the available net commands.

net help
net help help   Provides a description, syntax, and options for the net help command.

net help names   Defines all of the naming conventions used in the syntax of the net command.

net help syntax   Defines all of the conventions used in the syntax of the net command.

net help *command*Provides the description, syntax, and options for the net command you enter.

net *command* /? Provides syntax only for the net command you enter.

net help *command* /options*Provides detailed description of the options for the net command you enter.

Note: Individual net commands are described later in this appendix.

Maintenance Commands netevent(1m)

Name   netevent - sends an administrative or user alert to other computers.

Synopsis   netevent [-h | -?]
netevent -e admin -s *<service>* -t *<text>*
netevent -e user -s *<service>* -r *<recipient>* -u *<username>* -t *<text>*

Description   The netevent command is used to generate alert events. The types of alerts generated are an administrative alert, in which case, the alert goes to all registered names, or a user alert where the recipients user and machine name are specified.

Options   -s <service>   Is the server or person sending the alert.

-r <recipient>   Is the machine name of the recipient.

-u <username>   Is the username of the recipient.

-t <text>   Is the text of the message to be sent of length no greater than 148 characters.

Examples   To get help on the netevent command, type the following command at the UNIX system prompt:
```
netevent [ -h | -? ]
```

To raise an administrative alert, type the following command at the UNIX system prompt:
```
netevent -e admin -s <service> -t <text>
```

To raise a user alert, type the following command at the UNIX system prompt:
```
netevent -e user -s <service> -r <recipient> -u <user-name>
-t <text>
```

Note   If any argument is longer than one word, it must be enclosed in quotes.

Maintenance Commands passwd2sam(1M)

Name   passwd2sam - add or delete Solaris user accounts in the PC NetLink Server.

Synopsis   passwd2sam -l logon -p password [-h] [-i file] [-m connect]
[-n local path] [-o file] [-s logon script] [-u user
profile] [-y password]
passwd2sam -l logon -p password -r file [-h]
passwd2sam -l logon -p password -f [-h]

Description   The passwd2sam user account management utility enumerates user accounts stored in a Solaris name service (FILES, NIS, NIS+) into the PC NetLink Server Security Accounts Manager (SAM) database. All input files to passwd2sam must be formatted as /etc/passwd entries. See passwd(4) for details.

passwd2sam bridges Solaris name services and Windows NT Domain services. The bridge can be established only if you log on to the Windows NT Domain as Administrator and run passwd2sam as superuser. PC NetLink Server software must be up and running for passwd2sam to execute. passwd2sam supports three modes of operation:

1. Add Solaris user accounts into the PC NetLink Server Security Accounts Manager database (default).

2. Delete Solaris user accounts from the PC NetLink Server Security Accounts Manager database (see the -r option).

3. Find and disable Windows NT Domain user accounts added by passwd2sam, that subsequently have been deleted from a Solaris name service (see the -f option).

Mode 1, adding Solaris user accounts into the PC NetLink Server Security Accounts Manager database, can be performed using two methods. The default method is to enumerate nonprivileged user accounts in the running Solaris name service (FILES, NIS, NIS+), and to add each user account into the PC NetLink Server Security Accounts Manager database.

Another, more selective, method of adding Solaris user accounts to the PC NetLink Server Security Accounts Manager database is to use an input file formatted in the same way as /etc/passwd passwd(4).

Options for the passwd2sam utility support the User Properties of Windows NT Server's User Manager for Domains administration interface.

Mode 2, deleting Solaris user accounts from the PC NetLink Server Security Accounts Manager database, involves creating an input file of user accounts formatted in the same way as /etc/passwd passwd(4), and inputting this input file to passwd2sam using the -r option.

Mode 3 is used to find and disable Windows NT Domain user accounts that were added by the passwd2sam user account management utility, and later deleted from the Solaris name service. Using the passwd2sam utility in this mode produces an output file called /var/opt/lanman/dirsync/passwd2sam.disabled. This output file can be used as an input file to passwd2sam's delete operation (mode 2). This mode disables PC NetLink Server user accounts but does not delete them.

By default, passwd2sam produces randomly generated alphanumeric passwords for each user account and writes them to the transaction log /var/opt/lanman/dirsync/passwd2sam.log. The -y password option overrides this default behavior, allowing an administrator to assign a specific password to all user accounts, or no password at all.

All transactions, errors, and datafiles (except user-specified output files) are written to /var/opt/lanman/dirsync and prefixed with passwd2sam.

Options **-f**   Runs `passwd2sam` in mode 3, finding and disabling SunLink Server user accounts that were added by `passwd2sam` but subsequently deleted from the Solaris name service. Using this option disables PC NetLink Server user accounts but does not delete them. This option produces an output file called `/var/opt/lanman/dirsync/passwd2sam.disabled`, which is formatted the same way as `/etc/passwd passwd(4)`. The output file contains a list of disabled PC NetLink Server user accounts to delete. You cannot use this option in conjunction with the -m, -n, -o, -r, -s, -u, or -y options.

       -h   Displays a `passwd2sam` usage message.

       -i file Runs `passwd2sam` in mode 1, adding user accounts specified by an input file to the PC NetLink Server Security Accounts Manager database. Using this option overrides the default behavior of enumerating all user accounts from the running Solaris name service and adding each user account to the PC NetLink Server Security Accounts Manager database. You cannot use this option with the -r option.

       -l logon   Specifies a PC NetLink Server Administrator logon, and is required for all operations.

       -m connect   Creates a global PC NetLink Server home directory for each user account `passwd2sam` adds. The connect argument is a global home Directory path, which is a Universal fixed by a drive letter and colon. The drive letter and colon must be specified (for instance, H:). The UNC path can be a local or remote LAN Manager path to an existing network shared directory. Each user's logon name is automatically appended to the end of the Home Directory Connect path if not specified. Alternatively, using the %USERNAME% wildcard appends each user's logon name to the end of the UNC path. This option applies to all accounts in the add operation. You cannot use this option in conjunction with the -n option.
NOTE: When specifying UNC paths, you must substitute two backslashes for each backslash, to support Solaris command line shells (for instance, `-m H:\\\\SERVER\\USERS\\%USERNAME%`).

       -n local_path   Specifies a user's local home directory on the Windows workstation where the user logs on. This local directory path must be prefixed by a drive letter and colon (for instance, `-n C:\\USERS\\%USERNAME%`). Each user's logon name is automatically appended to the end of the local directory if not specified. Alternatively, using the %USERNAME% wildcard appends each user's logon name to the end of the UNC path. This add invocation parameter applies to all accounts in the add operation. You cannot use this invocation parameter in conjunction with the -m invocation parameter.

-o file Produces a user-specified output file that is formatted the same as `/etc/passwd`. This file contains a list of all Solaris user accounts added into the PC NetLink Server Security Accounts Manager database. This file can be used later to remove Solaris accounts from the PC NetLink Server Security Accounts Manager database. You cannot use this option in conjunction with the -f or -r options.

-p password   Specifies a PC NetLink Server Administrator password, and is required for all operations.

-r file Runs the passwd2sam utility in mode 2, enumerating an input file and removing each user account specified from the PC NetLink Server Security Accounts Manager database. This option deletes user accounts but does not delete users' home directories or files. You cannot use this option in conjunction with the -f or -i options.

-s logon_script   Sets up a network logon script that runs each time a user successfully logs on to PC NetLink Server software. The `logon_script` argument is a file name (for instance, `-s NETLOGON.CMD`) that contains commands to execute upon successful user logon. A network logon script is defined using relative pathing and pertains only to the authenticating PC NetLink Server. When a user logs on, the authenticating PC NetLink Server computer finds the specified logon script by following the PC NetLink Server logon script path `\\SERVER\NETLOGON`. This option applies to all accounts added by the `passwd2sam` user account management utility. You cannot use this option in conjunction with the -f or -r options.

-u user_profile   Specifies the User Profile Path, which is a Universal Naming Convention (UNC) path, that points to a roaming or mandatory user profile. The UNC path can be a local or remote LAN Manager path. Each user's logon name is automatically appended to the end of the User path if not specified. Alternatively, use the `%USERNAME%` wildcard to append each user's logon name to the end of the UNC path (for instance, `-u \\\\SERVER\\PROFILES\\%USERNAME%`). This option applies to all accounts added by the `passwd2sam` user account management utility, and cannot be used in conjunction with the -f or -r options.

-y password   Overrides the default randomly generated alphanumeric password and assigns a specified password to all PC NetLink Server accounts added by the `passwd2sam` user account management utility. Specifying NULL (for instance, -y NULL) assigns no password to user accounts. Specifying a password assigns the specified password to all user accounts added by `passwd2sam`. Password lengths are managed from Windows NT Server's User Manager for Domains administration interface under the Policies, Account panel. Assigning NULL passwords will only be successful if the radio button Permit Blank Password is enabled. All user account passwords are written to the `passwd2sam` transaction log `/var/opt/lanman/dirsync/passwd2sam.log`. These passwords are readable only by the superuser.

PC NetLink Server users will be prompted to change their password on the first successful PC NetLink Server logon. This option applies to all accounts added by the `passwd2sam` user account management utility. You cannot use this option in conjunction with the -f or -r options.

Examples   The examples following illustrate `passwd2sam`'s three modes of operation.

```
# passwd2sam -l Administrator -p password -m
H:\\\\SERVER\\USERS\\%USERNAME% -s NETLOGON.CMD
```

This example adds all Solaris user accounts found in the running Solaris name service (for instance, FILES, NIS, NISPLUS) into the PC NetLink Server Security Accounts Manager database. The -m invocation parameter creates a global home directory for each user at the specified UNC path. User account passwords are randomly generated characters. In addition, each PC NetLink Server user account will execute the network logon script specified by the -s invocation parameter upon successful logon.

```
# passwd2sam -l Administrator -p password -r passwd2sam.disabled
```

This example deletes all PC NetLink Server user accounts specified in the input file `passwd2sam.disabled`. This input file must be formatted in the same way as `/etc/passwd`. See `passwd(4)` for details.

```
passwd2sam -l Administrator -p password -f
```

This example disables PC NetLink Server user accounts that cannot be found in the running Solaris name service. This example also produces an output file `/var/opt/lanman/dirsync/passwd2sam.disabled`, which contains a list of the disabled PC NetLink Server user accounts. Directories and files owned by a disabled PC NetLink Server account are not deleted.

Files   `/var/opt/lanman/dirsync/passwd2sam.log`
                  `passwd2sam` transaction log.
          `/var/opt/lanman/dirsync/passwd2sam.error`
                  `passwd2sam` error log.
          `/var/opt/lanman/dirsync/passwd2sam.disabled`
                  List of disabled PC NetLink Server user accounts.

See also   `passwd(4)`,   `mapuname(1)`,   `sam2passwd(1M)`,
          `nisaddent(1M)`, `ypcat(1)`, `nsswitch.conf(4)`

Notes   When using `passwd2sam` arguments containing backslashes, you must substitute two backslashes for each backslash, to support Solaris command line shells.

Name   **regcheck** - enumerates all of the keys in the Registry, dumps the contents of the Registry, checks and repairs the Registry.

Synopsis   **regcheck -E | -D | -C | -R [-L]**

Description   The regcheck command is used to enumerate all of the keys in the Registry. It can be used also to dump the entire Registry for diagnostic purposes. If the internal format of the Registry becomes corrupt, it can be repaired.

Options   -C   Checks the Registry file.

        -D   Dumps the entire Registry in detail.

        -E   Enumerates the full paths of all Registry keys.

        -R   Checks and repairs the Registry file.

        -L   Locks the Registry while performing a specified action.

Notes   This command must be run as root. The check (-C) and repair (-R) options only check and repair the internal format of the Registry. No checking is performed on the validity of any of the data stored in the Registry.

The dump (-D) option outputs an exceptionally large amount of data, including information about the internal format of the Registry. This output is intended for diagnostic operations performed by product support personnel who have access to source code for the Registry. It is not intended for use by system administrators.

By default, the check (-C), dump (-D), and enumerate (-E) options do not lock the Registry. The advantage of this is that these commands can be executed without blocking PC NetLink Server if it is running. The disadvantage of this is that if PC NetLink Server modifies the Registry while a command with one of these options is being executed, the Registry may appear to be inconsistent. If the locking (-L) option is specified, commands containing the check, repair, and enumerate options are guaranteed to see a consistent snapshot of the Registry. However, PC NetLink Server will not be able to access the Registry while a command with the locking option is being executed. The repair (-R) option performs locking by default and thus is unaffected by the locking (-L) option.

Name   **regconfig** - sets or queries Registry key information.

Synopsis   **regconfig [-v] keyname**
regconfig [-b | -s | -v] keyname valuename
regconfig keyname valuename type value
regconfig keyname valuename REG_MULTI_SZ string1 [string2 ...]

Description   This command is used to query or set the value and/or the type of data item stored as a value entry in a key, or to obtain detailed information about a Registry key.

Options   -b   Displays a data item in binary format.

-s   Displays a data item in string format.

-v   Displays key information in detail.

<keyname>   Identifies the key by name on the local machine.

<valuename>   The name of the data item being stored as a value entry.

<valuetype>   Identifies the type of value. Valid options are REG_SZ (string), REG_DWORD (32-bit numeric value), REG_EXPAND_SZ (string), and REG_MULTI_SZ (multiple strings) and must be specified in uppercase.

<value>   The value to be assigned to the data item stored as a value entry. Do not set value entries of type REG_BINARY with this command.

Examples   To obtain information about a key, type the following command:
```
regconfig -v <keyname>
```

To display the value of a data item stored as a value entry in a key, type the following command:
```
regconfig [-b | -s | -v] <keyname> <valuename>
```

To store a data item as a value entry in a key, type the following command:
```
regconfig <keyname> <valuename> <valuetype> <value>
```

To display information about the System/CurrentControlSet/Services/Replicator/Parameters key, type the following command:
```
regconfig System/CurrentControlSet/Services/Replicator
/Parameters
```

Notes   Some values changed by this command will not take effect immediately. PC NetLink Server should be restarted after changing a value with this command. For lookup purposes, the keynames are case-insensitive.

Maintenance Commands   regload(1m)

Name　regload - initializes a Registry and, if necessary, creates it.

Synopsis　regload

Description　A number of Registry initialization and data files are installed in
`/var/opt/lanman/regfiles`. The regload command loads data from these
Registry initialization files and other data into the Registry. If a Registry store
does not exist, a Registry with default keys is created.

Note　The server must be stopped before running this command. The command must
be run as root.

Maintenance Commands   rmacl(1m)

Name　rmacl - Delete an entry/entries from Access Control List.

Synopsis　rmacl [objectname ... | -]

Description　The `rmacl` command deletes access control information associated with the
specified object(s). This will automatically do what acladm -P does implicitly.

Example　At a Solaris console, to delete an ACL entry for object `/home/foo/bar`, type
the following:

```
rmacl /home/foo/bar
```


Maintenance Commands   sam2passwd(1M)

Name　sam2passwd - create a passwd file containing PC NetLink Server user accounts
to add into a Solaris name service.

Synopsis　sam2passwd [-g gid] [-h] -l logon -p password [-s shell] [-t directory_path] [-
u uid] [-y password]
sam2passwd [-f] [-h] [-i file] -l logon -p password

Description　The `sam2passwd` import utility enumerates PC NetLink Server user accounts
and writes out a passwd(4) formatted file. This file contains PC NetLink Server
user accounts to add into a Solaris name service (FILES, NIS, NIS+).

The `sam2passwd` import utility is a PC NetLink Server application that
bridges Windows NT Domain services with Solaris name services (FILES, NIS,
NIS+). The bridge can be established only if you log on to the Windows NT
Domain as Administrator and run `sam2passwd` as superuser. PC NetLink
Server software must be up and running for `sam2passwd` to execute.

sam2passwd supports two modes of operation:

1. Creates a passwd(4) formatted output file containing nonprivileged PC NetLink Server user accounts to add into a Solaris name service (FILES, NIS, NIS+).

2.Finds deleted PC NetLink Server user accounts, created using sam2passwd, that have subsequently been deleted from PC NetLink Server but still exist in a Solaris name service (FILES, NIS, NIS+).

Mode 1, the default mode, exports all nonprivileged PC NetLink Server user accounts to a passwd(4) formatted output file called
/var/opt/lanman/dirsync/sam2passwd.passwd.

The sam2passwd utility checks each PC NetLink Server account name against the running Solaris name service (FILES, NIS, NIS+) passwd map. If the account name does not exist in the passwd map, it is written to the output file formatted as a passwd(4) entry. If the account name exists, or if it is a privileged account, it is skipped and logged as such.

Mode 1 produces two output files. The first output file
/var/opt/lanman/dirsync/sam2passwd.passwd is an passwd(4) formatted output file containing a list of PC NetLink Server user accounts to add into a Solaris name service. The second output file
/var/opt/lanman/dirsync/sam2passwd.mapunames is a Bourne shell script. The Bourne shell script is optional functionality that allows you to map PC NetLink Server user IDs to Solaris user IDs, after the PC NetLink Server user accounts have been entered into a Solaris name service (FILES, NIS, NIS+).

By default, sam2passwd produces randomly generated eight-character alphanumeric passwords for each user account and writes them to the transaction log /var/opt/lanman/dirsync/sam2passwd.log. The -y password option overrides the default behavior allowing an administrator to assign a specific password to all user accounts, or no password at all.

The PC NetLink Server HKLEY_LOCAL_MACHINE registry contains default values for Solaris user's /etc/passwd entry. These default registry key value pairs are located in
/SYSTEM/CurrentControlSet/Services/AdvancedServer/
UserServiceParameters
and
/SYSTEM/CurrentControlSet/Services/LanmanServer/Parameters,
and contain four fields in an /etc/passwd entry. An administrator can modify the default registry values or override them with sam2passwd invocation parameters.

The following are PC NetLink Server key/value registry pairs used to build each Solaris user's passwd entry.

Registry Key	Default Value	/etc/passwd **Field**
Exclude	0-100	pw_uid
UserComment	PC NetLink Server user	pw_gecos
userpath	c:\export\lanman	pw_dir
NewUserShell	/bin/false	pw_shell

Mode 2 is used to find deleted PC NetLink Server user accounts, created using sam2passwd, that have subsequently been deleted from PC NetLink Server but still exist in a Solaris name service (FILES, NIS, NIS+). Using this mode produces an passwd(4) formatted output file called /var/opt/lanman/dirsync/sam2passwd.deleted that contains a list of deleted PC NetLink Server user accounts still active in a Solaris name service. The Solaris name service administrator should delete or make inactive each Solaris user account contained in the list.

All transactions, errors, and data files are written to /var/opt/lanman/dirsync and prefixed with sam2passwd.

Options -f Accounts created using sam2passwd, that are still active in a Solaris name service. This option produces an output file called /var/opt/lanman/dirsync/sam2passwd.deleted, formatted as described in passwd(4). The output file contains a list of deleted PC NetLink Server user accounts to delete from a Solaris name service. This option can be used with the -i file argument specified in the following paragraphs. You cannot use this option in conjunction with the -s, -t, -u, or -y options.

-i file Used with the -f option, enumerates all Solaris user accounts specified in the input file against all PC NetLink Server user accounts, looking for deleted PC NetLink Server user accounts. You cannot use this option in conjunction with the -s, -t, -u, or -y options.

-g gid Overrides the PC NetLink Server default group ID of 10 (for instance, staff::10:) allowing a system administrator to specify a group ID (for instance, -g 99) for all sam2passwd created Solaris user accounts. This option applies to all Solaris user accounts created using sam2passwd. You cannot use this option in conjunction with the -f or -i options. See group(4) for details.

-h Displays a sam2passwd usage message.

-l logon Specifies a PC NetLink Server logon to the Administrator account, and is required for all operations.

-p password   Specifies a PC NetLink Server Administrator account
               password, and is required for all operations.

-s shell   Overrides the PC NetLink Server default shell value of
               /bin/false stored in the PC NetLink Server registry. This option
               allows a system administrator to specify a shell (for example,
               -s /bin/sh) for all Solaris user accounts created by sam2passwd.
               This option applies to all Solaris user accounts created by sam2passwd.
               You cannot use this option in conjunction with the -f or -i options.

-t directory_path Overrides the PC NetLink Server default directory path of
               c:\export\lanman in the PC NetLink Server registry, allowing a
               system administrator to specify a home directory path (for instance,
               -t /export/home). This option applies to all Solaris user accounts
               created by sam2passwd. You cannot use this option in conjunction with
               the -f or -i options.

-u uid Overrides the PC NetLink Server default starting user ID. By default,
               sam2passwd searches for the first unused user ID and starts adding
               Solaris user accounts at that UID, incrementing by one for each Solaris
               user account it creates. The PC NetLink Server registry contains an
               Exclude parameter where user ID ranges (for example, 0–100) can be
               excluded from the search. User ID boundaries for sam2passwd have a
               floor of 100 and a ceiling of LONG_MAX, which are the lower and
               upper user ID boundaries of Solaris. The -u invocation parameter
               overrides the sam2passwd default starting user ID, allowing a system
               administrator to specify a starting user ID (for instance, -u 1000), and
               incrementing by one for each Solaris user account sam2passwd creates.
               You cannot use this option in conjunction with the -f or -i options.

-y password   Overrides the default randomly generated eight-character
               alphanumeric password and assigns a specified password to all Solaris
               user accounts created using sam2passwd. Specifying NULL (for
               instance, -y NULL) assigns no password to user accounts. Specifying a
               password assigns the specified password to all Solaris user accounts
               created using sam2passwd. All Solaris user account passwords are
               written to the sam2passwd transaction log
               /var/opt/lanman/dirsync/sam2passwd.log. These passwords are
               readable only by the superuser. You cannot use this option in
               conjunction with the -f or -i options.

Examples The examples below illustrate `sam2passwd`'s two modes of operation.

```
# sam2passwd -l Administrator -p password -u 1000 -t
/export/home -s /bin/sh
```

This example creates two output files,
> /var/opt/lanman/dirsync/sam2passwd.passwd

and
> /var/opt/lanman/dirsync/sam2passwd.mapunames.

The `sam2passwd.passwd` output file contains the PC NetLink Server user accounts to add into a Solaris name service. The `sam2passwd.mapunames` output file is an optional Bourne shell script that maps PC NetLink Server user account IDs to Solaris user account IDs once the PC NetLink Server user accounts have been added into a Solaris name service.

Solaris user account IDs start at 1000 and increment by one for each user account created using `sam2passwd`. Each user's home directory is located at /export/home and each user will login to Solaris with a Bourne shell.

```
# sam2passwd -l Administrator -p password -f -i
sam2passwd.passwd
```

This example produces a passwd(4) formatted output file called /var/opt/lanman/dirsync/sam2passwd.deleted that contains deleted PC NetLink Server user accounts, that were earlier created by `sam2passwd`, and have subsequently been deleted from PC NetLink Server and still exist in the original output file `sam2passwd.passwd`. (The assumption is that user accounts in `sam2passwd.passwd` have been entered into a Solaris name service.) The output file named `sam2passwd.deleted` contains a list of PC NetLink Server user accounts to delete from a Solaris name service.

Files /var/opt/lanman/dirsync/sam2passwd.log
> `sam2passwd` transaction log.

/var/opt/lanman/dirsync/sam2passwd.errors
> `sam2passwd` error log.

/var/opt/lanman/dirsync/sam2passwd.deleted
> Deleted PC NetLink Server user accounts active in Solaris.

/var/opt/lanman/dirsync/sam2passwd.passwd
> PC NetLink Server user accounts to be added into a Solaris name service.

/var/opt/lanman/dirsync/sam2passwd.mapunames
> Bourne shell script mapping PC NetLink Server user account IDs to Solaris user account IDs.

See also passwd(4), group(4), mapuname(1), passwd2sam(1M), nisaddent(1M), ypcat(1), nsswitch.conf(4)

Maintenance Commands　　　　samcheck(1m)

Name　samcheck - checks, repairs, or dumps the PC NetLink Server account database.

Synopsis　**samcheck -s | -r [-v]**
　　　　samcheck -c | -a | -b | -l [-v] [-F filename]

Options　-s　　Checks the current account database.

　　　　　-r　　Checks and repairs the current account database.

　　　　　-v　　Verbose.

　　　　　-c　　Dumps the change log.

　　　　　-a　　Dumps the account file.

　　　　　-b　　Dumps the builtin file.

　　　　　-l　　Dumps the lsa file.

　　　　　-F　　Uses the filename specified rather than the default file.

Examples　To dump the PC NetLink Server account file, type the following command at the UNIX system console:
```
samcheck -a
```

To dump the PC NetLink Server account file including its internal control structures, type the following command at the UNIX system console:
```
samcheck -a -v
```

To dump a copy of the PC NetLink Server account file found in /tmp/pier3_dom, type the following command at the UNIX system console:
```
samcheck -a -F /tmp/pier3_dom
```

Notes　You must stop the server if you use the -s or -r options. If the account database on a backup domain controller is reported as corrupt, use the joindomain command to reinitialize it.

Maintenance Commands　　setdomainname(1m)

Name　setdomainname - changes the name of a PC NetLink Server domain.

Synopsis　**setdomainname [-n new-domain-name [-s]]**

Description　The setdomainname command is used to change the name of a PC NetLink Server domain. It is an interactive command but also accepts command line arguments. If an error occurs during processing or if you interrupt this command, it will restore the original domain name. You should run this command on the primary domain controller first, and then on any backup domain controllers. This command must be run on every server within a domain. Otherwise, domain-wide services will not work correctly. You must be logged in as root to run this command.

Options   -n new-domain-Name

Represents the new name of the domain.

-s   Prevents the server from starting automatically.

Example   If a server is a backup domain controller named `sales_bdc` in the domain sales, and you want to rename it to localsales, you can use the `setdomainname` command. You either can run the `setdomainname` command and respond to individual prompts, or you can type the following command:

```
setdomainname -n localsales -s
```

Maintenance Commands   setservername(1m)

Name   setservername - changes the name of a PC NetLink Server.

Synopsis   setservername [-n *newname* -p *password* -a *administrator* [-d *pdc_name*] [-s]]

Description   The `setservername` command is used to change the name of a PC NetLink Server. It is an interactive command but also accepts command line arguments. If an error occurs during processing or if you interrupt this command, it will restore the original server name. If you are changing the name of a backup domain controller, you need to supply the name of the primary domain controller, which must be running and connected to the network. You also will be prompted for the name of an existing administrative account and password in the domain. This permits the command to connect to the primary domain controller, to configure the new server name into the domain and to remove the old server name from the domain. You must be logged in as root to run this command.

Options   -n   Represents the new server name.

-p   Is the password for the administrative account.

-a   Is the name of the administrative account.

-d pdc_Name   Is (for a backup domain controller) the name of the primary domain controller in the domain.

-s   Prevents the server from starting automatically.

Example   If a server is a backup domain controller named `sales_bdc` in the domain sales, and you want to rename it to `sales2`, you can use the `setservername` command. You either can run the `setservername` command and respond to individual prompts, or you can type the following command:

```
setservername -n sales2 -p pass1 -a admin1 -d sales1 -s
```

User Commands   sjistoeuc(1)

Name   sjistoeuc - converts the encoding of characters from Shift- JIS (S-JIS) encoding to Extended UNIX Code (EUC) encoding.

Synopsis   **sjistoeuc [-ader] [file]**

Options   -a   If an input character has an invalid S-JIS encoding, the sjistoeuc command aborts.

-e   If an input character has an invalid S-JIS encoding, conversion to EUC cannot be performed for this character. However, the sjistoeuc command continues its conversion process for all subsequent characters.

-d   All conversions from S-JIS to EUC are performed within the input file.

-r   Converts a DOS file to UNIX system file format by converting all carriage returns followed by newline to newline. Additionally, the control-Z end of file marker is deleted.

See also   `euctosjis`

Examples   To convert all the S-JIS encoded characters files to EUC encoding in file-e, type the following command:

```
sjistoeuc file-s file-e
```

To convert all the S-JIS encoded characters in datafile to EUC encoding, type the following command:

```
sjistoeuc -d datafile
```

Maintenance Commands   srvconfig(1m)

Name   srvconfig - modifies the PC NetLink Server lanman.ini configuration file.

Synopsis   srvconfig [-v] -a section,keyword
srvconfig [-v] -d "section,keyword"
srvconfig [-v] -g "section,keyword"
srvconfig [-v] -i section,keyword
srvconfig [-v] -l section,keyword value
srvconfig [-v] -p
srvconfig [-v] -s "section,keyword=value" ["section,keyword=value" ...]

Description   The **srvconfig** command is used to display or modify the PC NetLink Server configuration file (lanman.ini). This command can be used interactively or it can be incorporated as part of a script. The PC NetLink Server does not need to be running to display or modify the lanman.ini configuration file.

Options   -a   Displays the maximum allowed value for the indicated keyword.

-d   Displays the default value for the indicated keyword.

-g   Displays the current value for the indicated keyword.

-i   Displays the minimum allowed value for the indicated keyword.

-l   Indicates whether value is valid for specified keyword. Returns 0 for valid value, -1 for invalid value. This option does not return output to the screen. Can be used in a shell script.

-p   Displays the default values for all possible lanman.ini file keywords.

-s   Changes the value for the indicated keyword(s).

-v   Turns on debugging for this command.

User Commands   ud(1)

Name   ud - converts text files between DOS, UNIX and Macintosh file formats.

Synopsis   ud [-d] [-u] [-m] [-z] *file*

Description   The ud command is useful if a file created in one operating system environment is to be used on a different operating system. This command is used primarily to convert files from DOS to UNIX format and vice-versa. Text files created on DOS usually have carriage return and newline characters at the end of the line, and may have control-Z character as the end of file character, while UNIX text files do not.

Options   -d   Converts the file to DOS format.

-u   Converts the file to UNIX format.

-m   Converts the file to Macintosh format.

-z   Ignores or does not emit the control-Z character at the end of the file.

Examples   To convert the DOS file foobar.txt to UNIX format, without preserving the DOS file, type the following command:

```
ud -d foobar.txt
```

To convert the DOS file foobar.txt to UNIX format, and to preserve the DOS file, type the following command:

```
ud -u foobar.txt > foobar
```

where *foobar* is the name of the file in UNIX format.

Maintenance Commands   winsadm(1m)

Name   **winsadm** - administers the Windows Internet Name Service (WINS) at the PC NetLink Server command prompt.

Synopsis   **winsadm** [-b] [-r] [-c] [-d]

Options   -b   Backs up the WINS database. The backup is placed in the default directory (/var/opt/lanman/wins) unless another one is specified in WINS Manager.

          -r   Restores the WINS database. The database is retrieved from the default backup directory (/var/opt/lanman/wins) unless another one is specified in WINS Manager. WINS must be stopped to use this command.

          -c   Compacts the WINS database. Periodic compacting of the WINS database is recommended to avoid unchecked database growth. WINS must be stopped in order to use this command.

          -d   Dumps the WINS database. Provides a convenient way of examining the WINS database. WINS must be stopped to use this command.

Note   You must be logged in as root to execute the winsadm command.

Maintenance Commands   winsconf(1M)

Name   winsconf - configure WINS servers.

Synopsis   winsconf [-v] [-f]
winsconf [-v] [-p prim_addr] [-t prim_timer] [-s sec_addr] [-T sec_timer]
[-x flag]
winsconf [-v] [-p prim_addr] [-t prim_timer] [-d 2] [-x yes/no]
winsconf [-v] [-s sec_addr] [-T sec_timer][-d 1] [-x yes/no]
winsconf [-v] [-d 1/2/3] [-x yes/no]

Description   winsconf is used for configuring WINS (primary, secondary and proxy) servers. When users call this utility from command line, it updates the file /var/opt/SUNWlznb/fnbwins.info based on options provided, and also passes this information to NetBIOS kernel. User can also give these configuration parameters interactively, through FMLI interface. winsconf takes timer input in terms of seconds. The timer input should be between 1 and 10.

Options   -v   View. This option displays the configuration details of primary, secondary and proxy servers.

    -f   Causes winsconf to configure WINS from the file /var/opt/SUNWlznb/fnbwins.info

    -p   Allows you to configure a particular node as primary name server.

    -t   Allows you to set timer associated with primary name server.

    -s   Allows you to configure a particular node as secondary name server.

    -T   Allows you to set timer associated with secondary name server.

    -x   Allows you to enable or disable the current node as proxy server by specifying yes or no as flag value.

    -d   Permits you to remove primary name server, secondary name server, or both by specifying 1, 2, or 3, respectively.

Defaults   If -t or/and -T options are not specified, it will use 3 as default timer value.

Examples   To configure primary server to 123.54.21.55 for 3 seconds you can use either of the following:
```
winsconf -p 123.54.21.55 -t 3
```

OR

```
winsconf -p 123.54.21.55
```

Files   /opt/SUNWlznb/sbin/winsconf
/var/opt/SUNWlznb/fnbwins.info

Net Command Help Files

The following documentation can be obtained by using the `net help` command. The documentation is duplicated here to act as a reference when a online PC NetLink server is not available.

NET Commands   NET ACCESS

Synopsis   NET ACCESS resource [/DELETE]
[/GRANT name:permission[...] | /CHANGE name:permission[...] |
/REVOKE name[...]]

Description   This command displays or modifies resource permissions on servers. Use this command only for displaying and modifying permissions on pipes and printer queues. Use `net perms` for managing permissions on all other types of resources.

Options   resource
    \PRINT (printer queue), or \PIPE (named pipe) for which permissions are to be manipulated.

name:permission[...]
    Name provides the existing username or groupname with one or more permissions. Do not use a delimiter when typing permissions (for example, type RWC). Separate multiple name:permission entries with a space. For a description of each permission, see .

name[...]   One or more usernames or groupnames. Separate multiple name entries with a space.

/DELETE   Removes all permissions for a resource.

/GRANT   Adds one or more user's or group's permissions to a resource. Separate multiple name:permission entries with a space.

/CHANGE   Changes one or more user's or group's permissions for a resource. Separate multiple name:permission entries with a space.

/REVOKE   Revokes one or more user's or group's permissions for a resource.

Comments   You must supply a resource name when using this command. Use the `net access` command to secure network resources by specifying who can use each resource and how. You can grant permissions to users and to groups.

When the server displays resource permissions, it designates groups with an asterisk (*).

If used on a print resource, the output of `net access \\print\\laser1` will look similar to the following:

Resource Permissions	Permissions
/print/laser1	
Administrators:CP	CREATOR OWNER:CP
Everyone:C	Print Operators:CP
Server Operators:CP	
Steve:(none)	

The following list shows the types of permissions that can be assigned for printers and pipes, and what each permission allows a user to do:

Code	Permission
R (Read)	User can read and copy files, run programs, and change from one subdirectory to another within the shared directory. User can also read the extended attributes of files.
W (Write)	User can write the contents and extended attributes of a file.
C (Create)	For DIRECTORIES and FILES a user can create files and subdirectories within a shared directory. After creating a file, a user with C permission (but without R and W permission) can read from or write to the file and its extended attributes only until closing it.
	For PRINTERS a user has "Print" permissions. Can submit print jobs.
D (Delete)	User can delete files and subdirectories within the shared directory but cannot delete the shared directory itself.
X (Execute)	User can run a file (but not read or copy it). X permission is not needed if R permission is assigned to the user for that directory or file. R permission includes all rights that X permission grants. DOS clients recognize X permission. For clients running DOS versions earlier than 5.0, files must have R permission for the clients to execute the files.
A (Change Attributes)	User can set the physical file flags of the file.

Code	Permission
P (Change Permissions)	For DIRECTORIES and FILES a user change permissions for the directory or file. For PRINTERS a user has "Full Control" permissions. Can administer print jobs. "P" permissions imply "C" permissions.
Y (Yes)	A user has RWCDA permissions. "Y" serves as an abbreviation for this set of permissions.
N (No)	A user has permissions of "(none)" and prevents the user from accessing the directory, printer, or file. Use this permission to exclude individual users from access to a directory or file, despite whatever permissions are assigned to the groups to which that user belongs. You can assign N permission only to individual users.

Notes   On PC NetLink Server, granting any of W, C, or A permissions results in granting of WCA combination of permissions to the resource. Also, if the resource has W permission on it, NET ACCESS will always show C and A permissions as well.

When assigning permissions information for a print or pipe resource (`\PRINT` or `\PIPE`), type the resource specification before the sharename (for example, `\\PRINT\\laser`). Then set `Y` (Yes), `N` (No), and `P` (Change Permissions) permissions for these non-disk resources. To give a print resource user `Y` (Yes) and `P` (Change Permissions) permissions, type `CP` as the permission string. To give non-disk resource users these permissions, type `RWCP` as the permission string.

When a server is installed, all resources are given default permissions. To modify permissions for a resource use the `/GRANT`, `/CHANGE`, `/DELETE`, and `/REVOKE` options.

Examples   At a UNIX system console, to grant `C` (Print) permissions for the group finance, `CP` (Full Control) permissions for the group `Print Operators`, and `N` (none) permission for the user "steve", to the "dot1" printer, type the following:
```
net access \\print\\dot1 /grant finance:c "print
operators":cp steve:n
```

To run the same command remotely (on server "market_asu"), type the following (replacing *"password"* with the password for "administrator":
```
net admin \\market_asu password /command net access\
c:/tmp/status /change jennyt:rw
```

See also   `net help`, `net perms`

Synopsis   NET ACCOUNTS [/FORCELOGOFF:{minutes | NO}]
                      [/MINPWLEN:length]
                      [/MAXPWAGE:{days | UNLIMITED}]
                      [/MINPWAGE:days]
                      [/SYNC]
                      [/UNIQUEPW:#]

Description   This command displays the role of servers in a domain and displays or modifies password and logon user requirements.

Options   /FORCELOGOFF:{minutes | NO}
         Sets the number of minutes to wait before ending a user's session with the server when the user account or valid logon time expires. The NO value prevents forced logoff. The default is NO.

/MINPWLEN:length
         Sets the minimum number of characters for a user account password. The range is 0 through 14; the default is 0.

/MAXPWAGE:{days | UNLIMITED}
         Sets the maximum number of days that a user account's password is valid. A value of `unlimited` sets no maximum time. The /MAXPWAGE option must be greater than /MINPWAGE. The range is 1 through 24855; the default is 42 days. For example, you set the maximum password age to 10 on August 20. Any user who had not changed his or her password since August 10 would be allowed to log on once and would receive a message that the password had expired. This user would have to change the password during this session in order to log on again. Users who had changed their passwords on August 19 would have until August 29, when their passwords would expire.

/MINPWAGE:days
         Sets the minimum number of days before a user can change a new password. A value of 0 sets no minimum time. The range is 0 through 24855; the default is 0 days.

/SYNC   When used on the primary domain controller, causes all backup controllers to synchronize with the primary. When used on a backup controller, causes only that controller to synchronize with the primary.

/UNIQUEPW:#
         Requires that a user's passwords be unique through number password changes. The range is 0 through 8; the default is 5 password changes. Password restrictions apply to the "net password" command. You can always change a password with the net user command.

Comments   Type net accounts to display the current settings for password and logon limitations and the role of the server. If the role of the server is backup, the name of the primary domain controller is displayed.

The net accounts command options also set the logon and password requirements for user accounts on a server. This information is stored in the server's datafiles, along with user accounts and resource permissions.

When the /FORCELOGOFF:minutes option is specified, the server sends a warning two minutes before it forces the user off the network. If any files are open, the server warns the user. If minutes is less than two, the server warns the user to log off from the network immediately.

Examples   At a UNIX system console, to display the current settings for forced logoff, the password requirements, and the server role, type the following:

```
net accounts
```

To set a minimum of seven characters for user account passwords, type the following:

```
net accounts /minpwlen:7
```

To specify that no password can be used more than every fifth time a password is changed, type the following:

```
net accounts /uniquepw:5
```

To prevent users from changing passwords more often than every seven days, and to force all users to change passwords every 30 days, type the following:

```
net accounts /minpwage:7 /maxpwage:30
```

To run the same command remotely (on server "market_asu"), type the following (replacing "password" with the password for "administrator":

```
net admin \\market_asu password /command net accounts
/minpwage:7 /maxpwage:30
```

See also   net help, net password

Synopsis   NET ADMIN \\servername [password | *] /COMMAND [command]

Description   This command runs an PC NetLink Server command or starts a command processor on a remote server.

Options   servername   Specifies a remote server.

password   The administrator's password for the specified server.

*   Produces a prompt for the password. The password will not be displayed when you type it. In the UNIX operating system, the asterisk (*) is a special character and must be preceded by a backslash (\ ).

command   A single network command.

/COMMAND   Runs a single non-interactive command, or starts a network command shell on a remote server.

Comments   To start a secondary command processor on a remote server, press return immediately following /COMMAND. Then, to return to the local server, type exit and press return.

When executing a command on a remote server, the command processor prompts for commands, executes them, and returns output to the local screen. If you do not include a full pathname for a command, the local server uses the \SYSTEM\CurrentControlSet\Services\AdvancedServer\NetAdmin Parameters\NetAdminPath
value in the Registry.

When you issue a net admin command to a server from a client, you must include all of the options on the command line since you will not be able to respond to the prompts that you would have received if you were working at the server. If the command is one that would normally prompt you for verification, you must include the /Y option. For example:
     net admin \\headqtrs /c net share printq1 /PRINT /y
will create and share a printer queue named printq1 on a server named headqtrs, but
     net admin \\headqtrs /c net share printq1 /PRINT
will fail.

Examples   To run the net group command remotely (on server market_asu), type the following (replacing "password" with the password for "administrator")
     net admin \\market_asu *password* /command net group

See also   net help

NET Commands

NET AUDITING

Synopsis NET AUDITING resource [/ADD name:options[...] |
/CHANGE name:options[...] | /DELETE name[...]]

Description This command displays and modifies the auditing settings of a resource.

Options resource Name of the resource on which the auditing is to be set or modified. To specify the remote resource name, prefix it with the name of the server on which this resource resides (for example, to access a local server's file FILE1 residing on the share SHARE1, you specify the resource name as \\SHARE1\\FILE1.

To access the resource with the same path on the remote server named SERVER1, the resource name should be specified as follows:
\\\\SERVER1\\SHARE1\\FILE1.

To specify the name of the root directory of the share (as opposite to the share itself), append "\\" to the share path, for example:
\\\\SERVER1\\SHARE1\\
will refer to the root directory of SHARE1 on SERVER1.

name:options[...]
Name provides the existing username or groupname with a combination of auditing options. The name must be a qualified user or group name (for example, sales_dom\\jennyt) for the users from the other domains.

Comments You must supply a resource name when using this command.

Use the net auditing command for auditing the use of files and directories by users and groups. For a particular file or directory, you can specify which groups or users to audit. You can audit both successful and failed actions.

When no options other than resource name are specified, the command lists the auditing information for the resource.

When the server displays auditing information, it designates groups with an asterisk (*).

If used on a directory \\server1\share1\dir1", the output of
net auditing \\\\server1\\share1\\dir1 will look similar to the following:

```
Resource:       \\server1\share1\dir1
Name:                          Events To Audit:
-----------------------------------------------------
MARKET_DOM\Administrator  R,SW,SX,SD
MARKET_DOM\user1          SP,FR,FW,FX
```

For every user or group, the following auditing options can be specified:

Code	Auditing option
SR	Audit successful read access of the resource.
FR	Audit failed reads of the resource.
SW	Audit successful writes of the resource.
FW	Audit failed writes of the resource.
SX	Audit successful executes of the resource.
FX	Audit failed executes of the resource.
SD	Audit successful deletes of the resource.
FD	Audit failed deletes of the resource,
SP	Audit successful permissions changes of the resource.
FP	Audit failed permissions changes of the resource.
SO	Audit successful changes to the ownership of the resource.
FO	Audit failed changes to the ownership of the resource.

When specifying more than one auditing option for the access to the resource by the user or group, separate the options by commas.

Note   Auditing options do not take effect until the audit policy of the domain is set to audit file and object access. Use Audit Policy menu to set the audit policy.

Examples   At a UNIX system console, to add auditing of successful read access by user jennyt from domain market_dom and failed write access by user samw from the local domain to the directory /tmp type the following:

```
net auditing c:/tmp /add market_dom\\jennyt:sr samw:fw
```

To change auditing settings for group users, whose access to the file file1 on share share1 on the local server is already being audited, to auditing of all failed accesses, type the following:

```
net auditing \\share1\\file1 /change
users:fr,fw,fx,fd,fp,fo
```

To add auditing of all write accesses to file file1 on share share1 of server server1 by user bobp from domain server1_dom, type the following:

```
net auditing \\\\server1\\share1\\file1 /add server1_dom
    \\bobp:sw,fw
```

To stop auditing accesses by user "jennyt" from the local domain to the root directory of share "share1", type the following:

```
net auditing \\share1\\ /delete jennyt
```

See also   net help, net perms

Synopsis   **NET BROWSER [/DOMAIN:domainname]**

Description   This command browses the list of domains visible from your computer or the list of computers active in the specified domain.

Options   NET BROWSER /DOMAIN:domainname
> Specifies the name of the domain to display a list of computers in. If this option is not specified, the list of all visible domains is returned.

domainname   Name of the domain.

Comments   This command displays only the list of those computers in the domain specified which are currently online. There may be other computers in the domain, which are currently turned off or not connected to the network. Use `net computer` command to display all computers in the domain.

NOTE: This command works only when the Browser service is running on the Primary Domain Controller of the domain to which your AS/U Server belongs.

To display the list of domains visible from your computer, type `net browser` without options. A display of domains visible from your computer looks similar to the following:

```
These domains are visible from your Domain Controller:
SALES_DOM                   LEGAL.DOM                 MARKETING.DOM
HELPDESK_DOM
```

Examples   To display a list of computers active in the domain called `product_dom`, type the following at a UNIX system console:
```
    net browser /domain:product_dom
```

The output of this request will look similar to the following:

```
These computers are active in domain product_dom:
PRODUCT1_ASU            PRODUCT2_ASU            TEST
SUPPORT1               SUPPORT2
```

See also   `net help, net computer`

Synopsis   NET COMPUTER [/DOMAIN:domainname]
\\\\computername { /ADD [/BACKUP] | /DEL } [/DOMAIN:domainname]

Description   This command displays or modifies the list of the computer accounts in the domain database of the specified domain.

Options   NET COMPUTER/DOMAIN:domainname
> Specifies the name of the domain being administered. If this option is not specified, the operation is performed on a local domain.

domainname   The name of the domain.

\\\\computername
> Specifies the computer to add or delete from the domain.

/ADD   Adds the specified computer to the domain being administered.

/DELETE   Removes the computer from the domain being administered.

/BACKUP   When used with /ADD option, specifies that the computer being added is a backup domain controller.

Comments   To display the list of the computer accounts in your domain database, type net computer without options.

The display of computer accounts in the domain database of the domain called sales_dom looks similar to the following:

```
These computers belong to domain sales_dom:
Computer                   Type

sales_asu                  Backup
salescenter                Primary
jenny                      Workstation
paul                       Workstation
```

Use the net computer command for adding or deleting a computer from a domain database. You can add a computer as Workstation (default), or as Backup Server, by specifying /BACKUP option. This command can be performed on domains other than the domain to which your AS/U Server belongs, by specifying /DOMAIN:domainname.

Examples To add a workstation called `sales_nt` to the list of computers of the domain called sales_dom, type the following at a UNIX system console:

```
net computer \\\\sales_nt /add /domain:sales_dom
```

To add a backup server called serv1_asu to the list of computers of your local domain, type the following:

```
net computer \\\\serv1_asu /add /backup
```

To delete a computer called product_asu from the domain called `manage_dom`, type the following:

```
net computer \\\\product_asu /del /domain:manage_dom
```

To display a list of computer accounts in the domain database of the domain called `market_dom`, type the following:

```
net computer /domain:market_dom
```

See also `net help, net browser`

NET Commands   NET CONFIG [SERVER]

Synopsis **NET CONFIG [SERVER]**

Description Displays configuration information or changes the configuration of a server service. When used without options, it displays a list of configurable services. The only available service is SERVER. To get help with configuring the server, type `net help config server`.

Options NET CONFIG SERVER
　　　　　　Displays information about or changes the configuration of a server.

See also `net help`

NET Commands   NET CONTINUE

Synopsis **NET CONTINUE {service | PRINT[=printname]}**

Description This command reactivates suspended services when typed at a server, and reactivates paused shared printers when typed at a client.

Options NET CONTINUE service
　　　　　　Specifies the service to be continued. These include the following services: Netlogon, Netrun, Server, and SNMP.

　　　　　　PRINT=printname
　　　　　　Specifies the UNIX system LP subsystem name for that printer (not the network queue name). Omitting `printname` continues all print devices on that server.

The net continue command can be abbreviated as net cont.

This command reinstates services or printers that were paused using the net pause command. When you continue a service or shared printer, you reactivate it without canceling users' connections.

Examples At a UNIX system, to pause the printer named hplaser, type the following:
```
net pause print=hplaser
```

To continue the hplaser printer services, type the following:
```
net continue print=hplaser
```

At a UNIX system, to pause the server service (thus preventing users from making new connections to the server's shared resources), type the following:
```
net pause server
```

To continue server service (thus allowing users to make new connections to the server's shared resources), type the following:
```
net continue server
```

To run the same command remotely (on server market_asu), type the following (replacing password with the password for administrator
```
net admin \\market_asu password /command net continue
server
```

See also net help, net pause, net print, net share, net stop, net start

NET Commands   NET DEVICE

Synopsis NET DEVICE [printname [/DELETE | /RESTART]]

Description This command lists device names and controls shared printers.

Options NET DEVICE printname
> Specifies the UNIX system LP subsystem printname (for example, laser or att495), not the network queue name.

/DELETE   Deletes the current print request.

/RESTART   Begins reprinting the current print job at a spooled printer from the beginning.

Comments   When used without options, the `net device` command displays the status of all shared printers at the specified server, as follows:

```
Device              Status          Time        User Name
-----------------------------------------------------------
laser Spooled     Printing        00:00:00

The command completed successfully.
```

This screen displays:

Column	Contents
Device	The printname of the shared resource.
Status	The status of the printer.
Time	This field is not applicable and always displays zero.
User Name	The system does not display the user name.

When used with only the `printname` option, the `net device` command displays only the status of the specified printer.

The name of a spooled print device is followed by the word `Spooled`. Because the server retains information about spooled printer queues you define, you can display information about a device associated with a spooled printer queue even if that printer queue is not currently shared.

The status of a device can be one of the following:

Status	Meaning
Idle	Not currently being used
Printing	The printer is active
Paused	The device has been paused with the "net pause" or "net print" command
Error	There is a problem with the device

At a UNIX system console, to list the status of the printer with the UNIX system LP subsystem printname `laser`, type the following:
```
net device laser
```

To delete the current print request from `laser`, type the following:
```
net device laser /delete
```

To run the same command remotely (on server "market_asu"), type the following (replacing "password" with the password for "administrator":
```
net admin \\market_asu password /command net device laser
         /delete
```

See also   net help, net print, net share

NET Commands   NET FILE

Synopsis   **NET FILE [id [/CLOSE]]**

Description   This command displays the names of all open shared files and the number of locks, if any, on each file. It may also be used to close shared files.

Options   id   Specifies the identification number of a file.

/CLOSE   Closes an opened file and releases locked records.

Comments   When used without options, the net file command lists all the open files at a server, as follows:

```
ID                Path                          Username       # Locks
-------------------------------------------------------------------
1073742661        C:\TMP\NEWFILE.BAT            LAURA             0
1073742637        C:\HOME\AL\MAIL.LST           SAM               0
1073742528        C:\HOME\KRM\LETTER.SLN        KAREN             0
1073722830        C:\HOME\KRM\MLIST.NDX         KAREN             1

The command completed successfully.
```

This screen displays:

Column	Contents
ID	The identification number assigned to the open file.
Path	The pathname of the open file.
Username	The username of the person using the file.
# Locks	The number of locks on the file.

You will receive one entry for each instance of an open file; therefore, if a file is opened three times (or by three different users), you will receive three separate entries.

The administrator has the ability to close files, which removes any locks, by using the `net file` command.

The `net file` command also can be typed `net files`.

There are a number of reasons why you may need to close an open file on the server. Sometimes you simply need to clean up after a program that left a file open. Other times, you may need to close a file in which somebody is working. For example, someone may use a word processing program to open a file and then leave his/her desk, leaving the file locked.

If you discover a security breach such as someone reading a confidential file, you can disable the account and then use the `net file` command with the `/CLOSE` option to close the file. If you use `net file /close` without first disabling the account, the person will automatically reconnect to the file.

Examples   At a UNIX system console, to display additional information on a server's open file, type the following:

```
net file 1073742661
```

where 1073742661 is the file id number.

To close the open file 1073742661, type the following:

```
net file 1073742661 /close
```

where 1073742661 is the id number of the file to be closed. This command closes the file and releases any file locks, making the file available for local area network use.

To run the same command remotely (on server `market_asu`), type the following (replacing `password` with the password for `administrator`

```
net admin \\market_asu password /command net file
1073742661 /close
```

See also   `net help, net share`

NET Commands   NET GROUP

Synopsis   NET GROUP [groupname [/COMMENT:"text"]]
groupname {/ADD [/COMMENT:"text"] | /DELETE}
groupname username[...] {/ADD | /DELETE}

Description   This command adds, displays, or modifies global groups.

Options   groupname
> The name of the group. To view a list of users in a group, type
> `net group groupname`. Groupnames can be up to 20 characters in
> length and can include any alphanumeric character, spaces, and the
> special characters except for the following:

> " / \ [ ] : ; | = , + * ? < >

> NOTE: groupnames containing spaces must be quoted.

username[...]
> Lists one or more usernames to add to or remove from a group. Separate
> multiple username entries with a space. Usernames containing spaces
> must be quoted.

/COMMENT:"text"
> Adds a comment for a new or existing group. The comment can have as
> many as 48 characters. Enclose the text in quotation marks.

/ADD Adds a group, or, when a username is supplied with a known group,
> adds a username to a group.

/DELETE   Removes a group, or, when a known username is supplied
> with a group, removes a username from a group.

Comments   To display the name of the server and the names of global groups on the
server, type `net group` without options.

To operate on a particular global group, type
```
net group groupname ...
```
OR
```
net group 'groupname containing spaces' ...
```
OR
```
net group "groupname containing spaces" ...
```

For example,
```
net group sales                    OR
net group 'domain admins'                  OR
net group "domain admins"
```

Use the `net group` command to group users who use the network in the same or similar ways. This is helpful when assigning resource permissions (net perms). When you assign permissions for a group, each member of the group automatically has these permissions.

This command can also be typed `net groups`. A display of global groups on the server is similar to the following:

```
Group Accounts for \\PRODUCT_ASU
--------------------------------------------------------
*Domain Admins     *Domain Guests      *Domain Users
```

Notice that each groupname is preceded by an asterisk (*). This distinguishes groups in displays that include both users and groups. When you type the `net group` command at a backup domain controller, changes to the user accounts database are automatically made at the primary domain controller and then copied to backup domain controllers. There is a delay before changes take effect.

Examples   At a UNIX system console, to display a list of all the groups on a server, type the following:
```
net group
```

To add a group called `sales` to the user accounts database, type the following:
```
net group sales /add
```

To add the existing user accounts `stevev`, `ralphr`, and `jennyt` to the `sales` group, type the following:
```
net group sales stevev ralphr jennyt /add
```

To display users in the `sales` group, type the following:
```
net group sales
```

To add a comment to the `sales` group record, type the following:
```
net group sales /comment:"The sales staff."
```

To run the same command remotely (on server "market_asu"), type the following (replacing "password" with the password for "administrator":
```
net admin \\market_asu password /command net group sales /
    comment:"The sales staff."
```

See also   net help, net perms, net user, net accounts, net localgroup

NET Commands   NET HELP

Synopsis
NET HELP [command [/OPTIONS] | topic]   -or-
NET command {/HELP | /?}

Description
This command provides a list of commands and topics for which you can get help, or provides help for a specific command or topic. command may be one of the following:

ACCESS	ACCOUNTS	ADMIN	AUDINTING
BROWSER	COMPUTER	CONFIG	CONTINUE
DEVICE	FILE	GROUP	HELP
HELPMSG	LOCALGROUP	LOGOFF	LOGON
PASSWORD	PAUSE	PERMS	PRINT
SEND	SESSION	SHARE	SID
START	STATISTICS	STATUS	STOP
TIME	TRUST	USER	
VERSION	VIEW		

Options
NET HELP command
> The command with which you need help. (Do not type net as part of command.)

The following options are not available for Basic DOS:

topic The topic you need help with. Help is available for the topics names and syntax.

/OPTIONS
> Displays the available options of the specified command.

/HELP
> Provides an alternate way to display the help text.

/?
> Displays the correct syntax for the command. In the UNIX operating system, the question mark (?) is a special character, and must be preceded by a backslash (\ ).

Comments
At a UNIX system console, to produce the same information about the net group command using two forms of the net help command, type the following:

```
net help group      -or-      net group /help
```

To view the SYNTAX from the UNIX system server, type the following:

```
net group /\?
```

To view information about the net logon command, type the following:

```
net help logon
```

To run the same command remotely (on server `market_asu`), type the following (replacing "*password*" with the password for administrator):
`net admin \\market_asu password /command net help logon`

See also `net helpmsg`

NET Commands   # NET HELPMSG

Synopsis **NET HELPMSG message#**

Description This command provides help for a network error message.

Options NET HELPMSG ####
     The number of the network error message you need help with.

Comments Use the `net helpmsg` command to get an explanation of why an error occurred and information about what action to take to solve the problem.

Examples At a UNIX system console, to get help for network error message NET2182, type the following:
     `net helpmsg 2182`

To run the same command remotely (on server "market_asu"), type the following (replacing "password" with the password for "administrator"):
`net admin \\market_asu password /command net helpmsg 2182`

See also `net help`

NET Commands   # NET LOCALGROUP

Synopsis **NET LOCALGROUP [localgroupname[/COMMENT:"text"]]**
     [/DOMAIN:domainname]
localgroupname {/ADD [/COMMENT:"text"] | /DELETE}
     [/DOMAIN:domainname]
localgroupname username[...] {/ADD | /DELETE}
     [/DOMAIN:domainname]

Description This command adds, displays, or modifies local groups in domains.

Options localgroupname
     The name of the local group to add, expand, or delete. Supply only a `localgroupname` to view a list of users or global groups in a local group. Localgroupnames can be up to 256 characters in length, and can include any alphanumeric characters, spaces and special characters except for the following:

          " / \ [ ] : ; | = , + * ? < >

/COMMENT:"text"

Adds a comment for a new or existing local group. The comment can have as many as 48 characters. Enclose the text in quotation marks.

DOMAIN:domainname

Specifies the name of the domain on which the operation is to be performed. When this option is not specified, the operation is performed on the local domain.

username [...] Lists one or more usernames or groupnames to add to or remove from a local group. Separate multiple entries with a space. Names may be users or global groups, but not other local groups. If a user is from another domain, preface the username with the domain name (for example, `sales_dom\\ralphr`).

/ADD Adds a groupname or username to a local group. An account must be established for users or global groups added to a local group with this command.

/DELETE Removes a groupname or username from a local group.

Comments To display the name of the primary domain controller of the local domain and the names of local groups in it, type `net localgroup` without options.

To display the name of the primary domain controller of the domain other than local and the names of local groups in this domain, type
```
net localgroup /domain:domainname.
```

To operate on a particular local group, type
```
net localgroup localgroupname ...OR
net localgroup 'localgroupname containing spaces' ...
```
OR
```
net localgroup "localgroupname containing spaces" ...
```
E.G.
```
net localgroup sales          OR
net localgroup 'Server Operators'          OR
net localgroup "Server Operators"
```

This command can also be typed `net localgroups`. A display of local groups in the domain is similar to the following:

```
Aliases for \\PRODUCT_ASU
-----------------------------------------------------------
*Account Operators      *Administrators      *Backup
Operators
*Guests                 *Print Operators     *Replicator
*Server Operators       *Users
```

Examples At a UNIX system console, to display a list of all the local groups on a local domain, type the following:

```
net localgroup
```

To display a list of all the local groups on a domain called market_dom, type the following:

```
net localgroup /domain:market_dom
```

To add a local group called sales to the user accounts database of a local domain, type the following:

```
net localgroup sales /add
```

To add the existing user accounts stevev and jennyt, and existing group mailusers to the sales group on a domain called market_dom, type the following:

```
net localgroup sales mailusers stevev jennyt /add
     /domain:market_dom
```

To display users in the sales group on a domain called market_dom, type the following:

```
net localgroup sales /domain:market_dom
```

To add a comment to the sales local group record on the local domain, type the following:

```
net localgroup sales /comment:"The sales staff."
```

To delete a user named jennyt from domain sales_dom from sales local group on a domain called market_dom, type the following:

```
net localgroup sales sales_dom\\jennyt /delete
     /domain:market_dom
```

See also net help, net perms, net user, net accounts, net group

NET Commands   NET LOGOFF

Synopsis **NET LOGOFF**

Description This command logs a username off from the network.

Options username   The name by which you are identified on the network (username can have as many as 20 characters).

password   The user's password.

*   Produces a prompt for the password. The password will not be displayed when you type it.

/DOMAIN:name The name of a domain (other than your local domain) in which you want to log on. This is called the "logon domain."

Comments Use the `net logoff` command to sign off a user who is currently logged on the network.

Logging off does not stop services that are running. It simply ensures that no one can use your username and password to gain access to shared resources, because logging off cancels all connections to shared resources.

Examples To logoff a user that is currently logged on the network, type the following:
```
net logoff
```

See also `net help`, `net logon`

NET Commands   NET LOGON

Synopsis NET LOGON [username [password | *]] [/DOMAIN:name]

Description This command logs on a username to the server and sets the username and password for the user's client.

Options username   The name by which you are identified on the network (username can have as many as 20 characters).

password   The user's password.

*   Produces a prompt for the password. The password will not be displayed when you type it.

/DOMAIN:name
The name of a domain (other than your local domain) in which you want to log on. This is called the logon domain.

Comments To get prompts requesting your username and password, type `net logon` without options.

Use the `net logon` command to establish your username and password. These are used to log you on to the network and verify that you can use network resources. Only one username can be logged on at a client.

If you do not specify a username with the `net logon` command, the default username is your UNIX logon name.

Examples To log on to the network and have the computer prompt for your username and password, type the following:
```
net logon
```

To log on to the network in the `account` domain with the username `felix` and the password `freddy`, type the following:
```
net logon felix freddy /domain:account
```

See also `net help`, `net logoff`, `net password`

NET Commands   NET PASSWORD

Synopsis   NET PASSWORD [[\\servername | /DOMAIN:name] username
oldpassword {newpassword | *}]

Description   This command changes the password for a user account on a server or in a
domain.

Options   servername   The server at which the password will be changed.

username   The username whose password is to be changed.

oldpassword   The current password.

newpassword   The new password, which can have as many as 14 characters.

*   Produces a prompt for the new password, which can have as many as 14
characters. The password will not be displayed when you type it.

/DOMAIN:name
The domain in which the password will be changed.

Comments   Use the net password command to change your password. To get prompts
for the name of the domain or server, the username, the old password, and the
new password, type net password without options.

If you forget your password, you cannot use this command to create a new
one. You must use the net user command to create a new password.

Examples   To change your password for the product server from miata to hctrebor
(your username is robertch), type the following:

```
net password \\product_asu robertch miata hctrebor
```

To make the same change, but have the server issue a prompt for a new
password which will not be displayed as you enter it, type the following:

```
net password \\product_asu robertch miata \*
```

To change the password in your local domain from miata to hctrebor, type
the following:

```
net password robertch miata hctrebor
```

To change the password for your user account in the account domain from
robertcx to hctrebor, type the following:

```
net password /domain:account robertch robertcx
hctrebor
```

To run the same command remotely (on server market_asu), type the
following (replacing *password* with the password for administrator):

```
net admin \\market_asu password /command net password
    /domain:account robertch robertcx hctrebor
```

See also   net help, net logon

NET Commands   NET PAUSE

Synopsis   NET PAUSE {service | PRINT[=printname]}

Description   This command suspends services or printers at a server.

Options   service   Specifies the service to be paused. This includes the following
services: Netlogon, Netrun, and Server.

PRINT=printname
Specifies the UNIX system LP subsystem name for the printer (not the
network queue name). Omitting `printername` pauses all print devices
on that server.

Comments   Pausing provides administrators with a way of suspending network services
and printers.

Pausing affects the network services in the following ways:

- Pausing the Netlogon service prevents the server from processing logon
  requests at that server. If the domain has other logon servers, users can
  still log on to the network.

- Pausing the Netrun service prevents users from running a program at
  that server. Programs currently running on the server are not affected.

- Pausing the Server service prevents users from making new connections
  to the server's shared resources and, if there are no other logon servers
  on the network, from logging on to the network. An existing connection
  is unaffected. Administrators can make connections to the server even if
  it is paused.

Pausing a printer makes that device unavailable to local area network users.
Jobs already in the queue remain there, and they will print when the printer is
continued.

If a job is printing, and the printer is paused, the job stops printing and moves
to the first position in the queue. When the printer is continued, this job prints
first.

Examples   At a UNIX system console, to pause all the shared printers at a server, type the
following:
```
net pause print
```

To pause only the printer named `hplaser`, type the following:
```
net pause print=hplaser
```

To continue the `hplaser` printer, which was paused, type the following:
```
net continue print=hplaser
```

To pause the `server` service (thus preventing users from making new connections to the server's shared resources), type the following:
```
net pause server
```

To run the same command remotely (on server `market_asu`), type the following (replacing *password* with the password for administrator):
```
net admin \\market_asu password /command net pause server
```

See also `net help`, `net continue`, `net print`, `net share`

NET Commands   NET PERMS

Synopsis NET PERMS resource [/GRANT name:permissions[...] |/CHANGE name:permissions[...] | /REVOKE name[...] |/TAKE]

Description This command displays or modifies resource permissions and ownership information on servers. The resources on which this command currently operates are shares, directories, and files.

Options resource   Name of the resource on which the permissions and ownership information are to be set or modified. To specify the remote resource name, prefix it with the name of the server on which this resource resides (for example, to access a local server's file file1 residing on the share share1, you specify the resource name as `\\share1\\file1`. To access the resource with the same path on the server named `server1`, the resource name should be specified as follows: `\\\\server1\\share1\\file1`. To specify the name of the root directory of the share (as opposite to the share itself), append "\\" to the share path, for example: `\\\\server1\\share1\\` will refer to the root directory of share1 on server1.

name:permissions[...]
        Name provides the existing username or groupname with a combination of individual or standard permissions. The name must be a qualified user or group name (for example, `sales_dom\\jennyt`) for the users from the domains other than the one to which the local server belongs. Separate multiple `name:permissions` entries with a space. For a description of each permission, see the Comments section.

name[...]   One or more usernames or groupnames. The name must be a qualified user or group name (for example, `sales_dom\\jennyt`) for the users from the domains other than the one to which the local server belongs. Separate multiple `name` entries with a space.

/GRANT   Adds the specified user or group with the specified permissions to the access list for a resource. The user or group name should not currently be in the access list for a resource.

/CHANGE   Changes the permissions for the user or group whose name is already in the access list for a resource. Separate multiple name:permissions entries with a space.

/REVOKE   Deletes all permissions for the user or group from the access list for a resource.

/TAKE   Allows the currently logged in user to take ownership of a resource.

Comments   You must supply a resource name when using this command.

Use the `net perms` command to secure network resources by specifying who can use each resource and how. This command allows the user to set and modify permissions for users and groups on a resource, and to take ownership of the resource.

When the server displays resource permissions, it designates groups with an asterisk (*).

When no options other than resource name are specified, the command lists the permissions and ownership information for the resource. This command can also be typed as `net perm`.

If used on a local share resource, the output of `net perms \\users` will look similar to the following:

```
Resource:      \users
Owner:
Name:                              Permissions:
-----------------------------------------------------------
*Everyone                          FullControl(All)
```

If used on a directory or file resource the output of
     `net perms c:/home/lanman`
will look similar to the following:

```
Resource:      c:\home\lanman
Owner:         sales_dom\Administrators
Name:                              Permissions:
-----------------------------------------------------------
*Account Operators                 Change(RWXD)(RWXD)
*Administrators                    FullControl(All)(All)
*Server Operators                  Change(RWXD)(RWXD)
*Everyone                          Read(RX)(RX)
*SYSTEM                            FullControl(All)(All)
```

You can specify combinations of individual permissions (for example, RWX for a file or RWX:RX for a directory) or standard permissions (for example, Change for a file or Add for a directory) for user or groups on the files and directories. You can set only standard permissions (for example, Read) on the shares.

The following list shows the types of permissions that can be assigned for a user's or group's access to shares, directories and files, and what each permission allows a user to do:

INDIVIDUAL PERMISSIONS(Directory or File)	
Code	**Permission**
R (Read)	User can display the file's data, attributes, and its owner and permissions.
W (Write)	User can change data in and append data to the file, change the file's attributes, and display its owner and permissions.
D (Delete)	User can delete the file.
X (Execute)	User can run the file if it is an application, change the file's attributes, and display its owner and permissions.
P (Change permissions)	User can change permissions on the file.
O (Take ownership)	User can take ownership of the file.

STANDARD PERMISSIONS (Directory)	
Code	**Permission**
NoAccess	User cannot access the directory in any way, even if the user is a member of a group that has been granted access to the directory.
List	User can only list the files and subdirectories in this directory and change to a subdirectory of this directory. User cannot access files in the directory.
Read	User can read the contents of files in this directory and run applications in the directory.
Add	User can add files to the directory but cannot read the contents of current files, change them, or list the files.
AddRead	User can add files to the directory and read current files but cannot change files.
Change	User can read and add files and change the contents of current files.
FullControl	User can read and change files, add new ones, change permissions for the directory and its files, and take ownership of the directory and its files.

STANDARD PERMISSIONS (File)

Code	Permission
NoAccess	User cannot access the file in any way, even if the user is a member of a group that has been granted access to the file.
Read	User can read the contents of the file and run it if it is an application.
Change	User can read, modify and delete the file. If the file is an application, the user can run it.
FullControl	User can read, modify, delete, set permissions for, and take ownership of the file. If the file is an application, user can run it.

STANDARD PERMISSIONS (Share)

Code	Permission
NoAccess	User cannot access the shared directory itself and the files and subdirectories in it in any way, even if the user is a member of a group which has been granted access to the share.
Read	User can display the names of subdirectories and files on the share, display the data and attributes of files, run program files and go to the directories on the share.
Change	User can read, write and delete directories and files on the share, can change attributes of files and directories on the share and run program files.
FullControl	User can read, write and delete directories and files on the share, can change attributes of files and directories, run program files and change permissions on the share itself and on its directories and files.

Displaying of Directory Permissions   When a directory permission is displayed, two sets of abbreviations for individual permissions are displayed next to it: the permissions set on the directory and the permissions which files in this directory will inherit. For example, when AddRead permission is set, you see (RWX), signifying Read, Write and Execute permissions on the directory, and (RX) signifying Read and Execute permissions which will be inherited by files in the directory.

When directory permission is shown as "Special Access", it means that the combination of directory and file individual permissions on this directory does not correspond to any of the standard directory permissions.

When access to the files in the directory is shown as (NotSpecified), that group or user cannot use files in the directory, unless access is granted by another means, for example, by setting permissions that grant access to individual files.

An asterisk (*) following the set of directory permissions, for example, (All)*, indicates that subdirectories do not inherit the permissions granted to that group.

Setting of Directory Permissions:
To set a standard permission on a directory, simply type the standard permission's name. For example, to set a Read permission for user `stevej`, type
> `stevej:read.`

You can also set a combination of individual permissions on a directory. It is possible to specify permissions for a directory itself and permissions to be inherited by the files in this directory separately. These permissions should be separated by a colon. For example, to set `RDPO` permission to the directory itself, and `RW` permission for the files in this directory for the user `stevej`, type
> `"stevej:rdpo:rw".`

By default, permissions on the directory itself will be inherited by its subdirectories. If you do not want to have permissions on the directory to be inherited by its subdirectories, specify an asterisk next to a directory permission. For example, to prevent subdirectories from inheriting directory permissions in the preceeding example, type:
> `"stevej:rdpo*:rw".`

Displaying of File and Share Permissions:
When a file or share permission is displayed, an abbreviation for individual permissions corresponding to this file or share permission appears next to it.

When file permission is shown as "Special Access", this means that the combination of individual file permissions on this file does not correspond to any of the standard file permissions.

To set a standard file permission or a share permission, just type the name of the permission. For example, to set a FullControl permission for user `administrator`, type `administrator:fullcontrol`.

To set a combination of individual permissions on the file, type the abbreviations for these permissions, such as `user1:rxp` to grant Read, Execute and Change Permissions permissions to user1.

NOTE: Groups or users granted FullControl permission on a directory can delete files in that directory no matter what permissions protect the files.

Examples At a UNIX system console, to grant `Add` permission for the user `mikeg`, `RWXD` permission for the directory itself, `RX` permission for the files to inherit for the group `Server Operators` and `FullControl` permission for the group `users`, to the `/tmp` directory on the local server, type the following:

```
net perms c:/tmp /grant mikeg:add "server operators":rwxd:x
    \users:fullcontrol
```

At a UNIX system console, to grant `Read` permission for the group `sales` and `NoAccess` permission for the user nobody from the `market_dom` to the file `f1`, residing on the share `share1` of the local server, type the following:

```
    net perms \\share1\\f1 /grant sales:read market_dom
    \\nobody:noaccess
```

To grant `RXP` permission to the directory, no inheritable permissions for the subdirectory, and `RD` permission to be inherited by the files in the directory, for the user `joanl` on the `root` directory of the share `sales_share` of the server `product_asu`, type the following:

```
net perms \\\\product_asu\\sales_share\\ /grant
joanl:rxp*:rd
```

To change permissions on the directory `dir` on the share `share` on the server `server1` for user `jennyt` to FullControl, type the following:

```
net perms \\\\server1\\share\\dir /change
jennyt:fullcontrol
```

To delete user `stevej` from the access list for the share `share1` on the local server, type the following:

```
    net perms \\share1 /revoke stevej
```

See also `net help`, `net auditing`, `net user`, `net accounts`, `net group`, `net localgroup`

NET Commands   NET PRINT

Synopsis NET PRINT [job# [/HOLD | /RELEASE | /FIRST | /LAST | /DELETE]]
sharename [/HOLD | /RELEASE | /DELETE | /PURGE]
    [/PRIORITY:#] [/SEPARATOR:pathname][/ROUTE:devicename[,...]]
    [/PROCESSOR:pmname][/AFTER:time] [/REMARK:"text"]
    [/UNTIL:time]
[/OPTIONS][/PARMS:"[COPIES=#] [EJECT=val] [BANNER=val]
[TYPES=type1[,...]]"]

Description This command displays or controls print jobs and printer queues, or sets or modifies options for a printer queue.

Options sharename   Name of the printer queue. For a client, when including the sharename with the servername, use a backslash (\) to separate the names.

job   Identification number assigned to a print job in a printer queue. A server with one or more printer queues assigns each print job a unique number. If a job number is being used in one printer queue shared by a server, that number is not assigned to any other job, not even to jobs in other printer queues on that server.

servername   Name of the UNIX system server sharing the printer queue(s).

devicename   Name of the device at the client computer assigned to the printer queue. Devicenames LPT1: through LPT3: are available in DOS.

/PRIORITY:#   Sets the priority for the printer queue (1 is the highest and 9 the lowest). Each print job is assigned a number based on the printer queue priority. If a printer has more than one printer queue routed to it, it prints jobs from the printer queue with highest priority first.

/ROUTE:printername1[,printername2...]
Routes the printer queue to one or more printernames on the server. Separate multiple printernames with commas (,). The printer names are LP subsystem printernames. In the UNIX operating system, the semicolon (;) is a special character that must be preceded by a backslash.

/AFTER:time   Prints jobs from the printer queue after the specified time. Use 24-hour time with the format hh:mm; or use 12-hour time with the format hh:mmam or hh:mmpm.

/UNTIL:time   Prints jobs from the printer queue until the specified time. Use 24-hour time with the format hh:mm; or use 12-hour time with the format hh:mmam or hh:mmpm.

/SEPARATOR:pathname
Instructs the printer queue to use the separator page defined in the pathname file. You can specify the full path to the file or only the filename. If only the filename is specified, the path is presumed to be lanmanpath (lanman/spool). The default is no custom separator page; the UNIX system LP subsystem banner page is printed instead.

/PROCESSOR:pathname
Instructs the printer to use the print processing program stored in pathname. You can specify the full path to the file or only the filename. If only the filename is specified, the path is presumed to be lanman/custom (which is the only acceptable path).

/PARMS:"keyword=value[:...]"
Specifies a set of options of the queue in the format keyword=value. Valid keywords include TYPES, EJECT, COPIES, and BANNER.

TYPES specifies the type of print data accepted by the queue, and is automatically set to match the printers in the queue.

EJECT specifies whether or not a formfeed command is issued at the between copies of a job; the choices are YES, NO, or AUTO; the default is AUTO (YES).

COPIES specifies the number of copies to print; the default is 1.

BANNER specifies whether to print a banner (separator) page before each job. The choices are YES and NO; the default is YES.

/REMARK:"text"
Adds a descriptive comment about the printer queue. Enclose the text in quotation marks.

/OPTIONS   Displays the options assigned to the printer queue.

/HOLD   When used with `job`, holds a print job waiting in the printer queue. The print job stays in the printer queue, and other print jobs bypass it until it is released. When used with `sharename`, all new jobs and all jobs presently in the queue are held except the one currently printing. Users can hold their own print jobs.

/RELEASE   Releases a print job or printer queue that has been held. Users can release their own print jobs.

/DELETE   When used with `job`, removes the print job from a printer queue. When used with `sharename`, removes a printer queue. At a client, users can delete their own print jobs.

/PURGE   Removes all print jobs from the printer queue except the print job that is currently printing.

/FIRST   Moves a print job to the first position in the printer queue.

/LAST   Moves a print job to the last position in the printer queue, then renumbers the job using the next available job number (therefore, the print job number will change). Users have permission to move their own print jobs (not someone else's) to the last place in the queue.

Comments   To display information about printer queues on the server, type `net print` without options.

Use the `net print` command to control printer queues and set options such as separator pages, print processors, and time limits. To share a printer queue, use the `net share` command. To display or control the status of a particular printer, use the `net device` command.

The net print command displays information about printer queues in several ways.

- To display all of the printer queues on the local server, use the form net print. You can limit the display to a particular queue by using the form net print sharename or to a particular device by using the form net print devicename. The following is a sample display of all printer queues:

```
Printer queues at product_asu.
Name            Job #        Size         Status
-------------------------------------------------------------
LASER Queue    1 jobs                    *Printer Active*
    JOHNSW          84       0              Spooling
LASER2 Queue   1 jobs                    *Printer Active*
    MARYSL          75       0              Spooling
POOL Queue     1 jobs                    *Printer Active
    ROBERTCH        45       129844        Printing on hplaser
```

- To display options for a single printer queue, type the following:
  net print sharename /options

  A display similar to the following appears:

```
Printing options for LASER2
    Status              Printer Active
    Remark
    Print Devices       hplaser
    Driver              PSI Driver for UNIX LP Version1.01
    Separator file
    Priority            5
    Print after         12:00 am
    Print until         11:59 pm
    Print processor
    Parameters          COPIES=1 TYPES=simple EJECT=AUTO
BANNER=YES
```

- To display a single print job, use the form `net print job#`. A display similar to the following appears:

```
Job #                   75
      Status            Waiting
      Size              3096
      Remark
      Submitting user   MARYSL
      Notify            CLIENT1
      Job data type     simple
      Job Parameters    COPIES=1 TYPES=simple EJECT=AUTO
BANNER=YES
```

To display printer queues and to control your own print jobs, use the `net print` command at a client.

- To display a printer queue on a server, type the following:
  net print \\\\servername\\sharename
- To display information about a particular print job on a remote server, type the following:
  `net print \\\\servername job`
- To send a print job to a printer queue, connect an LPT# to the printer queue with the `net use` command and do one of the following: submit the print job through an application program such as a word processor; send the print job to a printer queue with the copy command (for example, `copy job lpt1:`); or use the DOS print command.

Examples   At the UNIX system console, to display print options for the `laser1` queue, type the following:
```
net print laser1 /options
```

To list printer queues at the server, type the following:
```
net print
```

At a UNIX system console, to get information about job number 35 on the product server, type the following:
```
net print \\\\product_asu 35
```

At the UNIX system console, to make job number 263 the last to print, type the following:
```
net print 263 /last
```

At a UNIX system console, to hold job number 263, type the following:
```
net print 263 /hold
```

To release job number 263, type the following:
```
net print 263 /release
```

At the UNIX system console, to print from 7:00 A.M. until 6:00 P.M. (this example uses 24-hour time), in a printer queue named deptlaser, type the following:

```
net print deptlaser /after:07:00 /until:18:00
```

At a UNIX system console, to list the contents of the dotmatrix printer queue on the product server, type the following:

```
net print \\\\product_asu\\dotmatrix
```

To run the same command remotely (on server market_asu), type the following (replacing *password* with the password for administrator):

```
net admin \\market_asu password /command net print
       \\\\product_asu\\dotmatrix
```

See also   net help

NET Commands   NET SHARE

Synopsis   **NET SHARE sharename**
sharename=devicename[,...] [/PRINT] [/USERS:# | /UNLIMITED]
     [/REMARK:"text"]
sharename [/PRINT]
sharename=drive:path [/USERS:# | /UNLIMITED] [/REMARK:"text"]
sharename [/USERS:# | /UNLIMITED] [/REMARK:"text"]
{sharename | devicename | drive:path} /DELETE

Description   This command creates, deletes, modifies, or displays shared resources. Use this command to make a resource available to clients.

Before you can share a printer queue, you must configure your printer(s) through Solaris. Similarly, before you can share a directory, you must create it.

Options   sharename   Network name for a shared resource. Use the net share command with a sharename to display information about a resource. Do not use any of the following as a sharename:

COMM PRINT DEV QUEUE MAILSLOT SEM 1PIPE SHAREMEM

devicename   Specifies one or more printers shared by sharename. Separate multiple devicename entries with a comma.

pathname   Specifies the absolute path of a directory to be shared (including the drive id). A directory must exist before you can share it. The pathname must be the complete path to the directory, beginning with the root directory. For example, to specify the directory kate, which is a subdirectory within market, you would type the following:

```
net share research=c:/market/kate
```

/PRINT   Identifies the resource as a printer queue.

/USERS:# Sets the maximum number of users who can simultaneously access a shared resource.

/UNLIMITED Sets the maximum number of users who can simultaneously access a shared resource to the number maximum number allowed by the license of the server.

/REMARK:"text"
Adds a descriptive comment about the resource. Enclose the text in quotation marks.

/DELETE Stops sharing the resource.

Comments To display information about all resources being shared on the server, type net share. When you display all the shared resources at a server, it reports the sharename, the devicename(s) or pathname associated with it, and a descriptive comment. The display is similar to the following:

```
Sharename  Resource                           Remark
---------  -------------------------------    --------------------
IADMIN     C:\VAR\OPT\LANMAN                   Admin Share
IPC                                           IPC Share
C$         C:\                                 Root Share
D$         C:\VAR\OPT\LANMAN\SHARES           SystemRoot Share
REPL$      C:\VAR\OPT\LANMAN\SHARES\WIN       REPL MASTER
TOOLS      C:\VAR\OPT\LANMAN\SHARES\AST       PC NetLink
                                              Server Tools
DOSUTIL    C:\VAR\OPT\LANMAN\SHARES\DOS       DOS Utilities
LIB        C:\VAR\OPT\LANMAN\SHARES\LIB       Programming Aids
NETLOGON   C:\VAR\OPT\LANMAN\SHARES\WIN       Logon Script
                                              Directory
PRINTLOG   C:\VAR\OPT\LANMAN\SHARES\PRI       LP printer messages
USERS      C:\HOME2\LANMAN                    Users Directory
```

Most users have home directories on the server, a directory in which they can store files and from which they can share files.

There are two ways to create new home directories:

■ To create a new directory from a client, complete the following steps:

1. **Log on as a user with administrative privileges.**

2. **Link to the UNIX system server's C$ resource by typing**
   net use x: \\server_asu\c$

3. **Change directories to the path specified in the \SYSTEM\CurrentControlSet\Services\LanmanServer \Parameters\UserPath value in the Registry.**

   For example, UserPath could have the value c:\home\lanman.

4. Type mkdir directoryname and press return.

■ To create a new directory on the UNIX operating system, complete the following steps:

1. **Log on to the server console as root.**

2. **Change from the current directory, if you do not want the new directory to be in root's home directory.**

3. **At the system prompt, type** mkdir directoryname **and press** return.

4. **Change the permissions, ownership, and group for this directory to agree with the server's permissions, ownership, and group.**

   To change the permissions, type the following:

   ```
   chmod 775 directoryname
   ```

   To change the owner, type the following:

   ```
   chown lmxadmin directoryname
   ```

   To change the group, type the following:

   ```
   chgrp DOS---- directoryname
   ```

Use the following forms of the net share command to share resources:

■ To share an existing directory, type the following:

   ```
   net share sharename=pathname
   ```

■ To create and share a printer queue, type the following:

   ```
   net share sharename=devicename /print
   ```

■ To share a printer queue without assigning a devicename, or to share an existing printer queue, type the following:

   ```
   net share sharename /print
   ```

■ To establish security restrictions for a resource use the net perms command (for permissions) and the net user command (for users' passwords).

After you have configured your printer(s) on the UNIX system, you can share a printer queue. In this example, `acct_asu` is the name of the server; `laserprt` is the name of the shared printer queue; and `hplaser` is the name of the printer. From a UNIX system console, type the following:

```
net share laserprt=hplaser /print
```

To share the two printers with the UNIX system LP subsystem printernames `hplaser` and `att495` as a printer pool served by a single printer queue, type the following:

```
net share pool1=hplaser,att495 /print
```

To stop sharing a resource, type the following:

```
net share sharedir /delete
```

where *sharedir* is the name of shared resource to be disconnected.

To run the same command remotely (on server `market_asu`), type the following (replacing *password* with the password for administrator):

```
net admin \\market_asu password /command net share
    sharedir /delete
```

See also `net help, net perms, net print`

NET Commands   NET SID

Synopsis NET SID {/NAME:name | /SID:sidstring} [/DOMAIN:domainname]

Description This command performs translation between the account name and the corresponding Security Identifier.

Options /DOMAIN:domainname
DOMAIN specifies the name of the domain being queried. If this option is not specified, the operation is performed on a local domain. domainname is the name of the domain.

/SID:sidstring   Translate the Security Identifier to an account name in the domain being queried.

/NAME:name   Translate the account name to a corresponding Security Identifier in the domain being queried.

name Name of the account to be translated. It can be a user name, group name, etc. The name must be a qualified account name (for example, `sales_dom\\jennyt`) for the accounts from the domains other than the one to which the local server belongs.

sidstring   Security Identifier to be translated. It must start with `S-`, and have the form as in the output of the `net sid` command.

Comments   Use the `net sid` command for obtaining Security Identifiers for accounts in domains, and for translating Security Identifiers into account names.

The output of `net sid` command is similar to the following:

```
Account Name:    Administrators
Domain:          Builtin
SID:             S-1-5-20-220
Type:            Local Group
```

Examples   To display a SID of the account for the user `jennyt` in the domain called `pr_dom`, type the following at a UNIX system console:
```
net sid /name:jennyt /domain:pr_dom
```

To display a name of the account in your local domain for SID S-1-5-21-1765409576-1764449912-1520319331-1025, type the following:
```
net sid /sid:S-1-5-21-1765409576-1764449912-
1520319331-1025
```

To display a SID of the account for the user `annj` from domain `sales_dom` in your local domain, type the following:
```
net sid /name:sales_dom\\annj
```

See also   `net help`

NET Commands   NET START

Synopsis   **NET START [service [options]]**

Description   This command starts a service, or displays a list of started services.

Options   service   Specifies the service to be started. This includes the following services: Alerter, Netlogon, Netrun, Nvalert, Remoteboot, Replicator, Server, SNMP, Timesource, and UPS.

[options]   Specific to each service. For more information, see each `net start` command reference page. At the UNIX system server console, the options are ignored; the service uses only the keyword values from the `lanman.ini` file and the values from the Registry.

Comments   To display a list of running services, type `net start` without options.

Use the `net start` command to start various server services. Some services must be started before others. When you type a command that requires a service that has not been started, the server offers to start the required service.

You can start services automatically by including commands in either batch files or UNIX shell scripts. You can also modify the srvservices ([server] section) keyword in the lanman.ini file to automatically start services other than the Server service. The srvservices keyword specifies which services to start when the Server service is started. The Alerter, Netlogon, Netrun, Remoteboot, Replicator, Timesource, UPS and WINS services are possible values. Names of services cannot be abbreviated when listed in the srvservices keyword. When a service starts, the server reads values from the Registry and the lanman.ini file and uses them to configure the service.

Examples   At a UNIX system console, to list the services that are currently running, type the following:

```
net start
```

To run the same command remotely (on server market_asu), type the following (replacing *password* with the password for administrator):

```
net admin \\market_asu password /command net start
```

See also   net help, net stop

NET Commands   NET STATISTICS SERVER

Synopsis   NET STATISTICS SERVER [/CLEAR]

Description   This command displays or clears the statistics log.

Options   /CLEAR   Clears the statistics for the server.

Comments   To list the running services for which statistics are available, type net statistics without options.

When you type net statistics server, a display of statistics about the server appears, similar to the following:

```
Network Statistics for \\acct_asu
Statistics since July 27, 1995 at 13:12:23
Sessions accepted         1    Bytes received (KBytes)    503
Sessions timed out        0    Bytes sent (KBytes)
1225
Sessions errored out      0    Mean response time (msec)  0
Network errors            2    Network I/O's performed    43
System errors             0    Files accessed             1
Password violations       0    COM devices accessed       0
Permissions violations    0    Print Jobs spooled         0

The command completed successfully.
```

This screen displays:

- the date on which the statistics log was last cleared
- the number of sessions accepted, disconnected automatically, and disconnected by an error
- the number of bytes sent and received, along with the average server response time; for UNIX system servers, this value will always be set to 0
- the number of errors and violations of passwords and permissions
- The number of times shared files, and printers were used

Use the `net statistics` command to display performance information for the specified service.

This command can also be typed `net stats`.

Examples   At a UNIX system console, to display a list of statistics for a server, type the following:

```
net statistics server
```

To run the same command remotely (on server `market_asu`), type the following (replacing *password* with the password for administrator):

```
net admin \\market_asu password /command net
statistics server
```

See also   net help

NET Commands   NET SEND

Synopsis: NET SEND [alias | /DOMAIN[:name] | *] message

Note that text must be provided on the command line. `net send` cannot take message text from standard input.

Description   This command sends messages to other computers or users on the network.

Options   alias   Username, computername, or other alias to send the message to.

*   Sends the message to all aliases in your workstation domain.

/DOMAIN[:name]
Sends the message to all aliases in the workstation domain. If name is specified, the message is sent to all aliases in the specified domain.

/USERS   Sends the message to all users connected to the server.

message   Text to be sent as a message.

Comments   A UNIX system server can send messages, but it cannot receive them.

You cannot send messages to Macintosh client users.

To send a short message to someone else on the local area network, type the `net send` command as follows:

```
net send alias message
```

The text of your message may also be contained within quotation marks.

If the message you want to send is longer than one line, type the `net send` command followed by an alias and press `return`.

Clients have different limits on the size of messages they can receive. When the Messenger service is using expanded memory, the default size of messages is 16,384 bytes. If the Messenger service is not using expanded memory, the default and recommended maximum size of messages is 128 bytes.

If you use the `\*` option to send a broadcast message, the message is limited to 128 characters. If you try to send a longer broadcast message, extra characters are lost and the receiver is not notified that the message is incomplete.

To send a message to another user, the recipient's client must be running the Messenger service. When your message is successfully received, the server displays the following message: `Message successfully sent to username`. If you use an alias that the server does not recognize, or if the Messenger service is not running on the recipient's computer, an error message appears.

You can broadcast messages to all aliases in your local domain (use `\*` or /DOMAIN) or a different domain (/DOMAIN:name). Broadcast messages must be 128 characters or fewer. Use this feature with discretion.

If you wish to send a message to another computer, both computers must be running the same protocol stack. For example, if you send the broadcast message `net send \*`, the message is sent to the network represented by LANAO.

Examples   To send the message, "Meeting changed to 3 p.m. Same place." to the alias `jackst`, type the following:

```
net send jackst Meeting changed to 3 p.m. Same place.
```

To inform every user on the domain that a party is being held in the cafeteria, type the following:

```
net send \* Party in the cafeteria
```

To send a message to all users connected to the server, type the following:
```
net send /users This server will shut down in 5 minutes.
```

To run the same command remotely (on server `market_asu`), type the following (replacing *password* with the password for administrator):

```
net admin \\market_asu password /command net send/users
            This server will shut down in 5 minutes.
```

See also   `net help`

NET Commands   NET SESSION

Synopsis   **NET SESSION [\\computername] [/DELETE]**

Description   This command lists or disconnects sessions between a server and clients.

Options   computername   Client for which session information is displayed.

/DELETE   Ends the server's session with `computername`, and closes all open files for the session. If `computername` is omitted, all sessions for the server are canceled.

Comments   To display information about all sessions with the local server, type `net session` without options.

Use the `net session` command to display a list of users accessing a server (their computername and username), if they have files open, and how long each user's session is idle.

The `net session` command can also be typed `net sessions` or `net sess`.

The display is similar to the following:

```
Computer         User name       Client Type    Opens    Idle time
-----------      ------------    ------------   -------   --------
\\MARIEL         MARIEL          DOS LM 2.1        1       00:00:13
\\LYNNC          ADMINISTRATOR   DOS LM 2.1        0       01:05:13
\\KATE_42987     ADMINISTRATOR   DOS LM 2.1        0       00:00:00
```

Executing the `net session` command creates a session, so even if there are no other active sessions, at least one—the one created by this command—is always listed in the display. This session will appear similar to the last one displayedin the screen above.

When a display is for one user's session (computername is included with the command), the display includes a list of shared resources to which the user has connections.

A session is recorded when a user on a client successfully contacts a server. A successful session occurs when the two systems are on the same network, and the user has a username and password that are accepted by the server. A user at a client has to have a session with a server before being able to use the server's resources, and a session is not established until a user at a client tries to access a resource. A client and server have only one session, but they can have many entry points to resources (connections). To set how long a session can remain idle before being automatically disconnected, use the `\SYSTEM\CurrentControlSet\Services\LanmanServer\Parameters \AutoDisconnect` value in the Registry or the `/AUTODISCONNECT` option of the `net config server` command. An automatic disconnection is transparent to the user because the server reconnects the session when it becomes active.

If the user tries using the session after it is disconnected, the client tries to reconnect the session. If the username or password used to reconnect differ from that used to initially create the session, an error message is displayed.

To end a session with the server, use the `/DELETE` option with computername.

Examples   From the UNIX system console, to display session information for a client where `myclient` is the name of the client, type the following:

```
net session \\myclient
```

If you discover there is a problem with a session, notify the user currently logged on to `myclient` that you must disconnect the session in order to correct the error. Then, to disconnect all sessions between `myclient` and the server, type the following:

```
net session \\myclient /delete
```

To end all sessions between your server and other computers, type the following:

```
net session /delete
```

To run the same command remotely (on server `market_asu`), type the following (replacing *password* with the password for administrator):

```
net admin \\market_asu password /command net session
/delete
```

See also   `net help, net status`

NET Commands   NET STATUS

Synopsis   **NET STATUS**

Description   This command displays a server's computername, configuration settings, and a list of shared resources on the server.

Comments   The `net status` command displays the same information as the `net config` and `net share` commands combined.

Examples At a UNIX system console, to see the configuration values and shared resources for a server one screen at a time, type the following:

```
net status | more
```

To run the same command remotely (on server `market_asu`), type the following (replacing `password` with the password for administrator):

```
net admin \\market_asu password /command net status | more
```

See also `net help, net config server, net share,`
`net statistics server`

NET Commands   NET STOP

Synopsis **NET STOP** service

Description This command stops a network service.

Options service   Specifies the service to be stopped. This includes the following services: Alerter, Netlogon, Netrun, Nvalert, Remoteboot, Replicator, Server, SNMP, Timesource, and UPS.

Comment Stop a service to remove the network function it performs and to remove the software from memory. For example, when you stop the Server service, all sessions on the network end.

To stop the Server service, you must be logged on to the UNIX system at the server console as root.

Stopping the Server service prevents users from accessing the server's shared resources. If you stop the server when users are accessing resources, the server displays a warning message, requesting confirmation that you want to cancel the connections. A "y" response cancels all connections to the server.

Before stopping the Server service, you can

- Pause the service (to disallow new connections). The following services cannot be paused: alerter, nvalert, remoteboot, replicator, timesource, and ups.

- Send a message advising users to disconnect from the server's resources.

See also `net help, net start, net pause, net continue`

NET Commands   NET TIME

Synopsis   NET TIME [\\servername | /DOMAIN[:name]]

Description   This command synchronizes the client's clock with that of a server or domain, or displays the time for a server or domain. This command replaced the synctm command found in prior releases.

Options   servername   Name of the UNIX system server whose time will be displayed, or the server to which the client's clock will be synchronized.

/DOMAIN[:name]
Displays the date and time for the server designated as the domain's official time source. Use name to specify a different domain.

Comments   To display the current date and time at your domain's designated time server, type net time without options. From the UNIX system server, you can only view the time, not set it.

If you use this command without the servername option, or with the domain:name option, there must already be a time source server in your domain.

Examples   At a UNIX system console, to see the time and date in the account domain, type the following:
```
net time /domain:account
```

To run the same command remotely (on server market_asu), type the following (replacing *password* with the password for administrator):
```
net admin \\market_asu password /command net time/
domain:account
```

See also   net help, net stop, net start timesource

NET Commands   NET TRUST

Synopsis   NET TRUST [/DOMAIN:domainname]
domainname [/DOMAIN:domainname] {/DELETE | /DISALLOW}
domainname [/DOMAIN:domainname] {/ADD | /ALLOW} {password | *}

Description   This command establishes and breaks trust relationships between the domains, and lists the trust information for the specified domain.

Options   /DOMAIN:*domainname*
DOMAIN specifies the name of the domain being administered. If this option is not specified, the operation is performed on a local domain. *domainname* is the name of the domain.

/ADD   Adds the domain to the list of trusted domains for the domain being administered.

/DELETE   Deletes the domain from the list of trusted domains for the domain being administered.

/ALLOW   Adds the domain to the list of domains permitted to trust the domain being administered.

/DISALLOW   Deletes the domain from the list of domains permitted to trust the domain being administered.

password   Password used for the establishment of this trust relationship.

Comments To display the list of trusted and permitted to trust domains for the local domain, type `net trust` without options.

Use the `net trust` command for administering trust relationships between domains, enabling a user to have only one account in one domain, but be able to access the entire network.

A display of trusted and permitted to trust domains on the server is similar to the following:

```
Domain:      PRODUCT_DOM
Trusted Domains:
-----------------------------------------------------------
SALES_DOM                   LEGAL.DOM
Permitted to Trust this Domain:
-----------------------------------------------------------
SALES_DOM                   MARKET.DOM
```

Examples At a UNIX system console, to display a list of trusted and permitted to trust domains for the domain called `product_dom`, type the following:
```
net trust /domain:product_dom
```

To add a domain called `sales_dom` to the list of the domains permitted to trust domain `product_dom`, type the following (replacing "password" with the password used for setting up this trust relationship):
```
net trust sales_dom password /allow /domain:product_dom
```

To add a domain called `sales_dom` to the list of the domains trusted by the local domain, type the following (replacing "password" with the password the administrator of `sales_dom` chose for this trust relationship):
```
net trust sales_dom password /add
```

To delete a domain called `sales_dom` from the list of the domains permitted to trust by the local domain, type the following:

```
net trust sales_dom /disallow
```

To delete a domain called `sales_dom` from the list of the domains trusted by domain `product_dom`, type the following:

```
net trust sales_dom /delete /domain:product_dom
```

See also   `net help`

NET Commands   **NET USER**

Synopsis   **NET USER [username [password | *] [options]]**
username {password | *} /ADD [options]
username [/DELETE]

Description   This command adds, modifies, or deletes user accounts or displays user account information.

Options   NET USER *username*
Name of the user account (with as many as 20 characters) to add, delete, modify, or view. Usernames containing spaces must be quoted.

password   Assigns or changes a password (with as many as 14 characters) for the user's account. A password must satisfy any minimum length set with the /minpwlen option of the net accounts command.

*   Produces a prompt for the password. The password will not be displayed when you type it. Options are as follows:

/ACCOUNTTYPE:{Global | Local}—Specifies whether the user account is global (for regular user accounts in this domain), or local (for users from untrusted domains). The default is Global.

/ACTIVE:{NO | YES}—Deactivates or activates the user account. If the user account is not active, the user cannot access resources on the server. The default is YES (active).

/COMMENT:"text"—Provides a descriptive comment about the user's account. This comment can have as many as 48 characters. Enclose the text in quotation marks.

/COUNTRYCODE:#—Uses the operating system country codes to implement the specified language files for a user's help and error messages. A value of "0" signifies the default country code.

/EXPIRES:{date | NEVER}—Causes the user account to expire if date is set. NEVER sets no time limit on the user account. Expiration dates can be in mm,dd,yy format. Note that the account expires at the beginning of the date specified. Months can be a number, spelled out, or abbreviated with three letters. Year can be two or four numbers. Use a comma or slash to separate parts of the date (no spaces). If yy is omitted, the next occurrence of the date (according to your computer's date and time) is assumed. For example, the following date entries are equivalent if entered between Jan. 10, 1995 and Jan. 8, 1996:

> jan,9
> 1/9/96
> january,9,1996
> 1/9

/FULLNAME:"name"—Adds a user's full name (rather than username). Enclose the name in quotation marks.

/HOMEDIR:pathname—Sets the pathname for the user's home directory. The pathname can be an absolute path or a network path. The default USERPATH is found in the `\SYSTEM\CurrentControlSet` `\Services\LanmanServer\Parameters\UserPath` value in the Registry. For example, UserPath could have the value `c:\home\lanman`. This option does not create a home directory and does not check to see if one exists.

/PASSWORDCHG:{YES | NO}—Specifies whether users can change their own password. The default is YES.

/PASSWORDEXP:{YES | NO}—Specifies whether the password expires when the maximum password age is reached (YES), or never expires (NO). The default is YES.

/PASSWORDMUSTCHG:{YES | NO}—Specifies whether the user must change password at next logon. The default is NO.

/PASSWORDREQ:{YES | NO}—Specifies whether a user account must have a password. The default is YES.

/PRIMARYGROUP:[groupname]—Sets a primary group for the user. The primary group can be any of the global groups to which the user belongs. The default is Domain Users.

/PROFILEPATH:[pathname]—Sets a path for the user's logon profile.

/SCRIPTPATH:[pathname]—Sets a pathname for the user's logon script. This pathname is relative to the directory listed in the `\SYSTEM\CurrentControlSet\ Services\Netlogon` `\Parameters\Scripts` value in the Registry.

/TIMES:{times | ALL}—Specifies the times the user is allowed to use the server. The times value is expressed as day[-day][,day[-day]], time[-time] [,time[-time]], limited to 1-hour time increments. Days can be spelled out or abbreviated (M,T,W,TH,F,SA,SU). Hours can be 12- or 24-hour notation. For 12-hour notation, use AM, PM, or A.M., P.M. The value ALL means a user can always log on. A null value (blank) means a user can never log on. Separate day and time with a comma, and units of day and time with a semicolon (for example, M,4AM-5 PM;T,1PM-3PM). For 24-hour notation, the format must be hh:00. In the UNIX operating system, the semicolon is a special character that must be preceded by a backslash (\). Do not use spaces when designating /TIMES.

/USERCOMMENT:"text"—Lets an administrator add or change the ``User comment'' for the account. Enclose the text in quotation marks.

/WORKSTATIONS:{computername[,...] | *}—lists as many as eight clients from which a user can log on to the network. Separate multiple entries in the list with a comma. If /WORKSTATIONS has no list, or if the list is "*", the user can log on from any client. If you impose a restriction on a user's client, the user will not be able to log on at the UNIX system console.

/ADD   Adds a user account.

/DELETE   Removes a user account.

Comments To view a list of the user accounts on the server, type `net user` without options. To view information about a particular user's account, type `net user` *username*.

This command can also be typed `net users`.

Use the `net perms` command to define the users' permissions to use shared resources. When you type the `net user` command at a backup domain controller, changes to the user accounts automatically occur on the primary domain controller and then are replicated to backup domain controllers.

For security reasons, do not assign a null password to an account with administrative privilege.

Examples From the UNIX system console, to display a list of all user accounts for the local server, type `net user`. To view information about the user account `jimmy smith`, type `net user jimmy smith`. To add a user account for Henry James, with logon rights from 8 A.M. to 5 P.M., Monday through Friday, a mandatory password, and the user's full name, type the following:

```
net user henryj 0henry /add /passwordreq:yes
      /times:monday-friday,8am-5pm /fullname:"Henry
James"
```

To set `johnsw`'s logon time (8 A.M. to 5 P.M.) using 24-hour notation, type:

```
net user johnsw /time:M-F,08:00-17:00
```

To set `johnsw`'s logon time (8 A.M. to 5 P.M.) using 12-hour notation, type the following:

```
net user johnsw /time:M-F,8am-5pm
```

To specify logon hours of 4 A.M. until 5 P.M. on Monday, 1 P.M. until 3 P.M. on Tuesday, and 8 A.M. until 5 P.M. Wednesday through Friday for marysl, type the following:

```
net user marysl /time:M,4am-5pm\;T,1pm-3pm\;W-F,8:00-
17:00
```

To run the same command remotely (on server market_asu), type the following (replacing *password* with the password for administrator):

```
net admin \\market_asu password /command net user
marysl
        /time:M,4am-5pm\;T,1pm-3pm\;W-F,8:00-17:00
```

See also   net help, net stop, net perms, net accounts, net group

NET Commands   NET VERSION

Synopsis   **NET VERSION**

Description   This command displays the version of network software currently running on the computer at which the command is typed.

Examples   At a UNIX system console, to determine the version of network installed on a computer, type the following:

```
net version
```

See also   net help

NET Commands   NET VIEW

Synopsis   **NET VIEW [\\servername]**

Description   This command displays a list of servers or displays resources being shared by a server.

Options   servername   Specifies a server whose shared resources you want to view.

Comments   To display a list of servers in your workstation domain and other domains, type net view without options. The display is similar to the following:

```
Server Name              Remark
-----------              ---------------------------
\\PRODUCT_asu            Product file server
\\PRINT1_asu             Printer room, first floor
\\PRINT2_asu             Printer room, second floor
```

Examples   From a UNIX system console, to see a list of the resources shared by the product server, type the following:

```
net view \\product_asu
```

To run the same command remotely (on server market_asu), type the following (replacing *password* with the password for administrator):

```
net admin \\market_asu password /command net view \\product
```

See also   net help

Index

browser, 25
Browser cache files, 275
browser service, 23

C

chacl, 277, 283
characteristics
    loading, 108
    performance, 108
    server performance, 114
charge back, 178
CIFS, 8, 114, 267
class name
    Solaris, 33
Common Internet File System (CIFS), xxx, 4, 22
CPU, 73
    cache size, 117
    resource management, 186
    resources, 209
    sizing, 117
    speed, 117
CreateUnixUser, 142
cXtYdZ, 205

D

database file location, 57
default
    accounts, 141
default values
    memory, 79
delete ACLs
    acladm, 243
    rmacl, 243
delshmem, 277, 284
DHCP, 9, 23, 140
diff, 84
directory replication, 165
    configure the export server, 252
    configure the import server, 251
    set up roaming profiles, 254
    setting up, 248
    setting up between different domains, 249

directory replication service, 23
DiskSuite, 61, 64, 73, 206
DNS, 23, 139
domain authentication, 172
Domain login, 275
DOS attributes, 23, 236
dynamic reconfiguration (DR), 179
dynamic system domain (DSD), 179

E

elfread, 277, 284
end point mapper, 41
Enterprise Technology Center (ETC), 269
euctosjis, 277, 285
event vewer, 7
event viewer, 23

F

FC-AL, 61, 69, 70
file ownership, 255
file shares
    remove, 258
    set up, 256
files
    mapped, 125
fork, 188
FTP, 8, 181

G

GID, 40
GNU, 149
goals
    functional, 107, 111
    performance, 107, 110, 112
group ID, 38